# STRIKEBREAKING
# & INTIMIDATION

# STRIKEBREAKING

# & INTIMIDATION

## MERCENARIES AND MASCULINITY
## IN TWENTIETH-CENTURY AMERICA

### STEPHEN H. NORWOOD

The University of North Carolina Press  Chapel Hill & London

© 2002
The University of North Carolina Press
All rights reserved
Manufactured in the United States of America
Designed by Richard Hendel
Set in Charter and Champion types
by Keystone Typesetting, Inc.
The paper in this book meets the guidelines for
permanence and durability of the Committee on
Production Guidelines for Book Longevity of the
Council on Library Resources.

Portions of this book have been reprinted with permission
in revised form from Stephen H. Norwood, "Ford's Brass
Knuckles," *Labor History* 37, no. 3 (1996), and "The Student
as Strikebreaker: College Youth and the Crisis of Masculinity in the Early Twentieth Century," *Journal of Social
History* 28, no. 2 (1994).

Library of Congress Cataloging-in-Publication Data
Norwood, Stephen H. (Stephen Harlan), 1951–
Strikebreaking and intimidation: mercenaries and
masculinity in twentieth-century America / Stephen H.
Norwood.
p. cm.
Includes bibliographical references and index.
ISBN 0-8078-2705-3 (cloth: alk. paper)
ISBN 0-8078-5373-9 (pbk.: alk. paper)
1. Strikebreakers—United States—History—20th century.
2. Strikes and lockouts—United States—History—20th
century. 3. Strikebreakers—Recruiting—United States—
History—20th century. 4. Machismo—United States—
History—20th century.
HD5324.N67   2002
331.892'973'0904—dc21        2001059763

cloth  06  05  04  03  02   5 4 3 2 1
paper  06  05  04  03  02   5 4 3 2 1

Frontispiece:
Ford Servicemen assault
Richard Frankensteen during
the Battle of the Overpass,
May 26, 1937. Courtesy of
the Walter P. Reuther Library,
Wayne State University.

*To Eunice G. Pollack*

# CONTENTS

Acknowledgments *xi*

Introduction:

    The Emergence of the Anti-Labor Mercenary *1*

1 The Student as Strikebreaker:

    College Youth and the Crisis of Masculinity in the

    Early Twentieth Century *15*

2 Gunfighters on the Urban Frontier:

    Strikebreakers in the Car Wars *34*

3 Forging a New Masculinity:

    African American Strikebreaking in the

    North in the Early Twentieth Century *78*

4 Cossacks of the Coal Fields:

    Corporate Mercenaries in the Mine Wars *114*

5 Ford's Brass Knuckles:

    Harry Bennett, the Cult of Muscularity, and

    Anti-Labor Terror, 1920–1945 *171*

6 They Shall Not Pass:

    Paramilitary Combat against Strikebreaking in the

    Auto Industry, 1933–1939 *194*

Epilogue:

    Anti-Unionism in America, 1945–2000 *228*

Notes *249*

Bibliography *301*

Index *321*

# ILLUSTRATIONS

Confrontation occurs during the 1929 New Orleans strike  36

Strike sympathizers hurl missiles at a streetcar during the 1929
New Orleans strike  37

Strike sympathizers place obstructions on tracks, St. Louis
streetcar strike, 1900  41

Strike sympathizers hung "wire decorations" on trolley wires,
St. Louis streetcar strike, 1900  42

Policemen guard the streetcar route during the 1903 Chicago strike  57

Pearl Bergoff  67

African American strikebreakers, Chicago packinghouse strike, 1904  88

African American strikebreakers, Chicago teamsters' strike, 1905  96

Policemen escort African American strikebreakers, Chicago
teamsters' strike, 1905  98

Supporters of the 1913–14 UMW strike in Trinidad, Colorado  116

Daughter of a striking miner in Ludlow, Colorado, 1913 or 1914  117

Member of the Pennsylvania State Constabulary, 1916  124

Baldwin-Felts mine guards at Paint Creek, West Virginia, during the
1912–13 coal strike  134

Baldwin-Felts mine guards, southern Colorado coal strike, 1913 or
1914  143

Mounted Colorado militiamen surround women participating in a march
to support the UMW strike, Trinidad, Colorado, January 1914  145

Colorado National Guardsmen pose with drawn rifles after burning
the miners' Ludlow tent colony, 1914  148

Union miners and sympathizers in front of the Sebastian County jail
in Fort Smith, Arkansas, 1915  161

Harry Bennett  174

Ford Servicemen assault Richard Frankensteen during the
Battle of the Overpass, May 26, 1937  185

African American strikebreakers battle strikers, River Rouge plant,
   Ford strike, April 1941 *191*

Persons model Black Legion robes and display Black Legion weaponry,
   May 23, 1936 *198*

Detroit police fire tear gas to dislodge Yale & Towne sit-down
   strikers, 1937 *221*

Detroit policemen escort arrested striker or strike sympathizer,
   Federal Screw strike, 1938 *222*

Street fighting during Detroit's Federal Screw strike, 1938 *223*

Detroit police charge and club strikers and strike sympathizers,
   Federal Screw strike, 1938 *224*

# ACKNOWLEDGMENTS

Rose Norwood, my grandmother, veteran labor organizer and strike leader and president of the Boston Women's Trade Union League, introduced me to this subject. She vividly related many accounts of her confrontations with strikebreakers and stories of company detectives who trailed her in her organizing work. During her 1937 testimony before the Massachusetts legislature for a bill to prohibit labor espionage, she pointed to a detective who had followed her right into the committee chamber. As I write these acknowledgments, I am looking at three photographs taken during the 1930s of my grandmother leading a protest against the discharge of a worker who had attempted to organize a union at a food market in Boston's Dorchester section. As she pickets the store, she is flanked by several physically imposing bodyguards from the longshoremen's union. She knew what she was up against.

While living with my grandmother, I met many of New England's most energetic labor organizers of the early twentieth century, who during frequent visits recalled their past campaigns. It was through my grandmother and her friends, and through the work on my first book, *Labor's Flaming Youth: Telephone Operators and Worker Militancy, 1878–1923*, that I came to recognize the salience of strikebreaking and espionage to a full understanding of labor in the twentieth century.

As I began this study, I received encouragement from Victor Reuther, whose brother Roy had taught my grandmother public speaking at Brookwood Labor College; Doug Fraser; and the late Leonard Woodcock. They all provided insight into the methods management used to disrupt labor organizing and break strikes from the 1930s, when they were young worker-activists, to the 1990s.

I have benefited significantly from the criticisms and suggestions of Robert Zieger, whose scholarship I have always greatly admired. I would also like to thank Paul Avrich, another outstanding historian, for his helpful and perceptive comments. It was a pleasure to work with Chuck Grench, my editor at the University of North Carolina Press.

The book is dedicated to my wife, Eunice G. Pollack, who, in addition to profoundly transforming my life, has greatly contributed to this work, providing careful critiques of several sections, even while writing her own book.

# STRIKEBREAKING & INTIMIDATION

*Strikebreakers at a bar.*
*Courtesy of the Walter P. Reuther Library, Wayne State University.*

# INTRODUCTION
# THE EMERGENCE
# OF THE ANTI-LABOR
# MERCENARY

For 3,000 San Francisco streetcarmen preparing to strike in April 1902, "the lines of battle" were clearly drawn. They confronted an employer, United Railroads Company, whose elaborate labor espionage system denied them any job security and threatened their "manhood." Company agents, concerned largely with uncovering union organizers and sympathizers, spied on workers not only when they were on the job but also during their leisure hours. The carmen complained of being shadowed to their homes as though they were criminals. The union's central strike demand was the elimination of the company's practice of arbitrarily discharging an employee, without a hearing, on the uncorroborated statement of a "spotter," regardless of the quality of his work or his length of service. Management fostered a climate of such "fear and intimidation" that the carmen, in attempting to form a union, identified themselves with the "Nihilists of Russia." They were forced to meet in dark alleys and basements, and in "all sorts of secret places," to build up their organization "by day and night." The company even steamed open and photographed letters sent to union president Richard Cornelius.[1]

Aware of the extent of company surveillance, the ten motormen and conductors who had initiated the union effort had taken every precaution to conceal their identities at their first meeting in a little hotel back room in July 1901. Leaving their carmen's uniforms at home, they had each taken a different route to the meeting. They had each returned home alone "with coat collars turned up about their ears, and hats pulled down over their eyes." The next morning, the company discharged eight of the ten men, producing photographs of each of them on their way to the meeting.[2]

During the next eight months as organizing continued, United Railroads dismissed dozens more men, many of whom were blacklisted by every streetcar company in the country. United Railroads' general manager did agree to provide a letter of reference for some of the discharged men, but what appeared on the surface to be a "polite enumeration of qualifications" contained "a cipher sign whose meaning was known to all" of the nation's street railway superintendents. If the general manager merely suspected a man of union sympathies, he drew a single horizontal line at the bottom of the letter, which signified that "the bearer needed watching." If the company knew the man had actually joined the union, the general manager drew two horizontal lines. If the man was a union activist, he drew three lines.[3]

To the strikers, their battle against corporate authoritarianism was "as just as that . . . [of] our ancestors," who had fought with "Washington . . . against the oppression of King George," and for Lincoln in the struggle "to liberate the millions of black slaves." They were the "protect[ors] of womanhood," defending family and home against a corporation that had mobilized the "offscourings of society" against them, thousands of strikebreaking mercenaries from eastern city slums, ready for shipment across the continent, who resembled the Hessians that Washington and their forebears had fought in the Revolution. Contemptuous of the family, the corporation deprived wives of their husbands, and children of their fathers, by compelling the carmen to be on duty, away from home, sixteen to eighteen hours a day, for eleven hours' pay. The company's general manager in San Francisco had not even deigned to receive the union committee when it sought to present a demand for shorter hours. Instead a "red-haired office boy" had dismissed them as though they were pesky schoolchildren, forbidding them to penetrate beyond even the first of an elaborate series of entrances to the general manager's offices. To break the union, the corporation was prepared to replace "intelligent, responsible labor" with untrained and incompetent lumpenproletarians—"farmhands and hoboes"— who would endanger passengers' lives as they drove cars down "steep grades and around treacherous curves."[4]

By the early twentieth century, corporations' use of labor spies to prevent union organizing was widespread, and the supplying of strikebreakers and armed guards, often transported over vast distances, had emerged as a highly profitable business in the United States. An Interchurch World

Movement investigative report of the 1919 steel strike noted that "systems of espionage are an integral part of the anti-union policy of great industrial corporations." Labor espionage conducted by corporations or private detective agencies was unknown in Europe or any other advanced industrial nation, where such activity remained "a government monopoly." In 1933 a scholar of contemporary labor relations similarly observed that the "majority of large business and industrial establishments" employed labor spies "more or less regularly." The *Coast Seamen's Journal* in 1915 expressed an outlook widely held in the early twentieth-century labor movement when it equated American corporations' extensive use of "spies [and] informers" to combat union organizing with secret police tactics in czarist Russia, Europe's most repressive autocracy. Labor spies identified union sympathizers and reported them to the employer, undermined confidence in the union by spreading false rumors, and divided the labor force by stirring up ethnic and racial conflict.[5]

Even after the passage of the National Labor Relations Act, or Wagner Act, in 1935, which made corporations' use of labor spies an unfair labor practice, they remained common in American industry, and highly effective in undermining union campaigns. In 1937 the U.S. Senate's committee to investigate "violations of free speech and the rights of labor," chaired by Senator Robert La Follette Jr., found that labor spying was "almost universal."[6] Time and again, workers began an organizing drive with great enthusiasm, until they saw management identify and discharge the leading union activists. Then the workers, fearful of losing their jobs, ended any involvement in the campaign. A staff member of the La Follette committee recalled that the National Labor Relations Board (NLRB) had been "utterly ineffectual" in preventing management retaliation against union sympathizers during the late 1930s. He referred to a union local at the General Motors stamping plant in Lansing, Michigan, that had built up a substantial membership, until management began discharging workers who had joined it. Before long all that was left of the local were seven members, all officers. The La Follette committee determined that every one of them was a labor spy. But each was unaware that any of the others were engaged in labor espionage because they were all working for a different detective agency.[7]

The United States during the early twentieth century was the only advanced industrial country where corporations wielded coercive military power. In Europe, employers did not hire armed mercenaries. When force was applied in labor disputes, it was invariably by well-disciplined army troops or national police, neither of which was subject to private or local direction. As a result, spontaneous violence was far less common in European strikes. Paradoxically, the nation that never experienced feudalism and that pioneered in introducing civil liberties allowed corporations to develop powerful private armies that often operated outside the law, denying workers basic constitutional rights. For example, Baldwin-Felts guards employed by mine owners controlled the company towns and surrounding countryside in sections of West Virginia, Kentucky, and Colorado during the early twentieth century. Pennsylvania's private coal and iron police closed many mining towns to union organizers. During the 1930s, Ford Motor Company's Service Department, directed by ex-pugilist Harry Bennett, formed to suppress union organizing and strikes, constituted the world's largest private army, numbering between 3,500 and 6,000 men. The United Automobile Workers union compared it with both Mussolini's Blackshirts and Hitler's Gestapo.[8]

By the first decade of the twentieth century, a multitude of private detective agencies had emerged that specialized in recruiting and transporting strikebreakers and armed guards. These agencies often conducted business on a national basis, establishing branch offices across the country. One of the largest, Bergoff Brothers and Waddell of New York, promised it could supply 10,000 strikebreakers to a corporation within seventy-two hours, mobilizing probably more men more quickly than the federal government could. Given corporations' enormous demand for strikebreakers in the early twentieth century, the business of supplying them could prove very lucrative. R. J. Coach, head of a Cleveland detective agency that specialized in this service, during the 1910s wore "diamonds set in platinum," as he sat "amidst [the] splendor" of an office decorated with "rare oriental rugs." James Farley was allegedly paid more for providing the men that broke the 1905 New York Interborough subway and elevated strike than President Theodore Roosevelt received that year.[9]

Both labor espionage and the supplying and transport of strikebreakers and armed guards by detective agencies had begun during the late nineteenth century, coming fully to fruition as a business in the first two decades of the twentieth. The world renowned Pinkerton Detective Agency, founded by Scottish immigrant Allan Pinkerton in 1850, pioneered both in providing armed guards during strikes, to protect company property and strikebreakers, and in supplying labor spies. During the quarter century from 1866, when Pinkerton agents served as guards in a Braidwood, Illinois, miners' strike, through the 1892 strike against Carnegie Steel's mammoth plant at Homestead, Pennsylvania, Pinkerton guards were involved in about seventy labor disputes.[10]

Pinkerton had few scruples about whom it hired as guards, nor did the multitude of detective agencies that later emulated it. It recruited them by placing newspaper advertisements, by roaming the waterfront in search of men desperate enough to go to sea, and by combing army and navy recruiting offices for men not accepted for military service.[11]

In 1892 the role of corporate mercenaries received significant public attention for the first time when 300 Pinkerton agents, hired by Carnegie Steel to guard its Homestead works, became involved in a bloody gun battle with strikers and their supporters, after the river barges on which they had been transported were fired upon. In defeating the Homestead strike, with Pinkerton assistance, Carnegie Steel for all intents and purposes destroyed the Amalgamated Association of Iron, Steel, and Tin Workers (AAISTW), which had called it, and eliminated trade unionism from the steel industry for almost half a century.[12]

Pinkerton's spectacular success in infiltrating the Molly Maguires, a Pennsylvania Irish-American miners' secret society suspected of violent acts and sabotage against management, demonstrated the potential of labor espionage as an anti-union weapon, and led corporate business to implement it on a massive scale. At the request of Franklin Gowen, president of the Philadelphia and Reading Coal & Iron Company, Allan Pinkerton in 1873 sent an agent, James McParlan, disguised as a fugitive from a murder charge in Buffalo, New York, into the Pennsylvania coal fields. Not even Gowen knew McParlan's identity. McParlan's two and a half years of undercover work produced the evidence that resulted in the hanging of the leading Mollies. The Pinkerton agency "profited handsomely" from the affair; employers inundated it with requests for labor spies.[13]

By the turn of the century, drawing its spies in part from the Pinkerton agency, the Carnegie Steel Company under Henry C. Frick, who had broken the 1892 Homestead strike, had established such an elaborate labor espionage network that the United Mine Workers (UMW) union compared it to the "3rd degree of the Russian police system." Introduced immediately after the strike, it was so well concealed that the UMW's journal found it impossible to describe: "If it has a head, he is not known. It must have many branches or sections." The journal noted, "Time after time, men have been called to the office and told they were [fired] because they had become union men." Iron and steel workers in towns along the Monongahela lived in fear of a spy system that "lurks in the village store . . . reaches the preachers of their churches . . . searches the hearts of their children . . . hears the gossip of the old men and women [and] knows the mutterings of [the] half drunken." The constituent companies of the U.S. Steel Corporation all introduced labor espionage modeled on Carnegie's "perfect spy system." The infiltrators compiled files so extensive that corporate offices in Pittsburgh held lists of the leading union activists in all the large and small towns of Indiana. An investigator helping to conduct the "Pittsburgh Survey," a highly regarded sociological study of urban-industrial working-class life, in 1908 noted that fear of spies in Homestead was so pervasive that workers immediately terminated any conversation outside their homes when the steel company was mentioned.[14]

The first to recruit a permanent mobile mercenary force for strikebreaking, which could be transported quickly over a large distance, was Jack Whitehead, who by 1891 had gathered under his command forty skilled African American iron and steel workers from Birmingham, Alabama, known as the "Forty Thieves." Whitehead himself was an expert puddler, roller, and heater. In the newly founded iron and steel town of Birmingham, he was considered "a recognized authority on mechanical methods" in the industry. In 1891 Whitehead brought his force north to confront the AAISTW at what was considered its "strongest point," the strike-bound Clinton Mills on Pittsburgh's south side. With enough men to fill every skilled position in the plant, Whitehead broke the strike within ten days, handing the union its first significant defeat. The next year, Whitehead's mercenary band assisted Carnegie Steel in breaking the Homestead strike. Whitehead appears also to have supplied strikebreakers in Pittsburgh during the 1901 national machinists' strike.[15]

Jack Whitehead embodied the qualities the press and middle-class public associated with the professional strikebreaker and anti-unionist of the early twentieth century, like James Farley, Pearl Bergoff, and Harry Bennett: physical prowess and courage, pugnacity and daring, and a venturesomeness reflected in dramatic upward mobility. Of working-class origin, Whitehead had grown up in the shadow of Pittsburgh's south side iron mills and remained illiterate his entire life. But by age twenty-five, he was able to do "almost everything . . . about a mill." He achieved significant wealth as the first entrepreneur to recruit and transport African American labor from the South to a northern industrial center, allegedly receiving $10,000 for helping break a Pittsburgh steel strike.[16]

Although Whitehead bore "many scars" inflicted in brawls with union men, he was "devoid of fear," according to a major, turn-of-the-century mass circulation magazine. It noted that there had been occasions when Whitehead had "actually courted death." During the 1891 strike at the Clinton Mills, for example, Whitehead received word that a "gang of strikers" awaited him at a street corner, boasting that he would never again break a strike after they "got through with him." The "brawny" Whitehead immediately "went hunting for the gang that was thirsting for his life." Discovering the gang in a saloon, he marched in, and demanded to know who had threatened him. A "bitter fight" ensued, but when the police appeared, Whitehead, "standing with his back against the wall," was "sending down man after man."[17]

While Whitehead was the pioneering entrepreneur in strikebreaking, those who succeeded him as it emerged as a major business during the first two decades of the twentieth century amassed mercenary armies that were overwhelmingly composed of unskilled and semiskilled workers. As mechanization eliminated large numbers of skilled positions after 1870 and labor became increasingly homogenized, both the demand for craftsmen and the pool available for recruitment into strikebreaking diminished significantly. Employers desiring to hire craftsmen to replace strikers during the early twentieth century turned to college students, the subject of chapter 1.

The strikebreaking business of the early twentieth century was built from the "great industrial reserve army" of seasonally and permanently unemployed men, mostly unskilled. From 1870 until the early 1920s, employment in the working class was "chronically unsteady," and each year there were several hundred thousand persons who were unable to find work for at least a few months, even in relatively prosperous periods. Seasonal unemployment varied greatly but was considerable in many industries, like slaughtering and meat-packing, iron and steel, bituminous coal mining, brick and tile, garment manufacturing, and the building trades. Railroad construction jobs usually lasted only from March or April until November or December. Auto companies in the 1930s often laid off much of their labor force as they prepared for the annual model change. Seasonal fluctuations also terminated employment for a very large proportion of the labor force in the lumber industry, on the waterfront, and in agriculture. Logging camps, for example, which depended on snow, practically shut down during the summer. Common laborers, whose employment was notoriously unstable, continued to constitute a large and essential proportion of the labor force in many industries during the early twentieth century. They were often permanently laid off when a particular construction project was completed or production goal was reached.[18]

Aging also contributed significantly to unemployment. In many trades, management refused to hire men over the age of thirty-five, believing that they lacked the necessary strength or capacity for endurance required of heavy physical labor. Pensions were generally nonexistent for industrial workers, so there were always many middle-aged and elderly men desperately searching for work.[19]

Paid in cash wages and concentrated preponderantly in urban metropolitan areas, industrial workers lacked any nonmonetary source of income during periods of unemployment. They could not cultivate crops or maintain livestock, nor had they any access to fuel like coal and wood, necessary for heating during cold months.[20]

During the early twentieth century, neither government nor private sources made available any significant relief for the able-bodied unemployed. Before unemployment insurance was introduced under Franklin D. Roosevelt's New Deal, those out of work received no compensation from the state, and private charities generally provided only very limited sums for those physically incapable of holding a job—the elderly, orphaned or abandoned children, destitute mothers, the blind and crippled.[21]

Extensive seasonal unemployment resulted in considerable physical mobility among the working and lower classes, as workers were often compelled to move significant distances in search of jobs. Throughout this period, between 40 and 60 percent of the adult males in any American community, whether urban or rural, were likely no longer there ten years later. A U.S. Commission on Industrial Relations investigation in 1916 noted that several million American workers, "not definitely attached to any particular locality or to any line of industry," were "continually moving from one part of the country to another" in search of work. Employers deliberately glutted the labor market to drive wages down, often advertising with placement services in distant cities for more labor than necessary. This further contributed to the floating population, as many upon arrival found all positions filled, leaving them no choice but to continue their search for work elsewhere.[22]

During the winter months, the demand for labor tended to slacken, particularly in agriculture and construction, and travel, generally on foot or by hopping freight trains, proved more difficult, so much of the transient unemployed population congregated in the cities, awaiting warmer weather. A major mass circulation magazine noted in 1906 that the "problem of the unemployed and homeless man becomes every year more pressing in large cities." It estimated that on any given winter night in New York City, at least

50,000 homeless men slept in flophouses, saloon back rooms, in hallways and doorways, or just walked the streets. Sociologist Nels Anderson asserted in 1923 that the population of homeless men in Chicago varied from 30,000 in good times to 75,000 in hard times. During the Great Depression of the 1930s, the homeless situation worsened, as large shanty towns known as Hoovervilles became a significant feature of America's urban landscape.[23]

Jack London observed in 1905 that a large surplus army of laborers persisted even through periods of prosperity, which employers easily mobilized against strikers. In 1901, "a year adjudged the most prosperous in the annals of the United States," a strike of "large proportions," involving every Pacific Coast port had erupted, disrupting the "entire coasting service, from San Diego to Puget Sound." Thousands of men walked out, in many different trades, including seamen and longshoremen, teamsters, warehousemen, porters, and marine firemen. The unions believed that they held the advantage, because labor was relatively scarce. Military recruitment for the Philippines campaign and the Alaska gold rush had drawn large numbers of workingmen from the Pacific Coast. The strike had been called during the summer, when the demand for agricultural labor was at its peak. And yet, despite the physical risk involved in assuming a striker's position, "there remained a body of surplus labor . . . not only ready but anxious" to work, in any of the affected occupations. Even as strikebreakers were assaulted and the "hospitals were filled with [the] injured," men came forward to replace the strikers.[24]

The large population of unemployed in the early twentieth century gave rise in many of the larger cities to the "fink markets," where unemployed men were recruited for strikebreaking. Many considered signing up for strikebreaking the best available means of reaching another destination, or escaping monotony. The large agglomerations of men congregating at street corners or hotels recognized as recruiting points for strikebreaking enabled entrepreneurs to assemble large mercenary bands of "replacement workers" and armed guards on very short notice. The *United Mine Workers Journal* in 1914 identified the Mills Hotel on Bleecker Street in New York as a place where hundreds of men were stationed at any given time, awaiting assignment and transport as strikebreakers. The principal recruiting point for strikebreakers in Cleveland during the 1930s was the corner of 9th and Euclid Streets. In Philadelphia it was around the Reading railroad depot. Detroit's "fink market" was located at Grand Circus Park at Woodward Avenue, near the Statler Hotel. In Chicago, agents recruiting strikebreakers went to Randolph Street in the Loop or down to West Madison, "a port for homeless men," and the "most completely womanless and childless of all the city areas."[25]

The formation by a growing number of entrepreneurs in the early twentieth century of large mercenary bands for strikebreaking purposes, drawn largely from the ranks of unemployed men, greatly alarmed organized labor and its sympathizers. In 1909 the *Labor News*, organ of the Massachusetts State Federation of Labor, noted, "There are as many scab-[supplying] detective agencies [as] there are streetcar companies." The *United Mine Workers Journal* in 1916 denounced corporations' use of "the Private Army" as a "Menace to Democracy," because management's monopoly of armed force eliminated labor's ability to conduct strikes. American corporate business, instead of engaging in civilized negotiation with trade unions, hired mercenaries to intimidate and subjugate working people, like the "predatory robber barons of the Middle Ages." Sociologist Robert Hunter, reporting on this "commerce in violence" in 1919, noted that "there is no strike of any magnitude in which these hirelings are not employed."[26]

Organized labor repeatedly challenged the legitimacy of corporations' use of mercenaries by referring to their social marginality, implying that they were men who could not function in a society based on the family and the rule of law. John White, president of the UMW in 1916, labeled the strikebreakers recruited and supplied by detective agencies as "thugs and outlaws . . . penniless vagabonds gathered from the slums of the great cities, newly arrived immigrants unable to speak English, lawless men ready for any adventure that includes food and whiskey, [and] Negroes from the South." The Teamsters union journal in 1914 similarly described strikebreakers as "degenerates of the lowest kind . . . drug fiends and . . . thieves." It suggested that strikebreaking served as a major means for criminals to escape from the locality in which police were searching for them.[27]

Jack London, in his 1907 novel *The Iron Heel*, expressed labor's concern that the mercenary bands of strikebreakers could evolve into the shock troops of a movement that would suppress trade unions and democracy itself. Set in a near future when the large corporations responded to labor's increasing influence by establishing a brutal dictatorship, it assigned the strikebreaking detective agencies a prominent role in the new order. The Pinkertons, "fighting men of the capitalists" at the turn of the century, became a repressive armed force that "ground [the unions] out of existence."[28]

The significant involvement of youth in strikebreaking—college students, corporations' most reliable source, and the Boy Scouts, established in the United States in 1910—reinforced labor's increasing sense of vulnerability in the early twentieth century. The labor movement, at least prior to U.S. entry into World War I, considered the Boy Scouts' purpose the development of a new "armed guard" or "standing army" to suppress strikes. The organ of the American Federation of Labor's Western Federation of Miners declared that the Boy Scouts, clad in army-style uniforms, inculcating in youth an "idea of fealty to . . . employers [and] superiors," represented the greatest threat in world history "to capture the minds of . . . children for a military state." The *United Mine Workers Journal* identified the Boy Scouts with hostility to a free labor movement, noting that Europe's leading autocrat, Czar Nicholas II of Russia, had enthusiastically formed Boy Scout troops in his realm.[29]

Because the Boy Scouts helped on numerous occasions to break strikes, trade unions refused to permit any involvement in the scouts by their members. The Indiana UMW ordered the expulsion of any miner who supported or joined the Boy Scouts. The St. Louis Musicians Union refused to play in a parade planned as an escort for President Taft on his visit to that city in 1911 because the Boy Scouts were participating in it. The Chicago Federation of Teachers denounced the formation of Boy Scout troops in the public schools. In Des Moines, where the Boy Scouts broke a bootblacks' strike, the *Register and Leader* observed that "organized labor here has opposed each successive step in the upbuilding" of the Boy Scouts.[30]

Victor Reuther, born in 1912, noted that the Boy Scouts were used in strikebreaking in "some bitter and desperate struggles" in the West Virginia coal mines during the 1920s. Unaware of this, young Victor returned home from school one day and announced to his father, president of the Wheeling, West Virginia, central labor union, who had often traveled into the mine country to assist the striking miners, that he wanted to join the Boy Scouts. Because the Boy Scouts had developed a reputation for volunteering as strikebreakers, Reuther's father "went through the ceiling." Victor recalled that his angry father "gave me such a lecture. Thank God it wasn't a thrashing that day."[31]

Women were recruited for strikebreaking and were subjected to violence, particularly in the garment, textile, and laundry industries, but this study concentrates on men, who were recruited in greater numbers, mobilized in private "armies," and employed as armed guards. The detective agencies engaged in supplying strikebreakers do not appear to have devoted any significant attention to recruiting women. Men were also engaged in labor espionage much more frequently than women.

However, one of the most dramatic and well-coordinated long-distance shipments of strikebreakers during the early twentieth century involved women. This occurred in April 1913, when the newly organized, 2,200-member Boston Telephone Operators Union threatened to strike. Expecting management to hire replacements in the Boston metropolitan area, the union was stunned when hundreds of "volunteers" from the exchanges of associated Bell companies in major eastern and midwestern cities arrived in carefully guarded trains. The New England Telephone Company housed many of the strikebreakers at one of Boston's most elegant and expensive hotels, the Copley Plaza, where they enjoyed the great Jacobean sleeping rooms, plush velvet carpets, silken hangings, and scented baths. This constituted a sharp departure from the usual practice, where strikebreakers were lodged in squalid surroundings, like factories, packinghouses, or car-barns, or crowded on to ships or into flophouses. When, after a week, a settlement was negotiated, preventing a strike, the replacement operators were shipped back to their respective homes. In probably one of the most expensive importations of strikebreakers in American history, New England Telephone had brought in about 2,000 Bell system telephone operators from New York and northern New Jersey, Philadelphia, Pittsburgh, Baltimore, Washington, New England towns, and forty-one cities in Ohio, Illinois, Indiana, and Wisconsin.[32] Such a massive use of women strikebreakers was, however, highly unusual in the period.

Unlike men, women were not drawn to strikebreaking to express and demonstrate virility, a profound need for men in the early twentieth century. Indeed, a strikebreaker's masculinity was reinforced in violent encounters with women in strike crowds, where, as explained in chapter 2, they often assumed leadership roles. Moreover, the culture of strikebreaking had at its core a defiant, highly aggressive masculinity, in sharp contrast to family-based middle- and working-class society, shaped in significant ways by women.

This book is a social history of anti-unionism from the turn of the century to the onset of World War II. It focuses on corporate use of mercenaries, often organized as a private armed force, to disrupt union organizing and to break strikes, a phenomenon unique to the United States among the advanced industrial nations. The emergence of private armies whose members filled strikers' positions, protected and transported strikebreakers, intimidated and harassed workers attempting to organize, and infiltrated unions and workplaces as labor spies was a central part of an onslaught against unionization that management also pursued by other means. The book devotes less attention to the legal methods corporations employed to undermine unions and to assistance rendered corporations by the state, each of which is deserving of a study in its own right.

Chapter 1 examines why male students in a rapidly changing college environment constituted a major, often critically important, and highly reliable source of strikebreakers for employers between 1901 and 1923. Chapter 2 focuses on the conflation of masculinity with physicality in the early twentieth century and on why Americans identified the strikebreaker, a new soldier of fortune, with the valiant, self-reliant gunfighter of the Old West. It traces the development of strikebreaking as a well-coordinated business operating on a national scale and examines the significance of its emergence during a period in which the United States participated in no significant overseas military engagements.

Chapter 3 concentrates on the dramatic emergence of African American men from the South as a formidable strikebreaking force in northern labor conflicts, focusing most specifically on their role in the 1904 national packinghouse strike and the 1905 teamsters' strike in Chicago. It examines how strikebreakers constructed a new, assertive African American masculinity in a period when black vulnerability to violent assault and public humiliation steadily increased.

Chapter 4 analyzes the establishment in many of the country's major mining regions of repressive armed guard and labor espionage systems that trade unionists and reformers compared with those of czarist Russia. The chapter examines the "closed camps" that dotted these "forbidden lands," where mine corporations controlled local government and used armed mercenaries to enforce their dictate. Such communities often persisted for decades after mines were opened. From 1912 to 1915, the United States was torn by a series of bitterly fought armed conflicts between corporate mercenaries and union miners. Encounters between the rival forces at times resulted in casualties surpassing those of several skirmishes in the Spanish-American War and the border conflict with Mexico. Such armed conflicts occurred along Paint Creek and Cabin Creek in southern West Virginia in 1912–13, in Las Animas and Huerfano Counties in southern Colorado in 1913–14, along the Upper Michigan copper range in 1913–14, and in the Hartford Valley of western Arkansas in 1914–15. These were followed by another mine war in southern West Virginia in 1920–21. Chapter 4 also considers the role in suppressing unionism in Pennsylvania's coal counties of the uniformed coal and iron police, commissioned by the state but controlled by the mine owners, and the Pennsylvania State Constabulary, elite mounted units that constituted the nation's first state police force. Finally, the chapter also discusses how and why each side in the conflict depicted the other as savage, as a threat to civilized values.

The subject of chapter 5 is the Ford Motor Company's Service Department, directed by ex-navy boxer Harry Bennett. Bennett assembled the world's largest private army during the 1930s and early 1940s, and created the most extensive and efficient labor espionage system in American industry. The chapter examines the techniques Bennett employed to undermine the organizing efforts of the United Automobile Workers (UAW) at Ford, which the UAW compared with those of European fascism. It also analyzes the significance to this effort of Bennett's close ties with organized crime. Finally, it assesses Bennett's efforts to foment racial violence.

Chapter 6 analyzes the techniques and approaches the UAW elaborated to defend organizing efforts against General Motors, Chrysler, and the auto parts suppliers. It examines the anti-labor terrorism of the Black Legion and of GM-sponsored vigilante groups in the Flint, Michigan, and Anderson, Indiana, sit-down strikes. The chapter also discusses the anti-unionism of the Detroit police force. It concludes by assessing the diminution of anti-labor violence and strikebreaking in the auto industry during the immediate post–World War II era.

The epilogue examines the long-term impact of the delegitimation of anger, and the increasing divide between masculinity and physicality/aggression, on strikebreaking and labor militancy. It assesses how a widening generational divide affecting male workers, and a masculinity shaped by consumerism, have blunted union organizing efforts. It explains how legal and political developments in the late 1940s and 1950s hobbled organizing efforts and traces the emergence of "union avoidance" consulting as a highly lucrative business after 1970, evaluating its techniques. It details corporate business's shifting view of the African American worker, from member of a "scab race" to the most solidly pro-union member of the labor force. The epilogue also considers the persistence of corporate violence against organizing efforts in the post–World War II South, and the rising threat of "permanent replacements" in the strikes of the late 1980s and 1990s. It explains why organized labor's leaders today view the right to organize as a "legal fiction."

# THE STUDENT AS STRIKEBREAKER
## COLLEGE YOUTH AND THE CRISIS OF MASCULINITY IN THE EARLY TWENTIETH CENTURY

In March 1905 Columbia University students deserted their classes en masse to help break a strike of subway workers against the Interborough Rapid Transit Company (IRT), the biggest strike New York had ever experienced. Almost immediately after the walkout began, 300 Columbia students volunteered their services to the IRT as motormen, conductors, ticket sellers, and ticket choppers. Marching in squads from the subway exit at City Hall park to the IRT employment office on Dey Street, they gave the Columbia cheer and sang their college songs. The contingent included many of Columbia's top athletes, with the football "eleven," basketball and baseball players, crewmen, and bicycle racers all well represented. The college boys' "joyous exuberance" and "husky appearance" attracted considerable attention. Cries of "Scabs!" hurled at them by newsboys only put "ginger into their enthusiasm." One newspaper remarked that the students were "sublimely confident in their own strength" and "would have been more than pleased to start a rough house."[1] By the afternoon, Columbia's lecture rooms and laboratories were completely deserted. At day's end, the collegians had already achieved renown: the first subway train to make a successful run along the whole length of the Broadway line was one manned entirely by Columbia students.[2]

The IRT management was delighted that so many athletes had volunteered as strikebreakers, since it considered their physical prowess invaluable for the expected violent clashes with strikers and their allies. Led by Buck Whitwell, six-foot-three-inch star of the "eleven," the Columbia "delegation" constituted a "formidable array of strength and beef." As the *Evening Post* noted admiringly, the undergraduates were "big fellows" who could "easily hold the ticket choppers' gate" against attacks by strike sympathizers.[3]

The IRT company also specifically appealed to students at the New York area's major engineering schools, Brooklyn Polytechnic Institute, Stevens Institute of Technology in Hoboken, New Jersey, and the engineering colleges at Columbia and New York University, to enlist as strikebreakers. It needed them especially to replace skilled men involved with the subway's electrical power system, who had walked off the job. Many engineering students signed on as strikebreakers, and several almost immediately tasted combat. Stories circulated around Brooklyn Polytechnic Institute that "Poly" students working on the subways had "bested roughs a dozen times."[4]

Newspapers commented that the students regarded their strikebreaking as part of the frivolity of college extracurricular life, a "lark" equivalent to "stealing signs" or "class numeral painting." The collegians were surely not working on the subways out of any dire need for money, for observers were struck by the fact that many of them wore expensive attire. One policeman, for example, gaped in astonishment at the $75 overcoat and $6 tan boots of a young man from the University of Pennsylvania, up from Philadelphia to break the strike.[5]

Throughout the period between 1901 and 1923, college students represented a major, and often critically important, source of strikebreakers in a wide range of industries and services. Students had many attributes that employers particularly valued. Their youth and strength made them highly suitable for the arduous physical labor usually required on the job. Many students also possessed the kind of expertise much coveted by management. During a strike they often represented the only available pool of skilled labor.

Employers considered students to be the most reliable strikebreakers of the era. Most strikebreakers were unemployed, or members of racial or ethnic minorities shut out of the trade. Many were even transported to the strike scene without being informed they were to be used as strikebreakers. As workers or former workers, they were more likely to develop sympathy for the strikers, and desert their posts. But even students at state universities tended to be relatively affluent, with little or no work experience. Most identified with the privileged in their struggle against the working class. Collegians deliberately volunteered their services as strikebreakers and were the group least likely to be swayed by the pleas of strikers and their sympathizers that they were doing something wrong.

Finally, students projected an image that was far more presentable to the middle-class public than that of any other group from which strikebreakers were drawn. Nearly always, strikebreakers were perceived as a menacing, semicriminal element, recruited from the lower class. The socialist editor and labor organizer Oscar Ameringer described the "scab brigade" as composed of "riff-raff, slum dwellers, rubes, imbeciles [and] college students."[6] Journalists described the 1,500 strikebreakers shipped in from western towns to help break the 1905 New York IRT strike as unkempt lumpenproletarians, a "weird appearing lot," with "holes in their shoes," who "had not patronized [barbers] . . . for several days."[7] Clearly, the students stood out as the one group with which the middle class was comfortable. While the other groups tended to lessen the prestige of the struck company, the students could enhance it. Thus the student strikebreaker became a significant factor in capital's struggle against labor.

## THE COLLEGE VERSUS THE TRADE UNION

Students' antagonism to labor was not surprising during the first quarter of the twentieth century, because college was then an exclusive upper- and middle-class preserve, and few who attended had any understanding of the working-class experience. Through the 1920s college expenses remained prohibitive for most of the working class, even at state universities and polytechnic institutes. The vast majority of college youth had adequate financial support from their parents and did not need to work.[8]

By 1900 business leaders and middle-class parents considered college important in providing their sons with the higher level of training they needed in an increasingly specialized and bureaucratic society. Perhaps most important, college benefited the sons of the middle and upper classes by providing them with the social contacts that facilitated success in business and the professions after graduation.[9]

Not only was college inaccessible to working people, but the college culture was foreign as well. The students' world was so different and so distant from that of the worker, that relatively few ever developed any empathy for labor's plight. Many workers faced a life of grim, back-breaking toil. They often labored ten or twelve hours a day; for most, vacations were unknown.

Students, by contrast, regarded academic work as a "necessary evil" and considered college a period of "graceful leisure and gay irresponsibility."[10] The absenteeism, indolence, and frivolity permitted in college were never tolerated in the work world.[11]

The labor and socialist press were particularly contemptuous of student society and culture. They constantly ridiculed students as "rah rah sissies." This term deprecated students' enthusiasm for frivolous athletic and social pursuits and denied their masculinity, suggesting they lacked the maturity and work experience of "real men." The labor press also mocked students' indifference to learning, publishing, for example, an article by a former Harvard tutor detailing the methods the "little plutish boys" used to avoid studying. He claimed it was common practice for students to pay tutors to attend their classes and take their notes, and to write their term papers, while they lay in opulent rooms, beneath "silken sheets." A 1904 editorial in the *Worker*, revealingly entitled "The Barbarians of the Schools," asserted that "of intellectual atmosphere there is less . . . on the campus than in many a German beer-garden or . . . dingy workingman's clubroom on New York's poverty-stricken East Side." The *New York Call* claimed that students' conversations consisted only of trivialities like "What are our chances to win the ball game next Saturday?" or "How many positions on the Board ought to come to our frat?"[12]

The portrait drawn by these observers was quite accurate, for most students spent the bulk of their time vigorously pursuing extracurricular activities. Social and athletic pursuits, not learning, lay at the heart of "college life" as these students defined it. Eschewing the solitary life of the scholar, they spent their time in numerous group activities, participating frenetically in class "rushes," ribald parties, and drunken parades or riots to celebrate athletic victories. Occasionally they joined their classmates in building bonfires in vacant lots, into which they threw their schoolbooks and effigies of professors.[13] To these students, strikebreaking was just another group extracurricular activity, a romp.

Most college administrators and faculty considered students' extracurricular life frivolous and their behavior immature, but they strongly encouraged strikebreaking. Their hostility to labor was the result of corporate business's assumption of financial control over the college and university. By the early twentieth century, the boards of trustees of America's institutions of higher learning "read like a corporation directory."[14] So obvious was big business's influence in higher education that trade unionists referred to leading universities by nicknames that suggested they were mere instruments of their wealthy donors: the University of Chicago became "Standard Oil University," Stanford was known as "Southern Pacific University," the University of Minnesota was "Pillsbury University," and so on.

Many wealthy donors and boards of trustees in the early twentieth century displayed little understanding of, or commitment to, academic freedom, and pressured administrators to dismiss professors with pro-labor views. Although some university presidents became amenable to faculty tenure in the 1920s, it was not instituted on a wide scale until after 1938, so professors could never feel secure.[15] Any statement that displeased the donors or trustees could result in dismissal. As early as the 1890s, firings of pro-labor professors were common. Edward Bemis, economics professor at the University of Chicago, was dropped from the faculty in 1895 for publicly criticizing the railroad corporations during the Pullman strike. President William Rainey Harper informed him: "Your speech . . . has caused me a great deal of annoyance. It is hardly safe for me to venture into any of the Chicago clubs."[16] Scott Nearing was fired from the faculty of the University of Pennsylvania for making public speeches against child labor.[17]

In 1919 Harold Laski, then a young instructor at Harvard, came under fierce attack from prominent donors, alumni, and students for publicly declaring his support for striking Boston policemen. The *Harvard Lampoon*, a student publication, called Laski a "Bolshevik" and "scum," and ran sixteen pages of antisemitic poems, parodies, and caricatures mocking him. Harvard's president, A. Lawrence Lowell, refused to fire Laski, but told him, in confidence, that he would never be promoted. Soon after, Laski resigned his position at Harvard.[18]

Many of the nation's leading college presidents rivaled the corporate "robber barons" in their antagonism toward labor. Charles W. Eliot, Harvard's president from 1869 to 1909, was labeled in the labor press "the greatest labor union hater in the country." Eliot openly denounced the closed shop and the union label and offered panegyrics to the worker who broke strikes. In 1904 he pronounced the strikebreaker a "fair type of hero," a man possessed of an abundance of courage, who was even "willing to risk his life." Thus throughout the 1900s and 1910s, trade union newspapers regularly referred to strikebreakers as "Eliot heroes." Samuel Gompers, president of the American Federation of Labor, denounced President Eliot for "his inordinate desire to make the institution over which he presides the mentor and apologist for predatory wealth."[19] Eliot's successor, A. Lawrence Lowell, aggressively recruited students to break the Boston policemen's strike in 1919. Columbia's president Nicholas Murray Butler denounced the strike in general as "an act of war," while Yale's president Arthur Twining Hadley declared he did not see much hope "as to the good possibilities of labor organizations."[20]

Absorbed in their extracurricular activities, college students in the early twentieth century seemed rarely to think about politics, but whenever they did express their views, they tended to be conservative and anti-labor. Yale's freshman class conveyed not only its immaturity, but also its conservatism, in its response to a speech William Jennings Bryan delivered on its campus during his 1896 presidential campaign. Bryan intoned, "99 out of 100 of the students of this university are the sons of the idle rich." Bryan had inadvertently called out the class's "magic number," and the freshmen shouted down the "Great Commoner" by booming the class chant "9, 9, 99" over and over again.[21] Malcolm Ross, who attended Yale in the 1910s, recalled that "9 out of 10" of his fellow students subscribed "to anti-labor attitudes with fervor," as did students at "Harvard [and] California." There were students who became involved in the burgeoning settlement house movement, whose sympathies were with labor, but these constituted a small minority. More common were those who complained that modern society was "rotten with altruism."[22] Students voted like their fathers, although not as often or as enthusiastically. In October 1924 a nationwide straw vote among college students showed them to be "overwhelmingly conservative." They backed the Republican candidate Calvin Coolidge even more heavily than did the electorate that November.[23]

Progressives frequently compared the "reactionary" or "apathetic" American college students to their European and Asian counterparts, whom they credited with making major contributions to the liberation movements of their countries. In an article entitled "Why Don't Your Young Men Care?" Harold Laski portrayed the American student as the complete opposite of the European and Asian student. The American student was a "non-political animal," indifferent to the oppressed, whereas the Russian, French, Spanish, and Chinese students had all made "outstanding contributions" to progressive movements. (Laski even considered the British students far more progressive than the American, although they on occasion engaged in strikebreaking, most notably in the 1926 general strike.) Laski praised the heroism of the Russian student, who put his or her life on the line to defeat reaction: "I think of how the one cry which could drive back the Black Hundreds in pre-war Russia to their dens was the cry that the students were coming."[24] An American socialist traveling to Russia in 1906–7 noted that "Russian students are a serious lot. They can't understand our interest in athletics."[25] Even Samuel Gompers joined in the denunciation of the American collegian, claiming that students welcomed the opportunity "to exhibit themselves as scabs."[26]

To be sure, during the 1910s some dissident voices were heard in the student ranks. A "Bohemian revolt" developed on some eastern campuses, involving such youth as John Reed and Randolph Bourne, but it focused largely on cultural concerns like modern literature and avant-garde drama. There also appeared a small radical student group, the Intercollegiate Socialist Society (ISS). The ISS was, however, founded and led largely by non-student adults. The twenty-nine-year-old novelist Jack London was elected its president at its founding in 1905, and a six-person executive committee was established that included only one student. The ISS functioned mostly as a lecture and discussion group and gave little attention to strike support.[27] In fact, most radicals considered youth more conservative than adults. Emma Goldman, for example, looking back on the prewar period in 1934, claimed that finding a rebel in America under the age of thirty-five had been like coming upon a "pin in a haystack."[28]

In the 1920s there also appeared a national liberal student magazine, the *New Student*, but it openly admitted that most collegians were conservative and anti-labor. Even the greatest liberal crusade of the 1920s, the movement to defend Sacco and Vanzetti, aroused little interest among students.[29]

---

## FROM THE FIELDHOUSE TO THE ROUNDHOUSE: STRIKEBREAKING AND THE CULT OF MUSCULARITY

Students enthusiastically embraced strikebreaking during the early twentieth century not just to display antagonism to labor but also to prove their manhood. Strikebreaking provided the collegian with his best opportunity, short of military combat, to test his strength and nerve, by exposing him to severe danger and providing him with the opportunity to fight.

By the turn of the century, America's upper and middle classes—the classes from which the students were drawn—were in the midst of a "crisis of masculinity." Men of the old elite were increasingly anxious about being displaced in a rapidly changing and highly competitive society by newly made and more energetic men of wealth. The genteel norms of their class, the languor that came of being born into affluence, undermined their assertiveness and ability to compete. They felt ineffectual, even superfluous. Many reacted by craving intense, violent experiences that provided feelings of power and mastery.

This gave rise in the upper class to a "cult of muscularity," an emphasis on male virility and the "strenuous life," typified by America's president during the century's first decade, Theodore Roosevelt. It required that men perform daring deeds, court danger, and undergo tests of fortitude—like hunting in the wilderness and participating in violent sports.[30]

Just as insecure in its masculinity was the emerging middle class, white-collar salariat, consisting of clerks, professionals, engineers, and managers in the new corporate bureaucracies. Unlike the old "petty bourgeois," these men were not self-employed and controlled no productive property. Instead they were subordinates in an elaborate hierarchy, and their initiative was strictly limited by their superiors. Their sedentary, often routinized work did not permit them the opportunity to display any traditionally "masculine" qualities, like strength, courage, and autonomy. Like the old elite, these men compensated for their "loss of masculinity" by involvement in the "strenuous life" and the nation's violent sporting culture.[31]

The upper- and middle-class crisis of masculinity gave rise to the "Muscular Christianity" movement, which commanded significant influence by the turn of the century. Protestantism had become increasingly feminized during the nineteenth century; women vastly outnumbered men in most congregations. Long concerned about their inability to reach adolescent boys and men, some clergymen embraced an exaggerated masculinity and strongly endorsed violent sports, arguing that they built character and were consistent with Christian principles.[32]

Strikebreaking, performed in groups and providing the opportunity for intense male bonding, served the same purposes as violent sports and other "daring deeds." And it toughened college youth by introducing them to the work environment of the working-class male, where the traditional masculine qualities remained entrenched. Indeed, the single attribute of the workingman that the upper and middle classes envied was his masculinity, shown in physical and drinking prowess and exposure to danger at work.[33]

Early twentieth-century newspapers and magazines glamorized the courage and rough masculinity of the professional strikebreaker, who had emerged as America's "last frontiersman," combining the "daring of the desperado" with the "acumen of the businessman." Men like "Boss" Jim Farley, who specialized in breaking streetcar strikes, and Ed Reed, who had played football at Yale in the 1890s, maintained their own private armies and could send thousands of "soldiers" across the country at a moment's notice to break a strike. Farley took great pride in having taken the first streetcar out in a multitude of strikes, braving "howling," stone-throwing crowds. By 1905 the press claimed he had been shot at 100 times and carried a bullet in his body. But, like the marshal on the vanished western frontier, he stared down strikers with "mankiller eyes"; his jaw ran "straight . . . as the barrel of a Colt's forty-five."[34]

Male college youth devoted a considerable amount of their leisure time to the nation's most violent team sport, football, which had emerged in the elite eastern colleges during the 1880s. Even after the "brutality crisis" of 1905–6, sparked by a mounting toll of deaths and crippling injuries on the gridiron, forced rule changes, football remained an exceedingly dangerous sport. In 1911 a physician referred to it as "a prize fight multiplied by eleven."[35]

Football was, in fact, frequently equated with military combat. Walter Camp, the "father of football," saw a "remarkable likeness" between "great battles" and the "contests of the gridiron." His contemporaries talked of "field generals" and "soldiers" on the gridiron; after World War I, football linemen were said to "battle in the trenches." By 1900 college football stadiums frequently commemorated the nation's war dead. Stephen Crane, who had never gone to war, claimed his experience playing football allowed him to portray military combat so realistically in *The Red Badge of Courage*.[36]

Collegians became heavily involved in strikebreaking not just because they experienced severe anxiety about their masculinity but also because administrators at the turn of the century eliminated "cane rush" and other campus rituals that had allowed mass student participation in violence. Football was not an adequate substitute for the banned rituals, since it relegated most students to the role of passive spectator. By contrast, cane rush, intended to "cement a class union," had involved nearly the entire freshman and sophomore classes. It represented the ultimate test of manliness at both private and state colleges during the late nineteenth century.[37]

Cane rush had been conceived of as a mass "gladiatorial contest." Throngs of students, faculty, and alumni gathered at an open field, which became the "battleground." The contest lasted from five to ten minutes. The freshman and sophomore classes were each arranged in a line, with the heaviest men (*robustae*) in the middle. Every man was stripped to the waist, producing a "gladiatorial effect." At the signal, the two lines, consisting of hundreds of students, charged at each other, all reaching for a cane lying halfway between the lines. The object was for a class to have more of its men touching the cane at the end of the contest than the opposing class. Seconds after coming together with a "crash and a crunch," the combatants resembled "an immense octopus whose tentacles are human legs." Pullers (*avelli*), stationed around the edge of the pile, were charged with reaching into the mass of human flesh, dragging out opponents by the legs, and delivering them to the wrestlers (*palaestrae*). These men then pinned their captives down for the duration, thus providing "a realistic representation of the dead gladiators of the Coliseum." Midway through the contest the jumpers (*salturae*) entered, springing "high over the mass," driving "headlong into the central pit of heads," thrusting their hands toward the cane. At the judges' signal, the struggle ceased, and the combatants went to their rooms "displaying their battle scars." Victory gave the winning class the privilege of carrying canes for the year.[38]

Not surprisingly, students were often seriously injured in these debacles. Columbia's 1896 cane rush, for example, ended with four students lying on the ground unconscious, one "tossed in convulsions."[39] By 1905, nearly all colleges and universities forbade their students from engaging in "this relic of barbarism."[40]

Other similarly bloody rituals, like Yale's "Pass of Thermopylae," were abolished at the turn of the century. Thermopylae had required freshmen to run the gauntlet between long lines of upperclassmen. As class sizes increased, this became extremely dangerous.[41]

Strikebreaking was the perfect replacement for the banned violent rituals. It provided students with the opportunity for mass participation, denied in organized college athletics, and satisfied their pressing need for a "test of masculinity." And unlike cane rush and Thermopylae, it carried the blessings of college administrators and faculties.

The student strikebreaker first appeared in 1901, eager to take on a "man's job" on the docks of San Francisco. University of California at Berkeley students, including members of the "eleven," boarded the brig *William S. Irwin*, deserted by strikers, and unloaded its cargo. One of the athletes remarked that the work allowed the team to "harden up for football season." None of the students appeared in need of employment; one noted delightedly that the money he earned would be spent on "tobacco . . . for many days to come." After a day and a half of labor, excitement, and conditioning, the students had finished their task, and left the ship giving the California yell.[42] President Benjamin Wheeler of the University of California, answering the protest of the San Francisco Labor Council against the students' strikebreaking, announced that he fully supported what his students had done.[43]

In 1903 Great Lakes shippers recruited replacements for their striking ship stokers from the training camp of one of America's leading "Muscular Christians," University of Chicago football and track and field coach Amos Alonzo Stagg. Several football players, high jumpers, sprinters, and shot putters went on board three grain ships bound for Buffalo. One of the students summed up his manly adventure by declaring, "It was more fun than a track meet." Like Cal's president Wheeler, Chicago's president William Rainey Harper rejected labor's appeal that he order his students to desist from strikebreaking.[44]

Students demonstrated a few months later that there were massive numbers on the campus willing to risk life and limb for the employing class, when hundreds answered the Minneapolis flour millers' call for strikebreakers. Among the first to volunteer were varsity athletes from the University of Minnesota, who with a "lusty Ski-U-Mah" (the Minnesota cheer) formed a wedge, and blasted through the picket line at the Pillsbury-Washburn mill. Mill representatives established a hiring office at the university YMCA (the nation's leading "Muscular Christian" organization), and by the end of the week, over 100 students had "donned the white raiment" of the millers and were at work on six-hour shifts. After only a few days, University of Minnesota students made up fully one-quarter of the strikebreaking force.[45]

While university president Cyrus Northrup approved of the strikebreaking, the school newspaper, the *Minnesota Daily*, expressed concern that Minnesota's trade unions might pressure the state legislature to deny appropriations to the university. It argued that it was "well and proper" for students to become strikebreakers if they needed the money to pay for school but stated that "the great majority are not of this class." But few, if any, were influenced by the *Daily*'s appeal, and once again college students were instrumental in breaking a strike.[46]

Yale students in 1903 and 1905 found the opportunity to display their virility by helping to break strikes of team drivers and railroad workers, occupations associated with a tough, physical masculinity. In 1903 the *New Haven Evening Register* noted that "the spectacle of well-dressed collegians on the seat of drays attracted attention wherever they went."[47] Two years later, Yale contributed 200 students, including several football players, to the New York, New Haven, and Hartford Railroad, about 15 percent of the strikebreakers. Yale's president Arthur Twining Hadley, in effect, supported the students' actions both times.[48]

Collegians learned that strikebreaking provided the opportunity to imagine they were "soldiers at war" in 1912, when they joined the militia companies sent in to quell the Lawrence textile strike. Some of the battalions were composed entirely of Harvard and Massachusetts Institute of Technology (MIT) students. Students enjoyed the opportunity to precipitate violence, as they enthusiastically disrupted picketing and strike parades. Militia service also swelled the young collegians' sense of power. MIT's student newspaper claimed the news of the Tech battalion's arrival in Lawrence so frightened strike leader Joe Ettor that he counseled, "[R]etreat to the Hills of Wellesley College," where Professors Vida Scudder and Ellen Hayes had made speeches for the strikers.[49]

Student strikebreakers did not have to don the militiaman's uniform to feel they were "at war"; many strikes provided a sense of being in a combat zone. During the 1919 New England telephone operators' strike, for example, male sympathizers of the women strikers unleashed probably the bloodiest assault ever staged against collegians. In riots in the streets of Boston, Cambridge, Providence, and Malden, which were sparked by the strikebreaking of students from Harvard, MIT, Tufts, and Brown, the working class took its revenge on the collegians, badly mauling several. In Boston, for example, some student strikebreakers were beaten unconscious and one had his teeth knocked out. A union official in Providence gloated that a "good beating" administered by strike sympathizers had convinced some of the student "sapheads" to reconsider their new careers as strikebreakers.[50]

The striking operators waged psychological warfare against the students, who eagerly sought to prove their manhood, by constantly impugning their masculinity. In Providence, when a Brown University strikebreaker called out "Hello red head!" to a young woman on picket duty, she retorted with contempt, "Hello yellow!" And at the daily strike meetings in Boston, when pickets reported the number of strikebreakers at each exchange, Telephone Operators' Union president Julia O'Connor invariably asked, "Men or boys?" The assembled operators roared, "Lizzies!," suggesting they did not consider them members of the male sex. The women operators used the same approach to student strikebreakers during the 1923 New England telephone strike, labeling them "powder puff boys" and subjecting them to applications of women's face powder when they left the exchanges.[51]

The 1919 Boston policemen's strike provided students with probably the closest approximation to the atmosphere of combat for which they longed. Here, students were cast in the role of the "thin blue line" that protected "civilization" against hordes of thugs and ruffians intent on murder, rape, and robbery. Like soldiers at war, the students were energized by massive public support; few believed the policemen were justified in walking off their jobs when it meant Boston might lapse into barbarism. In the atmosphere of hysteria that prevailed during the "Red Scare" of 1919, much of the public also considered the students to be combatants in the war against Bolshevism.

Over 200 Harvard students answered the appeal of their university president, A. Lawrence Lowell, to volunteer as strikebreakers and patrol the streets of Boston, a city against which criminals (and some said "Bolsheviks") had declared war. Harvard Yard itself took on a martial atmosphere, with all gates barricaded.[52] The strikebreakers included nearly the entire Harvard football team. Coach Bob Fisher declared, "To hell with football, if the men are needed."[53] Like generals visiting their troops at the front, President Lowell and Dean Chester Greenough toured the streets of Boston, offering encouragement to their students.[54] The students, constituting 15 percent of the strikebreaking force, became a significant factor in the patrolmen's defeat.

Reinforcing students' feeling that strikebreaking was a "test of manhood" was the fact that women collegians almost never participated in it. This was in part due to the danger involved and to women students' aversion to violence. College restrictions on women students' leaving campus also remained much more stringent than at men's schools; as a result they were much less confident about exploring the outside world than men were. The Wellesley College student newspaper observed that "9 out of 10 girls know only the shopping district and theaters and would be quite lost anywhere in the city [Boston]."[55]

In addition, during the 1910s women's colleges were more open to prolabor views than were men's colleges, and there were even a few cases of strike support by women students. During the decade 1909–19, women's suffragism finally became a mass movement and women's labor militancy reached its all-time peak. The suffragists, who commanded significant support in many women's colleges, placed considerable emphasis on drawing working-class women into their movement. As a result, some college women came into contact with women workers; this exposure led them to develop greater sympathy for labor. The settlement house movement, in which women students were disproportionately involved, instilled pro-labor views in them, as it drew them into direct contact with working people. Finally, the Women's Trade Union League (WTUL)—a coalition of middle-class reformers, including settlement house leaders and workers established in 1903 to organize working women—developed influence at some women's colleges, although mostly among faculty.

Settlement house work and the open-air suffrage rallies that began in 1909 encouraged some women collegians to venture out from "'neath the oaks" into the public realm. In 1909–10, students from Vassar, Wellesley, Barnard, and Bryn Mawr Colleges left their campuses to demonstrate solidarity with New York's striking women garment workers. The collegians raised funds, gave speeches, picketed, and observed arrests in an effort to protect the strikers from police brutality. The Wellesley student newspaper openly announced its support for the "Uprising of the 20,000," noting that the strikers were "girls just our own age."[56]

During the 1912 Boston Elevated strike, Wellesley students challenged their male counterparts from Harvard and Yale, who signed on as strike-breakers, by rallying to the carmen's cause. Responding to an appeal from professors Emily Balch and Vida Scudder, both members of the WTUL, 100 Wellesley students donated $1,000 to the strike fund and agreed not to ride the streetcars until the strike was won. The students donned buttons that read, "We Walk to Help Organize the Car Men."[57]

However, the women who engaged in strike support work represented only a small proportion of the students at women's colleges, most of whom remained staunchly conservative. As late as 1911, students at Wellesley, probably the most liberal women's college, voted down women's suffrage in a campus referendum by a nearly two-to-one margin. In 1924 the *New Student* editorial board emphatically declared that the college woman was "highly conservative."[58]

Women had little involvement in strikebreaking even in the 1920s, when commitment to reform causes declined sharply. The 1920s collegian was indeed often willing to defy college rules that limited her access to the world away from the campus, but her energies were mostly devoted to social activities with men. Only during the 1923 New England telephone operators' strike, which occurred during the summer, when the usual opportunities for social interaction with other collegians were not available, did significant numbers of women students engage in strikebreaking.[59]

Working women were never comfortable even with pro-labor collegians, viewing them as dilettantes and resenting their condescension. Helen Taft, daughter of the president and part of a Bryn Mawr student delegation that came to New York to assist the garment strikers in 1910, gaped at the pickets as though they were animals at the zoo, describing them to reporters as "poor creatures." And with that, she and her party left for the opera.[60] Working women who had never known childhood, toiling long hours from an early age, perceived the collegians as self-centered and immature, drawn to the labor movement only because they felt bored and saw workers as exotic. They expected that the students would quickly return to lives of frivolity and material comfort. New York garment workers put on a play that portrayed the pro-labor college woman as a scatterbrained child; a "College Girl" asks WTUL leader Pauline Newman: "Could you please tell me all about the labor movement? I must have it for my paper at school. I'd like to organize the South or something."[61]

## THE ENGINEERING STUDENT AS STRIKEBREAKER

Engineering students were drawn into strikebreaking by their profession's new antipathy toward labor, not just by anxiety over masculinity. The engineering profession was now elaborating objectives that clashed directly with those of trade unions. And the engineering schools had begun to train their students in industrial management as well as in applied science. By the early years of the twentieth century the ideas of Frederick Winslow Taylor, the leading proponent of "scientific management," had attained wide influence in large-scale industry. For Taylor, efficiency in production required systematic management control over all aspects of production. Engineers, trained in scientific management techniques, restructured the work process by determining the "one best way" to perform any task. Their system undermined the autonomy of the craftsman and eliminated any worker initiative. As Taylor himself put it, "Under our system the workman is told minutely just what he is to do and how he is to do it." He and his associates were generally antagonistic to the trade union, viewing it as protecting workers' restriction of output.[62] Engineers also made every effort to emphasize their social distance from mechanics. By identifying with unions they would have blurred this distinction in status.[63]

During the early twentieth century, engineering colleges entered into close cooperation with corporations; supplying strikebreakers grew out of that relationship. Engineering colleges conducted research on a contractual basis for industry, often acting like private consulting firms. During the

1910s, for example, MIT's electrical engineering department did research for American Telephone and Telegraph, the Boston and Maine and the New York, New Haven, and Hartford railroad companies, and various electrical companies. At the same time business made heavy financial contributions to engineering colleges' research facilities.[64]

While the number of engineers expanded fivefold between 1900 and 1930, the profession remained predominantly the preserve of native-born Protestant middle- and upper-class men. By 1900 engineering schools like MIT were already challenging the elite liberal arts colleges as a training ground for America's corporate leadership. In the 1920s, for example, the chief executives of General Motors, General Electric, DuPont, and Goodyear, four of the world's most powerful corporations, had been classmates at MIT around the turn of the century.[65]

Engineering students made their first appearance as strikebreakers in the 1901 national machinists' strike, and they made a critical contribution to crushing the walkout in several localities. Steel, automobile, and shipbuilding plants in Chicago and Detroit hired University of Michigan students to replace strikers. The *Detroit Free Press* noted that the students were attracted by the "element of danger" and was certain they would be "right in" the fighting.[66] The Crocker-Wheeler Works in Ampere, New Jersey, the "storm centre" of the strike in the New York area, hired 100 Columbia University students, with the full approval of the school's president, Seth Low. As the *Free Press* proclaimed: "A new factor ha[d] entered into the battle between capital and labor. It is student labor."[67]

Because it was extremely difficult to find skilled machinists willing to replace strikers, the students were a godsend. Manufacturers like R. E. Olds, president of Olds Motor Works, rated the work of the student strikebreakers highly. Four years later, during the New York IRT strike, the *Columbia Spectator* noted that students from Columbia's School of Applied Science who had replaced striking motormen had "clearly demonstrated the practical value of the[ir] training."[68]

In 1913 the skills of engineering students from Stanford and the University of California at Berkeley proved invaluable to the Pacific Gas and Electric Company after its machinists, electrical and gas workers, and boilermakers walked out. After the strike was lost, labor leaders conceded that the students' contribution had been critical to the company's victory. David Starr Jordan, president of Stanford, and Benjamin Wheeler, president of the University of California, rejected labor's appeal that they order their students to return to their campuses.[69]

Engineering students were in the forefront of the massive collegiate strikebreaking effort against the railroad workers in 1920 and 1921, when the student struggle against labor reached its peak. The years immediately following World War I constituted a period of unparalleled class conflict, causing near hysteria among the middle and upper classes. Although the "Red Scare" subsided somewhat after 1919, many affluent Americans still equated strikes with "Bolshevik insurrection." As a result, when railroad workers threatened to strike across the East, students volunteered in massive numbers to assist the railroad companies. Like the Boston policemen's strike, these walkouts created a sense of public emergency—in this case the threat of food shortages in major cities—that resembled that of wartime. And students found glamor in the danger of railroad work.

College and university administrators recruited students for strikebreaking more openly and aggressively than ever before. At some schools in 1920 nearly the entire student body answered the call for strikebreakers, as at MIT, Stevens Institute, Columbia, and Princeton.

The railroad corporations particularly desired engineering students to fill in as engineers, firemen, brakemen, switchmen, and repairmen, although other students were hired in some of these positions, and also as trainmen and porters. In 1920 Stevens Institute suspended all classes as its students rushed to save the railroads from what the school newspaper called "Bolshevism." MIT's faculty strongly endorsed the decision of 3,000 students there to take strikers' jobs; they were certain they could "fill in efficiently."[70]

Administrators and the press acted as though the students were being summoned for military combat. The *New York Tribune* declared that Princeton "brought memories of that April day in 1917 when war was declared." Princeton's president John Grier Hibben notified the Pennsylvania Railroad that his undergraduates were "ready to serve" and that full credit would be given for strikebreaking. Dean Herbert Hawkes of Columbia helped recruit 5,000 student strikebreakers by telling them they were needed to fight an "insurrectionary movement."[71]

The railroad corporations fully appreciated the students' valuable contribution to breaking the strike less than ten days after they began volunteering. Corporation heads praised their "vigor" and "aptitude" and declared they were a "marvel to their supervisory officers."[72]

The colleges went a step further the next year, establishing special courses in railroad engineering on the campuses to help break the strike. MIT led the way, introducing the first "short course" in railroad work. The

Boston and Maine Railroad, for whom MIT had long done consulting work, placed a railroad track and a passenger car on campus for use in instructing strikebreakers.[73] Harvard established a similar course for 700 student strikebreakers. Engineering professors at Johns Hopkins University had no difficulty persuading their students to gain "practical experience" in railroading, which they claimed would prove more valuable than "theoretical work."[74] At Williams, the student newspaper clamored for the college to set up special courses in railroad engineering.[75]

This vast army of students, ready to don overalls for the corporations, helped undermine the unions' resolve. The railroad brotherhoods called off the strike before it began.

Students continued to engage in strikebreaking after the early 1920s but never on a scale resembling that of the first two decades of the twentieth century. Labor's quiescence from the early 1920s to the early 1930s provided few opportunities for strikebreaking, but the trade-union movement experienced a dramatic revival after 1933. The most prominent case of student strikebreaking during the 1930s occurred during the 1934 San Francisco longshoremen's strike, when a sizable contingent from the University of California at Berkeley's football team, at their coach's urging, went to work on the docks. University of Southern California football players also took strikers' jobs on the San Pedro docks. Harry Bennett, the ex-navy boxer who headed Ford Motor Company's "Service Department," a private army of thugs whose purpose was to beat up union organizers and strikers, also hired college athletes from the University of Michigan.[76]

However, the Great Depression transformed the campuses in ways that diminished strikebreaking's appeal to students. For one thing it radicalized many students, instilling sympathy for labor's plight. Beginning in 1932, when several busloads of collegians left the campus of Columbia University to bring aid to striking miners in Harlan County, Kentucky, students on many campuses demonstrated solidarity with strikers.[77] And more working-class youth enrolled in college during the 1930s, who were less likely to engage in strikebreaking than their more affluent counterparts. Hard times also turned students away from frivolous extracurricular pursuits, like strikebreaking, toward greater emphasis on academics. Faculty members, with greater job security after the onset of the tenure system in the late 1930s, were more likely to impart pro-labor views to their students.

Student strikebreaking also declined in the decades after the early 1920s as heterosociability took root on college campuses, replacing homosocial leisure life. The proportion of students attending coeducational residential institutions increased dramatically in the 1920s, so that they enrolled nearly two-thirds of all college and university youth. In fact, the term for woman college student became "co-ed." Instead of men socializing primarily with men and women with women, college social life centered around heterosocial activities of "play and pleasure," like dating, dancing, and fraternity and sorority parties. This was the case even at single-sex colleges, where social life focused on weekend encounters with students of the other sex from other schools.[78] College men continued to engage in frivolous extracurricular activities in the decades after 1920, but these focused much more on contacts with women than on contacts with each other. Strikebreaking, performed by men in groups, an activity of intense male bonding, greatly diminished as homosociability declined.

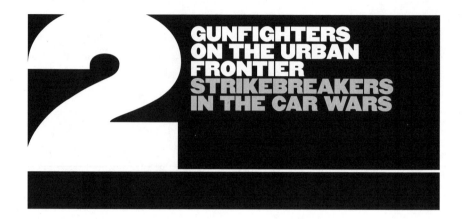

## GUNFIGHTERS ON THE URBAN FRONTIER STRIKEBREAKERS IN THE CAR WARS

Strikebreaking emerged as a new and highly lucrative business at the beginning of the twentieth century, organized on a national basis. It introduced to the American public a new soldier of fortune, one who embodied the traditional fighting qualities it associated with men of the vanished frontier. The large mercenary armies of the new strikebreaking agencies, transported on short notice over long distances, provided employers with a critical advantage in labor conflicts. During the first two decades of the twentieth century, strikebreaking agencies concentrated primarily on urban transit strikes, which were numerous and bitterly contested. The American city became the environment for romantic military adventure and a new form of guerrilla warfare, with hand-to-hand combat, night raids, cavalry charges, fighting from rooftops and behind barricades, and retreats in which the wounded were evacuated under heavy fire.[1]

With the Indian wars over and the United States involved in no significant overseas military engagements between the Spanish-American War and World War I, these labor conflicts provided the best opportunity for the conspicuous display of the more primitive and virile behavior that society increasingly valued in men because of its anxiety about "overcivilization" and "overrefinement." The middle class was redefining masculinity to emphasize the soldierly virtues of aggressiveness, courage and daring, and physical strength rather than self-restraint, character, and will.[2] Strikebreaking was society's most dangerous civilian occupation, most closely approximating that of the combat soldier.

The intense street fighting that erupted during all of these transit strikes led commentators to equate them with the land and sea warfare of the 1890s and early years of the twentieth century. The Reverend Thomas E. Sherman, S.J., son of the famed Civil War general William Tecumseh Sherman, called the 1903 Chicago streetcar strike "a war more barbaric than [that] in the Philippines" and declared that the strike disorder constituted a greater threat to the nation than "the southern confederacy ever was."[3] A detective who witnessed the "Washington Street Massacre" during the 1900 St. Louis streetcar strike, when citizen militia fired on union men marching behind a drum corps, commented: "I thought the battle of Santiago [was being] fought over," referring to a major engagement in the recently concluded Spanish-American War.[4] The *San Francisco Examiner* declared that the street fighting in that city's 1907 streetcar strike was "warfare as real, as vivid" as combat "between troops arrived on a [battlefield]." Society women even threw flowers at the cars of strikebreaking crews as they passed, as though they were soldiers going off to battle.[5]

Lecturing on "Substitutes for War" in 1903, settlement house leader Jane Addams cited that year's Chicago streetcar strike as a prime example of modern warfare, an expression of the "pugnacity [that] belonged to the childhood of nations" but that was "shameful [to them] . . . in their maturity." She condemned the "physical force" used by both sides in the strike, which she compared to two warring nations.[6]

During the 1903 Richmond streetcar walkout, commentators in the old Confederate capital even equated the strike violence with that which occurred during the Civil War. A Richmond attorney prosecuting a county sheriff for refusing to call for state militia to quell rioting asserted that the violence sparked by the city's streetcar strike was more terrifying than the "day about 40 years ago" when the Confederate capital, "a fiery veil," fell to the Union army: "Never before [was] there such disorder, midnight assassinations, [and] dynamite." The *Washington Post* also compared the strike to the Civil War, declaring that "such a . . . display of firearms . . . has not been seen since 1861." The *Richmond Times-Dispatch* noted that had electric streetcars existed in Richmond "in '60–'65," they "would have looked like" those stoned by crowds in 1903.[7]

The press also drew an analogy with naval warfare, referring to the streetcar piloted by strikebreakers as a "man-of-war" traveling through a hostile sea of strike sympathizers. As in the navy, a convoy system was sometimes used, in which several streetcars traveled in close formation along the tracks to ensure better protection against the crowds. And on some occasions when strikebreakers were housed on ships, they received

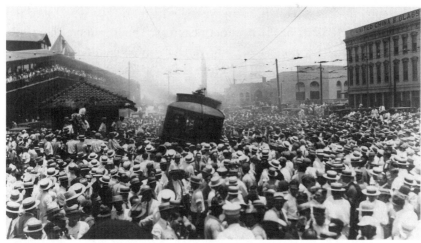

*A confrontation occurs after the streetcar company attempted to resume the running of cars during the 1929 New Orleans strike. Riots often occurred during early twentieth-century transit strikes when strikebreaking crews ventured out of protected carbarns into the streets. Crowds of strike sympathizers might surround and attempt to disable the cars or pummel the strikebreakers. Courtesy of the Walter P. Reuther Library, Wayne State University.*

orders to "land and take possession" of the streetcar barns vacated by strikers.[8]

During the first two decades of the twentieth century, nearly all the major American cities experienced major streetcar and subway strikes, marked by almost continuous and often spectacular violent conflict. Unlike a strike involving a factory or stockyards, strikebreakers could not be protected in a confined area. They had to venture out into the streets, where strike sympathizers, who frequently formed crowds as large as 5,000, and occasionally 15,000 or more, hurled rocks and other missiles at them, and sometimes pulled them from the streetcars and beat them. The thousands of miles of electric trolley wire and tracks could be easily sabotaged, causing accidents and posing further danger to strikebreakers. Deaths and injuries in urban transit strikes far exceeded those in most labor conflicts. The highest toll came in the 1907 San Francisco streetcar strike, when 30 were killed and 1,000 injured, but casualties ran into the hundreds in several other cities.[9]

Their inordinate violence would in any case have made the urban transit strikes a major focus of public attention, but it is also significant that the electric streetcar was the principal means of urban transportation in the

*Strike sympathizers hurl missiles at a streetcar run by a strikebreaking crew during the 1929 New Orleans strike. Courtesy of Associated Press/Wide World Photos.*

city between 1900 and 1920. As a result, any walkout seriously affected nearly all residents and major businesses.

Although streetcarmen seriously inconvenienced the public by walking out, disrupting the ability to get to and from work and making shopping and social life more difficult, the strikers invariably enjoyed wide public support, which extended beyond the working class. Much of the public resented the traction companies, in part because it considered them greedy monopolies, often absentee owned, which derived unreasonable profits at public expense, sometimes by bribing municipal officials. During the 1907 San Francisco streetcar strike, for example, that city's Hearst newspaper printed the union's denunciation of traction company management as "not of this town," men to whom "San Francisco is . . . as a Congo rubber plantation is to a European syndicate." Managerial officials "rolled around [San Francisco] in automobiles and spoke at big banquets . . . but . . . had never a thought for us." Their only concern was the "money they carr[ied] away" from San Francisco to the East.[10]

Passengers also developed a hostile attitude toward the traction companies because they found streetcar travel unpleasant. They were "buffeted and flung about" by "every jolt and jerk" in crowded cars, where many had to stand; accidents were frequent.[11] The *New York American* in 1906 branded Brooklyn Rapid Transit the "Kill 'em for a nickel company" and condemned its "murderous record" of eighty-five deaths, most of them children, during the first half of the year. It also complained of the company's "indecent" treatment of women, forced to ride with men in crammed cars.[12] Many believed that shorter working hours, a common strike demand, would promote public safety because an overworked motorman was more likely to have an accident.

In addition, regular riders often developed an attachment to the usually courteous conductor who not only collected their fares but conversed with them, looked out for their children, and assisted women in getting on and off the cars. The streetcarmen's union magazine, *Motorman and Conductor*, called the carman the "trusted confidant of the public," with "grave responsibilities" not only to "passengers, but pedestrians."[13]

In southern cities the streetcarmen's union was also able to mobilize fierce sectional emotion against the strikebreakers, who were generally imported from northern cities. In Richmond in 1903, speakers at the strike meetings told the carmen that the strikebreakers fighting them "were the same men . . . who fought their fathers in 1861." In New Orleans in 1902, pro-strike crowds denounced the strikebreakers as "northern murderers."[14]

Commentators described the urban transit strikes as among the most fiercely fought in the country's history and unprecedented in their impact on the city. *Motorman and Conductor* called Cleveland's 1899 streetcar strike "the hardest contested battle ever fought by our people in America."[15] St. Louis's streetcar strike the next year was the "most serious [streetcar] tieup . . . in the history of the world." Samuel Gompers, president of the American Federation of Labor (AFL), called it "the fiercest struggle ever waged by the organized toilers [anywhere]." The *St. Louis Globe-Democrat* observed that visitors to the city "might easily have imagined themselves in Central America" in the midst of a popular uprising, as "hundreds of armed and excited men surg[ed] through the streets, filling the air with bullets, bricks, and outcries."[16] The 1902 New Orleans streetcar strike was the first in which the entire transit system of an American metropolis was completely paralyzed, unable to carry a single passenger. The New York Interborough Rapid Transit (IRT) Company's strikebreaking force in the 1905 subway strike was larger than that previously assembled in any American strike.[17] During the 1910 Philadelphia streetcar walkout, union sympathizers broke so many streetcar windows that the city's stock of window glass was exhausted. The crowds in the 1929 New Orleans streetcar strike that menaced strikebreakers surpassed "the biggest swarm of Mardi Gras," at one point reaching an incredible 50,000.[18]

The intensity of the street fighting and the building of barricades led many observers to compare the early twentieth-century urban streetcar strikes to the French Revolution and the Paris Commune. As strikebreakers who had just shot twenty-five strike sympathizers abandoned their vehicles and retreated on foot down San Francisco's Market Street in 1907, firing into the pursuing crowd of 5,000, "the scene resembled those described in the French Revolution. . . . [T]he battle was no less serious than those fought on the streets of Paris over a century ago."[19] Reporting on the 1900 St. Louis strike, *Collier's Weekly* declared that the "scenes of disorder," unprecedented in the city's history, "took on the nature of the terrible orgies of riot and wantonness that characterized the early days of the French Revolution in Paris."[20]

The *New York Tribune* noted during the 1909 Philadelphia streetcar strike that families in the Kensington mill district were building barricades and declared that the "thirty hours of almost continuous rioting" early in the strike resembled the Paris Commune. The importation of strikebreakers had "kindled the fires of hatred," and the crowds lining the tracks were "so dense and so wild with anger" as to "give the scene the appearance of a revolution." The crowds drove back the police "like a whirlwind," in one incident burning two streetcars and turning three others crosswise on the tracks. Charges by mounted police failed to subdue the crowd, and "when the smoke of conflict cleared away," it was discovered that ten policemen had been injured. Kensington families gathered on their roofs to hurl stones down on passing streetcars; when the rocks gave out, they tore down chimneys and threw the bricks at the cars.[21]

Beginning with Cleveland's streetcar strike in 1899, the first in which explosives were freely used, strikebreaking crews faced the prospect of their cars being dynamited on the tracks. On what came to be known in Cleveland as "Bloody Sunday," a nitroglycerin bomb that had been placed on the tracks exploded beneath a Euclid Avenue streetcar, badly wounding ten passengers and ripping an ear off the motorman's head. Nitroglycerin bombs blew up several more streetcars during the next several weeks. In St. Louis's 1900 strike the dynamiting of streetcars was a "nightly occurrence."[22]

Strikebreaking crews also had to "run the gauntlet" along the tracks lined with hostile crowds, which hurled stones and other missiles from the street and from rooftops, capable of smashing through streetcar windows and sending flying glass everywhere. The companies sometimes, but not often, placed wire mesh screens over the windows to protect the crews. Crowds sometimes boarded the cars and beat the crews senseless, or burned and overturned the vehicles.

Increasing the strikebreaker's prospect of being injured during a streetcar strike were the frequent obstructions that strike sympathizers placed on the tracks. These obstructions might derail a car or prevent it from proceeding further, rendering it an easy target for missiles and making it possible for members of the crowd to board the cars and beat the motorman and conductor. In St. Louis in 1900 and in San Francisco in 1907, strike sympathizers piled mammoth stones and other debris on the tracks and built bonfires on them that burned day and night. Sometimes the flames reached even to the trolley wires. Crowds cut trolley wires and displaced rails, stopping streetcar traffic for hours. Downed trolley wires left dangling in the street could cause electrocution. Strike sympathizers in Cleveland in 1899 threw heavy ropes across the trolley wires to pull them down. They placed broken lampposts, troughs, iron and tin cans, and street refuse across the tracks, which they greased to cause derailment. In San Francisco, a "favorite practice" was to fill track switches with cement, which blocked traffic after hardening and had to be dug out by car crews.[23]

Teamsters also frequently assisted streetcar strikers by parking their wagons across the tracks, causing repeated blockades. They accounted for fully half the arrests during the 1903 Chicago streetcar strike. The strikers had men stationed at every carbarn, who reported to teamsters by telephone whenever the company attempted to move cars. At one point during the strike, a stockyards worker even drove a large flock of sheep on to the tracks, preventing any movement on the line for over an hour.[24]

Obstructions were sometimes placed across the tracks with the explicit purpose of harming the strikebreakers, not just to stop the streetcars, although that too put the crews at risk. In Richmond's 1903 strike, a streetcar traveling at night smashed into a heavy wire stretched across the track from pole to pole, which the motorman had been unable to discern in the darkness. Fortunately for him, he happened to be driving a vestibuled winter car, even though it was July. Had the front of the car been open, he would have been severely cut.[25]

Strike sympathizers also hung an assortment of objects known as "wire decorations" from the electric lines, designed to slow down or even halt the streetcars. In St. Louis in 1900, a reporter described the "cluster of obstructions" hung on the wires at one busy intersection as a "work of patience . . .

*Strike sympathizers place obstructions on tracks to impede the movement of streetcars, St. Louis streetcar strike, 1900. Baumhoff-Proetz Collection, Missouri Historical Society, St. Louis; photograph by J. Edward Roesch.*

genius and . . . toil worthy of the coral insect," so creative that "hours must have been devoted to the thinking of the combinations." The objects included wash boilers, dish pans, bread boxes, tea pots, coal scuttles, soup ladles, dinner buckets, water pails, fire shovels, lard cans, stove pipe, sugar boxes, barrel hoops, old shoes, clothes, gasoline cans, tin roofing, mosquito screens, and more, tied together with rags and old stockings. The hanging objects caused the wires to sag so low the streetcars could barely pass under them.[26] The *St. Louis Post-Dispatch* commented three weeks into the strike, "Apparently all the old clothes and retired kitchen utensils in the city [had] been used up in making . . . wire decorations."[27]

In working-class districts, strike sympathizers also hung effigies on the trolley wires to intimidate strikebreakers. By displaying an effigy of a strikebreaker or company official, a common practice in all the early twentieth-century streetcar strikes, the community was carrying out a symbolic execution. In fact, the "first ominous sign" a strikebreaking crew encountered was a "dangling effigy," or "perhaps a vista of them"—the sign that the crew was "going into the enemy's country."[28]

These displays often contained very explicit images of war and death. In one St. Louis neighborhood, 200 boys built a fort to warn strikebreakers away, using large rocks and cobblestones, which they also placed across

*Strike sympathizers hung "wire decorations" on trolley wires to prevent streetcars from moving, St. Louis streetcar strike, 1900. An effigy hangs in the foreground. Missouri Historical Society, St. Louis; photograph by George Stark.*

the tracks. Every ten feet along the tracks they placed a length of gutter spouting taken from nearby buildings, which were arranged to represent heavy artillery pieces, pointed in all directions. An effigy of a strikebreaker that the boys had hung on the wire wore a placard reading, "Any scab motorman passing here on a car will be shot." Another dummy bore the skull and crossbones, and a card on which was written, "Death to the scabs." A reporter noted that "from a distance it looked as if strikers during the night had lynched two men."[29]

Streetcar strikebreakers were, in fact, often threatened with lynching by pro-strike crowds, particularly after having fired on them. In Cleveland in 1899 a strikebreaking conductor who had fired two pistol shots from his car was immediately surrounded by a "maddened crowd" crying, "Lynch him, Lynch him!" The arrival of two police patrol wagons saved the strikebreaker from death, but only after many of the strike sympathizers had been "severely clubbed."[30] In 1902, after New Orleans police arrested two strikebreakers from Chicago who had drawn revolvers and fired at strike sympathizers when their car was halted by a plank barricade, an angry crowd chased the patrol wagon carrying them to jail, shouting, "Lynch the northern murderers!"[31] Crowds in Chicago and Waterbury, Connecticut, during the 1903 strikes there actually procured rope and prepared to string it up on poles. The arrival of police patrol wagons narrowly averted hangings.[32] In San Francisco, where the labor movement was as strong as in any American metropolis, strikebreakers arrested for firing into a crowd "huddle[d] . . . in their dark cells," fearful that "any noise signifi[ed] a mob attack" in which they would be lynched. They believed that San Francisco's police sympathized with the strikers and "would make but little resistance if their lives were demanded."[33]

The strikebreakers could not really feel safe even in the heavily guarded carbarns where they ate and slept, although in many cases the barns resembled "fortified arsenals." For this reason they were sometimes housed on ships anchored in outlying rivers, beyond the reach of attackers, as in New York's IRT subway strike in 1905. In San Francisco in 1907 the car windows were protected with wire mesh, and sandbags, barrels, and cable spools were arrayed around the barns to form barricades. The Turk and Fillmore Street barn was protected by a hastily built ten-foot-high wooden fence, topped with barbed wire. But crowds set siege to the carbarns, trying to starve out the strikebreakers by intercepting the company's food wagons.[34] In Chicago's 1903 streetcar strike, crowds surrounded the barns and "practically cut off [the strikebreakers] from the rest of the world." The company made several attempts to send in provisions wagons, but each time the wagons were captured and the food destroyed. Finally, seventy-five policemen managed to get food in to the beleaguered strikebreakers, but only after exchanging gunfire with strike sympathizers.[35]

The strike sympathizers' hit-and-run tactics, both those of the street crowds seemingly appearing out of nowhere to stone a car and the even more frightening night raids in the city's outlying districts, were frequently compared to contemporary guerrilla warfare, with which the American public had become fascinated because of the press's extensive coverage of the Boer War in South Africa and the Philippines campaign. Writers like Richard Harding Davis and Stephen Crane had made war correspondence a "great calling" during the 1890s, and the press drew frequent parallels between the battle tactics employed in the urban transit strikes and in these foreign "adventures."[36] From 1899 to 1902 the Boers, undisciplined farmers fighting without uniforms, made "full use of fog, smoke, and night" to launch surprise raids, a tactic their British enemy denounced as "unsporting." The British responded by forcing Boer women and children, along with men, into detention camps, an action that bore similarity to the mass arrests of women and children for stoning and obstructing streetcars during the early twentieth-century American transit strikes.[37] In 1902 the *New Orleans Daily Picayune* reported that the strikers "emulat[ing] the fighting methods of the Boers," as well as their "cunning," changed their "base of resistance," and struck at the streetcars "from an unforeseen direction." And in 1903 the *Richmond Times-Dispatch* remarked that because of the need to protect against guerrilla raids by strike sympathizers, streetcars on the city's Seven Pines line had come to resemble the "armored train[s] among the kopjes of Boerland."[38]

Guerrilla tactics proved most effective at night, and the strikebreakers became increasingly vulnerable the farther their car came to the city's outskirts, where few policemen were concentrated. At night the stone throwers and the occasional sniper became entirely invisible to the strikebreaking crew, and derailments and dynamitings were more easily carried out. For this reason, during strikes many streetcar companies suspended all service after dark. Strikebreakers taking a streetcar out on a night route bore some resemblance to American seamen on Mekong River patrol during the Vietnam War. In Cleveland's 1899 streetcar strike, a "systematic guerilla warfare [was] kept up from dusk until the last car was in the barns."[39] The *Richmond Times-Dispatch*, during that city's 1903 streetcar strike, also explicitly referred to "guerilla warfare" being waged in the "far

West End." Virginia state militiamen were assigned to ride streetcars sent through that section's "dark and dangerous fields," and often exchanged fire with strike sympathizers concealed along the tracks. Squads of militiamen patrolled the fields and hillsides in a usually unsuccessful attempt to ferret out snipers. For protection, streetcars entering the far West End were sometimes placed in total darkness, with all lights extinguished.[40]

The *Richmond Times-Dispatch* praised the strikebreaking crews on the night routes as "gritty men" who "take their lives in their hands on every run." It particularly admired the "cool daring" of one conductor on a night run through the far West End who climbed on top of the car when the trolley arm broke and held it against the wire, riding the rest of the way "silhouetted against the darkness," an easy target for stones and bullets.[41]

To be sure, strike sympathizers were in even greater danger than strikebreakers during these conflicts, because they were usually armed only with bricks or stones, whereas the latter often carried firearms and did not hesitate to use them. Selig Perlman, analyzing the 1913 Indianapolis streetcar strike for the U.S. Commission on Industrial Relations, noted that during the riots the "mob" used no firearms, whereas armed strikebreakers killed four men. In Bay City, Michigan, in 1905, strikebreakers on the cars even carried Winchester rifles, a "new departure" in streetcar strikes.[42] The *San Francisco Examiner* described strikebreakers in that city's 1907 strike as "desperate men," who "have no scruples of shooting to kill." On one occasion, strikebreakers opened fire on a crowd stoning cars, killing four and wounding over twenty. Twelve strikebreakers were arrested and charged with murder or attempted murder.[43]

In St. Louis during the 1900 strike, police indicated that anyone who joined a crowd containing persons throwing stones was fair game. When Frank Liebknecht, a twenty-one-year-old Spanish-American War veteran, was shot dead by a strikebreaker from a car, St. Louis's police chief remarked, "I don't know whether Liebknecht was stoning the car or not, but he was in the crowd and is therefore equally guilty."[44]

## THE PROFESSIONAL STRIKEBREAKER: AMERICA'S PRIMITIVE WARRIOR

Like the heavyweight prizefighter, who moved aggressively forward in the ring at great personal risk, the strikebreaker epitomized the new conflation of masculinity and physicality in early twentieth-century America.

As bureaucratization eroded their autonomy and increasingly confined them to sedentary jobs, middle-class men were drawn to the tougher, more boisterous behavior traditionally celebrated in the working class. They could engage in it at least vicariously by admiring the courage and physical strength of athletes, and the warriors and adventurers described by correspondents like Richard Harding Davis. Men's anxiety about the increasingly dominant role of mothers and female schoolteachers in socializing boys gave rise in the 1890s to a series of new terms of derision for those deemed insufficiently masculine, like "sissy," "mollycoddle," and "pussyfoot." Heavyweight boxing champion John L. Sullivan, the "Boston Strong Boy," a hard puncher and courageous battler who kept coming at his opponent even when hurt, by 1890 had become a national hero; he was adored not only by business and professional men but also by "nice" women, as well as by workingmen.[45]

By the 1890s the middle class had come to consider the ideal male body as bulky and heavily muscled rather than lean and wiry, as had been the case in the 1860s. Joining in society's "new fascination with muscularity," the middle class helped make celebrities of bodybuilders like Eugene Sandow and Bernarr McFadden.[46]

Newspapers often described professional strikebreakers as men of herculean strength, as fearsome as the top heavyweight boxers. The *Chicago Chronicle*, for example, during that city's 1903 streetcar strike, in profiling two strikebreakers from St. Louis, emphasized that the two "splendid physical specimens . . . like[d] trouble and thrive[d] on it." Each was of the "giant class," standing over six feet tall and weighing 220 pounds. The *Chronicle* observed that "[t]hey looked fit to enter a prize ring" or to "mix in a roughhouse argument with any half dozen men." One of them pulled off his hat to display "a couple big scars on his head," battle wounds from the 1900 St. Louis streetcar strike. He declared, "I can stand off 100 men with my brake lever and my fists, . . . and if it comes to the worst I will go to my hip pocket." Smashing his "big fist on the table until the glasses bounced in the air," his pal gleefully boasted: "Put us on a car and we'll take it to h—l and back if there's any rails to run on."[47]

The longing for a tougher and more independent model of masculinity led many Americans to identify the strikebreaker with the brave, self-reliant frontier gunslinger, celebrated in the immensely popular western novel, first introduced by Owen Wister with *The Virginian*, published in 1902, and most prominently associated with Zane Grey. Like the strikebreaker, the western gunman constantly moved from job to job, entering one dangerous situation after another; was not constrained by family life; took the law into his own hands; and solved problems with violence. The hero in the western novel proved his manhood by risking his life in violent confrontation, a climactic shoot-out that invariably required that he ignore the pleas of the woman in the story not to do so. To be truly a man, the hero must reject what the woman wants; he must prove that he is not under her control.[48]

That the professional strikebreaker was the modern-day cowboy was a recurrent theme in the nation's press. A mass circulation magazine described James Farley, the founder of the strikebreaking business and its dominant figure during the early years of the twentieth century, as a "native of the east [who] essentially . . . belongs to the west," and noted that he "does not seek trouble, but meeting it, invariably shoots first."[49] A writer who went undercover as a strikebreaker for Farley in the 1905 New York IRT subway strike to investigate the "new occupation" described many of the individuals he worked with as "bad men" from the West with "notches on their guns."[50] The *Philadelphia Inquirer* in 1910 reported that many of the strikebreakers in that city's streetcar strike were "Westerners" from "towns beyond St. Louis," who were "accustomed to breaking strikes by forcible methods." Some were cowboys, and others had lived on ranches. Driving the streetcars, they "acted in approved cowboy style," hanging out of the windows and firing their revolvers while "giving wild yells." Pedestrians "gaped in amazement" at the shop and office windows "broken by [the] flying bullets of the free shooting Western gunmen." The *St. Louis Post-Dispatch* directly linked the turn-of-the-century streetcar strike with the gun battles of the Old West by featuring a lengthy interview with legendary outlaw Frank James, asking him how he would handle the 1900 strike if he were Missouri's governor.[51]

Although it was obvious that many of the men recruited to break streetcar strikes came from the slums of the eastern cities, they were nonetheless often equated with western badmen. A journalist alleged that some of James Farley's "mercenary soldiers," shipped from the East to San Francisco to break the 1907 streetcar strike, had terrified the most fearsome western desperadoes. He recounted the tale of an overnight train carrying a carload of Farley's "eastern toughs" to San Francisco that was sidetracked at a sagebrush town out West. Within half an hour of the train's arrival, the main street was the scene of a "raging battle." Farley's strikebreakers quickly "chased all the local bad men to the tall timber." They gave the residents of the cow town an "exhibition of go-as-you please rough house such as they had never seen before."[52]

Riding a streetcar through hostile, stone-throwing crowds that piled obstructions in its path or threatened to seize and burn the cars like Indians attacking a wagon train, the strikebreaker seemed every bit as daring as the frontier gunslinger. Like an Old West wagonmaster, a strikebreaking motorman in the 1910 Philadelphia streetcar strike, spotting a bonfire raging on the tracks ahead, "turned on full power and drove his trolley through the flames." The press often depicted the strike crowds as "white savages," as menacing to civilization as the recently subjugated Indian "hostiles."[53] The strikebreaker also resembled the modern fighter pilot, braving enemy antiaircraft fire and often having to bring in a badly disabled craft, battered by bricks, with every window broken, struggling to stay on the tracks and reach the barn before being engulfed and set on fire by an angry crowd. Strikebreaking motormen and conductors were sometimes pulled off the car and held prisoner, like airmen shot down in enemy territory.[54] Like the modern fighter pilot, the strikebreaking carman knew that no sooner did he return from a successful mission than he again had to risk his safety and perhaps even his life by venturing out into the enemy's country.

Like the western gunslinger, the strikebreaker in the early twentieth-century urban transit strikes affirmed his masculinity by demonstrating that women could not control him. Newspapers frequently drew attention to the threat women posed to strikebreaking streetcar crews, because they made up a significant proportion of the crowds menacing the cars. Women frequently led the taunts directed at the strikebreakers and not only served as "brick passers" for the men who stoned the cars but often joined in themselves. Women in Chicago's stockyards district "danced with rage" during that city's 1903 streetcar strike and "poured forth a volley of abuse" at the strikebreakers. Elsewhere in the city, women broke car windows by hurling coal concealed under their shawls.[55] In San Francisco's vast refugee districts, in which tens of thousands of impoverished people lived after the 1906 earthquake and fire, women lined the tracks and helped wreck five cars that foolishly ventured into one of the camps. Women were instrumental in building the obstructions and bonfires on the tracks that forced the cars to halt in a "hail of stones" thrown "mostly . . . by women."[56] During the streetcar strike rioting in Bay City, Michigan, in 1905, women were in the "thick of the fight," charging strikebreaking crews with clubs and stoning cars. They helped set one car on fire and joined in kicking and beating the company's general manager when he was dragged from another car. The *New York Tribune* alluded to the castrating power of women strike sympathizers during New York's 1916 IRT subway strike by quoting a woman bragging that she had "bounced [a brick] off a fink's nut."[57]

Women's prominence in the attacks on strikebreaking crews was highlighted in newspaper accounts of "Amazons" leading the crowds. In Cleveland in 1899, a 280-pound Polish "Amazon" incited hundreds of men to stone a company crew sent to repair trolley wire pulled down by strike sympathizers. She was so formidable that police were unable to drag her through the gate of her yard; as they attempted to do so she instructed her husband to shoot the officers. In St. Louis during the 1900 strike, a "big woman" with "a determined countenance" declared, "I ain't afraid to say that I've . . . put rocks on tracks, and . . . thrown stones at scabs, and . . . tied tin cans to trolley wires," and vowed to do more: "We ain't doing half enough damage."[58] In San Francisco's refugee district in 1907 a "strong-armed Amazon" threw a heavy stone so hard that it passed clear through the streetcar and smashed against a building on the other side of the street. A crowd of women in New Orleans during that city's 1929 streetcar strike waited for the first trolley to pull out of the carbarn, tightly grasping bricks; they were unfazed by policemen who stood nearby holding sawed-off shotguns. As the car moved out, a woman gave a "derisive cry," and "quick as a flash" another "Madame Defarge" began the attack with a brick.[59]

The press also heavily emphasized the role of women in the humiliation of the State Fencibles, militiamen sent out by the mayor to quell rioting in Philadelphia's Kensington mill district during the 1910 streetcar walkout, the most serious that had occurred in any strike in the city's history. The Fencibles was an independent military organization of 200 members, which had served in the Spanish-American War. The city provided an armory for them, and they were obliged to perform police duty when the mayor called on them. They went into Kensington, the city's manufacturing center, heavily armed, with guns and bayonets and "plentifully supplied with ammunition, as in time of actual war."[60] But, according to *Collier's* magazine, the "youthful warriors" were assaulted by women and driven into the carbarns "with a severe loss of prestige." Making matters even worse, Kensington's young mill women had cut the brass buttons from their clothing, and stuck lemons on their bayonets. A disgusted mayor ridiculed the Fencibles as "picnic soldiers."[61]

But the press portrayed the professional strikebreaker as a fearless warrior, contemptuous of any woman's attempt to control or influence him. Whether married or not, he was always on the road, moving from one strike to the next, giving little or no attention to family life. Frank Curry had been married a year when he refused his wife's plea that he not take a streetcar out during the 1903 strike in Chicago. "Don't do it Frank, don't do it," she begged. "You might be killed and baby and I left alone." The *Chicago Record-Herald* reported that Curry "looked at her a moment without a word. Then his car shot out into the crowds that howled in the street."[62]

The stocky young man with the "bulldog jaw" and "steel gray eye," who had once been a cow puncher in Wyoming, gained a reputation during the strike as an "intrepid fighter," always taking out the first car when a "dangerous trip was in prospect." The *Record-Herald* praised him as the "Young Motorman who leads the way" and "does not fear death." The *Chicago Tribune* reported that "all day he stood at his post" at the front of his car, "eyes to the front," as he "pass[ed] through showers of stones and bricks," and quoted him as saying, "I am afraid of nothing. This is tame." As a brick crashed through the window close to him, Curry reached for his revolver. But "his eyes cowed the rioters" more than his gun. His face bleeding from broken glass, he brought his windowless car into the barn, and "was ready to go out again."[63]

When strikers encircled the 79th Street carbarn with a massive picket line, making Curry and the other strikebreakers there virtual prisoners, the young motorman again placed his "manhood" above his marriage and the interests of his child. He scorned his brother-in-law, who visited the barn and "begged [Curry] to throw up his position in accordance with the wishes of his wife."[64]

War correspondents' glamorizing of the mercenary soldiers, many of them Americans, who sought a new frontier by fighting in exotic locales around the turn of the century also fueled society's fascination with the professional strikebreaker. A veritable foreign legion fought within the Boer ranks in South Africa, for example, including a large Irish American contingent. Richard Harding Davis in 1906 published *Real Soldiers of Fortune*, a highly popular collection of biographies whose typical subject "for pay, or for the love of adventure . . . [sold] his sword and risk[ed] his life for presidents, pretenders, charlatans, and emperors," just as the strikebreaker would for any traction magnate, mine owner, or lumber boss. Professional strikebreakers like James Farley were described as the "condottiere of our days," early twentieth-century counterparts of the leaders of the mercenary bands in early modern Europe.[65]

The enormous sales of Edgar Rice Burroughs's Martian series, which began in 1911 with the publication of *Under the Moons of Mars*, is a further indication of the appeal of the primitive, roving warrior, whom many equated with the strikebreaker. The hero of the series, John Carter, on Earth had served in the armies of the Confederacy, three foreign republics, and an empire. On Mars he fights his way by sword "back and forth across a warlike planet, facing savage beasts and hordes of savage men."[66]

Like John Carter, who roamed the red planet armed with long sword and short sword, the early twentieth-century strikebreaker usually carried a weapon for use in hand-to-hand fighting. Patrick Kenealy told the *New York Times* during the 1905 New York IRT subway strike that he had carried a lead pipe with him "all across the United States" ever since becoming a strikebreaker, and declared, "[I] hope to die fighting with it." He paid tribute to a comrade from the 1895 Brooklyn streetcar strike, who had "died fighting [striking miners] at Cripple Creek [Colorado]," noting that "when they buried him I saw his lead pipe in his coffin."[67]

## JAMES FARLEY AND THE EMERGENCE OF STRIKEBREAKING AS A NATIONAL BUSINESS

Beginning at the turn of the century, entrepreneurs began creating what were, in effect, mobile mercenary armies composed of strikebreakers and guards, which they rented out to employers during strikes. The dominant figure in the strikebreaking business during its early years, when it was primarily involved with the streetcar and subway lines, was James Farley, who enjoyed a near monopoly from 1903 to 1907, when he retired. The business's leaders in subsequent years, men like Pearl Bergoff, who remained active until the late 1930s, Archie Mahon, and James Waddell, began their careers working for Farley. During the late nineteenth century various detective agencies, most importantly Pinkerton, Thiel, and Baldwin-Felts, had supplied armed guards to protect strikebreakers and intimidate unionists in the mining industry, but Farley was the first to maintain a large permanent army of professional strikebreakers. This army constituted the core of the strikebreaking force used in the urban transit strikes, supplemented by a far larger group of men hastily recruited by newspaper advertisements and word of mouth.

Farley developed a highly organized and specialized operation that broke strikes from the Atlantic to the Pacific. He allegedly commanded an

"Army of Forty Thousand Men Ready to do His Bidding," which he controlled "with almost military discipline."[68] He kept the names of these mercenary soldiers at his New York headquarters on cards in a set of drawers that "appeared precisely the same as a card catalogue of a library." Farley regularly communicated with a "captain" in every large city, who kept a record of the men in his "district" that he could send into a strike on a few hours' notice. At least seven traction companies around the country provided Farley with a list of about 200 of their employees available to him any time he needed them. Upon receiving a telegram from Farley, they immediately quit their employer and traveled to the strike scene.[69]

While he occasionally broke mill strikes, Farley concentrated almost exclusively on the urban transit sector. He declined requests to "take hold" of the 1904 packinghouse strike in New York on the grounds that "I know the street railway business and I don't know the meat business."[70]

Farley was the first to hold the strikebreaking force completely under his own control, rather than just furnishing men to the company. He also acted as both paymaster and commissary during the strike. Farley became a "general with absolute power," who assumed complete control over the operation of the lines, superior even to the company president. During the 1905 New York IRT subway strike, a reporter mentioned IRT president August Belmont, one of the nation's wealthiest men, to a strikebreaker, who responded, "Who the — is Belmont? Farley's runnin' this road." In complete command, Farley "seemed always to be sitting by the telephone, cigar in mouth, giving orders." He stood before his mercenaries, mostly tough lumpenproletarians from big city slums, "with the air of a potentate," wearing "a long Cossack overcoat," and the men "looked up at him with gaping mouths."[71]

The strikebreaking business was extremely profitable in the early years of the twentieth century, and Farley became exceedingly wealthy, retiring with a fortune estimated at anywhere from $750,000 to $6 million. He purchased a string of thoroughbred racehorses and divided his time between his upstate "palace" in Plattsburgh, New York, and a "magnificent suite" at the Hotel Astor in New York City. Farley owned four hotels of his own, two in Plattsburgh, one in Brooklyn, and one in Cincinnati. His earnings for some brief strikes equaled or exceeded the annual salary of President Theodore Roosevelt. Opponents claimed he was paid $3.25 million for breaking the 1905 New York IRT strike, and over $1 million for the 1907 San Francisco streetcar strike. The traction companies generally paid Farley $5 a day for each strikebreaker he supplied. In most cases, Farley paid the man half that sum as wages, and kept the rest as profit. The companies paid for round-trip railroad fare and room and board, usually housing the strikebreakers in their carbarns.[72]

Because strikebreaking was a new business where management directly interacted with a labor force of very low social status, composed largely of the unemployed and containing criminal elements, whose conduct was violent and boisterous, the elite chose not to become openly involved in it. Corporate magnates preferred instead to work through middlemen like James Farley. Entry into the strikebreaking business was not restricted by any social barriers, and it provided an opportunity for men of working-class and lower-middle-class background to achieve dramatic upward mobility. Farley himself was born into a lower-middle-class Irish American family in the upstate village of Malone, New York. At fourteen he ran away from home to join the circus. When it "went to the wall" in Monticello, New York, he obtained employment in a hotel there, first as a poolroom attendant and then as a bartender and clerk. He became uncontrollably violent when he accidentally swallowed an overdose of cocaine during a visit to the dentist and was chased into the woods, where he was hunted for weeks as a "wild man." Unemployed and penniless, he drifted to Brooklyn, where he found work as a detective.[73]

Detective work led Farley into a career in strikebreaking, which began in the 1895 Brooklyn streetcar strike, where the company put him in charge of fifteen special officers as a reward for being the only man to remain at his post one cold and stormy night early in the conflict. Soon after, he became a strikebreaker on the streetcar lines in Philadelphia, where the company put him in command of a "district." In 1899 he led a dozen of the Philadelphia strikebreakers into the Cleveland streetcar strike, where he demonstrated his daring by serving as motorman on the first car to go out.[74]

Having observed the chaos that resulted from the traditional practice of companies recruiting replacements from a half dozen competing detective and employment agencies, with no one in clear control of the situation, Farley concluded that successful strikebreaking required that a single general assume complete command from the company and supply all the men. Farley allegedly prepared himself for the task by working in Brooklyn for two years learning every branch of streetcar work, first as a conductor and motorman, then as an oiler in the engine house, a fireman in the power-house, and an inspector. However, a reporter for the socialist *Appeal to Reason* claimed that a former lieutenant of Farley had told him this was "one of the numerous myths [Farley] created for advertising purposes."[75]

Farley claimed to have broken over fifty strikes, nearly all of them in urban transit, without suffering a single defeat, in a career as a strikebreaking general that lasted only about five years. The press first identified him as having been accorded absolute power to break a strike in the summer of 1903, during the Richmond streetcar walkout. But he may earlier have had charge of breaking the 1902 Providence and February 1903 Waterbury, Connecticut, streetcar strikes.[76]

It was in Richmond's two-month long streetcar battle that Farley developed his reputation as "Lion-Heart," the "absolutely fearless" strikebreaking general who fought at the head of his troops, always taking the first car out himself. A mass-circulation magazine reported that Farley had "carried his life in his hands" during the Richmond strike, driving cars through a "fusillade of bullets." After one trip he retired to his quarters to pick birdshot left by the point-blank discharge of a ducking gun out of the side of his face. Like a frontier gunslinger, Farley openly displayed his "31" in a holster on his belt, and reporters claimed he did not hesitate to use it. When strike sympathizers stoned a car in which he was riding, he "sprang into the road" and the crowd fled "at the mere sight of him . . . with bullets from his revolver whistling about their ears."[77]

In Richmond, Farley demonstrated that successful strikebreaking required extensive preparation and planning prior to the walkout. By 1903, he had developed a national organization, and was able to send into Richmond men from New York, Philadelphia, Baltimore, and possibly "Western cities." Farley was in Richmond ten days before the strike began "look[ing] over the ground." It was his practice to determine the probable "trouble spots" in advance, the places along the routes where his men were most likely to be attacked, and to arrange with the police to station forces there.[78]

By November 1903, when the Chicago streetcar strike began, Farley was known as the "champion strikebreaker." America's metropolitan daily newspapers, few of which were sympathetic to labor, described him as possessing almost superhuman qualities. The *New York Tribune* declared that Farley had "had revolvers shoved in his face, but he never even blinked." When asked if he ever felt fear, "his sole answer is 'Fraid? Huh!'" The *Chicago Tribune* claimed that a "howling mob" that dragged other strikebreakers from their cars and beat them dared not "lift . . . a hand . . . to harm him." Reporters describing his physical appearance emphasized a rough masculinity: he was "tall, broad-shouldered . . . [and] extremely muscular, [with] steel-blue eyes, a square jaw, and a chin denoting great power."[79]

Chicago was Farley's toughest assignment to date, because it then rivaled London as the strongest trade-union city in the world, and the strikers could count on widespread public support. The streetcarmen hated Farley "more . . . than the millionaires who own[ed] the Chicago City Railway" and vowed that he would "meet a dog's death." During the strike, working people hung effigies of Farley from lampposts around the city. In 1903 Chicago also had more miles of street railway track than any other city in the world, which had to be guarded by a seriously understaffed police force.[80]

The intense working-class support for the strike was apparent on the first day when Farley sent out five cars on Wentworth and Cottage Grove Avenues "to test the temper of the crowds." With a "menacing yell," members of the crowd of 15,000 unleashed a torrent of bricks and stones at the cars. Strike sympathizers had blocked the tracks with "every conceivable obstacle," and cable slots were "choked with rocks and spiked by heavy wedges." Unable to move forward, the cars were surrounded by the angry crowd, who "batter[ed] and hammer[ed]" them until there was "little . . . left." Throughout the strike, the teamsters set up repeated blockades of the tracks to delay the cars and provided rides to as many people as they could carry, telling them: "We want no fares. Just . . . remember to sympathize with the strikers."[81]

The intense hostility of merchants in the neighborhoods surrounding the carbarns further isolated Farley's strikebreakers. A lunchroom near the 77th Street barn, for example, posted separate menus for union and nonunion men. The menu for union men was reasonable, but nonunion men were expected to pay "famine prices": $75 for ham and eggs, $100 for beefsteak, and $25 for oatmeal. Many barbers refused to shave strikebreakers.[82]

But Farley's quick and massive importation of strikebreakers from St. Louis, Cleveland, Terre Haute, Buffalo, and Texas, and his men's threats to use lethal violence against pro-strike crowds, along with the intimidative tactics of the Chicago police, achieved a "decisive victory" for the company in less than three weeks. Farley's men openly displayed "hammers, iron spikes, clubs, and revolvers," with which they threatened anyone who came too near the cars.[83]

According to the press, Farley's "imperturable demeanor" when confronted by crowds inspired the strikebreakers, and even "brave policemen . . . marvel[ed] at the coolness of this sphinx." When attacked, Farley proved as intimidating as any frontier sheriff. One night as he left the carbarn for his lodging house, he was attacked by six unarmed union pickets. Farley immediately "jerked a pair of revolvers from his pockets and fired a shot in the air," and then struck the pickets' leader over the head with one of the guns, knocking him down. The pickets fled.[84]

Farley also received major assistance from the Chicago police department, which placed at least eight heavily armed patrolmen on each streetcar. The hundreds of patrolmen who lined each side of the tracks in many neighborhoods, sometimes twenty-five to a block, "gave Chicago the appearance of a city under martial law." The mayor named Herman F. Schuettler, a six-foot-four-inch police captain with a reputation for physical prowess, deputy superintendent of police and placed him in charge of the strike detail. Schuettler set up twelve-man flying squadrons that "charged in . . . and broke up the crowds as they were forming." As was the practice in all streetcar strikes, plainclothesmen mingled in the crowds, identifying and arresting brick throwers and those who incited violence. They also closely watched the patrolmen themselves, to ensure that none fraternized with strikers or refused to assist strikebreakers remove obstructions from the tracks.[85]

Big city police departments, increasingly centralized and organized on quasi-military lines, considered strikebreaking among their principal responsibilities by the turn of the century. Numbering only a few dozen men in the mid-nineteenth century, the departments had grown to 500 to 1,000 men by 1900, and in the case of Chicago, to 2,000. Technological innovations during the 1890s permitted a police department to move its forces rapidly to trouble spots, greatly enhancing its ability to control strike crowds. Signal boxes placed every few blocks enabled a patrolman to report immediately any outbreak of disorder to headquarters. The introduction of the patrol wagon meant that ten to twenty policemen could be moved quickly to a location where strikebreakers were under attack, providing the mobility essential in controlling crowds, which formed suddenly and spontaneously. Moreover, a patrol wagon could be driven into crowds and used as a weapon to disperse them. During the 1903 Chicago streetcar strike, a patrol wagon, ready for action, was stationed every third block along the main lines in operation.[86]

Because no municipal police force had manpower sufficient to protect a streetcar or elevated system against sabotage, the traction companies often hired a "small army" of Pinkerton detectives to patrol the major routes to guard against tampering with the tracks, electric lines, or signal boxes. Pinkertons sometimes mounted searchlights, which shone at night on key bridges to detect saboteurs.[87]

*Policemen guard the streetcar route during the 1903 Chicago strike. Note the number of patrolmen positioned along the track. Courtesy of the Chicago Historical Society.*

By 1904 Farley's well-publicized success in breaking the Chicago and Richmond strikes by rapidly importing large numbers of strikebreakers over long distances and arming them to intimidate strike crowds caused him to boast that in two or three years, streetcar strikes "will be all but unknown." Speaking to reporters at a Park Avenue New York hostelry, surrounded by stuffed armchairs and "works of art," he "might have been taken for a prosperous merchant or banker." Farley noted that the emergence of the professional strikebreaking business during the previous few years, along with the recent consolidation of smaller traction companies into larger and wealthier corporations, enabled management to "fight it out" with the carmen whenever they walked off the job, "no matter what the cost." That was why, Farley declared, "a streetcar strike never is won nowadays—never can be won." Farley himself was already "known by name at least to every streetcar conductor and motorman from the Atlantic Ocean to the Pacific."[88]

A few weeks earlier, streetcarmen in San Francisco had lost their nerve on the eve of a strike when Farley appeared in the Bay on a steamer with 400 of his mercenaries, recruited from all over the country. On the night the carmen met to take a strike vote, Farley moved the steamer where they could view it and within signaling distance of shore. The carmen knew that if they voted to walk out, Farley's well-armed strikebreakers would immediately land and proceed to operate the road. They voted down a strike by a large majority. Farley had made his point: "[M]ake [them] know that cars are going to be run, and that anybody who gets in the way is going to be hurt."[89]

Farley's career reached its peak in 1905, when he "amazed" the public with the "prompt and effective way" he broke the IRT subway strike. Never in any American strike had so many strikebreakers been imported so quickly. His standing army of 4,500, drawn from all parts of the country, seemed to "appear from nowhere." He had the first train moving seven minutes after the strike began. Farley shipped men in from at least a dozen large cities in the East and Midwest, including St. Louis, Chicago, Cleveland, Indianapolis, Cincinnati, Louisville, Boston, Philadelphia, Baltimore, Washington, D.C., Richmond, and Columbus, as well as from other unidentified western cities and Texas. Farley's lieutenants were also reported to be "scouring the South." Street railway service in Pittsburgh was crippled as Farley drew away all the extra men and many of the regular motormen.[90]

The strikebreaking effort took on the appearance of a major military operation, as Farley housed 2,000 of his recruits on a triple decker, side-wheeled steamship, the *Northam*, which he docked on the Bronx side of the Harlem River, in "a position virtually immune from the possibility of attack." Most of the rest were stationed at the First Avenue powerhouse, which was converted into a barracks.[91]

Farley established his command headquarters in central Manhattan, and at 4:00 A.M. on March 7, when the strike began, both the subway and elevated lines passed under his "absolute control." The subway, which had been in operation less than a year, carried 400,000 passengers a day, while the elevated lines carried 750,000. In a room decorated with photographs of strike scenes and his upstate trotting horses, Farley directed by telephone "every move of the fight." Messenger boys were constantly coming in with telegrams from the field. Farley assigned a foreman to each section of the subway and elevated lines, who sent him reports every half hour. Serving under the foreman were "strong and hardy-looking men" whose job it was to "enforce [their] orders." Farley himself was "up and down the line all day, giving encouragement, and countering the efforts of strikers to get [strikebreakers] to desert." He even ran one train himself.[92]

Like the streetcar companies, the IRT considered passenger safety of much lesser priority than breaking the strike, and Farley's motormen, most of whom had never driven a subway or elevated train, caused several serious accidents. The worst occurred on March 7 when a strikebreaking subway motorman from Columbus, Ohio, ran four red lights and crashed into a train ahead of him, seriously injuring thirty passengers. Passengers endured "hair-raising trips," as motormen rounded curves at speeds that nearly lifted the cars off the rails. They brought cars clumsily into the station and often missed stops entirely. Jerking trains often threw passengers out of their seats. The company quickly gave up running express trains as too risky. Hearst's *New York Journal*, one of the few newspapers that supported the strike, editorialized that passengers made the subway journey downtown "only at imminent risk of their lives." Nor did it help matters that the company, fearing that strike sympathizers would pull the emergency brake cords to stop trains, had electricians remove the emergency cords and boxes, in direct violation of the law. As a further indication of the strikebreakers' lack of competence and experience at the job, motormen, many of them of the "wild Western type," applied and released the subway air brakes with too much force, resulting in many burned-out motors, ruptured tubes, and overheated bearings.[93]

The Hearst newspapers criticized Farley for recruiting men under false pretenses and for forcing the strikebreakers to live in squalor. The *New York American* charged that most of the men mobilized in Chicago, Indianapolis, Columbus, and Pittsburgh had arrived by train in Philadelphia, from which point they were sent to New York, without knowing their destination or purpose. But the anti-union *New York Herald* claimed that Farley had required each recruit to sign a contract stating that he "fully understands that this is for strike work in New York." One of the Columbus men complained of being "herded together like cattle" on the *Northam* and being fed spoiled meat. The *New York American* reported outbreaks of malaria and indigestion among the strikebreakers and warned of the impending arrival of a cholera-infected boatload of recruits from New England. It charged the company with violating sanitary, fire, and building laws in housing the strikebreakers on shore.[94]

Reports of epidemic disease spreading among strikebreakers crammed into the barns by the hundreds, sleeping on cots only inches apart, were common in early twentieth-century streetcar strikes, as were complaints from strikebreakers about being served spoiled and inedible food. A reporter who went undercover as a strikebreaker in New York in 1910 said the food was worse than stoker's grub on a liner. The bread was "hard as the pyramids and about as old," the beef stew was full of vermin, and "a tramp would throw away" the coffee.[95] In St. Louis in 1900 strike sympathizers circulated reports that smallpox had broken out among the strikebreakers in the carbarns and warned that schoolteachers riding the cars would spread the disease among their pupils. In New Orleans in 1902 strikebreakers were forced to eat "sourbelly"—that is, on the floor, not from tables—and their cots lacked mosquito bars.[96]

Breaking the New York IRT strike in less than a week was the most impressive triumph of Farley's career, but, as in Chicago, he had major assistance from the city's police department. Of the 5,516 men on the force, fully 3,200 were assigned to strike duty. A patrolman stood behind every motorman, with one at the center of the train and another in the rear, while between two and twelve were stationed on every subway and elevated platform. Crowds had far greater difficulty gaining access to the subway and elevated stations than to cars on the surface lines and that, combined with the police department's strong show of force, resulted in less violence than was usual in streetcar strikes. Several times, however, crowds did manage to pull strikebreakers from the trains and beat them.[97]

The notoriety he gained in breaking the IRT strike caused Farley to become a major issue in the 1906 New York gubernatorial campaign. The Hearst press "in shrieking type" charged that Farley had endorsed the Republican candidate, Charles Evans Hughes, and might become Hughes's principal labor adviser. Hughes's opponent, running as a Democrat, was publisher William Randolph Hearst, who repeated the charges in his campaign speeches. Hearst's *New York American* declared that Farley's declaration of support for Hughes was no surprise, because his mercenary army of 40,000 men was "in almost constant employment by trusts" all over the United States "either to break strikes or make a show of force when strikes are contemplated." It noted that a number of street railway corporations considered Farley so valuable that they paid him retaining fees, so they would have first call on his services if their employees went on strike. The *American* claimed that Farley had declared for Hughes because the Hearst press had consistently opposed and exposed his strikebreaking efforts. It also accused the Republicans of employing Farley to run Canadian floaters across the border into the state of New York, with the intention of having them vote repeatedly for Hughes in various localities.[98]

Farley vehemently denied the charges and claimed he had no preference in the election. The *New York Tribune* declared that Hearst had fabricated them in order to discredit Hughes with labor voters.[99] Nonetheless, that Farley became a major subject of campaign controversy underlined the new visibility of professional strikebreaking and its emergence as a highly significant political issue in Progressive Era America.

Farley's last strikebreaking effort came in 1907 in San Francisco, arguably the strongest labor city in America, where he "bludgeoned the union to death" in the bloodiest of all streetcar strikes. Farley had acquired a reputation for invincibility, combining a modern penchant for "direction and organization" with the primitive masculinity of a gladiator. The *San Francisco Chronicle* emphasized executive capability as the key to his success but at the same time described him as "a man who prefers hot blood to water as a beverage."[100]

Although Farley's agency was headquartered in New York, with another office in Chicago, he was prepared to intervene immediately in Pacific Coast strikes. He had many of his "regular soldiers" wintering in California towns, in frequent communication with the Chicago office. Two weeks prior to the strike, that office notified them to be prepared to travel to San Francisco at a moment's notice, and on May 1 it instructed them to go at once. These men were quickly joined by others Farley selected from his "chosen brigades" in New York, St. Louis, Chicago, and Milwaukee. Farley himself arrived on a train from Chicago on May 3.[101]

Because of Farley's reputation for violence, the United Railroads Company at first denied it had hired him, and he tried to keep his presence in San Francisco a secret. When a union carman recognized Farley, he unsuccessfully tried to buy his silence by thrusting a $20 gold piece into his hand. Reporters spotted Farley riding around the city with company officials, and the company publicly admitted he was in its employ. The company president also stated he was recruiting "large bodies of men in the East."[102]

Returning veterans of the Philippines campaign proved another valuable source of strikebreakers. Most of these men arrived by ship in San Francisco dead broke, having either spent what they had before leaving Manila or at intermediate ports in Japan, or else having gambled it away on board the vessel. Farley provided them with an immediate source of income.[103]

Farley proceeded to southern California to recruit more men, returning to San Francisco on May 7 to assist in bringing out the first car. The motorman was a trusted lieutenant from Chicago, "a veteran of four bloody strikes"; the conductor was another longtime mercenary from St. Louis. Second in command at the strikebreakers' largest barracks, the Turk and Fillmore Street carbarn, was a "heavy-set, low-browed fellow, [who] constantly chew[ed] on an unlighted pipe"—none other than Frank Curry, who had taken the first car out for Farley in the 1903 Chicago strike.[104]

The strike was marked by a level of violence unprecedented in transit strikes, as Farley's "armed braves" fought constant skirmishes with the crowds, one of which erupted into a major street battle in which the strike sympathizers were "shot down like dogs." Farley armed each strikebreaker riding the cars with a "brace of guns." The bloodiest confrontation occurred on May 7 after several cars were showered with bricks and forced to "retreat under fire" back to the barns. When more cars ventured out later in the day and were again pelted with missiles, Farley's men immediately opened fire with their revolvers, and "the battle was on." The strikebreakers "kept up an almost constant fusillade" and four strike sympathizers "dropped in their tracks," shot to death. Threatened by the "brick-armed regiment," Farley's men abandoned the cars and fled on foot back to the barns, "crouching behind fences and piles of lumber," and then "turning and firing into the crowd as they ran."[105]

During the strike, the streetcarmen's union accused Farley of deliberately placing explosives on the tracks to turn public opinion against the strikers, an "old detective agency [tactic]" designed to connect labor with terrorism. According to *Collier's Weekly*, the 1899 Cleveland strike, the first in which explosives were freely used, was lost when dynamite blew up a Euclid Avenue car, seriously injuring ten passengers, including several women. From that hour, "law and order was the only issue."[106] In San Francisco, Farley allegedly planted the dynamite in conspicuous places so that it would be discovered before it damaged cars or injured strikebreakers. The intention was to generate newspaper publicity that would cause the public to view the strikers as vicious saboteurs. During the Bay City, Michigan, streetcar strike in 1905, Farley had been convicted of placing obstructions on the tracks designed to cause wrecks that would be blamed on the union.[107]

Farley retired from professional strikebreaking after the 1907 San Francisco streetcar strike, having become fabulously wealthy after starting his career penniless in Brooklyn in 1895. Farley's decision to quit may have been motivated in part by the increasingly competitive nature of the business; his success was beginning to spawn imitators. Undoubtedly the constant tension and threat of physical harm associated with his work also took a toll. The *New York Tribune* in 1905 noted that Farley was "covered from head to foot with bullet wounds and scars from knives, clubs, pistol butts, blackjacks, cobblestones [and baseball bats]."[108]

That same year, 1907, the left-wing socialist Jack London published *The Iron Heel*, a novel in which he cast Farley as a leading hireling of the American capitalists who destroy the country's trade unions and violently install a dictatorship called The Oligarchy. The novel is drawn from a manuscript supposedly discovered in the twenty-seventh century, detailing how the capitalists subjugated the working masses seven centuries before. The professional strikebreakers of the early twentieth century, "hired fighting men of the capitalists," had evolved into "the Mercenaries of the Oligarchy," the dictatorship's repressive armed force. Farley "rose high under the rule of the Iron Heel," gaining admission to "the oligarch class." But in 1932 he is assassinated by a woman whose husband his strikebreakers had killed thirty years before.[109]

Farley actually spent his retirement years living in splendor in Plattsburgh, New York, where he devoted his entire time to handling his thoroughbred racehorses, "one of the finest strings of trotters and pacers in the United States." It was an interest he had first developed during his circus days. During his residence in Plattsburgh he "did more to advance light harness racing than any other man in Northern New York."[110]

Farley, once one of the best-known men in the United States, died of tuberculosis in 1913 at the age of thirty-nine. Although he had withdrawn into relative obscurity during his last years, Farley lived in constant fear, plagued by hallucinations that union men were trying to assassinate him. When he visited the racetrack he sat surrounded by ten armed bodyguards, and he kept several of them about him at all times, day and night. The labor press described him as "cring[ing] alone in his palace, suspicious of every new face, starting at every unusual sound, fearful even of his own special protectors."[111]

## LABOR MANLINESS AND MERCENARY COWARDICE

The labor movement attempted to subvert the press's image of Farley and other professional strikebreakers as fearsome, invincible warriors by impugning their masculinity, while associating the trade-union man with physical toughness. A pro-labor reporter who had gone undercover as a strikebreaker to write firsthand about "one of the lowest in the scale of dirty trades," declared that Farley, although "a man of herculean physique and fierce countenance," was "a notorious coward."[112] Labor writer John Kenneth Turner claimed that Farley began his strikebreaking career in 1895 by "running blabbing to [his] superintendent," instead of "standing with his fellows," and then proceeded to beat up "the smallest conductor he could find." Turner claimed Farley had quit the strikebreaking business in "a panic of fear" and suggested that the real cause of his death was not tuberculosis but a nervous disease brought on by fright.[113] New Orleans's striking carmen in 1902 ridiculed Alfred Clark, second-in-command of the Chicago-based Holmes Detective Agency, one of several strikebreaking firms hired by the company, for having "cried like a baby" after he was wounded in a clash with strike sympathizers. One striker called the "big bruiser," who had decided to return to Chicago, "one of the worst scared men I ever saw."[114]

Engaged in dangerous and exhausting outdoor work, exposed to all the inclemencies of weather, and entrusted with the safety of both passengers and pedestrians, the union streetcarmen elaborated a definition of manliness that strongly emphasized physical capability. Even to enter the occupation a man had to pass a stringent physical examination. Because the traction companies hired relatively few immigrants, the public viewed the carmen as "Americans, cool [and] determined."[115] The St. Louis press in 1900 noted the "muscularity and splendid" condition of the union carmen. The union president was of "powerful mold," a towering figure six feet two inches tall with "herculean" shoulders and legs like those of world heavyweight boxing champion Jim Jeffries. The strike leaders seemed "imperturbable, cool, and confident."[116]

Like their mercenary opponents, the union carmen embraced military forms of organization during strikes, identifying soldierly qualities with masculinity. In San Francisco in 1902, for example, the men detailed to picket the carbarns were divided into "squads" of twenty-four, each under the command of a "sergeant." St. Louis carmen in 1900 marched into their union hall like a "regiment," cheering and shouting "every foot of the way." And during the 1905 IRT strike, New York subway men set their strike song to the tune of the Union army hymn "Marching through Georgia," with a chorus of "Strike, Strike, Strike."[117]

## THE EXPANSION OF THE STRIKEBREAKING BUSINESS: BERGOFF BROTHERS AND WADDELL

Dominating the strikebreaking business in the fifteen years after Farley retired were two firms, Waddell & Mahon and Bergoff Brothers, both established by former hirelings of his. The firms merged in 1914 to become Bergoff Brothers and Waddell. Like Farley, these firms not only supplied strikebreakers and guards but assumed control of all operations from the employer during a strike. They went into a strike "thoroughly equipped, self-sustaining, like an army." They ran their own commissariat and housed the strikebreakers on company property. Bergoff's top aide, Harry Bowan, described by a labor reporter as "a large, cave-man type" and former "gun-man of fortune," explained: "We have our own baggage system. We carry our own portable shower baths. We carry along a physician, a boot-black, a barber, a lawyer." He claimed his agency could assemble an army of 5,000 men, ready for action, on forty-eight hours notice. Speed was critically important in strikebreaking as the business became more competitive, because an employer tended to hire from the agency that delivered most quickly.[118]

Unlike Farley, Waddell & Mahon and Bergoff Brothers became involved in several industries besides urban transit, principally railroads, shipping, and mining. Both firms helped break the 1909 and 1910 Philadelphia streetcar strikes, while Bergoff Brothers and Waddell broke the 1915 Chicago streetcar, the 1916 New York IRT, and the 1920 Brooklyn Rapid Transit (BRT) strikes.[119]

The Waddell & Mahon strikebreaking firm was established as a result of a chance encounter in a carbarn during the 1905 New York IRT strike between two men employed in James Farley's commissary department. James Waddell and Archie Mahon were aware that while the strikebreaking business required little initial capital investment, with one good contract an entrepreneur would be "wear[ing] real diamonds." The two men sat down on a case of canned goods and arranged to go into business together. Waddell was relatively new to strikebreaking, having worked for years as a salesman at Macy's department store. But Archie Mahon, son of the resident physician at Bellevue Hospital, had "been through the mill" with Farley. His background was sufficiently impressive to the owners of the New York Transportation Company, a large auto taxi firm, that in

1905 they awarded Waddell & Mahon its first contract, to break a chauffeurs' strike. By 1913, when it broke the Calumet copper strike on Michigan's Upper Peninsula, Waddell & Mahon had become the nation's leading strikebreaking agency, principally involved in metal mining and urban transit strikes.[120]

Bergoff Brothers was founded in 1907 by Pearl L. Bergoff, another soldier of Farley, whom *Fortune* magazine called "an exceptionally competent executive" who could "curse with the . . . fluency of a dock-walloper." His need to project an image of exaggerated masculinity may have been influenced in part by his carrying a girl's name, bestowed on him by a disappointed mother who had hoped for a daughter.[121] Bergoff entered the strikebreaking business with money he had earned by selling to the *New York World* the diary he had kept as Stanford White's bodyguard after the prominent architect's sensational murder by Harry Thaw in 1906. Bergoff obtained his first major contract from the city of New York, whose street cleaning commissioner paid him $24,000 to break a strike of municipal garbage cart drivers in 1907. He was hired to help break the 1910 Philadelphia streetcar strike when he promised to deliver 1,500 men in twenty-four hours, a bolder offer than any of his competitors dared make.[122]

Having merged with Waddell & Mahon after Archie Mahon's death in 1914, Bergoff's new firm, Bergoff Brothers and Waddell, expanded rapidly. Bergoff boasted of keeping a card index hidden in a safe deposit vault; it contained the names of 400,000 men he could call on for strikebreaking, classified according to skills and aptitudes. The firm also maintained an armory in New York with 1,100 rifles, and barracks where armed guards drilled. Bergoff Brothers and Waddell was hired to break the 1916 New York IRT strike, for which it received a gross profit of $750,000, and the streetcar strike in Havana, Cuba, the same year.[123]

Influenced by the New York East Side criminal gangs that supplied many of their recruits, Waddell & Mahon and Bergoff Brothers added a valuable sideline to their strikebreaking business by setting up gambling operations in the carbarns during strikes. The firms' owners derived sizable revenue from encouraging their strikebreakers to risk their earnings in games of chance with cards and dice, and at pool. Pearl Bergoff admitted that "a certain amount of graft" went on in the barns but insisted that he had to allow it to preserve harmony among the strikebreakers, because such distractions prevented them from "looking for mischief." Bergoff gained additional income from selling tobacco and cigarettes; he enjoyed a near monopoly because he severely restricted his recruits' movements.[124]

*Pearl Bergoff (center front) is surrounded by some of his strikebreakers. Courtesy of the Walter P. Reuther Library, Wayne State University.*

During the 1916 New York IRT strike, several strikebreakers accused Bergoff of forcing them to participate in the gambling. They testified to the New York City Public Service Commission that guards armed with "rods" (revolvers and automatics) and "jacks" (blackjacks), brass knuckles, and pieces of pipe, backed by the policemen on duty at the barns, who were in on the take, had warned them they would beat up anyone who tried to leave. Bergoff's men also brought in phony dice. His "thick-necked" assistants, called "crumb bosses," extracted a fee from the strikebreakers for blankets and bedding.[125]

However, streetcar strikes did provide the strikebreakers themselves with the opportunity for considerable extra income, because they often pocketed the fares, shortchanged passengers, and operated the cars only on the most lucrative routes. In fact, in the language of the strikebreaker, a streetcar strike was a "Christmas Dinner."[126] During the 1916 New York IRT and 1920 Brooklyn Rapid Transit strikes, which affected both the subway and surface lines, the strikebreakers showed a strong preference for working on the streetcars, where the conductors collected the fares. Many of those assigned to the subway protested vehemently and clamored for jobs in the "silver mines." Passengers riding the BRT lines in 1920 noted that conductors were operating the cars on a "co-partnership basis" with the motormen, splitting the fares with them, their pockets "sagging with the weight of the metal divided." The *New York Times* reported that conductors "moved through the cars tinkling like 10-mule teams coming down the mountain." On the subways, some of the strikebreakers even emulated the western outlaws of the late nineteenth century as they walked through the cars and demanded fares of passengers who had already deposited their nickels at the gate, threatening to put them off the train if they refused to comply.[127]

Bergoff Brothers and Waddell surpassed even Farley in recruiting strikebreakers from "all points of the compass." The men it imported to break the 1916 New York IRT strike represented not only "all parts of the United States" but "all the warring European nations." Its mercenary army included Swedes, Japanese, and even a "Hindu guard," who deserted a British steamer on which he had been a sailor when it came into New York to take on a munitions cargo. In breaking the IRT strike, Bergoff Brothers and Waddell benefited from its previous work for the railroad corporations. It had assembled large concentrations of men in Chicago, New Orleans, St. Louis, Philadelphia, and other cities in anticipation of a national railroad strike, which was called off when Congress passed the Adamson Act, granting the eight-hour day. The firm then immediately shipped these men to New York as strikebreakers for the IRT.[128]

Like Farley, Pearl Bergoff, James Waddell, and Archie Mahon became ostentatiously rich through strikebreaking. When Waddell arrived in New York in 1916 on a chartered train from Chicago to break the IRT strike, he was reported to have paid $500 in tips to the train crew. Chartering the train, which made the trip in ten hours less time than the fastest regular train, cost him $3,500. Journalists traveling with Waddell claimed that he telegraphed from Cleveland to Buffalo to have strawberries brought on the train there for his breakfast—in September, no less, when they were out of season. When the IRT company president was quoted as never having heard of him, Waddell told the press, "He'll never forget me after he gets my bill."[129] Bergoff's annual personal income from 1914, when he was already a millionaire, to 1924 was reputed to have been $100,000, with dividends of $200,000 to $400,000. He boasted that it cost him $100 a day just to open his office door, expressing contempt for "the smaller fry in his game who . . . 'carry their office around in their hat.'" When Archie

Mahon died in 1914, less than a decade after the $6-a-day commissary assistant first considered setting up a strikebreaking business, he "left a large estate."[130]

Bergoff Brothers and Waddell had consistent success in breaking urban transit strikes, failing only in Kansas City in 1918, but the demand for strikebreaking services declined dramatically after 1922, as the nation entered a period of relative labor quiescence. Bergoff, who from 1920 had full control of the firm, said that business was "atrocious" from 1924 until the onset of the Depression, and from 1929 to 1934 "it was even worse." He had to sell the firm's arsenal and all of its commissary equipment. *Fortune* magazine noted, "From 1924 to 1934 the Bergoff record of . . . achievement is all but a blank page." For much of the 1920s Bergoff focused on the Florida real estate business, losing $2 million when the land boom collapsed.[131]

In addition, the proliferation of the automobile in the late 1910s and 1920s greatly reduced the streetcarmen's union's leverage during a strike, rendering the prospects for walkouts in that sector much less likely. Automobiles were luxury items during the first decade of the century; the *San Francisco Examiner* noted during that city's 1907 streetcar strike that only the rich rode in automobiles. Most city residents were seriously inconvenienced during streetcar strikes, having to walk long distances, in often inclement weather, or rattle along the bumpy streets in an overcrowded butcher's or baker's wagon, or lumbering furniture van, hastily pressed into service as a taxi.[132]

As early as 1915, however, the *Chicago Tribune*, in a story headlined "Automobile Takes Edge Off Strike," stated that "the advent of the automobile . . . will show that a streetcar strike has been robbed of much of its hampering effect on transportation." After 1915, automobile ownership spread rapidly. In Chicago, for example, there was one automobile for every sixty-one residents in 1915, one for every thirty in 1920, and one for every eight in 1930.[133]

By 1929, despite the complete cessation of streetcar service in New Orleans due to a strike, mass ownership of automobiles prevented "the old-fashioned confusion, stagnation, and consternation." The *New Orleans Item* reported that "most Orleanians got to their work about the same time as usual." To emphasize that "Car Strikes Aren't What They Used to Be," the *Item* ran a cartoon showing fleets of automobiles whizzing by the streetcar barns. The *Item* noted that 58,000 motor vehicle licenses had been issued in New Orleans that year. Assuming that each car could carry four passengers, 232,000 people could be transported by automobile. To be sure, not all automobiles would be available to carry commuters. But only about 270,000 fares were paid on New Orleans's streetcars during weekdays in June 1929, both in morning and evening rush hours. The *Item* concluded: "Divide that by two and you see that the motor capacity is far beyond the passenger demand."[134]

## THE EMERGENCE OF STATE MILITIA AS A MAJOR STRIKEBREAKING FORCE

Although big city police departments were expected to assist in operating urban transit systems during strikes, superintendents were often unable to rely on their patrolmen to discipline crowds or arrest strike sympathizers, leading to the emergence of state militia as a major vehicle for strikebreaking by the turn of the century. Patrolmen often had relatives and friends among the streetcarmen, and, because both occupations were heavily Irish American in most of the major cities, there were shared ethnic bonds as well. The police, in any event, at least considered the carmen to be Americans, because few were immigrants, while they tended to scorn workers in many other sectors as foreigners.[135]

Police sympathy for streetcar strikers was dramatically evident in Pawtucket, Rhode Island, a factory town contiguous to Providence, and in New Orleans in 1902. In Pawtucket, the mayor clearly sympathized with the strikers, and the police made almost no effort to control crowds. As a result, Rhode Island's governor called out six companies of state infantry militia and two of cavalry to quell the disorder. In New Orleans, police sympathy for the strikers also led to intervention by the state militia. When a crowd surged on to a streetcar, like "wolves hungry for blood," and rained blows on the motorman and conductor, policemen drew their revolvers but did not shoot, because "their hearts were not in the task." The strike sympathizers cried, "Don't hurt the police boys! Kill the scabs!" The New Orleans press described policemen yanking strikebreakers off the cars, "slamming them about unmercifully," and then arresting them for carrying concealed weapons or shooting with intent to kill. Peter Johnson, agent of a Chicago strikebreaking firm, one of several hired by the company, accused policemen of deliberately holding up a car in which he was riding so that strike sympathizers could seize and beat his men.[136]

Police behaved similarly in other cities affected by streetcar strikes. In Richmond in 1903, patrolmen arrested a strikebreaker for drawing his revolver when he was hit in the head by a brick but let the brick-thrower go free. Virginia state militiamen sharply criticized the Richmond police for refusing to assist them in subduing riots. The *San Francisco Chronicle* complained during that city's 1907 streetcar strike of the strong police sympathy for the strikers: "conversations are frequently overheard between policemen [which] would lead the listener to believe he was attending a union labor meeting."[137]

Police superintendents often took disciplinary action against patrolmen for displaying sympathy for the strike and their unwillingness to break up crowds and arrest strike sympathizers. In Indianapolis in 1913 thirty-three patrolmen were suspended for refusing to board streetcars for the purpose of protecting strikebreakers.[138] Similarly, five New York policemen were suspended for refusing to act as train guards on the elevated during the 1916 IRT strike. Philadelphia's police chief ordered a general shifting of patrolmen out of their own neighborhoods because of the sympathy they expressed for the strikers. Assigning them to unfamiliar sections of the city at least reduced the possibility that they would be influenced by friendship or acquaintance with the union men.[139]

Some patrolmen just resigned their positions rather than carry out strikebreaking duties. In 1929 a New Orleans patrolman, one of five who quit on a single day early in the streetcar strike, expressing sectional animosity common in southern transit strikes, explained that he "didn't want to protect any Philadelphia and New York scabs" or "take a chance of shooting . . . [local] men . . . fighting to get back their jobs."[140]

In 1903 the sheriff of Henrico County, Virginia, which adjoined Richmond, was even put on trial for refusing to assist in breaking the 1903 Richmond streetcar strike. The Virginia Passenger and Power Company, owned by George Jay Gould of New York, which ran Richmond's streetcar system, preferred charges against Sheriff Simon Solomon alleging gross neglect of official duty and demanded his removal. The company charged that Sheriff Solomon had provided no protection for streetcars running through Henrico County and had refused to apply to the state militia for assistance. Moreover, he had arrested three strikebreakers "who had bravely fought in defense of their lives" against a crowd of strike sympathizers, handcuffed them, and thrown them into "a filthy and uninhabitable cell" in the Henrico County jail, as though they were "low, dangerous, and common criminals." Nor would the sheriff permit the company surgeon to inspect the cell.[141]

By subtly associating the strike with the Lost Cause and drawing on the strong county hostility to Farley's northern mercenaries, the defense won a 9 to 3 jury vote for acquittal, despite the appearance of Virginia's governor as a company witness. The case was not retried. Governor Montague testified that Sheriff Solomon had not responded to his suggestions to request state militia for Henrico County, forcing him to issue the order himself.[142] But defense witnesses convinced the majority of jurors that any disorder in the county had been precipitated by Farley's strikebreakers firing from their cars. Defense attorney Hill Carter proudly reminded the jury that he "rode behind [J. E. B.] Stuart" during the War between the States. Appealing to jurors who had "served with Lee and Jackson," the defense "laughed at [the] idea" that troops were needed to quell the "petty disorder" in the county.[143]

State authorities frequently determined during the early twentieth-century streetcar strikes that municipal police forces lacked either the size or the motivation to control and disperse the crowds of strike sympathizers, and imported militia to assist in breaking the strike, placing the city under martial law. State militia were composed of citizen-soldiers who trained at intervals while holding regular jobs, serving as an emergency force when called on by the governor. Alarmed by the intensification of labor strife during the late nineteenth century, state authorities and the more affluent citizens increasingly turned to state militia as a new "policeman of industry." Hundreds of armories sprouted up in American cities, designed like medieval castles, where militia stored their weapons and ammunition, drilled, and assembled when called on to suppress disorder.[144] Their fortress-like architecture suggested that many wealthier urban residents believed themselves to be under siege, threatened by an unruly working class whose strikes often provoked violent disturbances in the streets.

State militia, composed of both infantry and cavalry units, provided both the numbers and mobility that many municipal police forces still lacked. In 1899 Cleveland's police force of 295 patrolmen was the smallest of any American city of comparable size and proved completely ineffective in quelling disorder. The *Cleveland Plain-Dealer* remarked during the streetcar strike that "the appearance of so small a number of patrolmen had the same effect on the crowd that a red rug [has] . . . on a bull." But the importation of 1,200 Ohio militiamen, including 400 veterans of the Spanish-American War's Puerto Rican campaign, accompanied by huge army wagons carrying 10,000 rounds of ammunition, turned the tide in the strike. The strike sympathizers were well aware that "[i]f ordered to shoot, they shoot to kill."[145]

Rhode Island militiamen imported during the 1902 Providence streetcar strike proved similarly intimidating, forming an "invincible guard" in Pawtucket's downtown. Officers instructed infantrymen to first use their musket butts if they encountered resistance from strike sympathizers but to fire if necessary. When a crowd gathered as militiamen cut down effigies of strikebreakers wearing carmen's caps, the militia captain gave the order to load, and "cartridges dropped into guns with an ominous click." The soldiers turned toward the crowd, and "not another murmur was heard." The arrival of the highly mobile cavalry troops made possible the patrolling of a wide area, including outlying districts where the police presence had been minimal or nonexistent. Strike sympathizers fled from the galloping patrols, for fear of being trampled. Cavalrymen rode through working-class neighborhoods, ordering inside anyone standing in a doorway, and all windows closed, to prevent the throwing of objects at streetcars.[146]

In Richmond, 1,200 "grimly blue-coated" Virginia state militiamen imported during the 1903 strike provided formidable protection for the strikebreakers, some of them accompanying the strikebreakers on the streetcars. Officers were empowered to direct picked sharpshooters to fire at those throwing missiles at cars.[147]

The militia's firepower easily surpassed that of the police and the strikebreakers, armed with revolvers, automatic pistols, and clubs. Like the citizen-soldiers, the strikebreakers did sometimes carry rifles on the cars, but the militia also included heavy weapons units, which on several occasions effectively employed machine guns as a deterrent against crowd action. These units were most commonly equipped with the hand-cranked Gatling machine guns first developed in the 1860s. Although the American military made little use of the machine gun prior to World War I, it became "a standard weapon in the bitter struggle between management and organized labor" by the early years of the twentieth century, widely used by state militia during strikes.[148]

In the 1902 Providence streetcar strike a machine gun detachment dispelled the doubts of some brigade officers that the weapons were too unwieldy and difficult to move for effective use in urban riots. The detachment galloped quickly into position and trained the machine gun on strike sympathizers before they could disrupt streetcar traffic. The militia commander was "emphatic in his praise of the Machine Gun boys," and declared that by the time other units arrived at the trouble point all that remained of the crowd was "a collection of hats lying about the street, indicating the precipitate manner in which [it] dispersed" when confronted with a machine gun. The militia positioned four Gatling guns at key intersections in Providence and Pawtucket, "ready to sweep . . . in any direction" should a crowd rush forward. Militia also used Gatling guns in the Richmond and Waterbury streetcar strikes in 1903.[149]

Although the state militia provided management with an important advantage in several streetcar strikes, significantly augmenting the firepower of the strikebreakers, as an organization of citizen-soldiers it possessed the same shortcomings as the police. Because militia were to a great degree composed of working men, many of them union members, sometimes drawn from the same neighborhoods as the strikers, the citizen-soldiers often supported the strike. In New Orleans in 1902, where strikebreaker Alfred Clark lamented, "Almost every citizen you meet is in sympathy with the strikers," Louisiana militiamen actually donned civilian clothes and joined the crowds of strike sympathizers that impeded the passage of the streetcars. The strikers boasted that "[the] Militia are all with us," explaining that "the boys who belong to it have relatives and friends among the strikers."[150]

The first attempt ever to use the Connecticut state militia in a strike proved disastrous in Waterbury in 1903. A significant proportion of the militiamen were union members, and there were reports of soldiers stoning cars and encouraging strike sympathizers to fight the strikebreakers. The militiamen went so far as to post a sign in their armory bearing the strikers' motto "We Walk," and scores patrolled the streets wearing the strikers' buttons displaying that slogan. In fact, a dozen members of a company in the First Regiment were at that time on strike themselves in a shoe factory, while in another company fifteen men employed in a textile mill were also on strike. At the request of these companies' officers, militiamen were removed from the carbarns for making life "intolerable" for the strikebreakers there. When the First Regiment was withdrawn from Waterbury, many believed it was "because the large number of union men in it had not performed their duty properly."[151]

## PENNSYLVANIA'S BLACK HUSSARS

The inadequacy of state militia and municipal police in handling strikes led a few state governments to establish a full-time state police force. Aside from Texas, which established a frontier police, the Texas Rangers, in the nineteenth century, the first state to do so was Pennsylvania. Its State Constabulary was founded in 1905. Officially created to combat rural crime, its primary duty was suppressing public disorder during mining and streetcar strikes. Committed to keeping "the turbulent foreign element under control," its motto was "One state policeman should be able to handle 100 foreigners." The fraternization between Pennsylvania militiamen and miners during the 1902 coal strike had greatly alarmed state authorities and business leaders.[152]

The Pennsylvania State Constabulary consisted of 200 elite mounted troops recruited from around the state, and posted outside their home communities to eliminate the possibility that they could be friends or acquaintances of strikers. The troops were housed at four barracks, two of which were located in the anthracite coal region at Pottsville and Wilkes-Barre, and two in the bituminous region at Punxautawny and Greensburg. The state police force was subjected to strict military discipline. Such discipline was far easier to enforce than in the militia, since 90 percent of the men in the Constabulary were veterans of the regular army or navy. Most had held sergeant's commissions, the majority in the cavalry. Applicants had to pass a stringent physical examination. The Constabulary only recruited men who could ride, and the training included the use of horses in strikes.[153]

The black-uniformed, black-helmeted Pennsylvania Constabulary quickly developed a reputation as a highly mobile, efficient strikebreaking force, armed with automatic weapons, who "fire[d] to kill." They were hated and dreaded by Pennsylvania's trade unionists, who called them the "Black Cossacks" or "Black Hussars," nicknames that associated them with czarist and Habsburg brutality and despotism. In the 1910 Philadelphia streetcar strike, the Pennsylvania Constabulary put on "a demonstration of what mobility means." The entire squadron of nearly 200 arrived in Philadelphia only twelve hours from the time the governor issued his call, even though some of the men had to ride sixty miles from isolated substations to join the troops at the barracks.[154]

The Pennsylvania Constabulary replaced the disgraced State Fencibles, the independent militia that had been removed after being chased by strike sympathizers through the streets, and intimidated crowds with its "remarkable horsemanship," tight discipline, and willingness to use force. It was the first time the Constabulary had ever been sent into Philadelphia.[155] Its superintendent insisted that his men be kept together as a unit, under his command, rather than spread about the city working with municipal police under divided authority. He requested that all of his men be assigned to the most dangerous zone, the Kensington mill district. "Looking neither to the right nor the left, [with] not a flicker of nervous tension," the Pennsylvania Constabulary entered Kensington as a force of "grim, black-garbed riders," their "big, black holsters hanging heavy from the cartridge belt," each man displaying at his saddle a pair of shining handcuffs, which "clanked threateningly against the handles of hickory night sticks."[156] Troops were positioned at the key intersections, ready for a charge in any direction. Whenever a crowd began to form, state policemen rode into it, bringing their horses up on to the sidewalks and driving people from the doorsteps, using their riot sticks freely.[157]

Although workers in numerous other trades in Philadelphia staged a sympathy strike, the company's access to a national supply of strikebreakers and a highly disciplined paramilitary force, the Pennsylvania State Constabulary, resulted in the streetcarmen's union accepting a settlement the rank and file opposed. The State Constabulary left Philadelphia three days after it arrived, its mission completed. The union quickly collapsed, and the Philadelphia Rapid Transit Company remained nonunion for a generation.[158]

## CONCLUSION

The strikebreaking business became solidly established during the first decade of the twentieth century, as entrepreneurs assembled highly mobile mercenary armies available for quick transport across the country. Many Americans, lost in the anonymity of a rapidly urbanizing society, stifled by bureaucracy, sought escape from the mundane by vicariously identifying with the professional strikebreaker, who fought courageously, hand to hand, like the heroes of the pulp fiction they consumed. Unlike the turn-of-the-century mercenaries, fighting in far distant territory unfamiliar to the vast majority of Americans, the strikebreaker occupied center stage in a big-city arena, his every act reported by the metropolitan dailies. Aging veterans of the Civil War regularly gathered to commemorate heroic exploits that young and middle-aged men could admire but never experience themselves. Like the protagonist in Richard Harding Davis's 1896 short story "The Reporter Who Made Himself King," the latter felt at least a measure of disappointment when they "read the papers every morning . . . for war clouds," only to see them "always drift[ing] apart, and peace smil[ing] again."[159]

Simultaneously, African American men in the South emerged as still another source of strikebreakers that entrepreneurs effectively mobilized in northern labor conflicts. African American strikebreaking, which in several industries significantly reduced white workers' leverage on the job, appeared, by contrast, to provide new breakthroughs for black men. They hoped both to gain access to industries that had barred them from employment and to redefine black masculinity, highly important in a period of steadily increasing subordination to whites.

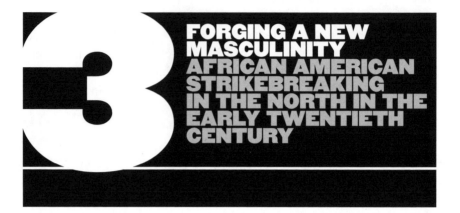

# 3

## FORGING A NEW MASCULINITY
## AFRICAN AMERICAN STRIKEBREAKING IN THE NORTH IN THE EARLY TWENTIETH CENTURY

The years immediately following the turn of the century marked the dramatic emergence of African Americans as a formidable strikebreaking force. Having recently developed the capability of hiring large concentrations of men and quickly transporting them over vast distances, northern corporations recruited "armies" of African Americans, largely from the Deep South and border cities, to break the national packinghouse strike in 1904 and the Chicago teamsters' strike of 1905. Employers' ability to recruit southern blacks so efficiently owed much to the recent emergence of strikebreaking as a business, as well as the South's full integration into the national railroad system, facilitated by its adoption of the North's railroad track gauge in 1886, and the technological progress and expansion of telegraphy and telephony. These strikes were critically important in forging an identity for African Americans as a "scab race," a perception widely held by the white public and in the labor movement until the 1930s.

Excluded by a strict color bar in hiring in most northern industries until the Great Migration of 1916–19, and from many occupations long after that, and largely shunned by northern trade unions until the 1930s, African Americans constituted a logical source of strikebreakers during the early twentieth century. Most southern blacks also lacked familiarity with trade unions, because they were largely concentrated in agriculture, and the rate of unionization in southern industry was significantly lower than in the North. Even as many African Americans agitated for an end to labor's discriminatory practices, many black leaders and newspapers condoned, and even encouraged, strikebreaking as a means of gaining access to industry.

During the early twentieth century, the labor movement's indifference to the African American worker, and the black elite's conservative and individualistic outlook on economic issues, facilitated northern employers' efforts to recruit significant numbers of African Americans for strikebreaking. By 1900 the American Federation of Labor (AFL), largely concerned with organizing skilled trades in which African Americans were greatly underrepresented, had abandoned its opposition to affiliated unions barring blacks from membership by constitutional provision. In any event, the AFL accorded the unions "complete self-government" and lacked the power to interfere with their membership requirements. Eight national unions excluded African Americans by a clause in their constitution or secret ritual, including the railroad brotherhoods, the Commercial Telegraphers, and the Machinists. Strict trade or apprenticeship requirements made it exceedingly difficult for African Americans to join other unions. Discrimination by union locals themselves was the most common reason for exclusion. Unions sometimes excused discrimination, or refusal to organize African Americans, by arguing that the public objected to the employment of blacks in the trade, as was the case with the Chicago streetcarmen's local. The unions' racially exclusionary practices stifled the development of a black labor leadership, which might have influenced African Americans against strikebreaking.[1]

The black elite in turn-of-the-century America was largely uninvolved in the emerging system of bureaucratic organization and maintained a faith in individual mobility and private enterprise that "sometimes bordered on naivete."[2] The outlook of Booker T. Washington, who encouraged blacks to develop alliances with white business leaders and to internalize middle-class values, was dominant. Washington had boasted in his famous Atlanta Compromise speech of 1895 that black labor was "not given to strikes" and in 1913 noted, not unapprovingly, that blacks had been "very willing strikebreakers."[3] Most black critics of Washington, while demanding more vigorous action to end segregation and secure voting rights, shared his conservatism on economic issues. W. E. B. Du Bois's journal the *Horizon* compared striking white miners and their supporters who attacked black strikebreakers at Pana, Illinois, in 1898 with the pro-slavery mob that murdered abolitionist Elijah Lovejoy.[4] African American newspapers, the largest and most successful of the nation's black business enterprises, for the most part also advanced Washington's pro-employer perspective and were primarily concerned with covering the activities of those in "Negro society."[5]

Reinforcing the economic conservatism of the black elite were the African American institutions of higher learning that trained much of it and were heavily dependent on the patronage of wealthy white benefactors. The "Negro college" in the early twentieth century, whose president was nearly always a minister, was largely concerned with "making professing Christians" and permitted faculty little or no academic freedom.[6] The prominent African American sociologist E. Franklin Frazier described black college students as "listless as the children of peasants," primarily concerned with social life and fraternities, institutions that symbolized blacks' achievement of middle-class status. He claimed that administrators, faculty, and students alike agreed that "money and conspicuous consumption are more important than knowledge."[7]

Equally conservative were the more numerous black schools of industrial education, like Booker T. Washington's Tuskegee Institute, which emphasized manual training. These instilled in students "a spirit of humility" and forbade faculty from "mention[ing] the existence of labor unions."[8] Black administrators from the manual training schools sometimes solicited donations from northern white philanthropists by offering their students as potential strikebreakers. In 1901, for example, a black administrator from a black manual training school in North Carolina, explained to Boston's Twentieth Century Club that "if you educate [the] million and a half of colored boys and girls and make skilled laborers of them," northern corporations no longer would have to make concessions to their workers, because the black youths "will take the place of . . . strikers."[9]

## FORGING A NEW BLACK MASCULINITY THROUGH STRIKEBREAKING

Strikebreaking also appealed to many African Americans because it provided the black man his best opportunity to assume a tough, combative posture in public and to display courage while risking serious physical injury or even death. Strikebreaking thus allowed African American men to challenge openly white society's image of them as obsequious, cowardly, and lacking the ability to perform well under pressure. It enabled them to violate the prevailing norms of conduct for black men in the South, which required that they act deferentially in the presence of whites, avoid eye contact, and step aside on the sidewalk.

In the two strikes with which this chapter is primarily concerned, African American strikebreakers assumed the role of soldiers in wartime, fre-

quently engaging in armed conflict with large crowds of white strike sympathizers, which sometimes threatened to lynch them. Newspapers ran
long daily columns listing the killed and wounded on each side, which the
African American *New York Age* remarked gave one the impression of "being on the edge of a battle-field."[10] The Chicago teamsters' strike in particular was "very bloody," as "pitched battles" between black strikebreakers
and white strike sympathizers raged in the streets throughout the city,
"claiming as many as 100 casualties in a single day." In fact, it was the most
violent labor conflict Chicago ever experienced.[11] In both strikes, a large
proportion of the African American strikebreakers armed themselves with
revolvers, clubs, and long knives, and during the latter employers supplied
the black teamsters riding the wagons with Winchester repeating rifles. As
in the U.S. Army, the black strikebreakers were supervised by whites, so
that their transformation into warriors did not challenge the prevailing
white belief that blacks were unfit for command. In both strikes, African
Americans were also hired in significant numbers as policemen, feared by
pro-labor forces because they were considered much more likely to shoot
to kill.[12]

During the early years of the twentieth century, African Americans
found themselves increasingly powerless, as the southern states elaborated
a full-scale system of legal segregation of public facilities and completely
disfranchised blacks, and northerners grew much more sympathetic to the
southern attitude toward race. Lynching, in the 1880s largely a phenomenon of the western frontier, became a highly significant feature of southern
life, an instrument of terror directed against African American men, often
used to punish black assertiveness. In the countryside, armed bands of
"white caps"—white farmers who coveted land rented or owned by blacks—
terrorized blacks in frequent nighttime raids.[13] Unlike during Reconstruction, when blacks as uniformed occupation soldiers or members of paramilitary self-defense squads could sometimes prevail in armed conflicts
with white supremacists, after 1890 southern blacks had been rendered
largely defenseless.[14]

As the turn of the century approached, anti-black violence in the South
intensified, assuming in the race riot a form in which a larger proportion
of the African American population was directly threatened with physical
harm than ever before in the post-Emancipation period. Unlike lynching,
which focused on individuals, the riots targeted entire African American
communities. Beginning in the North Carolina port town of Wilmington
in 1898 and climaxing in Atlanta in 1906, whites in several cities attacked

African American neighborhoods, killing and wounding many blacks, burning and wrecking black business establishments, and driving hundreds of blacks from their homes. Fully 10,000 whites joined in the Atlanta rioting, in which 25 blacks were killed and at least 200 seriously injured; more than 1,000 blacks fled the city.[15] Police in Wilmington and Atlanta, as well as in the New Orleans riot in 1900, either took no action to protect the victims or joined the rioters in the beating and pillaging. During the early twentieth century, until the period immediately following World War I, black self-defense was much less well organized and effective than during Reconstruction.[16]

The North not only acquiesced in the full-scale restoration and expansion of white supremacist rule in the South but also appeared increasingly inhospitable to African Americans in the early years of the twentieth century. Prejudice against the growing numbers of immigrants from southern and eastern Europe, and against the nonwhite populations of new possessions acquired in the Spanish-American War, caused many northerners to draw closer to the southern position on race. Even in the most racially liberal sections of the North, communities and institutions initiated measures that severely constricted blacks' rights. For example, Kansas's principal city Topeka passed a law requiring that blacks attend a segregated high school, and an increasing number of Boston's hotels and restaurants refused to serve blacks. Journalist Ray Stannard Baker noted in 1907 that "entire neighborhoods and even counties in Indiana and Illinois will not permit a Negro to pass in the country roads, much less become a resident." Blacks in some northern cities refrained from entering parks or using streetcars, for fear of assault.[17] At Northwestern University, outside Chicago, an African American student was unable to live in a new dormitory because all rooms housed two students, and no white student was willing to room with a black.[18]

Blacks' increasing insecurity and vulnerability in the North was dramatically illustrated in violent white attacks on African American communities in towns previously considered hospitable to blacks, and where they had long resided. Bloody, anti-black riots occurred in Springfield, Ohio, in 1906, which had been on the line of the Underground Railroad, and in Springfield, Illinois, in 1908, "within the pale of influence of the tomb and home of Lincoln the Emancipator." In the former town, a major center for the manufacture of farm machinery and tools, located near the nation's oldest black college, Wilberforce University, white workers demanded that African Americans be removed from positions as machinists, painters, and carpenters and employed only in menial positions. In 1906 a white mob there "did not content itself with burning a few hovels in the slums, but burned the homes of respectable and well to do blacks," resulting in the military occupation of the town. White mobs that rampaged through Springfield, Illinois, in 1908 killed 6 blacks and forced 2,000 more out of the city. Whites lynched an elderly black man said to have been a friend of Abraham Lincoln. The African American journal the *Horizon* observed "something . . . ominous" in the riot; it clearly demonstrated that "race antipathy" could be "as destructive and malevolent" in the North as in the South.[19]

The U.S. military had previously provided opportunities for African American men to gain respect from the white public, generally denied them in civilian life, by displaying the qualities it equated with masculinity: courage, aggressiveness, self-discipline, and the ability to withstand pain and physical discomfort without complaint. The armed African American soldier was deeply resented by white southerners because he undermined the stereotype of the humble, self-effacing black. Black soldiers' Civil War combat record and their leadership role in many southern communities during Reconstruction had significantly enhanced black self-esteem. The African American scholar Kelly Miller noted in 1908: "The soldierly spirit is incompatible with the status to which the black man has been assigned in [the southern] political and social scheme."[20]

But from 1890 until the United States entered World War I in 1917, opportunities for African Americans in the U.S. military steadily diminished. Black troops who had served in segregated regiments in the Indian wars in the West through the 1880s, under white officers, had convinced military authorities of their proficiency in combat. However, the army formed no new black regiments after 1869, while adding white ones, so that the two existing cavalry and two infantry regiments constituted a small and steadily shrinking part of the army. Whites not only in the South, but in the East and Midwest as well, did not want black troops stationed near them, so that from the end of Reconstruction until the 1890s, the black regiments had been "assigned exclusively to the West's dusty ranges."[21]

During the pre–World War I period, the requirement that African American troops serve under white officers, and the War Department's and Congress's refusal to consider black soldiers' requests to form artillery units, reflected the government's view that blacks' military role should be much more limited than whites'. The army high command probably assumed that blacks lacked the intelligence to operate more sophisticated weaponry. Assignment to the "big guns" might also impart to African Americans a sense of power and mastery the army believed unsuitable in blacks.[22] The navy was even more restrictive, allowing very few African Americans into the deck forces of the warships—the sailors and gunners assigned to combat. Nearly all African Americans in the navy were relegated to positions as messmen, stewards, cooks, and firemen. Men in these positions were not permitted the privileges of participating in the parades of crews of warships.[23]

The subjugation of the western Indians, and the end of concern about reservation uprisings, led to the transfer by 1900 of black troops from the frontier much closer to white population centers, resulting in mounting opposition to their presence by white civilians and military units, and precipitating calls in Congress to abolish the black regiments entirely. The army high command itself had been much more favorably disposed to black troops before 1890, when it desperately needed manpower to protect settlements scattered across the vast western expanses and was unable to recruit a sufficient number of whites. The black regiments did perform effectively in combat in Cuba during the Spanish-American War in 1898 and in the ensuing campaign against the guerrillas in the Philippines, but the former conflict lasted only a short time, and the latter was limited in scale. Black troops passing through the South on the way to Cuba in 1898 experienced harassment from whites in several towns and military encampments.[24]

The status of the African American soldier was further undermined as a result of the Brownsville Affair of 1906, when President Theodore Roosevelt dishonorably discharged from the army, without a trial, three companies of black regular infantry troops, 167 men from the Twenty-fifth Infantry Regiment, because of a ten-minute nighttime shooting spree committed by an unknown group of ten to twenty men, in which a white bartender was killed and a police lieutenant seriously wounded. War Department investigators were unable to identify the individuals responsible but claimed that the men in the companies had knowledge of the affair. Their dishonorable discharge meant loss of pension and the right to enter soldiers' homes. Nearly all of the men in the regiment had served more than one enlistment, and many had combat experience against Indians on the frontier. The regiment had also fought in the Spanish-American War.[25]

The black regiment had been stationed in Brownsville, Texas, only two weeks, having been transferred from Fort Niobara, Nebraska, but several serious altercations had already occurred between the soldiers and white and Mexican American residents. Townspeople had accused black soldiers of not stepping aside for whites on the sidewalk and of "behaving disre-spectfully" to them.[26]

Such friction was common in this period whenever black troops came into contact with white civilians or with white soldiers. The black soldiers of the Twenty-fifth Infantry Regiment had experienced serious harassment from white troops when stationed at maneuver camp at Fort Riley, Kansas, in 1903. The army command there had found it necessary to assign other soldiers to protect the blacks' encampment from a threatened attack by a white Texas National Guard regiment.[27]

The African American press considered the president's order to "dis-miss . . . in disgrace" the "noble" soldiers of the three companies an attempt to denigrate the reputation of the black soldier; it thus constituted a severe blow to "the race's honorable pride." Because "a few blacks were suspected of treating Southerners as Southerners treated them," the president had denied scores of black soldiers never accused of participating in the shoot-ing the American citizen's basic right to a fair trial and had sullied the "hitherto unblemished record of a soldiery who [had] saved the Union and saved Roosevelt himself on San Juan Hill."[28]

During the 1890s black troops assumed a prominent role in suppressing strikes by white workers, favored by management and government officials for that assignment because they were believed much less likely than white troops to fraternize with the strikers. Concern about fraternization was also significant in the decision of employers to import black strikebreakers during the early twentieth century. Black soldiers dispersed striking miners at Coeur d'Alene, Idaho, in 1892, and the War Department summoned them again to suppress the miners' strike there in 1899. In neither case was there any fraternization between the black troops and the striking miners, who were nearly all whites of British, Irish, Scandinavian, or Italian de-scent. Foreshadowing the response of many white unionists toward black strikebreakers during the 1904 packinghouse and 1905 teamsters' strikes, striking miners denounced the black soldiers as barbaric and accused them of excessive violence against the strikers. Black troops were also assigned to ride trains and guard tunnels, bridges, and switchyards during the 1894 Pullman railroad strike.[29]

According to the *New York Tribune*, the performance of the African American Ninth Cavalry Regiment in suppressing the Coeur d'Alene min-ers' strike in 1899 "completely upset" the widely held belief that blacks did not possess fighting ability. Reversing the prevailing stereotype of the black man as undisciplined, menacing, even semicriminal, it presented the "gallant and extremely effective" Ninth Cavalry as representing the forces of civilization against "fiends" (the striking miners) who had unleashed a wave of "unbridled lawlessness, of rap[e], of destruction of property, and bloodshed." It had appeared that the strikers would drive the mine owners out of Coeur d'Alene when the Ninth Cavalry miraculously appeared. Rushing off a train "with whoops and wild yells," the black soldiers seized a bridge before the miners could blow it up with dynamite. Like Teddy Roosevelt's Rough Riders at San Juan Hill, the regiment displayed "coolness and determination" as it then charged up a hill "crowded with strikers." When the miners opened fire, the blacks "replied without stopping their onward rush." Each soldier of the Ninth "was trying to get to the top of the hill first." Although the miners put up a determined resistance, the blacks took the hill, on which lay large numbers of dead and wounded from both sides. The blacks had demonstrated, according to the *Tribune*, that there was "no better fighter than the African, . . . when he is well-officered." The Ninth Cavalry Regiment remained in Coeur d'Alene until "order was restored."[30]

## THE BLACK STRIKEBREAKER AT THE CENTER OF ATTACK: THE NATIONAL PACKINGHOUSE STRIKE OF 1904

In the 1904 national packinghouse strike, for the first time in a major northern labor conflict, the black strikebreaker "was the center of attack from the moment the strike broke." The packinghouse companies transported massive trainloads of blacks from the Deep South and points in the border states, East, and Midwest to the major slaughtering and meatpacking cities. The strike, lasting two months, involved 23,000 workers in Chicago and over 40,000 nationally, primarily in Kansas City, Omaha, Fort Worth, Sioux City, East St. Louis, St. Paul, and St. Joseph. Both sides recognized that the success of the strike nationally hinged on the outcome in Chicago, the industry center. The massive importation of African American strikebreakers, who numbered between 10,000 and 18,000 in Chicago alone, resulted in a dramatic shift in the industry's labor force during the strike, from 95 percent white to 85 percent black within a month.[31]

Although the meat-packing industry was not well developed in the South, where over 90 percent of blacks resided, employers believed that African Americans would make suitable strikebreakers because most jobs were unskilled. The employers considered African Americans to be similar to the eastern European immigrants, who constituted the overwhelming majority of those entering the industry after 1900, capable of readily adapting to the extreme heat, filth, and stench of the packinghouses, and well suited for the heavy physical labor required. Michael Donnelly, president of the Amalgamated Meat Cutters and Butcher Workmen's Union and leader of the 1904 strike, declared that before the strike the packers had preferred to hire "husky foreigners who are able to pull thousands of pounds on a truck—a load that would make a mule bark."[32] Because the industry's labor force was 90 percent male, and there was almost no night work, there was little possibility of black men encountering white women in the slaughterhouses and in isolated situations. This would avoid the violation of a taboo, less emphasized in the North than in the South, but still a concern of many northerners. A leading northern journalist commented that the relative absence of women and night work in the industry removed "the possibility of those scenes of promiscuous immorality which have disgraced certain night-working twine mills in Illinois."[33]

In order to protect the strikebreakers, the employers housed them in the packinghouses. In Chicago, the industry and strike center, the settlement area became a vast, enclosed stockade, surrounded day and night by 1,200 armed deputies. The strikebreakers, isolated from the world, gave the appearance of an army under siege. Like soldiers at the front, they were regularly given time to "laboriously compos[e] letters [home]." Similar conditions, on a smaller scale, prevailed in the other cities affected by the strike.[34]

The strikebreakers were expected to endure the hardships of soldiers in war, eating and sleeping in squalid, highly uncomfortable surroundings. A journalist who accompanied Professor John Commons of the University of Wisconsin on a tour of the stockyards one night during the strike described the mostly black strikebreakers, mixed with some Poles and Italians, "huddled together" in a large dormitory in what had formerly been a hog house. In oppressive August heat, the men slept in their clothes, apparently for fear they would be otherwise stolen, "on the bare springs of small cots." Huge numbers could be accommodated, since the four-tiered bunks were placed so close together a man had to shuffle sideways to get between them. There were no windows, and the men got ventilation only through the door. Two barrels provided the only supply of drinking water. A sign warned that if a man were not in bed by 9:30 his cot would be taken "by the first applicant," suggesting that many strikebreakers slept on the floor elsewhere. Professor Commons commented, "In case of fire I should think

*African American strikebreakers are guarded by a policeman, Chicago packinghouse strike, 1904. Courtesy of the Chicago Historical Society, DN-0001021.*

certain death would be the fate of them all in this place." In the dining hall, a windowless room formerly used for meat stripping, hundreds of men ate from tin plates on long benches, as hordes of rats scurried about on the floor.[35]

Although the employers sought to isolate the strikebreakers in the stockades, violent conflict was frequent during the strike, occurring when the strikebreakers arrived at the railroad stations, were being transported through the city to the stockyards, or were being moved into the enclosures. In Chicago, the storm center of the strike, strikebreakers could gain access to the stockyard gates only by passing through very densely populated blocks, where the strikers and their families resided, containing probably the city's largest concentration of saloons, and where street life was intense. Under these conditions, large and boisterous crowds of strike sympathizers formed quickly. The union leadership, to be sure, urged that those participating in, and supporting the strike, refrain from violence, in order to prevent the intervention of militia to suppress the strike. To contain violence, it scheduled frequent mass strike meetings, allowing regular communication with the rank and file, and union picnics as diversions. But strikers and their sympathizers assumed a combative posture, rendered more intense by the racial character of the strikebreaking force, and initiated numerous assaults. At times crowds numbering in the thousands engaged in hand-to-hand battle with policemen and strikebreakers.[36]

The strikers' combativeness was also shaped by living and working in an environment where violence and pain were endemic and seemed natural. They were involved in the slaughtering of animals under dangerous conditions, covered with blood at work, and resided in neighborhoods lacking sewer connections, full of saloons, and surrounded by garbage dumps, resulting in a very high death rate. An observer noted that "monotonously plunging a knife all day long into the throat of the steer . . . inured to [its] pitiable shrieks" made a man "fierce." Unskilled workers engaged in heavy physical labor, like those in the packinghouses, tended to define masculinity in terms of physical and drinking prowess, courage, and boisterousness, all qualities associated with fighting. Early in the strike in Chicago, when some of the packinghouses put their clerks to work unloading hogs, strikers "in heavy boots and rough garb" looked on, laughing at their efforts, taunted them as "dandies" and ridiculed their panama hats and silk suspenders.[37]

African American strikebreakers arrived in Chicago and the other packing centers prepared for violence; many were armed. Some even stepped off the trains openly brandishing their weapons, like a group of 300 from Tennessee, hired by Armour & Company, who arrived in Chicago carrying squirrel rifles.[38]

From the beginning, black strikebreakers traveling through the city to the stockyards displayed a readiness to draw revolvers and to fire into crowds when threatened with sticks or stones.[39] Eight black strikebreakers who reached for their pockets when surrounded by strike sympathizers outside the Chicago stockyards early in the strike were immediately arrested by the police. When the police searched them, they found "a perfect arsenal." Each of the black men carried a "big loaded revolver," and several also had "long, keen-bladed knives."[40] When several hundred strike sympathizers stoned a train pulling into the railroad station in Chicago with sixty African American strikebreakers from Pittsburgh, "smashing windows and threatening serious assault," a black on the train opened fire on the crowd with his revolver. For the rest of the day police searched all trains carrying black strikebreakers into Chicago for firearms, confiscating "scores of weapons."[41] Later in the strike, black strikebreakers aboard a Black Diamond Special train, so named because it transported blacks for whom there was no room in the packinghouse dormitories every night to lodging houses elsewhere in Chicago, fired at a crowd of 500 that they believed was "pre-par[ing] to mob" the coaches. They killed a striker and seriously wounded three others. Police searching the train found "a dozen or more revolvers or knives" in each car. Chicago's Chief of Police O'Neill declared, referring primarily to the black strikebreakers, "There are more concealed weapons being carried in this strike than in any other within my experience."[42]

The metropolitan daily newspapers, largely sympathetic to manage-ment, frequently praised the African American strikebreakers for display-ing courage when assaulted by crowds of strike sympathizers, whom they denounced as cowardly.[43] The press's favorable depiction of the blacks was also influenced by the fact that they were usually outnumbered in these confrontations and sometimes threatened with lynching. On July 17, for example, Chicago police reinforcements barely managed to rescue a black strikebreaker from a crowd yelling, "Lynch the scab," after it had seized him from a patrolman attempting to protect him, but not before it had torn his clothes off and badly beaten him.[44] Two days later a crowd captured a black strikebreaker employed by Chicago's Libby, McNeill, & Libby pack-inghouse and procured a rope, amid cries of "Let him dangle!" At the last moment the black made a desperate break and escaped by jumping on the coupling bar of the last car of a passing freight train. Shortly afterward, another black strikebreaker was "treed" by a Chicago crowd of 2,000. His retreat having been cut off, he had climbed on to the roof of a porch, where police rescued him.[45]

African American strikebreakers faced similarly dangerous conditions in Omaha, where a "monster crowd of union men" surrounded a group of them as they were being escorted to the packinghouses by policemen and seized them as "prisoners of war." The Omaha unionists successfully car-ried out a similar operation again a week later, wresting a racially mixed railroad carload of strikebreakers from an armed contingent of mounted police and "march[ing] them triumphantly to union headquarters." The police chief declared that the crowd was so large his men had no chance to prevent the strikebreakers' capture, even though they put up "a fierce struggle": "They might as well have tried to hold up the waters of Niagara with a pitchfork."[46]

In Fort Worth, the only southern city affected by the walkout, it became clear that strikebreaking could undermine southern white authorities' in-tense hostility toward the armed black man. In a highly publicized trial, a black strikebreaker, charged by a group of white strikers with drawing a pistol when they urged him to refrain from working, was acquitted on the grounds that he had the right to self-defense. The packinghouse company that employed the strikebreaker supplied his attorney. The judge ruled that the black man had a "right to carry a pistol from his home to his place of business" and to draw it when threatened by white pickets, some of whom wielded sticks and "used vile language to him."[47]

In the town of Sheely, Nebraska, outside Omaha, the police force was augmented by the hiring of African American deputies, who did not hesitate to draw their guns and shoot when angry strikers, summoned by local residents who complained of police harassment, began hurling stones at them. Reflecting the deep racial antagonism that prevailed in the Omaha area, the residents of Sheely demanded that the black deputies be replaced by whites and refused to permit them to drink from their wells.[48]

In Kansas City the black strikebreakers displayed their solidarity and advertised their massive presence in an elaborate Emancipation Day celebration in Kerr's Park on August 1, commemorating the proclamation freeing all slaves in the British West Indian colonies on that date in 1834. The strikebreakers marked the occasion with speeches about emancipation, fireworks, and brass band performances.[49]

Although many newspapers praised the black strikebreakers' courage, their importation was protested by many Chicago businessmen, who feared that their retention by the packing companies would transform the stockyards district into a "negro settlement" or "black belt," driving out the white residents.[50]

The union sought to build public support for its cause by contrasting the "respectability" of its members with the alleged depravity and propensity for violence of the African American strikebreakers. It depicted the strikers as responsible family men, shaped by their wives' civilizing influence, struggling for their children's future, unlike the debauched African American strikebreakers from the "backward" South, working and living in an all-male environment in the packing centers, not subjected to women's moral restraint. On August 6, the union held a massive strike parade in Chicago, in which the strikers' children, marching in separate sections, were highly conspicuous, underlining the union's commitment to protecting the family. Little girls, dressed in white, symbolizing moral purity, carried banners proclaiming, "Give our fathers living wages so we may enjoy the benefits of the schoolroom" and "Take mother out of the packing house, so we can have her care at home." Fully 3,000 women participated in the procession.[51] Further underlining the strong bond between union and family were the "Bride's Dances" staged in the stockyards' Polish and

Slavonian communities, in which young women donated all of the proceeds from their wedding celebrations, often $400 to $500, to the strike fund. The union leaders also urged the strikers' wives and female relatives, as well as the relatively small number of women among the strikers, to use their influence to keep the men from drinking.[52]

Many observers were indeed impressed by women's moral influence over the strikers. The police captain of Chicago's stockyards district praised the women of the yards for "behaving with dignity" and noted that they were "a distinct influence for order and sobriety." Jane Addams expressed the same sentiment at an afternoon dance for "girl strikers" held at Chicago's University Settlement, reminding them that they had "great influence" over the men, and congratulating them for providing the men with an example of commitment to "law and order." The *Chicago Daily News*, impressed by the women's "fortitude" and loyalty to their men, and by their refusal to accept charity, compared them with "the Spartan mothers of old."[53]

The impact of female moral influence on the strikers was also illustrated when the prominent Chicago settlement house leader Mary McDowell, known as "The Angel of the Stockyards," persuaded the strikers to take down effigies of strikebreakers that they had hung on telegraph poles throughout Packingtown. She argued that the "ghastly sight" of boys performing a "war dance" around an effigy of an "executed" strikebreaker (or lynched black man) before large crowds gave the impression that the strikers were rowdy and might provoke the "thoughtless" to violence.[54]

Drawing on press reports of widespread gambling, drinking, and sexual debauchery among the African American strikebreakers in the packinghouses, the union and its supporters highlighted their "immorality" in an effort to influence public opinion. Union officials and supporters often employed racial stereotypes suggesting that African Americans were less capable than whites of self-discipline, more libidinous, and more prone to violence. Union president Michael Donnelly declared that the Chicago stockyards "looked like Southern plantations," with "hardly a white man [visible]." He claimed that the packers would never employ the blacks under ordinary circumstances. Donnelly charged, moreover, that because such men were working in the packinghouses, at least one plant had become a "house of prostitution," in which eyewitnesses had observed scenes so vile that, by comparison, "a levee dive is clean."[55] John Fitzpatrick, general organizer of the Chicago Federation of Labor, demanded that the mayor investigate the "[im]moral conditions in the plants." A. M. Simons, writing in the *Chicago Socialist*, which strongly supported the strike, asserted that inside the packinghouses "rages a saturnalia of beastly debauchery that beggars all description." He claimed that any woman who walked into the stockyards was "free prey of whatever brutalized negro who may care to use her for his purposes." Simons also reported that 200 cases of syphilis had been treated among the black strikebreakers in a single week.[56]

The image of black licentiousness promoted by the strikers was encouraged by press accounts of the strikebreakers' leisure activities in the stockyards, which seemed to primarily involve shooting craps, poker games, and nightly prizefights. The *Chicago Chronicle* described the stockyards on a Sunday afternoon as "a Mississippi River levee scene," as the "'down south' darkies" swarmed about. The *Chicago Record-Herald* reported that in the Armour plant "eight poker tables were in operation, while on every side the negroes were shooting craps." Out in the yards, crap games "could be found behind box cars, under loading docks, and in every shady spot."[57] The strikebreakers, craving instant gratification of their base desires, immediately gambled their earnings away rather than saving them.[58]

Strike supporters also denounced the boxing matches in which the strikebreakers engaged for evening recreation, for prizes as high as $6, as barbaric "gladiatorial exhibition[s]" fought by "human beasts." They proved the "negro [to be] of brutal, murderous disposition."[59] The combatants frequently broke their arms and ribs. Professor John Commons, touring one of the packinghouses, stumbled upon 5,000 blacks "whoop[ing]" and "cheer[ing]" as "two big naked black bucks" fought "fast and hard" in a makeshift ring. At Chicago's Libby, McNeil, & Libby plant, more than 1,000 blacks gathered for an evening program of "fistic entertainment" involving two bouts between men each put forward as champion of a particular locality from which strikebreakers had come.[60]

Further emphasizing the blacks' allegedly violent nature, the union leadership claimed they not only lacked competence in slaughtering but deliberately tortured the animals. Union president Michael Donnelly declared in East St. Louis that "cattle are being assassinated, not butchered." Whereas regular slaughterhouse workers were ordinarily able to immediately stun an animal with a pole axe or hammer, the black strikebreakers required as many as eight blows, sometimes allowing as many as six minutes to elapse between the first and second blow on the suffering animal. It was a veritable "bull fight on the killing floor."[61]

By late August, with many of the strikers and their families near starvation, union leaders appealed to Booker T. Washington to come to Chicago and use his influence to persuade blacks to discontinue strikebreaking. John Fitzpatrick, speaking for the Chicago Federation of Labor, declared that because the packers had been unable to recruit many whites to break the strike, "without the colored men and women now employed in the plants the companies would not be able to operate." The importation of African American strikebreakers "was fast bringing about a condition that may result in a race war in Chicago," with antagonism toward blacks so strong on the South Side that whites were dragging blacks not involved in strikebreaking off of streetcars and pummeling them. But Washington declined labor's request.[62]

After the strike ended in early September with the union's unconditional surrender, an AFL official expressed the view of the strike leadership, ascribing labor's defeat to the "importation of hordes of . . . negroes" from the southern cotton fields, "huge, strapping fellows, ignorant and vicious, whose predominating trait was animalism." The Amalgamated Meat Cutters and Butcher Workmen's Union was all but eliminated from the packing centers until the late 1910s. However, although African Americans were critical in breaking the strike, their strikebreaking could not alter management's prejudice against them as permanent employees, and they were unable to gain a foothold in the industry. Although over 10,000 blacks had been engaged as strikebreakers in 1904, in 1910 only 365 of over 16,000 packinghouse workers in Chicago were black, and a similar situation prevailed in the other packing centers.[63]

## TAKING THE OFFENSIVE:
## BLACK STRIKEBREAKERS IN CHICAGO, 1905

In the Chicago teamsters' strike of 1905, which began less than a year after the packinghouse workers surrendered, the African American strikebreaker, again imported in massive numbers from the South, appeared to whites even more menacing. No longer besieged and confined within walled enclosures, he boldly ventured forth through enemy territory, an aggressive and heavily armed warrior, "forc[ing] the fighting" and instilling fear in the city streets. The 105-day strike was the most violent labor conflict ever to occur in Chicago, and precipitated the bloodiest racial strife in the city until the Red Summer of 1919. Strike casualties totaled 21 killed and over 400 seriously injured, and there were over 1,100 arrests.[64]

Street fighting was so intense and widespread during the Chicago teamsters' strike that the press in both the United States and Europe equated it with the 1905 Russian Revolution, which occurred at the same time. The *Literary Digest*, for example, published a cartoon showing Czar Nicholas II reading a Chicago newspaper and Uncle Sam one from Moscow; the headline in each read "Striking! Rioting! Killing!"[65] Newspapers in Germany expressed astonishment at the level of violence in the Chicago strike, which they freely compared to the "bloodshed and riots in Russia." They noted that during the German miners' strike earlier that year far less violence had occurred, even though the entire province of Rhineland-Westphalia had been affected, a much larger strike zone, with fewer police than the city of Chicago.[66]

The high level of violence in Chicago in 1905 resulted both from racial antagonism, as African Americans replaced an overwhelmingly white force of teamsters, and from the nature of the work in which the strikebreakers were engaged. The armed black strikebreaker was highly visible, brandishing a Winchester rifle while riding his wagon to make deliveries of merchandise throughout the city. Deputy Police Chief Herman Schuettler, who had charge of the police strike force, claimed that "[t]he presence of negro strikebreakers increase[d] the trouble 500%." Chicago's patrolmen were widely believed to sympathize with the strikers for racial reasons and provided the blacks considerably less protection than they ordinarily accorded strikebreakers. The executive committee of the Employers' Association, organized by the stores and teaming contractors affected by the walkout, denounced the "shameful and open alliance between . . . policemen and strikers." Contempt for the black strikebreakers was openly voiced even by Chicago's superintendent of police, who denounced them as "damned hoodlums, picked up on the levees of New Orleans"—that is, no different from criminals.[67]

The black strikebreakers were also highly vulnerable to attack because of the nature of the work they performed. Teamsters' strikes were similar to those involving streetcars, requiring strikebreakers to drive wagons through avenues in which large and hostile crowds could quickly congregate. They could be even more dangerous, because violent crowd action was not confined to the area along streetcar lines or carbarns. Strikebreaking teamsters were also threatened by quick, hit-and-run guerrilla attacks by strike sympathizers concealed in doorways, behind buildings, or in alleys, described in the press as resembling Indian-style ambushes. Early in the strike the *St. Louis Globe-Democrat* reported: "Violence is rampant

*African American strikebreakers load a wagon for Montgomery Ward & Company, Chicago teamsters' strike, 1905. Courtesy of the Chicago Historical Society; photograph by Charles R. Clark.*

upon the streets of Chicago, surging through streets and alleys, springing from unsuspected places . . . hailing every opportunity to fall on a nonunion man and grind him into the pavement." Strike sympathizers constantly blockaded streets to prevent the movement of wagons. They also sometimes threw bricks or other objects from overhead windows and roofs. This was, moreover, an all-male, largely unskilled occupation involving rough, outdoor labor, including a considerable amount of lifting; as in dock work, physical and fighting prowess was associated with masculinity.[68]

The potential for violence was further heightened by the unusually high level of trade-union organization and commitment in Chicago and the fact that the strike was precipitated by employers' desire to destroy the teamsters' union. Chicago's labor movement was never as strong as during the first five years of the twentieth century, even though the near obliteration of the packinghouse unions in 1904, constituting about one-third of the city's union membership, had reduced its influence. The teamsters' unions constituted the "backbone of union strength" in Chicago. The strike was precipitated by the employers' refusal to renew closed-shop agreements after May 1, 1905, which amounted to "a declaration of war." When the right to organize or to maintain organization was the central issue in a strike, passions on both sides were usually most intense.[69]

In recruiting strikebreakers, as in the packinghouse strike, employers turned to African Americans in the South, where blacks had traditionally performed most of the teaming work. In Chicago, except for some coal teamsters, the men in the trade had traditionally been white. The affected merchants of the Employers' Association formed the Employers' Teaming Company, which immediately proceeded to purchase wagons and teams of horses to use during the strike. They contacted detective agencies and employment bureaus in all parts of the country to assist them in the task of recruiting and transporting strikebreakers.[70]

Early in the strike the Employers' Association relied heavily in recruiting on the services of professional strikebreakers Frank Curry and Thomas Dewar, head of a St. Louis detective agency. Both men appear to have been operating as agents of James Farley. In early May, Curry and Dewar shipped in trainloads of several thousand mostly African American strikebreakers from St. Louis, recruited there and from throughout the South by their personal representatives and through newspaper advertisements. Most of the blacks had been "picked up . . . along the levee"; many were roustabouts who had recently served on lower Mississippi River steamboats. They were, according to the newspaper reporters, "as lusty a set of men as one would find in a volunteer army."[71] The "black brigade" consisted of men who "were decidedly husky [and] looked like the 'real thing' in strikebreakers." While some carried belongings in valises or wrapped in newspapers, many, "like true soldiers of fortune," came with nothing except the clothes on their backs.[72]

Press accounts of the African American strikebreakers' arrival made considerable use of military imagery and gave the impression the blacks were courageous and capable warriors. The *Chicago Record-Herald* commented of the blacks that "[a]ll are said not to be afraid of a fight." The *Inter-Ocean* referred to the strikebreakers as the "colored battalions from the south" and noted that many of those gathered in St. Louis "declared their willingness to go to the front immediately."[73] While Thomas Dewar was inspecting the field in Chicago, his wife Rose, described as a "twentieth century Valkyrie," interviewed the prospective recruits in St. Louis, informing them, "This is strike duty . . . you may get shot at." To determine whether the applicant was "a fit subject for the battalion," Rose

*Policemen escort African American strikebreakers through the streets, Chicago teamsters' strike, 1905. Courtesy of the Chicago Historical Society.*

Dewar, while questioning him, assessed his "physical qualifications" and "estimat[ed] what value he would be in a fight." She warned applicants that strikebreaking was very dangerous, noting, "I don't promise any of them that they will ever come back."[74]

Rose Dewar, identified as the "doughty commandress-in-chief" of the black mercenary army, emphasized that the recruits were under strict, military-style discipline. Descended from Confederate soldiers buried "beneath the sod of Southern battlefields," she declared that she handled the strikebreakers "just as I would a crowd of volunteers in the army." Her guards, "acting under orders from headquarters," ensured that the blacks would "stand by the colors."[75]

Led by Frank Curry, who acted as Farley's field commander in Chicago, the strikebreakers immediately took the initiative, determined to "push war" on the union teamsters by establishing a massive, armed presence in the streets. Curry personally brought a large trainload of black strikebreakers into Chicago from St. Louis on May 1, many of them recruited from "down de ribber."[76] The next day Curry and his mercenaries came "under fire," as he led them in an imposing parade of wagons through the streets of the retail district. The "defiant attitude" of the forty African American guards Curry had posted alongside the wagons enraged a massive crowd of strike sympathizers that had quickly formed. The strikebreakers, both guards and teamsters, carried hickory canes and, in some cases, revolvers. They drove their wagons through a "constant gauntlet," as the pro-union forces fired some gunshots and hurled bricks, stones, eggs, and bottles filled with muriatic acid. Several of the blacks responded by hammering strike sympathizers into insensibility with their hickory canes. Downtown Chicago was in a "violent uproar" the entire day, with "every block in the downtown marked by rioting." Over fifty were injured in the clashes, and a white bystander was killed when a black strikebreaker hurled a cobblestone at him and struck him in the head.[77]

Frank Curry himself, "in the center of fighting all day," rallied his men until he was finally sent reeling by a blow to the head from a burly union teamster, which opened a jagged cut over an eye. Curry fired his revolver twice after having been struck, but the blood pouring into his eye ruined his aim, and his assailant escaped. Curry was carried to his office in a semiconscious state but nonetheless continued to direct the operations of his mercenaries by telephone, with his wounded head "swathed in bandages."[78]

The press described "field marshal" Curry as possessing the courage and steadiness under fire of a U.S. Army officer commanding African American soldiers in battle, as in the recent Spanish-American War, where all four black regiments saw action. The *St. Louis Post-Dispatch* described him as a veteran combatant "devoid of fear." His service as a strikebreaker dated back to a Milwaukee teamsters' strike in 1896 and included the 1900 St. Louis and 1903 Chicago streetcar strikes. While Curry's body bore many scars from previous strikes, caused by gunshots and clubs, he had never "been known to flinch."[79]

Setting a standard for his African American mercenaries, Curry embodied the qualities most in the working class and many in the middle class directly associated with masculinity: physical prowess, aggressiveness, and fearlessness. A former wrestler himself, he resembled swaggering heavyweight prizefighters like John L. Sullivan and Jim Jeffries, greatly admired for always advancing in the ring and for never giving up when seriously hurt. The "broad-shouldered" Curry "carrie[d] himself with his fists clenched and his shoulders squared, as if always ready to get in a blow." Let a striker "start something," and Curry fought with the fury of a "Kansas cyclone." He commanded instant obedience, because every man serving under him knew if he failed to carry out his orders, Curry would "beat him to a pulp." Curry warned the strikebreakers when he sent them out on deliveries not to return unless they brought their wagons back with them, "mean[ing] that they must defend the wagons with their lives." When the strikers did capture a wagon and placed the trophy in front of union headquarters, Curry led his men in a commando-type operation to recover it: "We made a charge to get it. We were resisted fiercely by the strikers, who threw bricks and rocks at us, used clubs, and at one time it looked like there would be shooting, but we got the wagon."[80]

According to most of the metropolitan dailies, the African American strikebreakers also epitomized this masculine ideal, a striking exception to the prevailing white view of black men. Even black prizefighters, while sometimes given credit for physical attributes, were believed to lack courage and to fold under pressure. In fact, largely because whites considered aggression a trait inappropriate in blacks, African American boxers in the Progressive Era tended to adopt a defensive style in the ring, emphasizing feinting and counterpunching, rather than the relentless attack and heavy punching favored by whites.[81] According to the *St. Louis Post-Dispatch*, the black strikebreakers in Chicago "took their lives in their hands" when they rode out into the street but "did not appear to have any emotions." They "looked straight ahead and fought stubbornly when they had the opportunity."[82]

The African American strikebreakers assumed the appearance of menacing Old West gunfighters when the Employers' Association armed them with Winchester rifles on the wagons, a throwback to "the old stagecoach days" on the frontier, when similarly armed men sat beside the drivers and "kept sharp lookout" for bandits and Indians. Aware that the carrying of concealed weapons was illegal, the Employers' Association was also concerned for the strikebreakers' safety, after Curry's parade had resulted in a "day of head-smashing," in which "ambulances . . . were in constant commission." The Winchester rifle was considered "one of the most effective weapons of destruction" at a range of "up to 300 or 400 yards," a "distance . . . quite sufficient for street fighting."[83]

The Employers' Association also adopted the caravan or convoy system used in streetcar strikes to deter attack, massing wagons together in tight formation, so that more guards and drivers would be on hand to afford protection. This method was more easily applied downtown but was less effective in outlying residential districts, where fewer wagons traveled.[84]

The sudden appearance in Chicago of hundreds of African American strikebreakers armed with Winchester rifles, aggressively confronting the crowds of white strike sympathizers in the streets, was strongly condemned by the International Brotherhood of Teamsters (IBT) leadership, and by leading southern newspapers, as dangerously provocative and degrading to whites. It caused public sympathy in Chicago to shift toward the strikers. IBT president Cornelius Shea declared that the employers had imported "worthless and shiftless" black men and "armed them to shoot white men," noting that this "would not be tolerated for a moment south of the Mason and Dixon line." A management spokesperson, the president of the West Side Liverymen's Association, charged that Shea had threatened that his men "would drive out every negro in Chicago and throw him in the lake."[85] The *New Orleans Times-Democrat* warned that "[t]he spectacle of armed negroes on wagons threatening white persons is one calculated to arouse the worst passions in the dominant race, and to lead to bloodshed and murder." Increasingly, white Chicagoans in the streets shouted for the employers to "[f]ight white men with white men."[86]

The southern press claimed that the rioting in Chicago against the African American strikebreakers exposed the North's hypocrisy in racial matters and demonstrated that the South was friendlier to blacks. The *Memphis Commercial Appeal* charged that Chicagoans' assaults on blacks were more brutal than any "ever witnessed in the South" and declared that they had "torn asunder the rotten cant of Northern pretension." After all, it editorialized, Chicago had "sneered at the South's conception of justice, condemned its charity [toward blacks] [and] misrepresented its customs," but now "[t]hey beat his black head into a quivering mass—in Chicago. They mash his limbs and crush in his ribs with stones—in Chicago. . . . And the public stands and cheers as he is mangled—in Chicago."[87]

Racial tension became exceedingly intense in the ensuing six weeks of rioting, as white crowds on several occasions procured rope and threatened to lynch African American strikebreakers, and the blacks on numerous occasions fired at strike sympathizers. For example, on May 6, a crowd of 6,000 swarmed around an African American strikebreaker whose wagon wheels had become stuck in streetcar tracks, screaming, "Get a rope!" "Smash him with brickbats!" and "Shoot him!"—these being the "mildest" of the crowd's demands, according to the *St. Louis Post-Dispatch*. Fifty policemen failed to drive the attackers back, and the black appeared doomed when a police patrol wagon, carrying fifty reinforcements, suddenly appeared, "with gong ringing . . . ma[king] a straight drive through the crowd," and accomplished a seemingly miraculous rescue. That same day a crowd of 5,000 strike sympathizers, which "seemed to rise up out of the ground," menaced black strikebreakers shoveling coal into wagons. A white policeman, waving his pistol, ordered the crowd back, but it pressed forward, even as he began firing in the air, and "it looked dangerous" for the strikebreakers. But when a black policeman suddenly appeared, with pistol drawn, a shout went up, "Cheese it! He's a nigger and he'll shoot to kill!" and the crowd immediately dispersed.[88]

The intense white antagonism toward the African American strike-breakers was reflected in a wave of strikes by pupils at grammar and high schools where black teamsters delivered coal. On May 10, over 700 of the 900 pupils at the Hendricks Grammar School refused to return to classes after the noon break because black strikebreakers had delivered coal there. During the morning, many of the boys had joined workers in a factory across the street in stoning the blacks. The superintendent of Chicago's compulsory education department rushed to the strike-bound school with his entire force of truant officers to prevent any further disturbances.[89] The pupils' strike spread two days later to Carter H. Harrison Grammar School, where 1,500 of the 1,700 pupils walked out. These pupils were even more belligerent, knocking the first black teamster off his wagon with stones, and dumping his entire wagon load of coal to the ground; the pupils later divided up the coal and took it home. The other black strikebreakers re-treated rather than attempt to unload.[90]

By May 14, pupils at seven schools had "quit [their] desks" and estab-lished picket lines, and school authorities responded by arresting seven-teen "ringleaders," including two eleven-year-old girls. A judge sentenced to reform school several of the boys accused of stoning the strikebreakers and posting "School Closed" signs.[91]

The Chicago City Council, convinced that employers' importation of black strikebreakers would result in a crime wave, passed a resolution early in the strike directing the Corporation Counsel to determine whether a law could not be invoked "to prevent the flooding of the city with this class of men." Alderman Hurt declared that the blacks' "conception of the duties of law-abiding citizens [was] as limited . . . as their educational qualifica-tions." The blacks, "illiterate, without a . . . trade, and of desperate charac-ter," would pose a serious danger to white Chicagoans when employers discharged them after the strike, as they clearly planned to do. Several days later the Corporation Counsel, citing Illinois law, informed the City Council that employers had the right to import and arm strikebreakers of whatever race, so long as the weapons were carried openly.[92]

The concerns of the Chicago City Council were echoed by white priests and ministers in sermons and speeches across the city. According to the African American *New York Age* this "pulpit invective" gave the impression that Chicago was filled with "burly Negroes plundering, terrorizing, and killing innocent and unoffending citizens."[93] A Catholic priest denounced as "reprehensible" the employers' importation of "half starved and wholly ignorant negroes," who would precipitate "a race war the like of which has never yet been seen in this country." A Methodist minister in a Sunday sermon charged that the employers' recruitment of black strikebreakers was designed to "foment race hatred" and was therefore "wicked."[94]

Leaders of Chicago's African American community, including several ministers, responded to the repeated attacks by strike sympathizers against the black strikebreakers and what it considered unfavorable press treatment of the "colored men" by scheduling a mass protest meeting at the Bethel African Methodist Church to denounce "Race Prejudice in the Strike." The gathering, attended by more than 1,000 people, adopted a resolution proposed by Ida Wells-Barnett, nationally prominent spokesperson for black rights, which praised the strikebreakers as "men who proved their value by risking their lives to obtain work." It denounced the brutality of police officers "who without the slightest provocation shamefully beat colored men . . . [allowing] rioters to go free, while their [black] victims [go] to jail or the hospital." The meeting endorsed the "constitutional right of all men to earn a living and to protect themselves in the exercise of that right." Dr. George C. Hall warned that Chicago's African Americans would not "ask other people to stop" the "infamous treatment" of the strikebreakers and other blacks: "We are going to stop it ourselves."[95]

The African American press was divided on the question of whether strikebreaking was in the black community's interest, although many newspapers believed that it had radically transformed white perceptions of black masculinity. The *New York Age* declared that the strikebreakers had undermined the strikers' assumption that the black man was "a coward who would turn and run out of town at the first shot." Instead, they had displayed "splendid courage" in the streets of Chicago. While strike sympathizers had sent many of the strikebreakers to the hospital, the *Age* gloated that "for every Negro wounded or maimed . . . [a] white . . . striker is likewise maimed and disabled." A reader of Indianapolis's African American newspaper the *Freeman* declared in a letter that the black strikebreakers had more of a right to work in Chicago than "foreigners," whom he claimed were "anarchists and plotters against our country."[96]

A significant segment of African American middle-class opinion, however, was concerned that the mass importation of black strikebreakers, drawn from the southern lower and working classes, would undermine the security of Chicago's resident black population. Chicago's African American newspaper *Broad Ax*, for example, complained of the employers' bringing to Chicago "from the rural districts of the South" men from "the lowest and the toughest element of the race," who were "armed to the teeth." The presence in Chicago of "this class of Negroes" threatened the status of "the respectable colored people." It was therefore the duty of African American preachers to "proclaim aloud from their pulpits against [the] flooding of Chicago" with black strikebreakers, especially because the major department stores using them were "Negro-hating concerns" that ordinarily would not hire blacks "even as cuspidor cleaners." Spokesmen for the Colored League of Illinois, an African American businessmen's association, also expressed concern that the black strikebreakers would become a serious economic burden on Chicago's black community after the strike ended.[97]

As in the packinghouse strike, the metropolitan dailies associated the African American strikebreakers with the lumpenproletarian culture of the levee districts of Mississippi River towns. On Saturday nights and Sundays the blacks' pay rapidly changed hands as they gambled at "tumbling 'bones'" (craps) and prize fights. On Sunday afternoon they allegedly "consumed innumerable 'gins,'" while looking forward to a dinner of "chicken wings and 'watermillion' [watermelon]" or "pig jowl and black-eyed peas." In the evening some might sing in a "plantation voice," while others gathered around.[98]

Because of the highly negative reaction of the white public and some newspapers, and the City Council's protest, the employers after a few weeks turned to hiring whites as strikebreakers rather than blacks, many of whom they discharged. However, many of these the city then hired as temporary policemen. Some of these had to be removed from the strike zone when white strikebreakers refused to be escorted by them. In fact, white strikebreakers from Cincinnati and Louisville actually walked off the job until the black policemen assigned to their wagons were removed— staging a strike against the employment of black policemen. In the Eleventh Ward, white property owners circulated a petition to the mayor protesting against the use of black policemen in their neighborhoods, and some storekeepers refused to sell to them.[99]

The white strikebreakers, who came to constitute about half those recruited, were drawn from a vast area extending from Omaha to Pittsburgh, and included many "fresh faced country boys" used to driving farm wagons. White men thrown out of work as a result of the recent closing of the St. Louis World's Fair became strikebreakers, as did Italians laid off from railroad construction jobs, and "Huns" and Lithuanians recruited from the southern Illinois coal mines. Many of the whites were young men who signed up in order to get free transportation to Chicago, only to desert after arrival.[100]

Employers' increasing reliance on white rather than black strikebreakers caused Chicago's policemen, 75 percent of whom were assigned to strike duty, to respond more vigorously to provocations from strike sympathizers. The police force was also augmented by the hiring of more than 1,000 special policemen; union membership disqualified a man from being hired. These were supplemented by 4,000 to 4,500 special deputies paid by the strike-bound firms. The police organized flying squadrons of 15 men each, composed of 10 uniformed officers and 5 plainclothesmen, to patrol the downtown. Their purpose was to "crash into mobs" as they were forming, and thus prevent large-scale rioting, and they proved effective. The flying squadron, which could be positioned anywhere in the Loop district in five minutes, swinging clubs freely, "le[ft] in its wake only the eddying remnants of a fleeing crowd." Policemen also marched alongside the convoys, arresting those who threw missiles, and searching suspicious persons for concealed weapons. Despite furious protest from the IBT and the Chicago Federation of Labor, they were also permitted to ride on the wagons. Policemen were also sent out in buggies to patrol outside the Loop.[101]

As in the packinghouse strike, employers' massive importation of strikebreakers, facilitated by the availability of large numbers of African Americans from the South and border cities, forced the union's unconditional surrender in July 1905. The strikers had to apply for their old jobs as individuals; employers reintroduced the open shop and prohibited teamsters from wearing union buttons.[102]

The strikebreaking by massive numbers of African Americans in 1904 and 1905 resulted in greater antagonism toward blacks, even though for many whites it undermined the image of black male passivity and obsequiousness. Probably not since the Civil War, when African American Union army troops had distinguished themselves in battles like that at Fort Wagner, South Carolina, in 1863, had black men received such fulsome praise for bravery and fighting capability, central to society's definition of manhood. The head of the Employers Teaming Company declared, "The Negroes did noble work. Their courage has seldom been surpassed."[103] Nonetheless, the employers did not want to retain the blacks as a permanent work force, and, as in the packinghouse strike, nearly all were discharged and replaced with whites. The 1910 federal census showed that there were even fewer African American teamsters in Chicago than in 1900.[104] White unionists were now more likely to resent African Americans for aligning so openly with the employers, while the reporting of the metropolitan dailies reinforced white stereotypes of blacks as licentious and prone to violence.

## BIRACIAL UNIONISM IN THE EARLY TWENTIETH-CENTURY DEEP SOUTH

Paradoxically, blacks' emergence as a potentially powerful strikebreaking force caused some white unionists in the Deep South to forge effective labor alliances with them, despite a rigid Jim Crow system, although none survived the immediate post–World War I period. Unlike in the North, blacks there constituted a sizable proportion, even a majority, of the labor force in some major industries, notably Alabama coal mining, the New Orleans docks, and Louisiana lumber. In these sectors, white unionists recruited blacks precisely because they knew employers could otherwise undermine their organization by mobilizing them as strikebreakers. They did not explicitly challenge segregation, organizing blacks into separate locals. But biracial union cooperation nonetheless represented a striking exception to the ever increasing racial division and antagonism in the region. The relative homogeneity in skill level and earnings in these sectors facilitated biracial organizing, because blacks were not stigmatized for performing distinctly undesirable "nigger work." Moreover, blacks gained legitimacy in these industries from having been in them from the beginning. Whites thus did not perceive them as intruders who threatened their jobs. In addition, the absence of females in the mines, on the waterfront, and in the forests and sawmills permitted biracial alliance because socializing at work did not violate the South's strongest taboo—black men having contact with white women.[105]

Black and white miners, longshoremen, and lumber workers were also drawn together by respect for each other's masculinity, as they observed each other performing jobs that required considerable strength and were highly dangerous. They were proud of their physical prowess and courage, which they believed set them apart from other men. Such attributes were central to their definition of masculinity, in sharp contrast to most craftsmen, who placed primary emphasis on self-control and steady employment.[106]

Unionization in the early twentieth century allowed African American workers to further enhance their masculinity. Redemption had destroyed southern blacks' newly gained civil rights, and their ability to participate freely in the political process and to vote, thereby depriving them of dignity and authority. The Jim Crow system, fully legalized by the end of the first decade of the twentieth century, regularly reminded blacks that whites did not consider them equal. Most black men in the South toiled for abysmally low pay, barely eking out a living. But the union provided them patriarchal status by securing a wage that permitted them to adequately care for their wives and children. The ability to provide for one's family was central to society's definition of manhood. Moreover, even though the unions blacks joined operated within the framework of the South's rigid Jim Crow system, and never openly addressed the issue of segregation, they often greatly reduced the social distance between the races. By lessening the black worker's subordination to both employers and whites in general, the union instilled a sense of self-worth, enabling him to feel more truly a man. During organizing drives black and white workers met together in the same halls, and even sometimes in each other's homes, where no formal physical separation was observed. On some occasions, fraternization between black and white unionists was so open that management accused them of displaying contempt for segregation, a system intended to foster a sense of inferiority in blacks.[107]

In the Louisiana lumber industry, corporations formed formidable mercenary armies to suppress union organization and break strikes. Employing gunmen from the Burns and Pinkerton detective agencies, the lumber companies crushed the newly formed biracial Brotherhood of Timber Workers (BTW) in the bitterly contested Louisiana-Texas lumber war of 1911–13. The mercenaries raided union meetings, flogged union activists, and drove union members and their families from their homes like "wild beasts." Faced with a "war of extermination" against what the BTW called "Black Hundreds"—referring to the reactionary paramilitary gangs of czarist Russia—the lumber workers armed in self-defense. The BTW newspaper even published a sketch of two crossed rifles, with the caption "The only argument a gunman understands." But although the companies proved unable to exploit racial divisions among the strikers, they prevailed because of superior firepower.[108]

In 1919 in Bogalusa, Louisiana, site of the world's largest lumber mill, the

Great Southern Lumber Company defeated a vigorous biracial AFL organizing campaign with similar terror tactics, eliminating unionism from the town for two decades. Since the founding of this company town in 1906, the employer's strong-arm force had had charge of law enforcement. For several months during the 1919 campaign, company gunmen beat union sympathizers, forcibly driving many of them, black and white, out of Bogalusa. Company violence drew blacks and whites together in common suffering, strengthening emotional bonds between the races. The climax of the campaign occurred when management officials ordered the seizure of Sol Dacus, head of the black sawmill and loggers' union, undoubtedly planning to lynch him. Dacus took refuge at union headquarters with several white unionists, who determined to protect him. The union men were vastly outnumbered by a company posse that surrounded the headquarters and shot four of the white unionists dead; Dacus managed to escape. The killings badly frightened Bogalusa's lumber workers and ended what the Louisiana State Federation of Labor called an anti-union effort that "had few, if any, parallels in this country for brutality and cold-blooded murder."[109]

The reign of terror that the Great Southern Lumber Company unleashed against the AFL's biracial union campaign in Bogalusa, culminating in the killings of union leaders, dramatically revealed the limits of paternalism. Bogalusa was considered a model company town, with housing deliberately spread over a wide area in order to provide residents "ample breathing space" and avoid "slum congestion." The Great Southern also built a hospital there, as well as YMCAs and YWCAs for each race, and sponsored elaborate sports programs, banquets, and picnics for the workers. From its founding, the Great Southern had touted Bogalusa as a showcase, a "New South City of Destiny" that contrasted sharply with the crude shack towns that had grown up around the South's smaller lumber mills. Yet the company responded immediately to the AFL organizing campaign with a massive display of force, as well as vicious race-baiting. Its gunmen brutally assaulted union activists, evicted large numbers from company housing, ransacked homes, and ultimately killed four men.[110]

## BLACK STRIKEBREAKERS AND THE DEFEAT OF THE 1919 STEEL STRIKE

The Great Migration of 1916–19 facilitated employers' recruitment of African American strikebreakers by establishing far more sizable pools to draw from in northern cities affected by strikes, but the next significant wave of black strikebreaking, in the period immediately following World War I, merely reinforced the pattern that had emerged in 1904–5. In the most important case in the postwar period, the nationwide steel strike of 1919, employers in recruiting strikebreakers again turned largely to African Americans because they assumed them to be more hostile to unions than whites and thus impervious to strikers' pleas to stop working. The white stereotype of the black worker as unusually loyal to management, conceived in slavery and fully elaborated in 1904–5, had been strongly endorsed by a wide segment of the black elite. It received even more reinforcement in the steel strike, because the "patriotic fervor" of the 1919 Red Scare sharpened the contrast between "loyal" blacks and "un-American" strikers, most of whom were immigrants from southern and eastern Europe. From 30,000 to 40,000 African Americans became strikebreakers in the 1919 steel strike, 8,000 in Chicago alone, where nearly all were recruited on State Street, in the heart of the city, most of them recent southern migrants.[111]

While employers hired many African American strikebreakers in the newly formed urban ghettos, they continued to recruit them in the South as well. As was the case with southern teaming in 1905, African Americans were significantly involved in the southern steel industry, so strikebound employers in the North were able to draw on experienced men. In Birmingham, Alabama, for example, where the southern iron and steel industry was centered, in 1917–18 about 89 percent of the unskilled workers were black, about 64 percent of the semiskilled, and 14 percent of the skilled.[112] Northern steel corporations sent agents into the South to hire strikebreakers, many of whom had experience recruiting workers there during the World War I labor shortage. In addition, these corporations used African American workers whom they had hired during the Great Migration to recruit their friends from the South to become strikebreakers.[113]

In the immediate postwar period, most African Americans regarded nearly all northern unions as either practicing outright racial discrimination or not interested in organizing them, so strikebreaking still seemed a feasible option for gaining access to employment in steel and other sectors. The executive secretary of the National Urban League, established in 1911 to assist the adjustment of southern black migrants to northern cities, complained in November 1918 that although African American leaders had already met with AFL president Samuel Gompers and the AFL Executive Council to discuss unions' exclusion and neglect of blacks, another conference was necessary because since then "numerous instances have shown themselves of gross discrimination against Negro labor on the part of local labor union[s]."[114]

The anti-labor prejudice of some southern black migrants intensified because they believed that southern white unionists resented their rising wartime wages, which in some trades had reached the level of whites. A black addressing a Sleeping Car Conductors' local meeting in Chicago claimed that "the white unionist in the South sought to have the Negro mechanic eliminated" in various trades because the African American worker's higher wartime wages shattered white confidence in black subordination. No longer were black workers' wives "compelled to wash and iron for the poor white southerner's wife."[115]

When a National Committee for Organizing the Iron and Steel Workers, in which twenty-four unions participated, began the campaign that culminated in the 1919 strike, it made only a very limited effort to attract African American support or use black organizers, even though blacks constituted about 11 percent of the steel mill labor force in Illinois, about 14 percent in Indiana, and about 11 percent in Pennsylvania.[116] Several of the locals affiliated with the National Committee did not admit black members. The white rank and file feared losing jobs to African American migrants from the South, resulting in serious tension between white and black steelworkers.[117] In addition, the African American migrants employed in northern steel mills were less likely to express discontent with wages and working conditions, because they compared them favorably with those in southern sharecropping. As a result, strike leader William Z. Foster was accurate in stating, "In the entire steel industry, the Negroes . . . gave the movement less cooperation than any other element . . . foreign or native." In Pittsburgh, the "storm center" of the strike, "the negroes . . . remained at work almost to a man."[118]

As in 1904–5, the black elite either supported strikebreaking or remained neutral in 1919. During the steel strike, A. Philip Randolph, editor of the African American magazine the *Messenger*, charged, "The Negro ministry is ignorant of the modern problem of capital and labor" and was "disinterested in unionism" as a means of improving the conditions of the black worker. He noted, "No conference of Negro churches has ever gone on record as endorsing the principle of unionism."[119] His colleague Chandler Owen had shortly before denounced the major nationally known African American leaders, including W. E. B. Du Bois, Archibald Grimké, and James Weldon Johnson, for failing to recognize "the necessity of the Negroes getting into labor unions." Instead, "we see Dr. Du Bois and all the other Negro editors and leaders herald in big headlines, 'Negroes Break Strike!' as though that was something to exult in. . . . [T]hey preach a gospel of hate of labor unions."[120] In Pittsburgh, black ministers "provided an anti-union influence" during the steel strike; many of their churches had received financial contributions from the steel corporations.[121] The Pittsburgh Urban League, highly influential in the African American community, had urged the National Committee to appoint black organizers but adopted a neutral position on the strike. Many local Urban League chapters, dominated by business and professional men, and dependent on the patronage of affluent whites, encouraged strikebreaking.[122]

The *Chicago Defender*, boasting perhaps the largest circulation of any African American newspaper in the country, had during the Great Migration "presented the North as a promised land" and often expressed anti-union views. Shortly before the strike it editorialized: "The unions in the main barred us from participating in the benefits of organization, yet it has never been clear how they expected us to be friendly . . . rather than fill a place left by a white striker."[123]

As the employers' ability to maintain production by recruiting massive numbers of African American strikebreakers became apparent, an alarmed union leadership urged Samuel Gompers to arrange a conference with black leaders, in the hope that they might persuade blacks to leave the steel mills, just as the packinghouse strike leadership had appealed to Booker T. Washington in 1904. But, like Washington, the black leaders did not respond.[124]

African American strikebreaking proved critical in defeating the two-month strike, a setback that delayed significant organizing in the industry for almost twenty years. Massive police and U.S. Army intervention, and the relative proximity of the blacks' residences to the steel mills, resulted in a significantly lower level of strike violence than in 1904–5. Samuel Gompers and strike leaders accused the U.S. Army of helping break the strike by disrupting picket lines and guarding black strikebreakers. In a complete reversal of the southern pattern, however, armed black deputies guarding the mills searched, hit, and knocked down white strikers. And, most important, African Americans again demonstrated that they were capable of seriously intimidating whites through strikebreaking. Employers credited them with a vital role in their victory: "Niggers did it," steel corporation officials remarked afterward.[125]

But again, strikebreaking resulted in little gain for African Americans.

Nearly all the blacks newly hired in northern steel mills as strikebreakers were discharged after the strike, while those already employed in them who had advanced to better jobs were returned to their old positions.[126]

## SERVANTS INTO MEN: ORGANIZING THE SLEEPING CAR PORTERS, 1925–1937

In 1925 A. Philip Randolph launched a campaign to organize the Brotherhood of Sleeping Car Porters (BSCP), a black union that, he argued, would not only improve working conditions but instill in black men a sense of dignity and assertiveness, transforming their masculinity through unionization rather than strikebreaking. The black porters displayed unusual courage in attempting to organize, because most of the African American press and most black churches opposed their effort, and the Pullman Company had recruited large numbers of loyal porters into an elaborate labor espionage system that resulted in the immediate discharge of men identified as union sympathizers. Randolph repeatedly reminded the porters that unionization allowed them to abandon a cringing posture and stand fully erect as men. He ran a cartoon in the *Messenger* showing the union porter talking directly to the white boss, man to man, while the unorganized porter remained in a corner, stooped over in a submissive posture, confronted by a little white office boy. The BSCP sought to eliminate conditions it considered "emasculating," including requiring porters to sleep next to smoking room toilets and tipping, which Randolph argued subordinated porters in a master-servant relationship. After a difficult struggle, the BSCP finally managed to win recognition from the Pullman Company in 1937.[127]

## AFRICAN AMERICAN AMBIVALENCE TOWARD ORGANIZED LABOR IN THE 1930s

Most employers and white unionists in the North continued to conceive of African Americans as a "scab race" until the 1930s. Only with the emergence of the Committee for Industrial Organization (CIO) in 1935, devoted to organizing mass production along industrial lines, did African Americans perceive a major sector of the labor movement as receptive, even friendly to them. Many AFL unions, along with the railroad brotherhoods, even then continued to exclude African Americans or place them in separate locals. The heavy concentration of African Americans in these industries, and the vulnerability of the easily replaceable white unskilled and semiskilled worker, required that CIO unions pursue a policy of racial inclusion. Many leaders and organizers in these unions, in any event, shared a racially egalitarian outlook.

The rise of the CIO created considerably greater support in the African American community for trade unionism than ever before, but many blacks during the 1930s still distrusted its intentions. To be sure, African Americans in 1936 abandoned their traditional allegiance to the Republicans, more sympathetic to business, and embraced the Democratic Party, with which the CIO was openly aligned. While the NAACP and the Urban League at the national level endorsed the CIO, the position of local chapters varied.[128] Chrysler in 1939 and Ford in 1941 employed black strikebreakers in sizable numbers, the last occasions where this occurred. Although many Detroit-area blacks nonetheless supported the union in these conflicts, significant African American suspicion toward organized labor lingered into the 1940s.

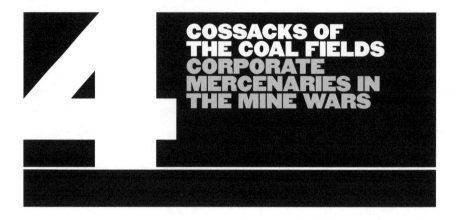

## 4

### COSSACKS OF THE COAL FIELDS CORPORATE MERCENARIES IN THE MINE WARS

During the early twentieth century, mine owners relied heavily on armed mercenaries to prevent union organizing and to break strikes, precipitating massive violence in bitterly contested shooting wars, with casualties at times surpassing those of Spanish-American War skirmishes. These mercenaries, employed directly by the mine corporations or supplied by private strikebreaking agencies, used advanced weaponry, including machine guns, sometimes mounted on armored-plated trains, and built elaborate fortifications. The miners, many of them veterans of the Balkan Wars, Italy's Tripolia campaign, or World War I, adopted military-style organization, with uniformed nurses to care for their wounded. These armed conflicts reached a peak between 1912 and 1915, when large-scale fighting, often lasting for days at a time, broke out along Paint Creek and Cabin Creek in southern West Virginia, in Las Animas and Huerfano Counties in southern Colorado, in the Calumet copper belt on the Upper Michigan Peninsula, and in the Hartford Valley of western Arkansas. The southern Colorado mine conflict culminated in the Ludlow massacre, the most renowned anti-labor atrocity of the twentieth century, and western Arkansas's constituted "the greatest industrial war in the history of the Southwest."[1]

In the coal districts of Pennsylvania, southern West Virginia, and Colorado, and in the Upper Michigan copper country, the mine owners' mercenaries suppressed miners' civil liberties, including freedom of speech, assembly, and the press, so vigorously and effectively that the labor movement accused the corporations of transforming many counties into "feudal baronies," where American constitutional rights and democratic procedures did not apply. The United Mine Workers Union (UMW), and even the American Federation of Labor (AFL) leadership, claimed that a military despotism prevailed in these "forbidden land[s]," as ruthless as in czarist Russia or in the Habsburg and Ottoman Empires, from which many of the miners had fled. In fact, organized labor denounced the armed mercenaries in these regions, as well as the State Constabulary in Pennsylvania, as "Cossacks," equating them with the czarist autocracy's most repressive and brutal armed force.[2]

Identifying itself as the defender of civilized values, the early twentieth century UMW, the Western Federation of Miners (WFM), and their labor allies portrayed the mine owners' mercenaries as invading or occupying armies, composed of desperate lumpenproletarians, men living outside of families, who threatened the sanctity of the home. Trade unionists accused the mercenaries of breaking into miners' homes without warning at any hour of the day and night, ransacking them, and beating their occupants. They charged that the mercenaries often committed acts of sexual debauchery and even rape, against mothers surrounded by their small children, or young preadolescent girls, accosted in the fields or on the public highways. Union miners and their supporters repeatedly invoked the imagery of feminine virtue and childhood innocence, venerated by labor, defiled by the mine owners' barbaric hirelings, and by state militiamen. A pro-labor correspondent, reporting on the 1913 copper strike from the "war zone" in Calumet, Michigan, declared, "I . . . looked on the fair white breasts of girls beaten black and blue with . . . sabres [and] rosy-cheeked children with the marks of horses' hooves on their tender bodies." Strike sympathizers also alleged that the mine corporations further corrupted the moral standards of surrounding communities by importing hordes of prostitutes "to satisfy the lust of the invaders."[3]

The UMW drew attention in its propaganda to the horrifying consequences of the mercenaries' abuse of the miners' daughters, claiming that it might prevent them from ever becoming mothers and nurturers. Referring to the sixteen-year-old schoolgirl kicked in the breast by the adjutant general of the Colorado militia in 1913, a UMW leaflet observed: "As a mother she may never be able to nurse her babes."[4]

Even as a profound cultural reorientation occurred during the 1910s in America's larger cities, in which women claimed the right to sensual pleasure previously reserved for men, highly traditional views about gender identity and relations continued to prevail in the mining communities. Defending a woman's virtue and the home in which she was anchored

*Supporters of the 1913–14 UMW strike in Trinidad, Colorado, include little girls carrying American flags and a young mother with an infant in her arms. The mine workers' unions were strongly committed to defending the family and female virtue, and this was reflected in the extensive involvement of women and girls in pro-strike demonstrations. Courtesy of the Denver Public Library, Western History Department.*

remained a central defining attribute of manhood. In the cities, by contrast, women were considered much less vulnerable. New commercialized forms of recreation, most notably dance halls, amusement parks, and movie theaters drew young working-class women out of the home, away from family and adult supervision. These rapidly expanding new leisure opportunities encouraged women to become more adventurous, to expand their physical boundaries greatly and to remain out at night. The huge department stores emerging at the turn of the century, glittering "palaces of consumption" centered in the downtown district, appealed primarily to women, who flocked in droves into a section of the city previously considered a male domain. This greatly increased casual contact, and flirtation, between the sexes. A new heterosocial youth culture was being elaborated in the rapidly expanding urban high schools, attended for the first time by a significant proportion of the eligible working-class population. In the high school, youth shifted their emotional commitment from the family to the peer group, which encouraged contact between the sexes. High school youth tolerated a greater degree of assertiveness and initiative by girls in these relations.[5]

*A daughter of a striking miner in Ludlow, Colorado, 1913 or 1914, poses with her doll in front of a window with lace curtains, again identifying the union with the defense of innocent girls, future mothers, and the comforts of home. Courtesy of the Denver Public Library, Western History Department.*

Yet gender relations in the mining communities remained largely untouched by these changes, still governed by the system of separate spheres, in which men assumed responsibility for work and women for the home. The sexes were considered to possess opposite qualities, with women perceived as delicate and less sexual than men, on whom they relied for protection. The mining economy provided almost no opportunity for women to work outside the household, forcing them into economic dependency on men. In the daytime men were underground, leaving women alone on the surface. The extreme danger and physically exhausting nature of mine work further separated the sexes, causing miners to spend much of their leisure time in male institutions like taverns and gambling dens, while women remained at home. The mining communities lacked the department stores and commercialized recreational facilities that drew women in the cities out of the home and were devoid of night life. Few in the mining communities attended high school, where the new heterosocial youth culture that flourished in the cities was centered.[6]

In addition, many of the miners were Slavic, Magyar, south Italian, or Greek immigrants, among whom traditionalist concepts of gender roles and relations were strongly entrenched. Among these ethnic groups, family reputation depended to a significant degree on the females' sexual purity. Catholicism, the religion to which most of these groups at least nominally adhered, strongly emphasized the importance of virginity for females prior to marriage.[7]

Reinforcing the perception of female vulnerability in the mining camps was the fact that the miners viewed corporation mercenaries as pleasure-seeking agents of a ribald, seemingly unrestrained new urban culture, whose weapons and aggressive orientation made them especially threatening. Moreover, community sanctions used to pressure men who became sexually involved with young women into marriage could not be applied to these outsiders.

Reflecting the intensity of antagonism in the mine wars, the mercenaries, militia officers, and other supporters of the mine owners, largely native-born Americans of British or west European background, depicted the miners, largely immigrants from southern and eastern Europe, or of Irish background, except in West Virginia, as racially inferior savages, accusing them of atrocities similar to those attributed to American Indians in the nineteenth century. During the 1902 Pennsylvania anthracite strike, a commentator sympathetic to management declared, "The brute aroused in the Slav's breast is as fierce as the red-clawed beast of the forest." In fact,

"Nothing in the annals of savagery exceed[ed] in brutality" the Slavic strikers' violent acts, which allegedly included marking nonunion men by mutilating their ears. The Celt, "when excited," was capable of similar behavior. In Colorado in 1913, where a U.S. Labor Department investigator noted that "race hatred has contributed in surprising degree to the bitterness between strikers and militia," a Colorado Fuel & Iron Company spy reported to John D. Rockefeller Jr. from Trinidad that the strikers were "bloodthirsty Greeks . . . just returned from the Turkish War." Colorado National Guard officers involved in suppressing the 1913–14 coal strike accused union miners of mutilating the bodies of slain militiamen, tearing off military insignia, and removing valuables. National Guard spokespersons commented, "In such a way does the savage bloodlust of this southern European peasantry find expression."[8]

A U.S. Labor Department investigator who interviewed Karl Linderfeldt, commander of the militia responsible for the Ludlow massacre, and previously a gunman employed by the Baldwin-Felts strikebreaking agency, noted his "intense hatred for the Greeks . . . southern Europeans, [and Slavs] who predominated in the tent colony." He commented that Linderfeldt considered them "unworthy of consideration as human beings."[9]

Mine company management also implied that when on strike, miners degenerated into uncouth lumpenproletarians, denying their claim to moral superiority over the corporations' mercenaries. A labor spy operating undercover in Republic, Pennsylvania, during the 1922 coal strike, for example, described most of the strikers as "loafing about the pool rooms and bowling alleys." Many begged for tobacco money, while others operated illegal stills in their homes. Another labor spy in Fairchance, Pennsylvania, stated that the strikers there drank openly on the streets, discussing the "buying and selling of moonshine." Strike leaders consorted with Italian "black-hand gangsters," who each day placed notices on miners' porches warning them not to return to work, and who encouraged strikers to engage in violence.[10]

The mine owners also sought to overturn the miners' identification with defense of the family and female virtue by disparaging Mother Jones, the elderly union organizer who served as a unifying and inspirational figure for the miners in West Virginia, Colorado, Pennsylvania, and Michigan, symbolizing maternal dignity, strength, and empathy. They referred to her as the "Old Hag." Organized labor highlighted the mine guards' and militiamen's abuse of the elderly woman, jailed several times during miners' strikes, arguing that it revealed their contempt for core values of civilized society—respect for, and protection of, women and the aged. The UMW issued a pamphlet during the 1913 Colorado coal strike with an illustration of the eighty-two-year-old Mother Jones shivering in a "damp, filthy" cellar cell in the Walsenburg jail in Huerfano County. Snow poured through the window, rats scampered across the floor, while a guard viciously jabbed the old woman with a bayonet through the bars of the cell.[11] During the 1912–13 Paint Creek/Cabin Creek strike in West Virginia, the UMW reported that the mine owners' Baldwin-Felts guards had forced Mother Jones to walk in ankle-deep water in a creek for over a quarter of a mile, refusing to permit her to travel on the county road or railroad track, located on company property.[12]

While labor revered Mother Jones as an ideal maternal figure, who slept among the miners' children on the bare floors of their shacks, using her handbag as a pillow, the mine owners counterposed the image of an ex-prostitute and procuress. A Colorado newspaper sympathetic to the mine owners originated the charge that Mother Jones had once been a prostitute in a Denver brothel in 1904, when she became involved in the first major strike in the state's southern coal fields. Linking social protest to sexual debauchery, it also claimed she had acted as a procuress in Denver for Coxey's Army. Newspapers across the country reprinted these articles, and a Colorado Congressman close to the mine owners read the accusations into the *Congressional Record* during the 1913–14 coal strike. Adjutant General Chase, commander of the Colorado National Guard during the 1913–14 strike, in his report to the governor alluded to these charges against Mother Jones and claimed that her speeches, presented in "vulgar and profane language," appealed "to the lowest passions of mankind."[13] Mine guards from New York's Ascher Detective Agency, hired to help break the 1913 Calumet, Michigan, copper strike, similarly suggested that strikers' wives lacked virtue for demonstrating in the streets, taunting that "they would be better off in a house of prostitution."[14]

## PENNSYLVANIA'S COSSACKS

Mine corporations first established private armed forces to suppress union organizing and break strikes in Pennsylvania, the largest anthracite and bituminous coal-producing state, in the early twentieth century. Known as coal and iron police, their presence caused organized labor and its sympathizers through the 1920s to compare Pennsylvania's mining districts to "czar-ridden Siberia." Under Pennsylvania's Coal and Iron Police Acts of 1865 and 1866, the state permitted railroad and coal-mining corporations to hire as many policemen as they desired, who were commissioned by the state for a small fee, but supervised and paid only by the employers. The state gave the coal and iron policeman no indication that he owed it any allegiance; to him, the employer was the law. Coal and iron policemen were uniformed and carried revolvers, nightsticks, and sometimes Winchester repeating rifles. During the 1920s, they were also equipped with machine guns and tear gas. By 1902 the coal and iron police had assumed much of local police's role during strikes. The state "issued . . . every one of the commissions blindly," failing to investigate the backgrounds of the applicants, who were not required to appear in person at its offices, or to provide references or any information about themselves. In fact, the state did not even know whether the applicant signed up under a real or an assumed name.[15]

Because the state allowed employers a free hand in hiring coal and iron policemen, commissions were issued to "criminals of the deepest dye," including "gunmen from the slums of New York . . . not long . . . out of jail," as Pennsylvania governor Gifford Pinchot noted during the 1920s. Governor Pinchot considered the coal and iron policemen "thugs."[16] Many coal and iron policemen in the 1902 Pennsylvania anthracite strike testified before a federal investigating commission that they had not been questioned about their character or background when hired and admitted having served prison terms for offenses including assault and battery with intent to kill, larceny, and burglary.[17]

Countering labor's charge that management sought to break the strike by mobilizing lumpenproletarian criminal elements, another mine corporation spokesperson described the miners as "The scum and off-scourings of the slums of Europe," who had come to the Pennsylvania coal regions "with the odor of the steerage not shaken out of their garments." While the UMW accused the coal and iron police in the 1902 anthracite strike of brutality and gratuitous violence against men, women, and children, as well as sexual "outrages" against women and girls, management charged that the "barbarous . . . foreigner[s]" committed atrocities against strikebreakers. These included murder, and humiliation of the deceased by refusing to permit burial of the corpse, insisting that it should be "exposed to the sun until decomposition sets in."[18] Both sides repeated similar charges through the 1920s.

The coal and iron police first emerged as a significant force during the

UMW's 1902 anthracite strike, the largest work stoppage the world had ever experienced, involving 140,000 miners and lasting nearly six months. The coal and iron police committed many of the fourteen killings during the strike.[19] Contributing to the war atmosphere was the mine corporations' transformation of the collieries into armed barracks, around which they built high wooden fences topped with five strands of barbed wire. Within these well-guarded grounds strikebreakers were protected from contact with strikers. The men recruited into the coal and iron police, and as strikebreakers, included many recently discharged veterans of the Philippines campaign, a significant proportion of whom returned to the United States penniless.[20]

The mine corporations employed 5,000 coal and iron policemen during the 1902 anthracite strike, "armed with the most improved breach-loading and repeating rifles and revolvers," some of whom they organized into an elite "Flying Squadron," which could be moved rapidly by special train, at any time of day or night, to any point where management anticipated trouble. The Flying Squadron was garrisoned at Hazleton, and maintained telephone connections with every colliery in the anthracite district.[21]

Believing that the "whole anthracite region" was "in a state of lawlessness," the governor sent into the strike zone all of the Pennsylvania National Guard, whose commander further angered the mine workers' communities by ordering his men to shoot to kill anyone throwing stones, and to arrest anyone, including children, who called the soldiers or strikebreakers names. Guardsmen further inflamed passions by shackling three elderly men they caught gathering coal for the winter at an abandoned drift, and marching them through the streets between files of fifty mounted soldiers. At Wilkes-Barre, miners accused drunken Guardsmen of insulting their daughters in the streets.[22]

During the first three decades of the twentieth century, the coal and iron police prevented union organizers from entering many of the towns in the state's coal belts, whether or not a strike was in progress. They watched the railroad stations, riding up to meet incoming trains, and carefully observing all who got off. Roads leading into coal towns were often in very poor condition, making it very difficult to enter by automobile. Powers Hapgood, a leading UMW organizer, recalled he was "hailed from behind" only minutes after arriving in Vintondale, Pennsylvania, in 1922 by a "young man in riding breeches and a gray shirt," who had a "revolver protruding from his hip pocket and a visored cap on his head," which had an insignia with the initials C & I—a uniformed coal and iron policeman, who demanded to know why he was in town.[23] George Medrick, another UMW organizer, working in the Banning, Pennsylvania, area in 1927, noted in his diary: "I was not long on the road before coal and iron police began keeping track of me." Five coal and iron policemen stopped cars entering Banning to inquire about the occupants' business.[24] A reporter for the *New York Daily News* who visited Rossiter, Pennsylvania, a bituminous town in the central part of the state, in 1928, found its residents living "in abject poverty, in utter fear of the coal and iron policemen." He commented, "It seemed as if a person were transferred back into the Middle Ages, among a crowd of serfs."[25]

Concerned that soldiers of the Pennsylvania National Guard, which was mostly drawn from the working class, had fraternized with union miners during the 1902 anthracite strike, the Pennsylvania state legislature in 1905 established the Pennsylvania State Constabulary, the nation's first state police force. The legislature was also influenced by the fact that calling out the National Guard had cost the state nearly $1 million. When it began operating in 1906, the State Constabulary consisted of 228 men, 90 percent of whom were U.S. Army veterans. Governor Samuel W. Pennypacker had implied that the State Constabulary would assume the responsibility for preserving order during strikes from the coal and iron police, whose interference, he noted, "was more likely to cause than to prevent violence." But the latter never diminished in significance, even expanding to include 6,000 men during the 1920s.[26] Corporate mining interests benefited from the creation of an additional standing army available to disperse crowds of strike sympathizers and to protect strikebreakers.

Governor Pennypacker conceived of the State Constabulary as an elite, "well-uniformed, finely mounted" paramilitary force, consisting of skilled horsemen, modeled on the British constabulary in Ireland. He consulted with British government officials when establishing it. Those serving in the State Constabulary were expected to give undivided attention to their tasks, and thus were required to be single. Members who married often became coal and iron policemen.[27]

Pennsylvania's State Constabulary troopers were rigorously trained in both fighting skills and horsemanship. They attended a School of Instruction at Hershey, where the course of study included cavalry drill and mob control techniques, as well as the use of firearms, jujitsu, wrestling, and boxing. They took constant target practice. The troopers carried the

*A member of the Pennsylvania State Constabulary, the elite mounted force that suppressed coal and streetcar strikes, equipped with bobby-style helmet and long hickory baton, 1916. Courtesy of the Pennsylvania State Archives.*

Colt .38 caliber revolver and twenty-two-inch hickory baton on regular patrol duty, and the Springfield .45 caliber carbine in situations of "extreme disorder."[28]

The State Constabulary highlighted its status as an elite force in dramatic public exhibitions of horsemanship. At West Pittston's golden jubilee celebration in 1908 or 1909, for example, spectators thrilled as riders picked up handkerchiefs from the ground as their horses dashed along at full speed. The *Philadelphia North American* reported, "The charge of the troop with drawn clubs against an imaginary mob was especially well executed."[29]

The Pennsylvania State Federation of Labor and the UMW regarded the State Constabulary as a strikebreaking force, whose members "by training and environment" were incapable of "hav[ing] any sympathy with working people," calling it "an imitation of the Russian Cossacks." Such a force was "out of place under a republican form of government."[30] Residing in isolated barracks, and recruited largely from outside the working class, the men in the State Constabulary, like the Cossacks, had "no connections or friendships with the masses."[31]

Always referring to the State Constabulary as "Pennsylvania's Cossacks," trade unionists equated it with Europe's most brutal anti-democratic paramilitary force, whose atrocities in the 1905 Russian Revolution against peaceful demonstrators, including women and children, received extensive coverage in the American press. The *Chicago Inter-Ocean*, for example, under the headline "Cossack Ghouls Rob Dead Women," explained how the Cossacks shot down women in the streets, then stripped their corpses of jewels and other valuables, while the *Topeka Daily Capital* reported that a Cossack pursued a ten-year-old boy who had jeered him "and cut him from the shoulder to the waist with one blow of his saber."[32]

The State Constabulary almost immediately gained a reputation for using strong-arm methods against crowds in 1906, when the entire force was called to strike duty for three months in Pennsylvania's anthracite and bituminous districts. Having quelled a riot at Cornwall by what it called in its report "lawless foreigners," the State Constabulary's Troop C proceeded to Mt. Carmel where, besieged by more than 1,000 miners and strike sympathizers hurling bricks and rocks, it fired into the crowd, wounding "quite a number."[33] J. B. Cheyney, the manager of the *Wilkes-Barre Times*, complained to Governor Pennypacker that a State Constabulary lieutenant, stationed at nearby Wyoming, when asked whether his men had made any arrests there, had replied, "We don't make arrests; when there's any trouble we will go in and club hell out of them."[34]

During the Westmoreland County bituminous coal strike in 1910, the UMW accused the State Constabulary of terrorizing the strikers and their families to force the miners back to work, shooting up their towns "in true western style," and committing other violent acts so brutal and barbaric they "would put to shame a Chinese heathen."[35] State Constabulary troopers, along with coal and iron police, killed sixteen strikers and their wives, some of whom were shot to death as they lay sleeping in hillside tents, after having been evicted from company housing. Charles Maurer, a Pennsylvania State Federation of Labor official, claimed that State Constabulary, like Cossacks, "drove their horses up on the sidewalks, and knocked people in all directions," and on other occasions rode into groups of strikers "on the gallop," forcing them to scatter or be "trampled to death under the horses' feet." The police chief of South Bethlehem, Pennsylvania, stated that State Constabulary troopers broke into miners' homes without warrants and badly beat people standing on street corners, ignoring the pleas of local police officers to desist.[36]

Mrs. George Morton, a Berwick, Pennsylvania, hotelier, added charges of sexual debauchery against the State Constabulary, in addition to brutality and excessive violence. Addressing a UMW convention in Scranton in 1919, she announced that the State Constabulary troops from the Wyoming, Pennsylvania, barracks who stayed at her hotel kept and drank the liquor they had confiscated in speakeasy raids, giving some of it to prostitutes they entertained in their rooms. She heard "oaths and vileness and lewd talk" coming from the troopers' rooms at all hours. When she ordered a corporal, a married man who shared his room with two "sporting women," to leave the hotel, he responded "with a laugh that was satanic": "Do you think you can put out a state cop?" Not only did the commanding officer refuse to take any action, but when Mrs. Morton persisted in her accusations he had her arrested for criminal libel, because three newspapers had printed them.[37]

When Mrs. Morton exclaimed that "[t]he Spanish Inquisition would be mild" compared with what she had experienced, the convention delegates "stood as one man" to thank her for her testimony, vowing to use it in their campaign against legislation to increase the size of the State Constabulary. Several weeks later at another UMW convention in Wilkes-Barre, Mrs. Morton denounced the State Constabulary for practicing white slavery, informing the delegates that troopers had attempted to force one of her hotel maids to accompany them to Bloomsburg and stay all night with them at a rooming house there.[38]

During the 1922 coal strike, the Pennsylvania State Federation of Labor passed a resolution condemning the "Cossacks of Pennsylvania"—in this case the coal and iron police—for forcibly entering the home of John Rykala, a Hungarian miner, in a midnight raid, and raping his wife, Katherine Rykala. The couple had been awakened by ten uniformed coal and iron policemen, waving revolvers, shining flashlights in their faces, and announcing that they were searching for concealed moonshine liquor. Katherine Rykala claimed that nine of the men ushered her husband downstairs, while the remaining one violently brushed aside her seven-month-old baby and raped her. Then the coal and iron policemen left, taking with them the

Rykalas' $50 gold watch. Although the man Katherine Rykala identified as the rapist was arrested, the case was ultimately dismissed.[39]

Portraying the coal and iron police during the 1928 Pennsylvania bituminous strike as an uncivilized occupying army threatening a family-based mining community that highly valued the dignity and protection of women, miners' wives and daughters detailed before a U.S. Senate committee numerous acts by the invaders of rape, sexual abuse, and white slavery. A sixteen-year-old girl from Pricedale, Pennsylvania, for example, testified that a coal and iron policeman had dragged her into his car and taken her to Smithton, Pennsylvania, where his cohorts kept "any number of girls" for sexual purposes. For three weeks she was held there against her will, while coal and iron policemen came nightly and spent several hours with the girls. A Pittsburgh Coal Company attorney, however, portrayed the girl as a willing prostitute with a "notorious" reputation, explaining that that was why a justice of the peace had only fined the coal and iron policeman accused of abducting the girl $25 for fornication. Another young woman from La Belle, Pennsylvania, informed the committee that a coal and iron policeman had persuaded her to enter his car after she learned that her brother had fallen ill and had offered to drive her to his home. Instead, he parked the car in an isolated area where, she said, he "grabbed me in his arms, and held me and kissed me. . . . He tried to get his hand up my clothes."[40]

Governor Gifford Pinchot abolished the coal and iron police, known as Industrial Police after 1929, in 1931, at the beginning of his second term. Pinchot believed that the purpose of the coal and iron police had been to "foment disturbances" in order to provide an excuse for the governor to call in the State Constabulary to suppress a strike. Alarmed that coal and iron policemen were mostly "thugs and gunmen of the most desperate type," Pinchot during his first term as governor (1923–27) had required a state official to investigate the backgrounds of men applying for commissions and had reduced their numbers from 6,000 "promiscuous and largely criminal characters" to 2,000 "reasonably decent officers."[41]

However, Pinchot's successor, Governor John S. Fisher, immediately dismissed the state official he had placed in charge of the investigations and, in Pinchot's words, revived the "old mine thug system." Pinchot charged that Governor Fisher had again sanctioned the employment as coal and iron policemen of "gunmen and other bad characters," who "committed . . . numerous assaults on men, women, and children."[42]

Through the 1930s, the State Constabulary, wearing the black uniform and bobby-style helmet of the 1905 era, but now equipped with machine guns and tear gas bombs, also remained a significant presence in the coal districts. Horses and riders were often transported by truck to trouble points. On numerous occasions during the 1930s the State Constabulary escorted strikebreakers through picket lines and were often engaged in dispersing crowds that hurled epithets, and sometimes stones, at cars and trucks transporting the strikebreakers to the mines.[43]

## BALDWIN-FELTS GUNMEN IN "RUSSIANIZED" WEST VIRGINIA

Samuel Gompers noted in 1913 that the mine operators had "Russianized" southern West Virginia with armed mercenaries supplied by the Baldwin-Felts Detective Agency, so that "the coal operators and the Government [were] one and the same," and "personal freedom was . . . a farce." The mine corporations had reduced the coal miners to "peonage and almost to slavery."[44] Hired to suppress union organizing and to break strikes, the Baldwin-Felts Detective Agency also developed an extensive labor espionage system "probably never equaled outside Russia." Its agents worked undercover in the mines or operated small businesses in the mining communities, their identities kept secret even from company officials. The Baldwin-Felts mine guard system during the early twentieth century "grew to such gigantic proportions" in southern West Virginia "as to become the chief law enforcement agency in the coal counties." According to the UMW, the Baldwin-Felts mine guard exercised "all the authority of a Russian Cossack." Recruited primarily from the West Virginia and Virginia hill country, many of the Baldwin-Felts guards had criminal records, "fearless mountain gunmen" who "would not take off [their] hat[s] to the desperado[s] of the wildest town of the wildest West."[45]

The rugged terrain and paucity of passable roads and the prevalence of company towns in the southern West Virginia coal counties provided a favorable environment for the emergence of what was probably the nation's most formidable mine guard system. Mountain ranges shut off the mining communities from the outside, and few inhabited the surrounding countryside. Unlike in Pennsylvania, there were no large cities or alternative industries nearby. In the Kanawha River valley, comprising much of the coal mining area, and site of the 1912–13 Paint Creek/Cabin Creek strike, the numerous creeks flowing into the river were separated from each other by mountains, so a mining town on one creek was very much isolated from one on another, even if the towns were only a few miles apart. Traveling from one town to another was generally possible only by going to the mouth of one creek and then from there moving up the next creek. Company mine guards could therefore operate unnoticed by state authorities, the press, or the general public.[46]

A significantly higher proportion of West Virginia miners lived in company towns than in other mining regions, fully 80 percent as late as 1922, allowing the mine guards to function without any outside interference. Company towns were unincorporated, meaning the mine owners were the only governing officials. The company owned the miners' houses, the stores, and usually all the land, including the roads and bridges. "No trespassing" signs were even posted along the railroad right of way. Miners and their family members could go from their homes to those of others only at the sufferance of the mine owner, unless they used the county road, which did not reach half the houses.[47] To prevent organizing, company towns were built without plazas or squares, so that no public meetings could be held. Moreover, Baldwin-Felts guards forbade the miners to assemble in groups larger than three at night.[48]

The mine company's ownership of the store and supervision of the post office, usually located inside it and managed by one of its bookkeepers, facilitated its control of the labor force. It usually required that the miners shop only at the company store, known as the "pluck me" or "grab all," because its prices were about 30 percent higher than at an independent outlet. Baldwin-Felts guards enforced the company store's monopoly by keeping traveling salesmen out of town. Running the post office enabled the company to inspect the residents' mail, preventing miners who wanted to retain their jobs from ordering goods from mail order houses. Those who attempted to flee were pursued by Baldwin-Felts guards as though they were fugitive slaves and forced to return until their debt was paid. The UMW's journal reported in 1903 that six Italian miners who had fled Beckley, West Virginia, because of "bad treatment," had been bound together with ropes when captured, and then hitched to a mule in a public street, in the presence of local officials and the whole town. They would have been dragged back to camp in this manner, "like beasts," had a justice of the peace not intervened, but he nonetheless ordered them back to the mine until their debts were worked off.[49]

Gino C. Speranza, appointed by the Society for the Protection of Italian Immigrants in New York to investigate alleged abuses against Italian miners in West Virginia in 1903, who visited numerous coal camps in the Paint Creek and Cabin Creek sections, stated that because mine operators and labor contractors had invested significant sums to transport men from New York and other eastern cities, it meant a "clear [financial] loss" if miners wanted to leave, and the "temptation was therefore to hold men." Labor contractors misrepresented wages and working and living conditions in West Virginia and, in an effort to recruit as many men as possible, sent "tailors, barbers, waiters, and other men unfit for the work," who often tried to leave. Speranza noted that the "employment of armed guards to prevent men from leaving and otherwise intimidate them" was "abundantly proven" by affidavits he secured.[50]

As in Pennsylvania, the coal corporations considered the southern West Virginia miners as racially inferior, justifying harsh treatment, even though many were native-born and of British ancestry. These men were stereotyped as having come from "wild stock," primitive mountaineers and moonshiners who harbored an "antagonism toward the restraints of civilization." They were innately contentious, unruly, and violent. The eastern and southern Europeans, constituting over 25 percent of the mine force, were "not inclined toward self-government," while the African Americans, perhaps 25 percent, wanted "3 meals a day and the rest of the time off."[51]

By 1902 the Baldwin-Felts Detective Agency, formed as a partnership between William G. Baldwin (1862–1936) and Thomas L. Felts (1868–1937) in 1892, was significantly involved in disrupting labor organizing and in strikebreaking in southern West Virginia, and by 1910 its guards were operating in nearly every company town. Headquartered at Roanoke, Virginia, the agency was initially employed to protect railroad corporations from freight car and payroll theft, but by the late 1890s it had expanded its operations to policing the new, isolated mining communities of southern West Virginia, where counties lacked the funds to provide this service. Baldwin managed the Roanoke office and had charge of railroad policing, while Felts opened a new office in Bluefield, West Virginia, in 1899 and supervised the agency's work for the mining corporations. Bluefield, which called itself the "Capital of the Black Diamond Empire," was strategically situated on the mainline of the Norfolk and Western Railroad, allowing Baldwin-Felts guards to move quickly to trouble spots across the southern coal fields. Thomas Felts's brother Albert Felts managed a subsidiary office in Thurmond, West Virginia, on the mainline of the Chesapeake & Ohio Railroad, and another brother, Lee Felts, also worked for the agency.[52]

Like James Farley, the press attributed to Thomas Felts the courage and fighting skills of the nineteenth-century frontier gunslinger, along with enormous perseverance and entrepreneurial ability that enabled him to rise from relatively humble beginnings and amass a fortune. The *Huntington (W.Va.) Herald-Dispatch* declared in his obituary that "[h]is name for 30 years spelled either death or capture to the outlaws of the South" and credited him with having "shot it out" at least twenty times with "lawbreakers." It claimed that he was once left for dead with four bullets in his body after such an encounter.[53] The *Bluefield (W.Va.) Daily Telegraph* praised Felts as "the most fearless officer who ever packed a gun in these parts," noting that "he carried with him to the grave bullets he stopped in countless encounters with killers." Its obituary emphasized that Felts, who had begun as a claim department clerk for the Norfolk and Western Railroad, had enjoyed a "spectacular career" with the Baldwin-Felts Detective Agency. Because of it, he attained prominence in the "political, farming, and banking circles of southwestern Virginia" and was elected to the Virginia House of Delegates in 1920 and the Virginia State Senate in 1927. When he died in 1937, Felts was president of the First National Bank of Galax, Virginia, and the owner of a vast landed estate in Carroll County, Virginia, the "fruits," according to the *Daily Telegraph*, of "his courageous enterprise."[54]

Like Pennsylvania's coal and iron police, Baldwin-Felts guards assumed prominence breaking a strike in 1902, which the UMW had called largely to prevent nonunion West Virginia coal from taking over the eastern markets ordinarily supplied by the struck Pennsylvania anthracite fields. A union miner observed during the strike that Baldwin-Felts guards were "more numerous than mosquitoes in a Southern swamp."[55] The UMW hoped not only to gain the right to organize and the eight-hour day, but to prevent the transformation of the southern West Virginia miners, "primitive as the Boers," but "as indomitable," into "labor serfs." It hoped to undermine the power of the company stores by demanding pay in cash, rather than scrip redeemable only at the store. John Gehr, a member of the UMW's national executive board, who visited the strike zone, reported that three Baldwin-Felts guards followed him "day and night" everywhere he went.[56] Mother Jones entered West Virginia "as an outlaw," and miners spoke to her under threat of discharge and eviction. A journalist accompanying her into West Virginia shortly before the strike stated that it was very difficult for them to travel, because the mine companies owned the ferries used to cross the rivers and creeks, and the ferrymen refused to carry them.[57]

The UMW accused the Baldwin-Felts guards of not only savagely beating its activists but also seizing an unarmed African American organizer near Bramwood, West Virginia, shortly after he arrived at the railroad depot, taking him deep into the forest, and then executing him with a revolver—a defenseless prisoner of war. The UMW's journal, however, announced that union miners had ambushed the mine guard responsible on his way home from the killing and shot him dead, firing 114 bullets into his body.[58] In the intermittent armed labor conflict of the next two decades, each side exacted revenge in this manner for the killing of its men.

Throughout the strike zone, Baldwin-Felts guards roughly evicted strikers and their families from their company-owned homes, recklessly tossing about household goods, which they placed along railroad tracks, the only place outside company property. For the southern West Virginia miners, eviction was the companies' most feared weapon, because the overwhelming majority rented company dwellings. Eviction also meant that miners lost access to the gardens that many had planted in their yards, an important source of food. In addition, it drained the union's financial resources, because it often provided tents for the evicted families. To illustrate the mine guards' alleged brutality toward women and contempt for the family, the UMW's journal reported that they had evicted a miner and his wife with a two-day-old baby in her arms, even though a physician warned them it would endanger the health of both mother and child, who were then, in their frantic search for refuge, "jolted in a farm wagon over rough mountain roads."[59]

The UMW highlighted the working-class respectability of the strikers, defending home and family against "Turkish" provocations by lumpenproletarian, semicriminal mercenaries, drawn from "the lowest and most depraved class of desperadoes," whom the mine operators had recruited "from the dives and slums of everywhere." Rather than promote stable, family-based communities where miners owned their own homes, the mine companies and their mercenaries had created an environment where vices of all kinds flourished. Typical were communities like Pocahontas, a major company town in the southern fields, with a population between 2,500 and 4,500, full of saloons and "painted women," and nearby Keystone, where "the end of your cane will burn off if you stick it in the earth, so near it is to hell."[60]

For almost a decade after the 1902–3 strike, which resulted in the unionization only of a small area in the Kanawha district, the Baldwin-Felts mine guard system effectively prevented union organizers from entering southern West Virginia. In 1910 Thomas Felts defined his agency's main task as "protecting the interests of the coal operators against organized labor." He boasted that his agency had completely eliminated miners' unionism in the southern West Virginia fields: "[T]here is not a single local maintained in the territory represented by [us], and no semblance of organization." When he "undertook this work" in 1902, there had been more than 3,000 union miners in the Pocahontas district alone.[61] Felts informed a mine company general manager in 1907 that his company's purchase of Winchester rifles for its Baldwin-Felts guards had a "good effect" on the miners: "They are afraid if they raise any disturbance, they will be killed or sent to jail."[62]

The only exception to the Baldwin-Felts monopoly in southern West Virginia was in Logan County, whose Coal Operators' Association relied on the county sheriff and his deputies, paid by the mine owners, to perform the same functions. From 1908 to 1925 Don Chafin, who served two terms as sheriff and held other high county offices, ruled Logan County like a "feudal barony." His deputies, stationed at every railroad depot, required all strangers entering the county to identify themselves and state their business.[63]

During the Paint Creek/Cabin Creek coal strike of 1912–13, one of the bloodiest labor conflicts in American history, the southern West Virginia mine operators significantly increased their reliance on Baldwin-Felts guards, employing about 2,500. These mine guards engaged in several large-scale gun battles with strikers, involving hundreds of combatants on each side. Both sides also resorted to "bushwhacking" tactics, and "men were shot in the back without the slightest chance for their lives."[64] U.S. news agencies that had recently dispatched reporters to Mexico City to write about the revolution in progress there, where "streets were . . . mowed by . . . [the] cannons of contending armies," failed to cover many of the proceedings in West Virginia, because they did not consider it safe "for newspapermen to enter that field."[65]

The strike began when the mine operators on Paint Creek, unionized since 1902, repudiated the UMW, refusing to sign a new contract when the old one expired in April 1912. It then spread to non-union Cabin Creek. Paint Creek included fifteen mines and a population of 6,000; Cabin Creek forty or forty-five mines and a population of 14,000. The miners demanded union recognition, the reduction of the workday from nine to eight hours, and the abolition of the mine guard system. The Paint Creek miners had prepared for the strike by buying up old Springfield rifles, discarded by the

*Armed Baldwin-Felts mine guards were employed at Paint Creek, West Virginia, during the 1912–13 coal strike. Courtesy of West Virginia and Regional History Collection, West Virginia University Libraries.*

government. Strengthening the mine guard force, the mine owners imported machine guns that shot 300 bullets a minute at a distance of five miles, mounting them in hurriedly built forts. Powerful searchlights were set up around the forts to protect them against night attack.[66]

Journalists emphasized the menacing, lumpenproletarian character of both the new Baldwin-Felts guards and the strikebreakers, recruited from the slums of eastern and midwestern cities, including New York, Philadelphia, Cleveland, Chicago, and St. Louis, and from the rural South. The new mine guards resembled a "division of . . . Coxey's army," shabbily dressed, "unwashed [and] unshaven," but each one "carried a brand new repeating rifle, and at his hip a blue-banded Colt's."[67] A reporter visiting Mucklow, who noted that Baldwin-Felts guards scanned everyone who arrived at the railroad station, commented: "It is a weird sensation for a stranger to get off a train . . . and find himself obliged to run the gauntlet of a line of armed men!" Always making a show of their arms, the guards patrolled Mucklow's streets with rifles, and "loung[ed] on . . . porches . . . with the ever present gun."[68] John Kenneth Turner, covering the strike for the socialist *Appeal to Reason*, claimed to have seen the "yellow legs" search train passengers' baggage, confiscate whiskey in the flask, and later drink it themselves. He declared that Ernest Gaujot, whom the strikers called the "Human Hyena," captain of the Baldwin-Felts guards on Paint Creek, was "a chronic inebriate." The UMW journal identified the strikebreakers as "Bowery cubs and barroom artists and gutter snipes."[69]

In January 1913 the head of a Wilkes-Barre, Pennsylvania, detective agency that supplied strikebreakers to the Paint Creek and Cabin Creek mines was arrested as a white slaver. He was charged with recruiting girls to work in boardinghouses in the West Virginia strike zone and forcing them, on their arrival there, "into lives of shame" as prostitutes for the strikebreakers and mine guards.[70]

John Kenneth Turner considered the situation in West Virginia to be as dangerous as that in revolutionary Mexico, where on three occasions he had been lined up to be shot a short time before. Turner had come to West Virginia questioning the wisdom of contemporary American workers resorting to arms, but commented: "I had not been in West Virginia 72 hours before I myself had a gun in my hand and was on the point of shooting." Baldwin-Felts guards shadowed him in Charleston and in the strike zone, and they badly beat up a companion in an adjoining hotel room. In Charleston, he called on various persons sympathetic to the strike, "all of whom impressed upon me the unwisdom of being seen with them on the street." When Turner and an organizer named J. C. Rodgers arrived at Oak Hill, a "free" town (that is, incorporated, not a company town) in the New River field, they noticed some "hard-looking loiterers" hanging about the ramshackle train station, and Rodgers muttered, "Baldwins." After registering at the town's only hotel, Turner walked out on to the porch and saw a tall man, standing across the street, take a notebook from his pocket and begin writing in it. A hotel boarder remarked to Turner, "In an hour your description will be in Thurmond"—the nearest Baldwin-Felts headquarters. Soon, three or four other Baldwin-Felts guards appeared, "muscular men, with the look of fourth-class prize fighters." They "swaggered up and down" the main street, glaring at Turner and "shoving out their chins belligerently." A union miner told Turner that this was the safest town in the district, remarking, "Now you ought to see Mount Hope! I live there, but I can't go home."[71]

Again in West Virginia, the UMW during the strike identified itself as the protector of family and home, while charging the Baldwin-Felts guards with widespread abuse of women and children. In September 1912 Mother Jones brought hundreds of strikers' children down from the mountains to Charleston, the state capital, to march through the streets carrying banners proclaiming, "We Want to Go to School and Not to the Mines," and, referring to the massive evictions, "We Are the Babes That Sleep in the Woods." To illustrate alleged mine guard savagery, striking miners marched in the procession with a banner that stated, "Death to the Human Hyena, the Baldwin thug, who cut a woman's breast off at Kayford," a town on Cabin Creek.[72] The strikers complained that in several cases Baldwin-Felts guards kicked miners' wives who were "in delicate condition" and subjected miners' daughters to "outrageous insults and indignities." An Italian striker's wife testified before a U.S. Senate committee investigating the strike that Baldwin-Felts guards broke into her house early one morning searching for firearms, punched her in the face, and kicked her in the stomach, using profane language. Six months pregnant at the time, she claimed that, as a result of the beating, her baby was born dead. Another striker's wife testified that a Baldwin-Felts guard had grabbed her by the throat and hit her several times when she appealed to strikebreakers arriving at the railroad station not to go into the mines. When a bystander called out to the guard, "Watch out, that is a lady you are striking," he responded, "God damn the lady."[73]

Strike supporters claimed that the Baldwin-Felts guards attempted to force the miners back to work by starving, freezing, and terrorizing their wives and children. A man who repaired pianos and organs for the miners wrote to the pro-strike *Labor Argus* of Charleston that he had seen Baldwin-Felts guards drive a striker's wife away from a well, forcing her babies to drink creek water, which was dangerous and "not fit for a cow." The mine guards prevented miners' children from gathering sticks in the woods, or coal along the railroad tracks, so that the strikers could not heat their dwellings in the winter. In addition, he reported that a striker's wife had told him that the Baldwin-Felts guards would enter houses without permission when the women were alone "and have all kinds of indecent talk to them," and that some had "attempted to even go farther than that."[74]

It was not surprising, declared the strike's supporters, that "when a man's little children were cursed and threatened upon the public highway, when his daughter was insulted or made to wade the creek, [and] when his pregnant wife was kicked in the abdomen," a striker would be aroused and reach for his rifle, for he was "a man, and not a worm." The *National Rip-Saw* reported that after a group of Baldwin-Felts guards, for the purpose of sexual titillation, forced two miners' daughters to wade a stream, holding their skirts above their waists, the miners ambushed three of the guards in the woods and retaliated by "unsexing" them.[75] Many miners kept their rifles hidden in the brush during the daytime, then gathered in the hills as soon as night fell, to launch guerrilla attacks on the mine guards. They also fired from the hillsides on a train transporting strikebreakers into the district. By February 1913 all Chesapeake & Ohio trains sent into the strike zone were equipped with machine guns to counter these attacks, manned at all times and ready for use.[76]

A large-scale battle between two well-organized armed forces at Mucklow in July 1912 caused Governor Glasscock to order state militia companies into the strike zone. About 500 miners had surrounded Mucklow, taking up positions in the mountains, from which they could see the lights in their old homes, now occupied by Baldwin-Felts mine guards. The miners advanced on the town as an "organized army," divided into squads and companies, each under its own commander. When the miners began their attack, the "mountain sides . . . burst[ing] into flashes of fire," the mine guards aimed their machine gun at the "smoke jets in the hills." They were unable to telephone for help, because the miners had cut the wires. But the gunfire was so loud and intense that it could be heard by the Baldwin-Felts guards three miles away in Wacomah, and "King" Gaujot rushed to Mucklow with sufficient reinforcements to force the miners into retreat. Two men may have been killed on both sides.[77]

As armed clashes between miners and Baldwin-Felts guards continued, Governor Glasscock ordered the entire state militia into the strike zone, declaring martial law on Paint Creek and Cabin Creek in early September 1912 and establishing a military commission to try "offenders." The militia immediately began to disarm both sides, searching miners' cabins and Baldwin-Felts forts, although many strikers and mine guards managed to move beyond the militia's reach. Nevertheless, within a period of twelve hours, the militia confiscated over 200,000 rounds of ammunition, 7 modern Colt machine guns (from the mine guards), 1,500 rifles, and "bushels" of pistols. A reporter noted that "much of the confiscated ammunition savors of barbarism"; it included dum-dum and poisoned bullets, banned by The Hague Peace Conference.[78]

Although the miners had at first assumed they would benefit from the militia's presence, believing it offered their families protection from the mine guards' depredations, the soldiers soon began carrying out mass arrests of miners, while largely ignoring the mine guards, becoming, in effect, a strikebreaking force. A strike sympathizer commented when the militia arrived that it would enable the miners' families to sleep "without fearing that they will be dragged from bed and kicked out into the mud in the middle of the night by armed thugs." While the militia's occupation of the strike zone resulted in a cessation of hostilities during the winter of 1912–13, under martial law habeas corpus, trial by jury, and civil law were suspended. The military commission court-martialed and imprisoned more than 100 union miners, whom the soldiers had arrested without warrants, primarily for alleged involvement in shooting incidents and destruction of property. With the situation quiet, Glasscock withdrew the militia in December 1912 and granted Christmas pardons to 7 of the 20 men, including 2 mine guards, whom the military commission had sentenced to penitentiary terms of from one to five years.[79]

During the strike, the Baldwin-Felts Detective Agency recruited many of its guards from the West Virginia militia. In fact, officers and enlisted men were permitted to resign from the militia for the express purpose of becoming Baldwin-Felts guards. Three high officers in the militia became commanders of three sections of the Baldwin-Felts "army" in the martial zone. The militia background of many of its members undoubtedly contributed to what John Kenneth Turner called the mine guard force's "military nature": "They go about in squads and companies."[80]

A renewal of armed conflict in February 1913, sparked by one of the worst atrocities ever committed by Baldwin-Felts guards against miners and their families in West Virginia, resulted in Governor Glasscock's reimposition of martial law and further mass arrests of union miners by militia. On the night of February 6, 1913, at 11:00 P.M., a special train with an armored-plate car, known as the "Bull Moose Special," carrying the Kanawha County sheriff and twenty-four deputized Baldwin-Felts guards, armed with a machine gun and rifles, and at least one coal mine owner, pulled into the strikers' Holly Grove tent colony on Paint Creek and opened fire on the encampment from one end to the other. The attack occurred shortly after a "sharp engagement" between strikers and Baldwin-Felts guards, which left two guards dead.[81] Union machinists and boilermakers in the Chesapeake & Ohio shops had refused to cover the special car with steel plates when told to do so, "guessing the errand for which [it] was intended." But members of a religious sect called the Holiness Union had agreed to do it. In the attack, which occurred when most of the colony was asleep, tents were "shot all to pieces," a union miner was killed as he was taking cover under his shack with his six-year-old daughter, and an old woman lying in bed was shot in both feet. The miners, seeing themselves under fire, shot back as best they could but inflicted no casualties. In denouncing the attack on the tent colony, strike sympathizers impugned the mine guards' manhood, declaring that the car was armored so "that the hides of the cowardly murderers might be protected."[82]

A mine guard who had been in the armored car on the Bull Moose Special when the tent colony was fired on, testified before a U.S. Senate Committee that the attack had been carefully planned. As the train approached Holly Grove, the brakeman walked through the cars and turned down the lights. The guard was positive that the shooting had begun from the armored car.[83]

Enraged by the most recent Baldwin-Felts assault on their wives and children, 300 to 400 miners attacked a company of mine guards, and at least sixteen men were killed in the several hours of fighting that ensued. The miners attempted to establish positions behind trees and boulders on the mountainside, from which they could fire on the town of Mucklow beyond the range of the Baldwin-Felts machine guns. But they were unable to do so, and the guards, joined by strikebreakers who volunteered to fight with them, "swept the mountain side" with the machine guns, "and a veritable rain of death showered on the strik[ers]." The miners finally retreated into the mountains, carrying their eleven dead and fifteen wounded with them.[84]

A wave of arrests by militia of strike leaders and union miners followed, with nearly 200 herded into bullpens and makeshift jails and then tried by the military commission at Pratt, West Virginia. Most prominent among those confined was Mother Jones, arrested when she went to Charleston to see the governor. Also arrested that day was Charles Boswell, editor of the Charleston pro-strike weekly *Labor Argus*. Soldiers demolished his office, wrecked the newspaper's printing equipment, and confiscated the mailing galleys. Not long afterward, soldiers closed down another West Virginia newspaper that supported the strike, the *Huntington Socialist and Labor Star*, destroying its plant and jailing its five-member staff. After arresting and removing editor W. H. Thompson, they entered his home after midnight and searched and burglarized it, in the presence of his "ill and terrified wife."[85]

In an effort to demoralize the strikers, the militia held those they arrested for excessively long periods of time pending trial by the military commission, denying them habeas corpus proceedings. Many captured strikers were kept locked in freight cars at Paint Creek Junction. Thirty-eight men were confined in a small, second-story room, measuring sixteen by forty-six feet, in the Chesapeake & Ohio railroad station there, where the "big herd of bullpenned" was held. The militia deliberately isolated anyone it believed to be a leader, capable of advising the prisoners. Mother Jones was isolated in a cottage two blocks from the station, where she was kept under guard day and night. Charles Boswell was held in an old stone building at the edge of the settlement.[86]

Five of the arrested strike leaders, including Mother Jones, defiantly refused to recognize the right of the military commission to try them, declining to enter a plea. They also demanded habeas corpus proceedings, on the ground that they had been arrested by civil officers outside the martial law district, and then taken there for trial by the military commission. The West Virginia Supreme Court denied the writ of habeas corpus and ruled that the governor had the right to arrest and detain persons "aiding and abetting insurrection" until order was restored, including those outside the martial law district "who wilfully give aid, support, or information to persons who break laws within the district." In March 1913, the new governor, Henry Hatfield, did release forty-five of the about sixty-five persons convicted by the military commission, including Boswell, although he required some of these to leave the strike district.[87]

The strike was ultimately settled in July 1913, with no discrimination against union miners on Paint Creek and Cabin Creek, and the workday set at nine hours, although it soon became apparent that many of the coal companies were not observing the agreement. The strike left the miners with bitter memories, of their people "sent wholesale to filthy bullpens," of a harsh militia occupation, and of the climax "of Holly Grove and the Supreme Court decisions," a horrible atrocity against a sleeping community of families, and denial of their basic constitutional rights. And it confirmed to the miners that they had to respond to the mine guards' provocations with violence.[88]

The Baldwin-Felts mine guard system not only persisted but was expanded after the strike. In fact, coal companies even began to surround their towns with barbed wire fences to keep out union organizers. Writing shortly after the strike, Samuel Gompers declared that mine company absolutism remained entrenched throughout southern West Virginia, and its people were still "naught but serfs."[89]

## COLORADO'S COSSACKS AND THE "MASSACRE OF INNOCENTS": BALDWIN-FELTS GUNMEN IN THE WEST

The southern Colorado coal strike of 1913–14 was in many ways a repetition of the Paint Creek/Cabin Creek "war" in West Virginia. The mine corporations hired the Baldwin-Felts Detective Agency to protect strikebreakers and carry out evictions on a massive scale and equipped an armored-plated car with machine guns to terrorize the strikers' tent colonies. The miners complained that mine guards constantly harassed their wives and daughters. The Colorado state militia, in which many Baldwin-Felts guards served, intervened on the side of the mine owners. Regular armed skirmishes occurred between the strikers on one side and Baldwin-Felts guards and militia on the other. Like West Virginia, Colorado was "a state in [a] state of war . . . with front lines and battlefields." Casualties in the Colorado strike exceeded those sustained by U.S. forces in the border conflict with Mexico. Albert Felts, Thomas Felts's younger brother, previously in charge of the Baldwin-Felts office in Thurmond, West Virginia, served as the coal corporations' "military and campaign director."[90]

The southern Colorado bituminous coal district, comprising Las Animas and Huerfano Counties, was so similar to that of southern West Virginia that the UMW referred to the two states as "Hell and Repeat." Most southern Colorado coal miners lived in company towns built in isolated canyons, policed by armed mine company guards with the power to make arrests, who had been deputized by the county sheriffs. The company owned everything in the town, including the movie theater, the saloons, the gambling dens, and the brothels, and company scrip was used in all of them. Mine guards protected the company store monopoly by preventing farmers from selling their produce in town and refusing access to peddlers. Mine company officials considered union organizers "worse than criminals"; if they attempted to get off a train at a company town, they were "immediately deported or beaten up" by mine guards. There were sixty-five mines, employing 8,000 miners, in the district, which was dominated by three companies, Colorado Fuel & Iron (CF&I), the largest, owned by the Standard Oil Corporation; Victor-American Fuel Company; and the Rocky Mountain Fuel Company. Trinidad and Walsenburg, the Las Animas and Huerfano county seats, respectively, were the only towns of any size in the district.[91]

When the UMW launched a major organizing campaign in southern Colorado in early 1913, the three major mining corporations there, impressed by the Baldwin-Felts Detective Agency's strikebreaking activities in West Virginia, imported a large number of its mine guards, commanded by Albert Felts, who was deputized in February. They included many of the men who had participated in the Bull Moose Special attack on Holly Grove in West Virginia. This force was steadily augmented after over 90 percent of the miners of Las Animas and Huerfano Counties walked out on strike in September 1913, until it numbered between 500 and 700 men. Felts brought at least eight machine guns to Colorado from West Virginia, with a killing range of two miles.[92]

As in West Virginia, the UMW depicted the strike as a moral struggle between a respectable, hard-working, family-based community of miners and unscrupulous absentee mining corporations, which had hired a sizable force of vicious, lumpenproletarian mercenaries to break the strike with massive violence. Contemptuous of civilized values, the mining corporations forced the miners to live in squalid company towns that promoted immorality and corrupted young children. A UMW official who had visited these towns in southern Colorado wrote that he had seen ten- and twelve-year-old boys and girls "coming out of the company saloon so drunk they could scarcely walk." He emphasized that "[t]he saloons, gambling joints, and houses of prostitution were never closed, not even on Sunday." Swelling the ranks of its Baldwin-Felts guards from West Virginia was a "derelict horde" of "desperadoes" and "saloon bums" that the mining corporations had hastily recruited in Denver's Larimer Street dives, "their faces scarred, and their breath strong with whiskey."[93]

Indicative of the rage many miners harbored because of mine guards' sexual harassment of their wives and daughters, the strikers drew first blood only four days after the walkout began by gunning down Bob Lee, a CF&I gunmen since 1904, who had long "terrified certain miners' wives into submitting to him by the authority of his star." Lee had been known to warn women that he would have their husbands discharged if they resisted his advances. Women residing in mining communities were especially vulnerable to such abuse, because the mine guards were generally the only men around during the daytime, when the miners were in the pits, and there was no one to police them—they were the police.[94]

When the mine corporations, as in West Virginia, initiated massive evictions, the UMW established eight tent colonies on land it leased near the approaches to the mines, both to minimize families' difficulties in moving and to facilitate the miners' interference with the movement of strikebreakers. The largest tent colony was located at Ludlow, eighteen miles north of Trinidad, with a population of more than 1,000. To harass strikers and their families, the mine guards swept the tent colonies with high-powered searchlights throughout the night, to interrupt sleep.[95]

When Albert Felts had an automobile covered with steel plate three-eighths of an inch thick, mounted two machine guns on it, and had it driven through the streets of Trinidad, where UMW headquarters were

*Baldwin-Felts mine guards, with machine gun and rifles, ride in an armored car, the "Death Special," during the southern Colorado coal strike, 1913 or 1914. Courtesy of the Denver Public Library, Western History Department.*

located, and by the tent colonies, in an attempt to frighten and intimidate the miners and their families, the strikers impugned the Baldwin-Felts guards' masculinity, dubbing the so-called Steel Battleship a "Coward's Castle." Pro-union spokesmen scoffed at the idea that men who risked their lives every day underground from cave-ins and gas explosions would be afraid of men who refused to show themselves in the open.[96]

Following armed clashes between mine guards and strikers at some of the major mines, Governor Ammons brought in troops of the Colorado National Guard, who were recruited, according to the UMW, largely from "barrel-house bums and Baldwin-Felts thugs," and also included mine superintendents and mine clerks. The National Guard commander, General John Chase, ordered the strikers to surrender their weapons, but they gave up very few, being unwilling to put them in the hands of their enemies, the mine guards, now an integral part of the militia. In searching for weapons, the militiamen entered miners' tents and hundreds of private homes, whether or not the residents were there, often smashing trunks with their bayonets, overturning furniture, and tearing up mattresses and floors. Miners accused them of carrying away items other than firearms, and even stealing money from them. Militiamen also escorted strikebreakers to the mines, who were recruited from as far away as Pennsylvania.[97]

Identifying the militia as an alien presence, hostile to the community it policed, the UMW accused the "mounted Cossacks" of extorting services from small businesses, as would an invading army of occupation. It reported, for example, that the militia had not paid the Elite Laundry in Trinidad for washing the soldiers' dirty clothes. When the Elite's manager refused to deliver the laundry then in the establishment, a lieutenant and four privates backed a four-horse team and wagon up to the entrance, broke down the door, and walked out with the laundry on which they owed $75. The UMW claimed that the militia committed the "same form of robbery" against feedstores, and had failed to pay hotel and boardinghouse bills. A U.S. Labor Department investigator also reported that militiamen repeatedly stole whiskey from saloons and wholesale liquor houses in Walsenburg and bootlegged it.[98]

Strike sympathizers accused the militia of undermining the moral standards of the towns they occupied, terrorizing the residents, and requiring strikers to perform forced labor for mine companies. Throughout Las Animas and Huerfano Counties, women had to endure the militiamen's "brazen and vulgar ogling" and "uninvited attempts at 'mashing.'" At Aguilar, an incorporated town relatively independent of the mine companies, the militiamen rode their horses on the sidewalks, "filled . . . the town . . . with profanity," and insulted "respectable" women. Their presence attracted "stained women," who "paraded shamelessly upon the streets." The night after the militiamen arrived, they "went on a big drunk and did a lot of indiscriminate shooting"; by damaging the fire engine lamp and waterhose, they left Aguilar without fire protection. Captain Garwood, second in command in Aguilar, arrested three striking miners without charging them, and made them dig a ditch for the Empire Mining Company for several days, under guard. In Trinidad, militiamen frequently stopped people at gunpoint on the streets and shoved their rifles "against the breasts of women," in a deliberate attempt to strip them of their respectability.[99]

In January 1914 saber-wielding Colorado militiamen brutally suppressed a demonstration of more than 1,000 women strike sympathizers in Trinidad, called to protest General Chase's arrest of Mother Jones there for "incendiary utterances." Probably fearing that the demonstrators, assisted by strikers nearby, planned to liberate Mother Jones, General Chase ordered the procession to halt, but it did not. When Chase, at the head of 100 mounted soldiers, rode up to block it, his horse brushed against a sixteen-year-old schoolgirl named Sarah Slaton, and his spurred boot struck her in the breast. The UMW charged that he had deliberately kicked her there,

*Mounted Colorado militiamen surround women participating in a march to support the UMW strike and free Mother Jones, Commercial Street, Trinidad, Colorado, January 1914. Courtesy of the Denver Public Library, Western History Department.*

denouncing him as not only "a tyrannizer of men" but "an outrager of womanhood." Chase's horse suddenly became frightened and stumbled, and he fell off, causing the women in the procession to laugh derisively. Angered, Chase remounted and ordered his men to ride down the women. Slashing with their sabers and bayonets, the militiamen, resembling Cossacks, almost severed one woman's ear from her head and smashed a fifteen-year-old girl's foot with a rifle butt. A militiaman struck a woman in the face with his fist, blackening both her eyes. Eighteen people were arrested.[100]

By 1914 the Colorado militia units, most of which were heavily armed and uniformed, confronted what a U.S. Labor Department investigator called "the strangest . . . organization of military character upon the American continent," companies composed of veterans of conflicts in the Balkans and North Africa, officered by men who had commanded troops in those wars. Mostly, as at Ludlow, Slavs, Italians, Greeks, and English-speaking miners maintained their own companies, using the drill of their respective countries, although at some camps the companies were mixed. Whether a company was foreign-speaking, English-speaking, or mixed, it carried the

American flag as a symbol of opposition to mine corporation "feudalism," which the UMW considered fundamentally un-American. The Labor Department investigator was highly impressed with the military proficiency and experience of the men in these companies, noting that they "take their position on the field only as veterans can." He stated, "They know how to run and fall, charge, and retreat, and are perfectly familiar with the latest science of entrenchment. I watched them maneuvering. . . . [T]hey covered miles of prairie." They could keep concealed and move quickly.[101]

Concerned about the heavy financial cost the state incurred in maintaining a large militia presence, Governor Ammons in late February 1914 withdrew all but 200 troops from the coal fields, but the remaining units were well armed and commanded by men with considerable military experience. Major Patrick Hamrock, a Denver saloon owner and a veteran of the U.S. Army's campaign against the Sioux that had ended in the Wounded Knee massacre of 1890, was in nominal command of the existing forces. In April 1914 these forces were divided into Troop A, consisting largely of mine guards, foremen, and clerks from CF&I and Victor-American, under Edwin Carson, and Company B, originally composed of Denver business and professional men and clerks, but now including mostly mine guards, under Karl Linderfeldt. Carson, a sixteen-year veteran of the British army, had served with it in the Boer War and in its campaign against the Dervishes in the Sudan.[102] Linderfeldt, commanding Company B, posted near Ludlow, was a soldier of fortune strongly influenced by his service in the Philippines campaign, waged against an opponent considered racially inferior and involving the burning of homes by U.S. forces and the murder of prisoners of war. He had served as a mercenary soldier in the Boer War and in the Madero revolt against President Diaz in Mexico. Linderfeldt had joined the militia as a Baldwin-Felts guard, commissioned as a lieutenant.[103]

The violence in the southern Colorado coal fields reached a climax on April 20, 1914, when a militia force led by Linderfeldt launched an attack against the strikers' Ludlow tent colony, resulting in a fourteen-hour battle that culminated in a massacre. State Senator Helen Ring Robinson later testified that while visiting the coal fields shortly before the attack, she had heard militiamen threaten to wipe out the Ludlow colony. The colony was strategically important, because it had been deliberately situated where two branch lines of the Colorado & Southern Railroad led up to southern Colorado's most important coal mining valleys. By picketing the train station at Ludlow, the strikers had seriously interfered with the movement of strikebreakers into those mines. The now outnumbered militia force may have believed that the strikers were planning to seize the mines and drive out the strikebreakers.[104]

Riddling the tents with rifle and machine gun fire, the militiamen killed six men and a boy, with one of their own killed by strikers' fire. Hundreds of women and children "were driven terror stricken into the hills," while many others huddled in pits the miners had dug beneath the tents to shelter them in case of a battle. The militiamen shot dead three strikers they had taken prisoner, including Louis Tikas, leader of the Greeks in the colony. Lieutenant Linderfeldt inflicted a mortal, or very serious, wound on Tikas by bashing his head with his rifle butt, and militiamen then finished Tikas off by shooting him three times in the back as he lay unconscious on the ground. In a final act of humiliation, militiamen shook hands with the corpse, wishing Tikas well in the next world.[105]

Late in the day, the militiamen, under orders from their officers, poured coal oil on the tents, setting them on fire, driving out their screaming occupants and then looting them of clothing, money, jewelry, tools, and bedding. Witnesses described militiamen carrying away stolen trunks and "dancing with stolen blankets about their heads, to the music of a stolen accordion." Many women, driven from the tent colony, wandered in the hills all night, "crazed by fear." Some, "to save the babies at their breast," had been forced to abandon their older children.[106]

When the "Black Hole of Ludlow" was discovered the next day, a pit underneath the charred remains of tents, containing the bodies of two women and eleven small children who had suffocated to death during the fire, newspapers across the country labeled the attack a "massacre of innocents." They charged that Colorado militiamen had burned and shot women and children "like rats." The *Rocky Mountain News* of Denver, with the largest daily circulation in Colorado, asked in an editorial: "Does the bloodiest page in the French Revolution approach this in hideousness?" Not since the frontier depredations committed by "pitiless red men" against white women and children, had the West witnessed "so foul a deed." The editorial blamed the massacre on the mine corporations' employment of armed guards, and their recruitment into the militia. It described these mine guards as "the offscourings of humanity."[107]

By contrast, the military probe committee, composed of three Colorado National Guard officers, charged with investigating the attack on Ludlow, chose to blame not uncivilized conduct by lumpenproletarian mine guards,

*Colorado National Guardsmen, called in to suppress the UMW strike, pose with drawn rifles after burning the miners' Ludlow tent colony, 1914. Courtesy of the Denver Public Library, Western History Department.*

but the coal corporations' importation into Colorado of "a numerous class of ignorant, lawless, and savage South-European peasants." A military tribunal acquitted everyone in the militia who had participated in the attack, including the commander, Karl Linderfeldt, who came to be known as the "Butcher of Ludlow."[108]

The Ludlow massacre caused the leaders of organized labor in Colorado to issue a call to arms, urging union members to acquire "all [the] arms and ammunition legally available," and a large-scale guerrilla war ensued, lasting ten days. In Trinidad, UMW officials openly distributed arms and ammunition to strikers at union headquarters. Believing their women and children to have been "wanton[ly] slaughter[ed]" by the militia, 700 to 1,000 inflamed strikers "attacked mine after mine, driving off or killing the guards and setting fire to the buildings." At least fifty people, including those at Ludlow, were killed in ten days of fighting against mine guards and hundreds of militia reinforcements rushed back into the strike zone. The fighting ended only when President Wilson sent in federal troops.[109]

After the federal intervention, the strike was defeated, and the mine guard system remained in place in the largely unorganized southern fields. The Victor-American Company did sign a contract with the UMW for its dozen large Colorado mines in 1917, but the southern fields as a whole were not unionized until the 1930s.[110]

## WADDELL-MAHON AND ASCHER GUNMEN
## IN THE CALUMET COPPER WAR

While the southern Colorado coal strike raged, the Waddell-Mahon and Ascher Detective Agencies of New York supplied gunmen to the Calumet & Hecla mining corporation and the Houghton County sheriff on Michigan's Upper Peninsula copper range, where miners affiliated with the Western Federation of Miners, also overwhelmingly of southern and eastern European birth, staged an eight-month strike for union recognition, a wage increase, and an eight-hour day. Although lacking the large-scale gun battles of West Virginia and Colorado, the Upper Michigan copper strike of 1913–14 resembled those conflicts in many ways. The miners condemned the Michigan National Guard for intervening on the corporation's side, viewing it as an invading army undermining their communities' moral standards by sexually threatening their wives and daughters and bringing with them vast numbers of prostitutes. They also accused the corporation's supporters of an atrocity against their women and children, similar to the Ludlow Massacre or the Bull Moose attack on Holly Grove: deliberately causing a stampede at Christmas Eve festivities in Red Jacket, Michigan, resulting in the deaths of fifty-nine children and fifteen adults. As in Colorado and West Virginia, the mine corporation imported a large number of strikebreakers—in this case, at least 1,600—from the industrial and mining centers of the East and Midwest.[111]

Like the southern West Virginia and southern Colorado coal counties, Michigan's Upper Peninsula copper range was a closed society of company towns, where the mine corporations owned most of the schools and controlled a press that trade unionists referred to as "copper-collared." Most of the mines were absentee-owned, property of corporations headquartered in Boston, the largest of which was the Calumet & Hecla. According to Kate Richards O'Hare, who came to the copper range to report on the strike, "There is no more freedom there than in Mexico, [and] no more enforcement of written law . . . than in West Virginia or the Balkans." U.S. Labor Department investigator Inis Weed stated that "the region resembles a feudal country rather than a republic."[112]

The mining corporations initially tried to protect their strikebreakers by having 200 of their employees deputized and armed with clubs, not firearms, but they quickly proved inadequate to the task, failing to intimidate the miners. Reacting to the deputies "with jeers and contempt," the strikers tore their badges off, grabbed their clubs away from them, and chased them from the streets.[113]

As a result, the Houghton County sheriff, James Cruse, entered into a contract in July 1913 with James Waddell to import gunmen from his Waddell-Mahon strikebreaking agency in New York to train the deputies, protect the strikebreakers, and help evict 60 percent of the miners' families from their company houses. These gunmen were "muscular men of the prizefighter variety." Houghton County paid Waddell $5 a day for each gunman, whom he in turn paid $3 a day, allowing him a profit of $2 a day per man. Having anticipated the strike, Waddell had been on the copper range for about two weeks "looking for business." The sheriff granted the mining corporations a blanket license, allowing them to arm as many men as they saw fit. Shortly afterward, the corporations made a similar arrangement with New York's Ascher Detective Agency.[114]

The strikers charged that James Waddell had assumed the powers of Houghton County sheriff and "dictated everything the sheriff did." According to the WFM, Waddell-Mahon gunmen were heavily engaged in arresting strikers, usually without cause, and transporting them to jail, often roughing them up in the automobiles on the way.[115]

As in West Virginia and Colorado, the strikers accused the state militia of openly siding with the mining corporations, aggressively protecting strikebreakers and disrupting picketing. At the request of Sheriff Cruse, the governor almost immediately ordered the entire force of the Michigan National Guard, 2,700 men, into the strike zone. They established camps all along the copper range. The militia's arrival caused the two largest towns on the copper range, Calumet and Hancock, to assume the appearance of a battlefield: "The streets swarmed with deputies, the hotels were full of . . . gunmen, and soldiers clattered by on horses." Strike sympathizers considered the militiamen "green young fellows," easily corrupted by the Waddell-Mahon and Ascher gunmen, many of them hardened ex-convicts from the New York City slums. For Kate Richards O'Hare, "the most sickening sight of all was that of fresh-faced high school boys [the soldiers] consorting with vicious criminals," who filled "their plastic boyish minds [with] . . . filth."[116]

Miners and strike sympathizers agreed with this assessment, complaining that both the militiamen and the Waddell-Mahon and Ascher gunmen delighted in harassing the women, children, and elderly in the mining communities. They alleged that mounted militiamen deliberately rode down a nine-year-old girl, a striker's daughter; knocked down a seventy-year-old man; and threw a baby out of a buggy onto the pavement. A Finnish striker testified before a congressional committee that when he and his wife were walking home from a dance with two or three other couples, drunken soldiers out in the road tried to chase the men away, because "[t]hey wanted us to leave the women for them." The soldiers, acting like "livery bum[s]," called out to the women, "Hello chicken," and "You are a pretty little girl. How would you like to go along?"[117]

Expressing the union's desire to identify itself with the maintenance of high moral standards, and to portray the corporations and their hirelings as menacing them, O'Hare claimed that she had come into contact with thousands of striking miners since her arrival on the copper range and had never "see[n] a miner under the influence of drink," in sharp contrast to the company gunmen, who frequently appeared on the streets inebriated. She also declared that the mine guards and militiamen had brought prostitution to Calumet, a "clean, decent little city," where it had been previously "almost unknown," with no red-light district.[118]

Strikers and their family members and supporters accused the militiamen and the imported gunmen of violently assaulting women who were peacefully picketing and demonstrating. William Palmeter, a WFM member, testified that the militia captain commanding soldiers escorting strikebreakers from the mines became "very . . . incensed" when women and children in the crowd that formed every night at that time began yelling "scab." Palmeter claimed that the captain struck one of the women twice across the shoulders with his saber. When another woman called the captain a coward, he "seized her . . . and . . . kneeled on her with his knee, and . . . called for a tie strap . . . [which] he put . . . around her neck . . . and . . . undertook to tie her to a horse." Another woman in the crowd attempted to protect her, but a soldier struck her in the breast with his rifle butt and knocked her into a pit. Kate Richards O'Hare reported that deputized gunmen dragged "beautiful young girls" through their ranks, "subjected [them] to vile insults, and jammed them into jail." Soldiers attempting to wrest an American flag from a Slavonian miner's daughter carrying it in a parade slashed her hands with their bayonets as she clung to it.[119]

The Croatian funeral for eighteen-year-old Alois Tijan, a striker shot dead by Waddell-Mahon gunmen, highlighted the latter's undermining of marriage and the family, institutions that the strikers strongly valued. According to Croatian custom, when a man died before he could marry, at his funeral a young woman in bridal dress, accompanied by ten veiled girls dressed in white, followed a white hearse carrying the deceased.[120]

Reacting to charges in Houghton County's three English-language newspapers that the WFM was "lawless," responsible for terrorist acts in the West, the strikers alleged that absentee corporations had disrupted a peaceful, family-oriented community by importing gunmen of lumpenproletarian, criminal background. Every day, strikers paraded through village streets and county roads, carrying placards reading: "WFM headquarters—Denver; Calumet & Hecla headquarters—Boston; Waddell thugs headquarters—Sing Sing."[121]

In an attempt to offset the corporations' implication that the miners, 80 percent of whom were immigrants from eastern and southern Europe, were un-American subversives, the strikers prominently displayed the American flag in their demonstrations and aggressively defended it when militiamen attempted to wrest it away, even accusing the soldiers of wanting to desecrate it. Management spokespersons viewed the "predominant elements" in the copper strike, the Finns and Poles, as not really assimilable, "liable to have extreme socialist or anarchist tendencies."[122]

The strikers blamed the Citizens' Alliance, an organization largely composed of small businessmen, for the worst atrocity in the strike, the Italian Hall tragedy on Christmas Eve, 1913. The mining corporations controlled the banks on the copper range and determined whether or not they extended credit to small businesses. Thus small-business owners not wishing to have their credit cut off sided with management. Nearly all of them leased their automobiles to the mining corporations to transport the Waddell-Mahon and Ascher gunmen about, and their sons often served as drivers. Citizens' Alliance members, deputized by the sheriff, conducted several raids on union and socialist offices on the range, breaking down doors without search warrants, arresting large numbers of unionists, and confiscating weapons.[123]

Strikers claimed that a man wearing a Citizens' Alliance button had deliberately yelled "Fire!" when there was none in Red Jacket's Italian Hall, packed with wives and young children of strikers gathered for Christmas Eve festivities, in yet another assault on the family. The accusation could not be proved, and was probably untrue, but reflected the strikers' view of the corporations' supporters as grossly immoral men willing to use any means to break the strike, including the deliberate murder of small children. The WFM had appropriated $500 to purchase a present for each of the children, distributed to them by Santa Claus. When someone shouted "Fire, fire, fire" a "scene of the most indescribable panic" ensued. As men, women, and children stampeded down the stairs, many fell and were trampled to death. The pro-strike Finnish newspaper *Tyomies* claimed that deputies wearing Citizens' Alliance buttons had placed obstructions at the foot of the stairs to prevent those inside from escaping, then jeered as the victims suffocated. A witness testified to a congressional committee that "every little hand held in its stiffening fingers the present that Santa Claus had brought them." Seventy-four persons died as a result of the stampede, fifty-nine of them children under sixteen. The victims were primarily Finns, but also included Croats, Slovenes, and Italians.[124]

There was no question, however, that the Citizens' Alliance did not hesitate to commit violent assault and kidnapping, when two days later many of its members formed a mob, seized WFM president Charles Moyer, and forcibly deported him from the copper range, in what a *Collier's Weekly* reporter called "an act of outlawry." The act was clearly intended to intimidate and demoralize the strikers. A large group of men entered Moyer's Hancock hotel room without knocking and began beating and kicking him. One of them hit Moyer with a revolver, which discharged, wounding him in the back. The intruders then forced Moyer down the stairs and dragged him one and a half miles through Hancock's streets. Moyer identified his abductors as Citizens' Alliance members, joined by some Waddell-Mahon gunmen. When the mob approached a bridge, some proposed hurling him off it or hanging him. Moyer claimed that at the railroad station, a mob leader pointed out Calumet & Hecla corporation president James Mc-Naughton to him, indicating they were acting at his instruction. Choking and cursing Moyer, the mob forced him on to a Milwaukee-bound train, warning him that if he returned to the copper range they would hang him. Before he left, they took his wallet and all the money in it except for $10. On the train Moyer informed a doctor that he had been wounded by gunshot, and he was removed at Chicago and hospitalized there for ten days.[125]

Given the mine corporations' influence over law enforcement and the courts on the copper range, it was not surprising that no member of the mob that beat, shot, and abducted Moyer was indicted, even though none were masked. More than twenty-five people outside the mob had witnessed the abduction, but when brought before a grand jury they were "mum as oysters."[126]

The copper corporations' ability to import large numbers of strike-breakers under the protection of their armed gunmen and the militia ultimately doomed the strike, which was called off after eight months in April 1914. Charles Moyer declared that "Gunmen Defeated [the] Copper Strikers." The strike pushed the WFM deeply into debt and dashed its hopes for significant growth in the East. Unionization was a "dead issue" on the copper range for about thirty years. The miners on the Upper Peninsula copper range did not finally organize until 1943, winning recognition through the CIO's Mine, Mill, and Smelter Union, but by then the industry there was in serious decline.[127]

## MINE GUARD MERCENARIES IN
## ARKANSAS'S HARTFORD VALLEY MINE WAR

In Arkansas's Hartford Valley in 1914–15, the absentee-owned Bache-Denman Coal Company's importation of Burns Detective Agency guards to assist in opening several previously organized mines with nonunion labor, and to break the resulting strike, precipitated a massive arms race between the UMW's District 21 and the company. The miners were determined to protect their wives and daughters from alleged indecent treatment by the mine guards and from another Ludlow massacre. A series of clashes climaxed in a large-scale, six-hour gun battle. While the armed conflict itself resembled that in West Virginia in many ways, the Hartford Valley miners benefited significantly from residing in an area without company housing and stores, where local government officials and constables strongly supported the union. Their mobilization against mine guard violence was particularly effective because UMW District 21 in which they were located, comprising western Arkansas, eastern Oklahoma, and north central Texas, maintained nearly 100 percent organization from their 1903 victory in the "long strike" until 1924.[128]

The mining communities in the nine-mile long Hartford Valley, located in Sebastian County near the Oklahoma border, were especially close-knit not only as a result of union solidarity but because the merchants and professionals were aligned with the UMW. Imported mine guards thus appeared even more alien. Unlike in the company towns that predominated in southern West Virginia and southern Colorado, where the churches were controlled by the mine corporations, the ministers in the Hartford Valley generally sympathized with the union, further legitimizing the charges about mine guard degeneracy. Sebastian County was also the major Socialist Party stronghold in Arkansas, and a significant majority of the valley's miners were probably party sympathizers. In fact, Pete Stewart, District 21 president in 1914, had been elected mayor of Hartford, "the metropolis of the Arkansas coal belt," with a population of 2,500, as a socialist in 1912.[129]

Bureau of Investigation agents working undercover in Hartford during the 1914 coal strike, in an apparent effort to combat sabotage of mine property, listening to conversations in barber shops, pool halls, and Italian restaurants, described the whole population as solidly against the open shop. Hartford, along with Huntington the only town of any size in the valley, was one of a half dozen "pitiful settlements" of one-story shacks, with a "few discouraged-looking stores," built along narrow dirt roads. One agent claimed that "half the town of Hartford was anarchists." Another, reporting from nearby Fort Smith, the Sebastian County seat, which he described as "strictly union," heard a hotel proprietor denounce Franklin Bache, the owner of the principal Hartford Valley mines, as "a boss driver, a dirty old SOB, and crooked," indicating widespread support for labor militancy among the area's merchant class.[130]

The Arkansas mine war began on April 6, 1914, when a crowd of 2,000 assembled at the Prairie Creek mine in Hartford Valley to protest the decision of Franklin Bache, owner of the Bache-Denman mining corporation, to operate it on an open-shop basis. Bache-Denman, which for eleven years had employed only union labor, owned six other mines in the area, closed until the fall, which it also planned to reopen with nonunion labor. The 800 miners at Prairie Creek had been working under a closed-shop agreement, not scheduled to expire until July 31, 1914, but Bache, who resided for much of the year in Philadelphia, shut down operations on March 27 and fenced off the property with wire cable, planning to reopen in April using nonunion labor. Bache had hired Burns Detective Agency guards to protect the site, armed with high-powered Winchester rifles. Commanding the guards was Roland Barnes of Burns's Minneapolis office, who had had considerable experience breaking strikes in coal fields across the country. Barnes had served as a mine guard in the Calumet copper strike the year before. The crowd consisted of "practically the entire citizenship of the Hartford Valley" and included its "best citizens"—"merchants, doctors, lawyers, and farmers." Those assembled appointed a committee headed by Hartford constable Jim Slankard, a former miner, to meet with the mine superintendent in an effort to get him to close the mine.[131]

The Arkansas commissioner of labor informed the governor that no trouble would have developed had the Burns mine guards not openly displayed disrespect for the women and children in the crowd, cursing at them and "using [the] vilest oaths." He observed that the corporation seemed to have selected the guards more "for their abilities as fighters than for maintaining peace."[132]

When a Burns guard jabbed a boy in the breast with his gun, a riot resulted, as the crowd broke through the cables, disarmed and badly beat several guards, and drove away the twenty or thirty nonunion miners working at the site. A union miner kicked the mine foreman's teeth out; proudly displaying the bloody shoe he had used, he revealed the intensity of the community's hatred of strikebreakers. The foreman claimed the crowd had "barbarously" assaulted him with sticks, stones, and coal chunks and had threatened to throw him into a fire. A Hartford physician in the crowd refused to dress the foreman's wounds, declaring that he would not treat "a God damn scab." Shutting down the mine, the crowd hoisted an American flag on a tipple, unfurling alongside it a huge banner proclaiming, "This is a Union Man's Country."[133]

Soon after the confrontation, the corporation began secretly moving in nonunion miners from Texas, Oklahoma, and Tennessee, heightening tension in the valley. U.S. Western District judge Frank Youmans on May 9 made permanent a temporary injunction prohibiting union forces from interfering with the corporations' mines, further angering the valley's residents.[134]

Reflecting the near universal support for the strikers throughout the valley, the mayor's court in Midland heavily fined three mine guards bringing in supplies by wagon for disturbing the peace by displaying firearms—a charge they denied—ordering them to pay $100 each, plus court costs. Two UMW members arrested for stoning their wagon were discharged when the guards, "afraid to attend the trial," did not show up in court. A local observer commented that it would have been foolish for them to brandish firearms, "as Midland is full of union men."[135]

As the number of mine guards and strikebreakers in the valley steadily increased, union miners' wives and daughters complained they were committing sexual "outrages" against them. Union supporters like Eugene V. Debs portrayed the intruders as bringing the immorality of the urban lumpenproletariat into a previously stable, family-based working-class community; he referred to Bache's mine guards as "red-light gunmen." The Arkansas State Bureau of Labor Statistics in its biennial report stated that the strikebreakers had been recruited from "the worst class of citizens" and called them "undesirable."[136] Elberta Johnson, the twelve-year-old daughter of a union miner in 1914, stated that mine guards were always passing by her family's house "cussing and using all kinds of bad language." One of them accosted her when she was chasing a cow in a field and called her a "little freckled face slut," refusing to let her proceed unless she acceded to his sexual demands. The girl claimed that three armed mine guards or strikebreakers had surrounded her and two other young girls when they were up on a hill using an outdoor toilet for schoolchildren and had "taken their pants off, or half way off there, and offered us money" to have sex with them. Her friends Jessie Howard and Mary Manick confirmed that three armed "scabs" had propositioned them when they were preparing to use the outdoor toilet, offering them money for sex. They claimed mine guards insulted the "young ladies and girls every time we go out every day" at Prairie Creek schoolhouse and would gather at the schoolyard at "play time" to ogle them. No constable then lived at Prairie Creek whom they could ask for protection.[137]

On May 25, UMW District 21 president Pete Stewart, accompanied by a local district attorney, made a speech in Midland in which he charged that nonunion employees were insulting the women and girls of the mining communities on the public highways. Warning the audience that there was danger of another Ludlow massacre occurring in the Hartford Valley, he advised everyone to arm himself.[138]

On June 1, U.S. attorney general McReynolds sent fifty to sixty marshals to the Prairie Creek mine to enforce Judge Youmans's injunction, but withdrew all but three after a few days, over the protest of the corporation, which feared an armed confrontation with miners who enjoyed nearly universal support throughout the region. The valley's merchants and hotelkeepers refused service to the marshals. Two of the marshals who remained claimed they had encountered two union miners on a railroad platform and asked them about a sign posted there inscribed "Remember Ludlow." In reply, the miners warned the marshals to bury their rifles or "stick them up your ass."[139]

In mid-June 1914 the corporation charged that UMW District 21 president Pete Stewart, Hartford constable Jim Slankard, and five other unionists and sympathizers had violated Judge Youmans's injunction by planning violence, and the federal district court in Fort Smith ordered the accused to appear there July 1 to show why they should not be tried for contempt. Nearly the entire town of Prairie Creek moved to Fort Smith to appear as witnesses. The corporation submitted affidavits stating that Stewart had declared, while in Midland, that "he would arm every union miner in the

Hartford Valley" if mine guards continued assaulting miners' wives and daughters, and that "if they wanted a Colorado down there . . . they could get it." In a surprise development, the corporation produced a McAlester, Oklahoma, hardware merchant who testified that he had shipped twenty to twenty-five rifles, with 100 rounds of ammunition for each, purchased by District 21 secretary-treasurer Fred Holt, to Oscar Layton, a UMW leader in Midland.[140]

The prospect of a major armed conflict developing loomed when a large crowd of mine guards on July 15 launched a night attack on the Frogtown mining camp between Hartford and Prairie Creek mine 4, where 300 to 400 union miners and their wives and children lived. In an attack lasting several hours, the nonunion forces fired with high-powered Winchester rifles into the miners' houses, as women and children fled in panic toward Hartford. There were no casualties, possibly because the attackers were positioned on an elevation and aimed too high. Again emphasizing the mine guards' lack of respectability, the UMW claimed their assault on Frogtown had been motivated by their anger at the miners' forbidding them to continue buying liquor from "an illicit booze joint" there. They had come to Frogtown "in droves" earlier in the day from Prairie Creek mine 4. Upon learning that they would be "cut off from booze," they determined to "shoot up the town in revenge."[141]

Enraged by the attack on Frogtown and the perceived threat that lumpenproletarian mine guards and strikebreakers alien to the Hartford Valley posed to the moral fabric of the family-based union mining communities, armed miners on July 17 staged a massive attack on Prairie Creek mines 1, 3, 4, and 6. Between 10:00 P.M. and midnight, the miners cut the electric power lines near the mine, plunging it into darkness, so that they could advance undetected. Realizing an attack was impending, the nonunion men tried to call for help but were unable to do so, because the UMW forces had cut all the telephone and telegraph wires. At daybreak the attackers, estimated to number anywhere from 50 to several 100, began shooting at the 60 to 100 guards and strikebreakers at mine 4.[142]

A Southwestern Telephone Company lineman four miles from the site stated that the ensuing conflict sounded like "an immense naval battle." The union miners were plentifully supplied with ammunition, which they had carried out from Midland in racks on horseback, passing it out in the thick of battle. They brought more in on the train from Hartford to Frogtown, unloading it on to handcars and moving it along the tracks to the battle zone. Union miners from Frogtown crossed through the woods to the number 3 tipple, "conceal[ing] themselves by going from one tree to another," and then shooting into the company's camps, after which "firing started from all sides." Union forces quickly captured the number 3 tipple, and blew it up with dynamite. At the number 4 mine, guards and strikebreakers dug in behind breastworks fashioned from loaded coal cars and rock piles.[143]

The battle continued for hours "in savage intensity" until the nonunion forces ran out of ammunition at noon, when they fled "through tall grass and the timber" toward Fort Smith, leaving the unionists in control of the mines, which they proceeded to destroy. During the afternoon and into the night "the sky over the valley glowed from the destroying fires at the mines," while the "hills shook with the detonation and shock of dynamite that tore buildings, shaft, and slopes apart." Practically all the Bache-Denman mine corporation property was wrecked.[144]

Anti-union forces charged that the union miners had executed in cold blood two mine guards they had captured and burned their bodies. They were identified as J. E. Sylesberry, twenty-three, son of number 4's mine boss, and John Baskins, forty-five, of Johnson County, Tennessee. Franklin Bache claimed that their captors had included several local peace officers. For the next two days refugees from the dynamited mine camps, many of them strikebreakers from Johnson County, straggled into Hartford, many displaying bullet holes in their clothing.[145]

Socialist Party leader Eugene V. Debs depicted the battle as a moral conflict between respectable union miners committed to "defend [their] homes and families" and a corporation's private army consisting of "the most detestable of degenerates," capable, as at Ludlow, of "murder[ing] women about to be mothers, and suffocat[ing] and roast[ing] babes." Debs noted that in recent years big corporations had "established . . . thug-recruiting agencies in all the large cities" that "drag[ged] the slums" to enlist mercenaries for their private armies. He praised Fred Holt's shipping guns from Oklahoma to the Arkansas miners; it was the only possible defense against a mercenary army that, like a savage horde, had been "sent out to slaughter honest men [and] pillage their homes."[146]

As the Bache-Denman Company began active preparation to reopen the mines destroyed on July 17, union miners attacked again in the night on October 29, firing over 3,000 shots into the Prairie Creek mine camps. The mine guards and strikebreakers had anticipated the attack and had barricaded the walls of their houses with sheet iron. Two U.S. deputy marshals who had been at Prairie Creek during the attack stated that the sheet iron had saved the nonunion men's lives, as bullets fired by miners concealed behind trees and rocks 100 yards away riddled the houses. A deputy declared that the miners had been shooting to kill, not just to frighten, as the bullets came in low, forcing the nonunion men to the floors.[147]

Because the Hartford Valley's population, including local constables, solidly backed the UMW, federal authorities had considerable difficulty arresting the union miners they believed had led the October 29 attack. The U.S. marshal in Fort Smith issued warrants for thirteen union miners, five of whom his deputy located in Hartford and arrested. But as the deputy and the arrested men sat on the train at the depot waiting to go to Fort Smith, fifty masked men carrying rifles boarded it and freed the miners. They warned the deputy not to return to the mining district again to serve warrants on union men. The U.S. marshal in Fort Smith advised the Justice Department that it would be futile to increase the number of deputy marshals in order to recapture these defendants, because "in the present spirit the attempt would undoubtedly mean death."[148]

Believing that the situation in the Hartford Valley had become "almost uncontrollable," President Wilson ordered four U.S. cavalry troops from Fort Sheridan in Chicago to proceed to the Arkansas strike zone, causing the violence to diminish sharply. These troops were composed of about 260 men, including two machine gun platoons, whose five guns each fired 600 shots a minute. They were seasoned campaigners, having recently returned from patrolling the Arizona border with Mexico.[149]

After several weeks of deliberations, a federal grand jury in Fort Smith returned thirty-five indictments against union miners and their sympathizers, inaugurating one of the greatest legal crises the South's labor movement ever confronted. Those indicted were charged with conspiracy against the U.S. government, violating a federal injunction by participating in the "mine riots" that had occurred in the Hartford Valley. They included prominent District 21 officials. The UMW, which could count on acquittals in the local courts, believed the federal court was prejudiced in favor of the corporation, citing the fact that the grand jury foreman, C. E. Speer, president of one of the largest wholesale hardware companies in the Southwest, was a stockholder in the Bache-Denman Coal Company. He had sold Bache-Denman the guns for its mine guards.[150]

Fearing that a hostile court would convict all the defendants, the UMW accepted a deal in which eleven men would plead guilty to conspiracy against the government in exchange for dismissal of the charges against the rest, some of whom were women. Yet again citing its commitment to

*Union miners and sympathizers arrested after disturbances at the Prairie Creek mine pose in front of the Sebastian County jail in Fort Smith, Arkansas, 1915. The well-groomed, immaculately dressed defendants project an image of respectability, befitting defenders of women and the family against the depredations of "red-light" gunmen. Third from left, standing, is Sandy Robinson; sixth from left, standing, is Jim Slankard; second from left, seated, is John Manick. The man seated at the left appears to be the jailer. "Prairie Creek Mine," Picture Collection, number 4069, Special Collections Division, University of Arkansas Libraries, Fayetteville.*

protecting the home and female virtue, the UMW explained that it accepted the deal in order to prevent many men from being separated from their families, and so that the women among the defendants would be spared the hardship and indignity of imprisonment. Those pleading guilty included Fred Holt, secretary-treasurer of District 21, who had recently resigned that office to run as the Socialist Party nominee for governor of Oklahoma; Pete Stewart, former president of District 21; James McNamara, financial secretary of Hartford's UMW local, and a leader in the July 17 battle; and James Slankard, Hartford constable.[151]

These individuals, proclaiming themselves political prisoners, were sentenced to prison terms of varying lengths and assessed fines. Holt, charged with shipping guns and ammunition from Oklahoma into the Hartford Valley, was sentenced to six months in prison and fined $1,000; Stewart was fined $1,000 for making inflammatory remarks after the issuance of the federal injunction; James McNamara was sentenced to two years in Leavenworth penitentiary and fined $1,000 for sending word for the July 17 assault on the Prairie Creek mines and for being present at the execution of the two mine guards. James Slankard was sentenced to six months in prison and fined $1,000 for failing to "do his duty" during the disturbances. Four others received the same sentence for being part of the masked group that freed the prisoners from the U.S. deputy marshals. The UMW paid the fines.[152]

Holt, writing from the "filthy . . . 10 by 13 feet" cell in which he and eight of the others imprisoned in Fort Smith were confined, declared that he was proud to have shipped "all the high-powered rifles" he could procure "and plenty of ammunition" to help men "protect their homes." The corporation had imported 100 gunmen into a peaceful community, and they had begun "their usual tirade of abuse against . . . helpless women and children." Had the miners not been heavily armed, the corporation might have reenacted another Ludlow.[153]

The trial of Jim Slankard and a union miner named Bee Trout at Greenwood, Arkansas in January 1915 for the murder of the two mine guards, Clarence Sylesberry and John Baskins, at Prairie Creek on July 17, 1914, revealed the sharp contrast between federal and local courts, where community pressure guaranteed labor an acquittal. Most of the state's witnesses could not be found when the case came to trial, leaving only three mine guards or strikebreakers who had been captured with the slain men. They testified that neither defendant had committed the killings but had been present in the group and had done nothing to prevent them. A jury composed almost entirely of farmers found the defendants not guilty.[154]

The Arkansas mine war was ended inconclusively, with the Hartford Valley miners preserving their organization for several more years after their shooting battles with the mercenary forces. But as the UMW's membership declined precipitously during the 1920s, the union collapsed in the Hartford Valley. By 1927 nearly every coal mine in Arkansas was running on an open-shop basis. To be sure, the UMW did suffer financially from a lawsuit the Bache-Denman corporation's receivers filed after it went bankrupt in 1915, as legal fees drained its resources. The plaintiffs charged that the union had destroyed mine property and violated the Sherman Antitrust Act of 1890 by conspiring to restrain interstate commerce by interfering with mine production. The UMW argued that the destruction of the mines had resulted from the corporation's importation of gunmen who "assaulted . . . women, and insulted children, upon the streets" and "shot up" the miners' settlement at Frogtown, causing the "entire community" to rise up "in righteous indignation." After several appeals the lawsuit was finally settled out of court in 1927, with the UMW paying the receivers $27,500, by which time it had been permanently displaced from the Arkansas coal fields.[155]

## BALDWIN-FELTS GUNMEN IN SOUTHERN WEST VIRGINIA FROM MATEWAN TO THE AGENCY'S DEMISE

The bloody shoot-out between union miners and Baldwin-Felts guards at Matewan, West Virginia, in May 1920 served as a prelude to a massive, military-style march by thousands of miners on Logan and Mingo Counties that resulted in "the greatest domestic armed conflict in American labor history." The Baldwin-Felts Detective Agency sustained serious losses at Matewan, where seven of its men were killed, including two of its leaders, Albert Felts, director of its Thurmond, West Virginia, office and its field commander in the southern Colorado mine war of 1913–14, and Lee Felts, also a younger brother of Thomas Felts, and a veteran gunman. The Baldwin-Felts Agency a year after the shoot-out dramatically revealed it had infiltrated the UMW leadership in southern West Virginia, achieving the most spectacular success in anti-labor espionage since Pinkerton agent James McParlan penetrated the Molly Maguires in the 1870s. And the agency survived as a significant armed force for more than a decade, participating actively in the 1920–21 southern West Virginia mine war that followed Matewan. Between 10,000 and 20,000 men fought on both sides in the armies of the miners and the Baldwin-Felts guards, deputy sheriffs, and anti-unionists who opposed them. President Harding ordered 2,500 U.S. Army troops into the battle zone, along with military aircraft, the first time they had been used in a labor conflict.[156]

Speaking for the Baldwin-Felts Detective Agency, Albert Felts declared it would smash the UMW's organizing campaign in southern West Virginia, initiated in late 1919 because shipment of coal from the nonunion region threatened to undermine the national coal strike. The UMW quickly formed thirteen or fourteen locals in Mingo County, with 3,000 members. Baldwin-Felts guards began evicting union miners and their families, forcing hundreds into tent colonies.[157]

The confrontation at Matewan, a town with a population of about 500 in the Tug River coal field, was precipitated by Baldwin-Felts evictions near the town earlier in the day. The Stone Mountain Coal Company had posted a notice on the window of its company store that any miner joining the union must leave company housing. Believing the evictions were illegal, Matewan police chief Sid "Two Gun" Hatfield, a strong UMW sympathizer, backed by the town's mayor, Cable Testerman, informed Albert Felts, his brother Lee, and eleven other Baldwin-Felts guards who had carried them out that they were under arrest, as they prepared to board a late afternoon train for Bluefield. Albert Felts responded by producing a warrant to arrest Hatfield, on a charge of having taken a prisoner from his guards some time earlier, informing him he would have to accompany the guards back to Bluefield. As armed union miners stood nearby, or watched from windows overlooking the street, gunfire almost immediately broke out. Each side later claimed the other had fired first. Albert Felts and Mayor Testerman were killed within seconds, and in the next several minutes six more mine guards were shot dead, including Lee Felts, along with two union miners, and several others were wounded. Thomas Felts blamed Sid Hatfield for the "massacre" of his brothers, claiming he had drawn first, killing Albert, and vowed to exact revenge. But Hatfield charged that Albert Felts had begun the shoot-out by gunning down Mayor Testerman.[158]

Each side identified itself as highly respectable, while charging that Matewan had revealed the other as wholly uncivilized. Thomas Felts claimed that the violent conflict had been caused by the "Bolshevistic teachings" of UMW organizers who had invaded a district that, until their arrival, had been "[at] peace and enjoying . . . prosperity." Implicitly comparing the union miners with nineteenth-century Indian frontier marauders, Felts declared that they had "maltreated and robbed" the bodies of the Baldwin-Felts guards at Matewan and had left them lying in the street for an inordinate length of time. He accused them of stealing the masonic shriner's pin from Albert Felts's body, "in their greed for plunder." Howard Lee, a writer unsympathetic to the union, described Sid Hatfield and a "howling . . . shrieking" pro-labor mob drunk on moonshine whiskey "dancing around the bodies" for hours, firing hundreds of bullets into them. Felts's hometown newspaper, the *Bluefield Daily Telegraph*, praised his brothers Albert and Lee as men of "high standing and good character," noting that Albert had been both a Shriner and a life member of the Bluefield Lodge of Elks. The latter organization in fact passed a resolution mourning the deaths of Albert and Lee Felts, "two loyal citizens, who were members of an organization which has always championed law and order." The *Huntington Herald-Dispatch* declared that "all were forced to admit [Albert Felts's] courage."[159]

The UMW and its sympathizers, by contrast, expressed the hope that the Matewan killings marked the beginning of the end of "thug rule" and depicted Albert and Lee Felts and their "gang" as "outlaws," who had brought a machine gun from West Virginia to Colorado to use in the Ludlow massacre. A Mason's widow expressed shock in a letter to West Virginia governor John J. Cornwell that "a man of the Albert Felts type" had been "discovered dead in the street at Matewan wearing a Masonic shriner's pin," since the "Masonic order stands for law and order and the protection of women and children." She noted that Felts and his "thugs" had taken the law into their own hands by evicting workingmen from their homes near Matewan. Most importantly, she emphasized that the Baldwin-Felts "murderers" had outraged the "whole . . . civilized . . . world" at Ludlow by "mow[ing] down innocent women and dear little children with . . . machine guns."[160]

When Sid Hatfield and twenty-two other miners and union sympathizers were brought to trial in Williamson, the seat of what was now known as "Bloody" Mingo County, the UMW was stunned when one of its own adherents, Charlie Lively, declared on the stand that he was an undercover agent for Baldwin-Felts. Lively, a longtime UMW member, had arrived in Matewan from the union office in Charleston at the beginning of the organizing drive and opened a restaurant that became the favorite meeting place in town for UMW leaders and activists. He rented the floor above to the union for its Matewan office. Lively in the evening sent his reports of the unionists' conversations he heard to the Baldwin-Felts office in Bluefield, under the code name "Number Nine." The "man without nerves" had shared drinks with union miners at his restaurant, celebrating the killing of the Baldwin-Felts guards the evening of the shoot-out.[161]

Lively was a longtime protégé of Lee Felts, whom he had met as a youth about ten years before in a saloon near a Western copper mining camp, which Lee and Albert Felts and several of their gunmen had entered searching for "agitators." Lively recalled that as the "door burst open" all the men in the saloon "went for their guns," and a classic frontier-style shoot-out ensued. Lively was hit and fell to the floor badly wounded. Suddenly Lee Felts lifted him up, pulled him through a window, and placed him on the back of his horse, riding with him for miles to a doctor, an act that Lively believed had saved his life. From that day on, Lively "worshiped the ground Lee Felts walked on."[162]

When he recovered from his wound, Lively joined the Baldwin-Felts Detective Agency, undergoing intensive training in which he "learned . . . how to shoot from the hip, . . . [a] lightning fast draw, and deadly accuracy in firing six-guns with both hands." Like the legendary frontier gunfighters "under fire he became cold as ice." He became one of the agency's most valued operatives in the West but was transferred to West Virginia by 1920, along with most of Baldwin-Felts's western force.[163]

Lively prevailed upon Tom Felts, who had "raved like a maniac" when he learned that his brothers had been gunned down at Matewan, to assign him the task of avenging the killings, which he carried out a year later. The jury in Williamson, composed of men sympathetic to the UMW, had acquitted all the defendants, but Sid Hatfield knew Tom Felts had targeted him for death. Felts was able to have Hatfield, along with thirty-five others, indicted for participating in an attack on a nonunion mining camp at Mohawk, in McDowell County, in August 1920. The union accused Baldwin-Felts guards of staging the attack in order to frame Hatfield and force him to appear for trial in anti-union McDowell County. Unlike rapidly organizing Mingo, McDowell County remained "a complete industrial autocracy," where the Baldwin-Felts Detective Agency enforced the law.[164]

In August 1921 Hatfield appeared in Welch, the McDowell county seat, where Lively and a "deadly reception committee" of Baldwin-Felts guards waited. The Baldwin-Felts agency had positioned armed guards behind drawn shades on the second floor of every building that overlooked the courthouse. Lively later described the atmosphere of extreme tension when he walked into the Busy Bee restaurant about 7:00 A.M. for breakfast and saw Hatfield and fellow defendant Ed Chambers, son of the man believed to have killed Lee Felts at Matewan, with their wives at a table in the center of the room. "Never taking his eyes off the group," Lively sat down at a nearby table and ordered his breakfast. He recalled that the "deadly enemies" ate silently only a few feet apart, watching for one "false move," each man "keeping [his] hands well above the table."[165]

As Sid Hatfield and Ed Chambers ascended the courthouse steps, Lively and two other Baldwin-Felts guards standing alongside opened fire on them, killing them instantly, while another fired several shots into the courthouse wall to make it seem as though Hatfield and Chambers had fired first but missed. Neither Hatfield nor Chambers had been armed, but

Baldwin-Felts guards placed pistols in the corpses' hands. Crowds of union sympathizers quickly gathered at the site, but "the silent threat of the second floor windows" kept them in check. Howard Lee, writing in 1969, recalled that he had asked I. C. Herndon, judge of the circuit court for McDowell and Mercer Counties, why he had not called a special grand jury in his court to investigate the killings, and Herndon had replied that if he had announced he planned an investigation, he would have been killed before a grand jury could even assemble.[166]

The Baldwin-Felts murder of Hatfield and Chambers precipitated a massive march by armed miners from unionized Kanawha County, angered by the coal corporations' use of violence and eviction to disrupt their organizing drive in Don Chafin's Logan County fiefdom and in Mingo County, where the miners, 90 percent organized, had walked out on strike. Their objective was to overturn the governor's recent martial law proclamation and spread their organization across southern West Virginia, driving out the Baldwin-Felts guards. Chafin vowed he would use force to prevent the miners from marching across his county, mobilizing a volunteer anti-union army, largely from Logan and McDowell Counties, including Baldwin-Felts guards, which felled trees and dug trenches to block the unionists' advance. At the end of August 1921 fighting broke out along a ten-mile front near Blair Mountain, at the border of Logan County.[167]

The West Virginia mine conflict of 1921, like those at Paint Creek and Cabin Creek, in southern Colorado, in Michigan's Upper Peninsula, and in Arkansas's Hartford Valley, resembled a wartime military engagement. A Spanish-American War veteran who fought at Blair Mountain stated that the amount of shooting there was comparable with what he had experienced at Manila. Several hundred Logan County deputies and volunteers at Blair Mountain fired their rifles from behind breastworks and employed machine guns. Chafin even sent out three airplanes, first to track the unionists' movements, and then to drop crude bombs, hastily built out of gas piping stuffed with powder and iron nuts. Many of the miners went into battle wearing their World War army uniforms, organized into "companies" based on their union locals. Casualties were impossible to determine with any real accuracy, because both sides made every effort to conceal the number. Refugees from the Logan County battle zone reported Chafin's forces transporting stacks of corpses in trucks from the front, resulting in estimates of 100 to 300 killed on his side.[168]

In early September, citing the president's powers to suppress an insurrection, President Harding signed a proclamation prepared by Secretary of War John Wingate Weeks ordering the miners to disband, and sending 2,500 U.S. troops to West Virginia, along with seventeen military aircraft. Although many of the miners attempted to continue their advance, the army's show of force caused a cessation of the fighting within a short time.[169]

The outcome represented a serious defeat for the union, leaving the mine guard system intact and Sid Hatfield's killers free, continuing to work for Baldwin-Felts. In Mingo County the miners held out on strike until October 1922, by which time District 17 was effectively bankrupted. Demoralized by losing the long, drawn-out strike, and without financial resources, the UMW in West Virginia fell from 50,000 members in 1920 to 600 in 1929, as organized labor suffered a precipitous decline nationally.[170]

The Baldwin-Felts Detective Agency remained a significant presence in southern West Virginia well into the 1930s. Because of the UMW's near collapse in West Virginia after 1921, there was little or no strikebreaking work, but the agency remained in charge of law enforcement throughout much of southern West Virginia and engaged in labor espionage for the coal companies. A state police force, numbering 100 to 150 men, had been established at the urging of Governor Cornwell in 1919, over the UMW's opposition, which feared its use as a strikebreaking force, but it was too small and poorly funded in the 1920s to assume primary responsibility for law enforcement.[171]

Until Tom Felts dissolved the Baldwin-Felts Detective Agency in May 1937, four months before his death, its agents continued to work undercover in the mines, reporting on workers involved in organizing or displaying pro-UMW sympathies. They shadowed union organizers who entered the southern West Virginia coal districts, and sometimes roughed them up, and intercepted and destroyed pro-labor newspapers brought into the region. Baldwin-Felts detectives occasionally acted as agents provocateur, dynamiting mine facilities, or nonunion miners' homes, and making it appear that pro-union forces were responsible, in an effort to discredit the UMW by identifying it with terrorism. Earl McKee, who confessed in 1937 that he had "Thugged for 18 years" for the Baldwin-Felts Agency, when not spying undercover in the mines, had worked as a piano player, using that talent to mix with coal miners in beer gardens, dance halls, their union hall, and at private affairs.[172]

The coming of the New Deal, which created a more favorable environment for union organizing than had ever existed in West Virginia, resulting in an upsurge in the state's UMW membership to 100,000 by 1934, caused the Baldwin-Felts Agency to shift its focus away from "open activities" of intimidation toward subterfuge. Earl McKee noted in 1937 that while the "day of the blackjack artist [was] about over," the Baldwin-Felts Agency had increased the number of undercover operatives after UMW organizing began in earnest in 1933. Baldwin-Felts spies not only reported those joining the union to management but attempted to sow dissension within union locals by spreading false rumors about UMW leaders' misdeeds and financial mismanagement, and bribing members on votes to provoke debilitating splits. McKee claimed that "usually, a half hour after a local meeting has adjourned, the operator [i.e., management] knows everything that took place at the meeting."[173]

When Tom Felts dissolved the Baldwin-Felts Detective Agency, the UMW had solidly organized West Virginia. Felts's partner, William G. Baldwin, who ran the Roanoke, Virginia, office and managed the agency's railroad business, had died in April 1936. Both men had attained prosperity and middle-class respectability through careers in strikebreaking and union busting. Baldwin, who began his career as a small storekeeper in the 1880s, sat on the board of directors of several Roanoke banks and owned the Martha Washington candy factory in Roanoke, as well as a funeral home. Felts had also "made . . . a fortune"; when he died he was president of a bank in Galax, Virginia, and a large landholder. Both men were members of Masonic orders and the Rotary Club.[174] But the UMW's successful unionization of West Virginia under Roosevelt, the election of governors and legislatures sympathetic to labor, who would no longer tolerate the massive deputizing of mine guards, and the steady expansion of the state police, along with the deaths of Baldwin and Felts, finally ended the decades-long rule of southern West Virginia by the mine corporations' armed mercenaries.

## CONCLUSION

The mine conflicts of the early twentieth century resembled military campaigns against a foreign enemy, involving significant battle casualties, the use of advanced weaponry, and attempts to stigmatize the other side as uncivilized. The conflicts in Colorado, Michigan, and West Virginia produced atrocities similar to those that shortly afterward were ascribed to German forces during the invasion of Belgium—the butchering of innocent women and children at Ludlow and Red Jacket, and the armored train assault on the Holly Grove tent colony. The union miners cited them, along with the mine guards' surprise night attack on Frogtown, Arkansas, that had driven the women and children from the settlement in panic, as evidence that the corporate mercenaries were sadistic killers, lacking any self-discipline, who delighted in terrorizing the helpless and murdering prisoners. The miners viewed the mercenaries as marauding troops, representing the debauchery of contemporary urban society, despoiling family-based communities by sexually harassing their wives and daughters, violating the sanctity of their homes, and tormenting the elderly. These "red-light gunmen" drew streams of prostitutes into the communities they invaded, like the camp followers of wartime.

By contrast, the mercenaries considered the miners racially inferior savages, because they were southern or eastern European immigrants, or wild mountaineers of native ancestry, long isolated and steeped in primitivism. To the mercenaries, these men resembled the Indians of the nineteenth-century frontier, a people apart, unassimilable, capable of the cruelest depredations, including the mutilation of corpses.

Well-organized, heavily armed private armies permitted mine corporations to exercise dictatorial control in many sections, controlling government functions, and denying inhabitants any civil liberties. But permanently established private armies wielded such power not only in these relatively isolated mining regions and in the "piney woods" lumber camps of east Texas and Louisiana. The largest was based in one of the world's most industrialized cities, Dearborn, Michigan, contiguous to Detroit, a highly modern center of technological innovation. Known as the Ford Service Department, it was founded on Henry Ford's instructions and directed by ex-navy boxer Harry Bennett. The power of Bennett's private army, and its suppression of workers' civil liberties, persisted after that of the armies of the mining and lumber corporations had waned. In 1937, CIO leader Adolph Germer remarked that "Logan County and Mingo County, West Virginia have been civilized. . . . Now the task remains to civilize Dearborn, Michigan . . . and annex [it] to the United States."[175]

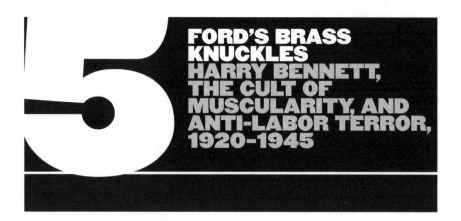

# FORD'S BRASS KNUCKLES

## HARRY BENNETT, THE CULT OF MUSCULARITY, AND ANTI-LABOR TERROR, 1920-1945

On August 9, 1937, Rudolph Rutland, production manager of the Ford Motor Company assembly plant in Dallas, summoned a 232-pound wrestler named "Fats" Perry, who had charge of his "outside" squad, a group of employees of "large stature and . . . unusual muscular development" drawn from the plant's champion tug-of-war team.[1] Established a few months before on instructions from Harry Bennett, who directed Ford's labor policy from its headquarters in Dearborn, Michigan, the outside squad was designed to prevent Committee for Industrial Organization (CIO) organizers from entering Dallas. Bennett encouraged Rutland to use violence in this effort. Supplied with blackjacks manufactured in the plant, the outside squad worked in pairs, watching the bus and railroad stations, domino parlors, and barber shops, and shadowing suspected union sympathizers. Some of the squad acquired pistols, whips, and lengths of rubber hose called "persuaders." Bennett also ordered the formation of an "inside" squad to spy on workers inside the plant.[2]

Both squads were part of Harry Bennett's Service Department, an integral unit in every Ford plant, whose purpose was the suppression of unionism through physical intimidation and espionage. Dallas Ford's Service Department was assisted by spies recruited from among the city's gas station operators, grocers, and restaurateurs, whom it paid to listen in on conversations and report any sign of union activity.[3]

Rutland instructed Perry to break up a CIO meeting scheduled for that evening in a city park, and to destroy the pro-labor film *Millions of Us* that the organizers planned to show. He also ordered the inside squad to participate in the disruption.[4] Ford's Service squads launched their well-coordinated assault right after the CIO film showing. Perry's men stormed the stage, knocked down the CIO speaker just beginning his remarks, and upended his table. They then overturned the CIO sound truck and destroyed the union film projector. Ford Servicemen surrounded CIO organizer George Lambert, slugging him with brass knuckles and kicking him repeatedly after he fell to the ground.[5]

One of Perry's lieutenants knocked Herbert Harris, the other CIO organizer, unconscious, and carried him out of the park to his automobile, where Ford Servicemen blindfolded him. They drove him to "one of the usual whipping places" at the Trinity River bottoms. They told Harris, as he regained consciousness in the car, that he would be burned at the stake.[6] At the "whipping place," "Fats" Perry ordered Harris to remove his clothing. Servicemen then applied two coats of tar from his neck to his ankles, and covered him with feathers. They then drove the still blindfolded Harris back to Dallas and dumped him in front of the *Morning News* building, where they had arranged for a photographer to take his picture. The next morning the Servicemen presented their superintendent with a specimen of the tar and feathers they had used and were congratulated for a "damn good job."[7] Harris had to be hospitalized for three days.[8]

The disruption of the CIO meeting in Dallas and the tarring and feathering of Harris represented merely one incident in what the NLRB called Ford's "war" on unionism.[9] Ford's war effort against the United Automobile Workers (UAW-CIO) was directed by Harry Bennett from his basement office near the company's massive River Rouge plant in Dearborn. The Dallas Ford Service Department had acted on direct orders from Bennett.[10] During the late 1920s and 1930s Harry Bennett personally assembled the world's largest private army and established the most extensive and efficient espionage system in American industry. His Service Department was the largest department in the Ford Motor Company. Bennett's private army ensured that Ford remained the "citadel of the open shop" through the 1930s, the last of the auto companies to be organized.

All of the automobile manufacturers and their parts suppliers were hostile to unionism and used systematic espionage and sometimes violence to discourage it, but none fought it as ruthlessly and violently as Ford, which was alone in establishing a private army. Victor Reuther noted that General Motors (GM) and Chrysler were "much more careful to try to not implicate the corporations *per se* in the dirty work, but rather contracting it out, [while] permitting it to enjoy full corporate official support and protection and funding."[11] GM and Chrysler both paid professional labor spying agencies to place operatives in their plants, particularly after Section 7A of the National Industrial Recovery Act sparked union campaigns in 1933. GM became the Pinkerton Detective Agency's biggest industrial client, and spent about $1 million on labor espionage in 1934–36 alone. It controlled municipal police in Flint, Michigan, where its major plants were located, and promoted an armed vigilante organization in Anderson, Indiana, which ransacked union headquarters and terrorized strikers.[12] Chrysler hired spies from Corporations Auxiliary Service; sit-down strikers who inspected the corporation's files in 1937 uncovered extensive "stool pigeon" reports.[13]

The Ford Motor Company, the first manufacturer to introduce the mechanized assembly line, epitomized modernism and efficiency in production; the term "Fordism" was synonymous with industrial achievement. The colossal River Rouge plant in Dearborn was the world's largest industrial complex during the 1930s. Yet Henry Ford entrusted labor policy to Harry Bennett, truly a marginal man in the modern bureaucratic-industrial system. Bennett was poorly educated and wholly lacking in business experience. He knew nothing about production methods and did not even like to drive a car. He possessed neither the interpersonal skills nor the ability to work in a group that was expected of American business executives. Bennett openly expressed his contempt for "the white-collar officials up in mahogany row," preferring the company of gangsters, ex-convicts, and athletes. He resembled a "fight manager," rather than a corporate executive.[14]

During the 1930s and early 1940s, Harry Bennett was one of the most powerful executives at the Ford Motor Company, and during the last years of Henry Ford's reign, the most powerful. *Time* magazine called him "the apple of old Henry's eye." Henry Ford referred to Bennett as his "loyal right arm." Bennett himself stated that: "During the thirty years I worked for Henry Ford I became his most intimate companion, closer to him than his only son."[15]

In fact, Henry Ford was drawn to Harry Bennett precisely because he found in him the qualities he felt were lacking in his only son. Bennett was tough, aggressive, and seemed self-assured. He was willing to carry out any order from Ford. Bennett had known deprivation in childhood, having grown up without a father. His father, a house painter, was killed in a brawl when Bennett was an infant. His mother had remarried, but Bennett always remained estranged from his stepfather. For a time after his stepfather's death, which occurred when Bennett was about ten, he was "orphaned out" to an uncle. He eventually rejoined his mother in Detroit,

*A jaunty Harry Bennett. Courtesy of the Walter P. Reuther Library,*
*Wayne State University.*

where she ran a roominghouse. Edsel, by contrast, at least since adolescence, had been raised in luxury. Henry Ford, a self-made man, believed that his son lacked the "iron" necessary for success in business; he was too soft, too conciliatory. According to Bennett, Edsel Ford "was a nervous man; when he got angry he threw up. He was just a scared boy."[16] Although Henry Ford gave his son the title of company president in 1919, Edsel possessed little influence except in the areas of product development, sales, and advertising.[17] Bennett worked hard to exacerbate the tension between father and son, constantly belittling Edsel to Henry and "deliberately [setting] him up to embarrass him."[18] As a result, the fatherless Bennett established himself as Henry Ford's "surrogate son," and a "spoiled son at that."[19]

Bennett himself seems to have had a lifelong need to affirm his masculinity, due no doubt to his not having known his father, his frustration over being short—he was only five feet seven inches tall and weighed 145 pounds, although he wore a size 17 collar—and his having been "brought up like a sissy, Buster Brown collar and all."[20] From a young age Bennett was drawn to men who displayed physical prowess. He spent many afternoons as a child watching University of Michigan football and baseball games and field sports. As an adolescent in Detroit, where he attended the School of Fine Arts, he often encountered sailors, and became enthralled by their tales of life on the "salt water." Under age, he tried to enlist in the navy, but suffered humiliation when he could not secure his mother's consent.[21]

But in 1909 Bennett ran away from his mother to Cleveland, lied about his age, and successfully enlisted in the navy. He was persuaded to do so by a burly sailor named Sam Taylor, who promised to teach him how to box. Assigned with Taylor to the battleship *Ohio*, Bennett became one of the best lightweight boxers of the Atlantic fleet, fighting under the name "Sailor Reese." During his tour of duty he trained under "Kid" McCoy, one of the classiest middleweights of his time, a "clever, sharpshooting" boxer who had fought Gentleman Jim Corbett, Jack Root, and Joe Choynski. Bennett fought professionally every time he came ashore.[22]

During his navy days, Bennett advertised his masculinity by acquiring tattoos in New York, Paris, and Cuba. His "gnarled fists" looked "formidable"; he broke all his fingers and knuckles boxing.[23] Facial scars and a "suspicion of a twist in his jaw—broken in a navy ring scrap," added to this image of toughness.[24]

Having finished two enlistments in the navy, and still feeling the need to test his manhood, Bennett in 1916 signed on as a deep-sea diver for a ship doing salvage work and charting the West African coast for the French government. At Port St. Louis, Senegal, a below-deck explosion caused the ship to burn to the waterline. Suspicion fastened on Bennett and another sailor, who fled inland and made their way to Dakar. When they emerged from the swamps a week later, bearded and exhausted, they told of being attacked by a "crazed native," who slashed Bennett's face and cut off his companion's ear lobe before the two seamen managed to push him into a bog. Securing passage on a Spanish tramp steamer, they made their way to Vera Cruz, and then to New York.[25]

It was Harry Bennett's scrappy performance in a street brawl almost immediately after his arrival in New York that first brought him to Henry Ford's attention. The young ex-gob "gave a good account of himself" before police arrested him. Luckily for Bennett, the prominent journalist Arthur Brisbane had witnessed the brawl and admired his fighting prowess. He persuaded police to drop the charges and then took Bennett to meet Henry Ford at his New York office. Ford liked Bennett's navy stories and hired him on the spot. Shortly afterward Bennett began work at the River Rouge plant in Dearborn protecting from sabotage the Eagle boat submarine chasers being built there for use in World War I.[26]

It was an opportune time to arrive at the Rouge; the Ford Motor Company was about to begin a phenomenal expansion. When Bennett arrived it was little more than a "blast furnace and tractor factory." But by the late 1920s it had surpassed the older Highland Park plant and become Ford's major production center. With open access to the Detroit River the Rouge could more easily bring in production materials. And, unlike Highland Park, its physical expansion was not blocked by contiguity to residences and other businesses.[27]

As the Rouge's labor force swelled to 100,000 by the late 1920s, managerial control and discipline tightened considerably. After Henry Ford introduced a profit-sharing plan in 1914 permitting a Five Dollar Day for workers who attained a certain standard of efficiency and personal conduct, his company briefly enjoyed a reputation for paternalism in labor relations. But by the early 1920s, Ford had abandoned the effort to "elevate" its work force morally, terminated profit sharing, and displayed concern only for production. The company embraced the view, as one Ford executive put it, that "men are more profitable to an industry when driven than led, that fear is a greater incentive to work than loyalty."[28]

By 1921 Harry Bennett had been given a significant role in enforcing the Ford Company's new "drive system." Impressed with his swagger and tough talk, and his defeat of much bigger men in brawls at the Rouge, Henry Ford placed him in charge of its plant police, called the Service Department.[29]

Bennett's power grew enormously after 1927, when Ford shifted to production of the Model A and the Rouge became the center of the company's operations. Bennett greatly increased his staff of Servicemen, most of whom could be described as "plug-uglies—ex-boxers and wrestlers, with cauliflower ears [and] crooked noses." Their chief concern in patrolling the plant was to let the workers know they were being watched, and that those not working fast enough, or showing any sympathy for unionism, would be discharged.[30]

During little more than a decade, Bennett's duties expanded to include not just plant policing but full control over personnel matters at Ford, including the hiring and firing of workers. His rise to power was facilitated by Henry Ford's highly personal, impulsive, and disorganized approach to management. Ford distrusted nearly everyone, and had difficulty delegating authority. Managerial positions were not well defined; most officials lacked titles and were unsure of their exact duties. Charles Sorensen, Ford's production chief, recalled that "[c]onstant turmoil was Henry Ford's idea of harmony. By keeping things stirred up, no one else could swell with importance."[31] Obviously, this situation provided Bennett with a better opportunity for upward mobility in management than would the more clearly defined and impersonal bureaucratic hierarchy typical in most large corporations.

Bennett also benefited from the fact that Ford was much more likely to place men with little formal education, and from working-class backgrounds, in managerial positions than were most of the other automobile companies. Before 1930 auto manufacturers tended to produce for their social peers. Companies selling expensive cars, like Packard, tended to recruit managerial executives from the upper class, while those competing in the middle-priced field, like Hudson and Chalmers, were more likely to hire executives from the middle class. Ford, which produced low-priced cars for skilled workers and farmers, drew more of its leadership from lower in the social structure; before 1930, 22 percent were sons of working-men. Only 24 percent had attended college, against an industry average of 45 percent. Henry Ford's own background was relatively humble, and he was not comfortable with Detroit's elite families.[32] Ford, who had little schooling, held the college-educated in disdain. Willis Ward, a Ford executive during the 1930s, recalled that "one of the best ways not to get anywhere in the Ford Motor Company at that time was to have a college degree."[33]

Bennett's ascendancy also owed much to his ability to exploit Henry Ford's fear that his grandchildren would be kidnapped. Since the early 1920s Bennett had cultivated close personal ties with gangsters, and he convinced Ford that he thereby had the power to protect his family. Ford had real cause for concern; in the early 1920s he frequently received letters threatening his family with bodily harm. In 1924 Detroit police arrested extortionists who had threatened to blind his grandchildren.[34]

Many of the leaders of Detroit's underworld were Bennett's friends. The city had become a major organized crime center during the 1920s because its proximity to Canada made it a major port of entry for bootleggers. Using his contacts among Detroit's "criminal gangs," Bennett was able to get word of several kidnapping plots targeting the Ford family before they could be implemented. Traveling from one gang hideout to another, he warned "flint-eyed" men that Ford would unleash a "cutthroat war" if any harm ever came to his grandchildren.[35] In 1928 the father of a kidnapped boy named Jackie Thompson appealed to Henry Ford for help after police failed to turn up any leads. Ford turned the matter over to Bennett, who in short order brought about the boy's return.[36] Ford, who "had a small boy's awe of outlaws," was terribly impressed by Bennett's friendships with gangsters.[37]

Bennett felt he could ensure better protection for the Ford family, and strengthen his Service Department, if he provided favors to gangsters. He gave Chet La Mare, "supreme overlord of Detroit's racketeers," the lucrative fruit and vegetable concession at River Rouge, even though "Chet didn't know a banana from an orange." Besides bootlegging, La Mare was involved in truck hijacking, robbing freight cars, prostitution, and drug trafficking.[38] Bennett gave Detroit mobster Anthony D'Anna the contract to haul away cars from the Rouge plant. He also provided both D'Anna and La Mare with Ford dealerships.[39] Bennett granted Brooklyn gangster Joe Adonis a monopoly on delivering cars assembled at Ford's Edgewater, New Jersey, plant. Adonis was Brooklyn's "top man" in narcotics, waterfront hijacking, floating crap games, loan sharking, and counterfeiting. Bennett also supplied legal assistance to mobsters.[40] In exchange for all these favors, he was able to recruit large numbers of gangsters into Ford Service.

Henry Ford's alarm over the attempts to unionize auto workers during the 1930s guaranteed Harry Bennett's rise to the pinnacle of power. Ford detested unionism and was determined to defeat it by any means necessary. He had Bennett transform the Service Department into the world's largest and most formidable private army. For a full decade from 1932 until 1941, Bennett's army considered itself in a state of war against unionists and combined bloody assaults with systematic espionage to keep Ford nonunion.

While highly effective in disrupting organizing in the short term, Ford

Service further degraded an already very unpleasant work environment, giving added credibility to the union appeal. Assembly line work was monotonous and physically exhausting and allowed the worker no freedom of movement. He could not leave the line even to go to the bathroom without a foreman's permission. Jobs for auto workers were never secure, and seniority meant nothing. The auto market's seasonality made work highly irregular. The yearly model changes caused plants to shut down; after a layoff of several weeks, companies rehired workers at the entry-level wage, regardless of what they had been earning previously. Bennett himself identified this custom as "the real motive power for the union movement." Irregular employment became an especially serious problem for auto workers during the Depression, when they could no longer find other jobs during layoffs. Because auto companies preferred vigorous men under thirty-five for assembly line work, experienced men older than that were often the first dismissed and last rehired.[41]

Perhaps the most humiliating aspect of auto work was having to perform personal favors for foremen in order to retain one's job. Foremen never recognized seniority and rehired workers based on whether or not they liked them. As a result, workers were often called upon to paint their foreman's home or do his repairs there. Sometimes foremen even demanded favors of workers' wives. Doug Fraser recalled Richard Frankensteen telling him about a worker at Dodge Main who asked a co-worker to punch him out a few minutes early so he could go home for lunch. Upon arriving home, the worker discovered his wife in bed with his superintendent. The worker slipped out unseen and returned to the plant. The next day, when his co-worker asked him if he wanted to be punched out again, he replied, "No, I almost got caught yesterday."[42]

Conditions at Ford were considered the worst in the auto industry. The Rouge plant itself was "dull, gloomy, and forbidding."[43] Wages were about 10 percent lower than at GM and Chrysler. Workers were given only fifteen minutes for lunch, which they had to eat standing, or sitting on the oil-soaked floor. One Ford worker recalled that his wife peeled his oranges for him the night before, to make it possible for him to finish eating in time.[44]

Because of Bennett's Service Department, Ford employees toiled under more exacting supervision and were more vulnerable to arbitrary discharge than workers in other auto companies. Ford Servicemen had the authority to discharge any worker without the approval, even over the objection, of a foreman or superintendent. These "ex-pugilists and otherwise tough hombres" walked up and down the aisles, glaring at the workers and watching for any infraction of the rules. Those they caught were often fired on the spot and bodily ejected from the plant.[45] Workers were required to maintain absolute silence on the line. One man, John Gallo, was fired at the Rouge because a foreman saw him laugh. Workers caught smoking were also discharged.[46] Ken Bannon, who worked in the Rouge Motor Building, recalled that Servicemen followed workers to the bathroom to check whether they were really going to the toilet and that it was not unusual "for a Serviceman . . . to ask you to stand up if you were sitting down [on the toilet seat] to see if you were lying or not." No wonder that Ford workers frequently referred to themselves as "Ford dogs" and "slaves."[47]

In March 1932 Harry Bennett received major public attention for the first time, when he helped to suppress brutally the Ford Hunger March, dramatizing Ford's determination to use violence against those demonstrating for labor rights. The courage—some said foolhardiness—that Bennett displayed won him Henry Ford's undying admiration and drew the two men closer together than ever. Sponsored by the small, Communist-led Auto Workers' Union and the Detroit Unemployed Council, the march sought to draw attention to the plight of the unemployed. The marchers, mostly former Ford workers, planned to present Ford officials with demands to rehire laid-off workers and to improve working conditions at the Rouge. When the procession, which had begun in Detroit, reached the Dearborn border, Dearborn police unsuccessfully tried to halt it with tear gas. They then retreated to the Rouge gates, where they were joined by armed Ford Servicemen.[48]

The upshot was a "sharp, bloody battle," as police and Servicemen fired on demonstrators armed with only sticks and stones, fatally wounding two. Suddenly a Ford car carrying Harry Bennett drove through a factory gate into the crowd, which pelted it with rocks. Bennett got out of the car, intending to address the marchers and disperse them. But he was immediately hit in the head with a brick and knocked to the ground, blood gushing from the wound. Believing Bennett had been shot, Servicemen and police fired hundreds of bullets into the crowd. Bennett himself rose to his feet and joined in the shooting; when his gun ran out of bullets he grabbed a policeman's and continued firing. In all, four marchers were killed and twenty-eight were wounded.[49]

Bennett's Servicemen and the Dearborn police had turned a peaceful demonstration into a horrible massacre. But this only confirmed to Henry Ford that Bennett was the right man to spearhead his drive against labor. Detroit's press, always highly favorable to the auto companies, sang the praises of their new hero, a "born fighter," who instead of directing his men by telephone from the safety of his office, had "charged [the] mob bare-handed . . . swinging his fists."[50]

By 1936–37, when the UAW-CIO began a serious effort to organize the auto industry, Harry Bennett had employed many of the methods of the European fascists to turn River Rouge into a "gigantic concentration camp, founded on fear and physical assault."[51] A similar situation existed in the satellite plants. Liberals and trade unionists referred to Bennett's Service Department as "Ford's Gestapo." It numbered between 3,500 and 6,000 men.[52] Ford workers could never escape surveillance inside the plant, where about one of twenty-five men was a Serviceman. They sometimes posed as workers, picking fights with suspected union sympathizers and getting them discharged as a result. They also rifled lunchboxes and even opened sandwiches to find union fliers. Bennett also recruited as spies many of the sweepers, who moved freely about the plant. Sweepers searched coats hanging on racks for union buttons and leaflets. Workers who had been laid off were sometimes forced to spy as a condition for being rehired.[53]

Bennett's spies maintained a careful watch in the workers' communities as well. Bennett mapped out the Detroit region into small areas and instructed his Servicemen to form "neighborhood units" in each. Not just the Servicemen but their wives as well spied on the Ford workers, listening in on conversations in grocery stores, meat markets, bars, restaurants, gambling dens, and even churches. Workers' wives waiting to make purchases in stores might discuss their husbands' discontent at work or sympathy for unionism. If they did, Bennett heard about it.[54]

Bennett's Servicemen carefully watched union meetings and the homes of suspected unionists. When they could not gain access to meetings, they recorded the license plate numbers of cars parked nearby.[55] They visited wives of men suspected of attending union meetings and warned them that their husbands not only would be fired but might never come home again. The UAW-CIO instructed its members not to tell their spouses and children the location of the union meetings they attended, because Ford Servicemen might attempt to squeeze it out of them. It also urged members not to travel to meetings alone, to protect against assault by Servicemen.[56]

Bennett even posted spies at auto dealerships throughout the Detroit area to make sure that Ford workers bought only Ford cars. Any Ford worker reported to have purchased any other make of car was promptly fired. In some Ford plants, such as Hamilton, Ohio, Ford workers were told not to do business with any concern—milk companies, laundries, grocers—that did not deliver in Ford cars.[57]

So thorough was Bennett's espionage system that Ford workers could not escape the scrutiny of the Service Department even after being laid off. Tens of thousands of Ford workers were forced onto Works Progress Administration (WPA) projects during the 1930s. Because Ford management expected that it might sometime have to rehire some of these men, it arranged with friendly politicians for Ford Servicemen to be appointed as foremen or subforemen on WPA projects where discharged Ford workers constituted a majority of those hired. These ex-Ford workers were reminded that the Ford Company was "still keeping a watchful eye over them."[58]

Making Bennett's private army even more menacing to unionists was the fact that a significant proportion of it consisted of men paroled from prison, many of whom had been convicted of violent crimes. Henry Ford had been convinced by prominent Detroit social workers in the 1910s to give jobs to ex-convicts as a means of rehabilitation, and by 1920 he had 400 to 600 on his payroll.[59] But Bennett greatly expanded the policy in 1935 after Michigan governor Frank Fitzgerald appointed him to the Michigan Parole Board. In this manner, he recruited scores of murderers, rapists, armed robbers, and drug pushers as strong-arm men for his Service Department.[60] These men were well aware that if they did not follow Bennett's orders unquestioningly, they would be "right back smack [in] the clinker." And they also knew that Bennett had agents in the prisons who could inflict severe punishment on them if they went back.[61]

Bennett was also drawn to athletes and made a concerted effort to recruit them into the Service Department. Like the ex-convicts, he valued them for their fighting abilities, and for the rough camaraderie they provided, so lacking in conventional business executives. The athletes also made useful spies. Bennett had them make frequent visits to boys' clubs, where they plied unknowing youths for information about their fathers' union activities.[62] His personal assistant was Stan Fay, captain of the University of Michigan football team in 1933. He hired Kid McCoy, the ex-boxing great who had taught him how to handle himself in the ring in his navy days, when he was paroled from San Quentin, where he had served seven years for manslaughter as a result of killing his "reputed sweetheart." McCoy, until his suicide in 1940, worked for Bennett in the Service Department. Bennett placed Eddie Cicotte, the former Chicago White Sox pitcher disgraced in the Black Sox scandal, in charge of the Service Department at Ford's Highland Park plant.[63]

Bennett, advertising his freedom from the constraints of modern bureaucratic life and his disdain for conventional business executives, ate lunch every day with flashily dressed gangsters and athletes at a special table in Ford's Administration Building. There he engaged with them in boisterous, working-class style repartee that contrasted sharply with the stiff formality and almost childlike deference required of the other top executives who ate at Henry Ford's own table in the Engineering Laboratories Building. Bennett's regular lunch companions were men like Detroit Tigers catcher Mickey Cochrane, University of Michigan football coach Harry Kipke, pro football star Harry Newman, and gangsters like Chet La Mare and Joe Tocco. They were joined by certain executives loyal to Bennett. Conversation was relaxed and centered on sports and crime, never on automotive affairs.[64]

Such easy informality and manly posturing were entirely foreign to the executives who assembled every day at 12:55 P.M. at Henry Ford's table. Like dutiful schoolboys, they rose to greet the Old Man, who entered at precisely 12:59 P.M. They all had to eat some of Henry Ford's experimental food, like soybeans, or his "rabbit food," raw vegetables. Conversation was serious, and concerned engineering or production. Only Henry Ford, his son Edsel, or production chief Charles Sorensen could initiate conversation.[65]

Like Henry Ford, Bennett viewed both corporate management and the labor relations arena as a "jungle" in which only the strongest survived. Instead of advising Ford officials desiring promotion to concentrate on teamwork, he asked them, "Can you lick the guy [above you]? If you can . . . go in there and take his chair."[66] Consorting with gangsters and pugilists reinforced the reputation for fearlessness he had gained confronting the Hunger Marchers. So did playing with ferocious animals. Bennett kept cages of lions and tigers at the end of a tunnel leading away from his brick castle near Ann Arbor, one of his five homes. In 1937 he even added a professional lion tamer to his Service Department staff.[67]

In 1937 the new UAW-CIO, energized by its stunning victory in the General Motors sit-down strike and by U.S. Steel's recognition of the CIO a few weeks later, determined to take on Bennett's private army, and began the first major campaign to organize Ford. But Bennett easily thwarted the campaign during its early stages by unleashing massive violence and by using his control of Dearborn's government, and his strong influence in other cities, to deny the UAW the ability to recruit in the open. The UAW's lack of momentum in its Ford campaign contrasted sharply with its successes at GM and Chrysler, where it won a significant degree of recognition in 1937. Although those corporations hired private detective agencies to spy on their workers and engaged in explicit violent intimidation of unionists, Ford surpassed both in the amount of violence it inflicted and in the extent and efficiency of its espionage.

Hoping that the courage and commitment of its organizers could inspire River Rouge's workers to overcome their terror of Bennett's Service Department, the primary obstacle to organization, the UAW planned a massive leaflet distribution at all the main factory gates for May 26, 1937. But Bennett brutally suppressed the union's effort to bring its message to the workers, dealing the UAW a serious, short-run defeat.

To ensure that no violence would occur, UAW leaders obtained a city permit to distribute handbills and assigned most of the actual leafleting to women, whom they believed Servicemen were less likely to attack. But Bennett's aide Everett Moore warned ominously that "loyal employees" might resent the leafleting and that the company would not be at fault if fighting broke out. On May 26 journalists observed "brawny men" guarding each gate.[68]

Even so, the UAW activists never anticipated what Bennett had planned for them. As Walter Reuther and Richard Frankensteen, leaders of the Ford drive, and three other UAW activists stood on the overpass that led to the Rouge's main gate, they were confronted by a group of Servicemen, who told them, "Get the hell out!" The Servicemen included Bennett's old navy buddy Sam Taylor; Angelo Caruso, boss of Detroit's infamous Down River gang; two professional wrestlers; the welterweight boxing champion of Michigan; and a man carrying handcuffs in his trousers. Several of the Servicemen wore bandages around their hands to conceal brass knuckles and other hard objects.

Giving the UAW activists no opportunity to leave, the Servicemen immediately began a systematic beating. Twelve or fifteen Servicemen pounced on Walter Reuther, knocking him to the concrete, where they kicked his head again and again. Seven or eight times they dragged him to his feet, and repeatedly punched him in the face. Then they hurled him down three flights of stairs. Using the technique of professional hoodlums, the Servicemen pulled Richard Frankensteen's coat above his head, rendering him completely defenseless, and beat him nearly unconscious. Bennett's thugs broke the back of UAW activist Richard Merriweather. They tore the leaflets from the hands of UAW women attempting to distribute them; some they punched and kicked in the stomach. A reporter testified that "everywhere he looked, four or five [Service]men were kicking some unionist

*Ford Servicemen assault Richard Frankensteen during the Battle of the Overpass, May 26, 1937. Courtesy of the Walter P. Reuther Library, Wayne State University.*

around." To prevent the public from learning of the brutal assault, Servicemen ripped the film from photographers' cameras.[69]

The Battle of the Overpass made dramatically clear Harry Bennett's control of Dearborn's police force. In 1929 Bennett had Dearborn's mayor Clyde Ford, Henry Ford's cousin, appoint Carl Brooks, one of his former Servicemen, chief of police. Brooks served in that capacity until 1941, when he was indicted for taking bribes from Dearborn brothels, gambling houses, and slot machine syndicates.[70] As police chief, Brooks, in collusion with Bennett, sold jobs at the Rouge to men desperate for work, for $50.[71] Brooks commanded the police who fired on the Hunger Marchers in 1932. During the Battle of the Overpass his mounted police watched the beatings and never intervened. Their only action was to arrest a group of UAW women leafleters for "overloading" a car into which Servicemen had pushed them.[72]

Because Dearborn's municipal government was controlled by Bennett, the UAW failed miserably in its attempt to force a city investigation of police conduct during the Battle of the Overpass. UAW representatives appeared before the Dearborn Safety Commission, which supervised the police department, the city council, and the mayor to present evidence that Dearborn police had witnessed the beatings and had not intervened to stop them. But each branch of government refused to take any action. In fact, shortly afterward, on Bennett's instructions, the city council passed an ordinance banning leafleting near the Rouge, which severely hampered organizing efforts until a judge declared it unconstitutional in November 1940. Dearborn officials also pressured the landlord of the UAW's Ford Organizing Committee to evict it from its headquarters, forcing the committee to move to Detroit.[73]

Bennett's private army, fully backed by municipal officials, forced the UAW to call off its Ford organizing campaign in Dallas and Memphis by savagely beating union organizers and sympathizers, often on busy streets in broad daylight. Both city administrations shared Bennett's intense hostility to the CIO. The local politicians also knew that if they in any way displeased Ford, he might transfer its assembly plants elsewhere.[74] The tarring and feathering of CIO organizer Herbert Harris by Ford Servicemen in August 1937 climaxed weeks of fist maulings, whippings, and kidnappings in Dallas, in which at least twenty-five CIO sympathizers were injured. Ford Servicemen assaulted UAW-CIO attorney W. J. Houston at noon in the heart of Dallas's business district, knocking him to the pavement and kicking him in the head, stomach, and groin. After his release from the hospital, Houston closed his office and left Dallas. Servicemen abducted a man they suspected was a UAW member in front of his wife, drove him to an isolated spot, and administered "50 licks." Ford thugs smashed the face of union organizer George Baer with blackjacks, knocking out several teeth and blinding him in one eye. Dallas police not only did nothing to stop the assaults, they also assisted Ford Servicemen in tracking down labor organizers. None of the Servicemen involved in the beatings was ever punished.[75]

Ford Servicemen, some imported from Dearborn, terminated the UAW effort in Memphis in less than two months. In September 1937 UAW organizer Norman Smith opened an office in Memphis and announced his intention to organize its Ford plant. City officials, however, declared they would not tolerate CIO organizers. A month after his arrival, six or seven Ford thugs dragged Smith from his car and beat him over the head with hammers and pistol butts, fracturing his skull and nearly killing him. Memphis police made no arrests, despite having eyewitness reports and the assailants' car license number. When Smith recovered from the beating, the UAW withdrew him from Memphis.[76]

Bennett escalated his war against the UAW-CIO in 1938 by ordering the kidnapping of Walter Reuther, leader of Detroit's large West Side local. Reuther had just led a successful strike against Federal Screw, a Ford parts supplier in Detroit. The evening after the settlement, two of Bennett's hirelings, with drawn revolvers, burst into Reuther's apartment, shouting, "Okay, Red, you're coming with us!" Fortunately for Reuther, he had invited a large group of friends over to celebrate his sister-in-law's birthday (Sophie was the wife of brother Victor). One of them quite defiantly told the gunmen that they could shoot some of them, but they themselves would not escape. When another guest slipped out the window and called for help, the gunmen fled. Fearing that Bennett had marked them for death, Walter and Victor Reuther both purchased .38 revolvers to protect themselves. For a long time afterward, Sophie Reuther carried Victor's revolver under her apron when she took the garbage out to the alley.[77]

Bennett's violent tactics, while stalling the Ford organizing drive for a time, in the long run strengthened the union's resolve, increased its public support, and precipitated federal intervention on its behalf. The UAW could now portray itself as fighting not just for recognition and better wages and job conditions, but for democracy and civilized values, for freedom of speech and assembly, for basic human dignity. It was able to portray its opponent as fundamentally "un-American," an "industrial autocracy" that openly defied the Wagner Act, suppressing its workers' civil liberties with the methods of European fascism. Days after the Battle of the Overpass, the UAW announced that "Fordism is really gangsterism, fascism, and feudalism." It labeled the Service Department as "Ford's Gestapo" and "Dearborn's Blackshirts" and portrayed Servicemen as troglodytes.[78] The UAW prominently featured the battered faces and black eyes of its organizers on its recruiting leaflets.[79] Making the UAW's accusation that Ford was "fascist" even more credible were Henry Ford's rabid antisemitism and membership in the America First Committee, and Harry Bennett's financial contributions to Gerald L. K. Smith's antisemitic and pro-fascist radio broadcasts. Walter Reuther later reported that Bennett had owned a swastika banner and a "Gestapo control map."[80]

The Battle of the Overpass itself provided inspiration to UAW activists impressed with the courage of those who had survived ferocious beatings; along with the sit-down strikes at GM and Chrysler that same year, the battle allowed the UAW to claim almost immediately a "heroic past." It became the UAW's "Alamo," and the memory of it helped energize the second Ford organizing drive that began in 1940. Bennett's Servicemen failed in their effort to destroy all the photographic evidence of the assaults, and pictures of the bloodied but defiant Reuther and Frankensteen were widely circulated in the mass media. Doug Fraser recalled that years afterward, when he spoke at retired auto workers' meetings in Florida, "every Ford worker [would] come up . . . and say, 'I was on the Overpass with Walter!'" Of course, as Fraser noted, "if all those wonderful people [had been] on that Overpass with Walter, that goddamn bridge would have collapsed."[81]

Bennett's use of violence was so overt, his disregard of the Wagner Act so blatant, that the federal government entered the fray on the side of the union. After the Battle of the Overpass, the NLRB issued a sweeping condemnation of Ford's labor tactics, and ordered the company to "cease and desist" discouraging unionization by assaulting and discharging workers. The NLRB also found Ford guilty of unfair labor practices at many of the assembly plants, including Dallas; St. Louis; Kansas City; Somerville, Massachusetts; and Long Beach, California. After a series of appeals, the NLRB decisions were upheld by the U.S. Supreme Court in February 1941, providing further substantiation for the UAW's claim that it championed "Americanism" against a company that denied workers the basic rights of citizenship. "Uncle Sam Cracks Down on Ford," proclaimed one UAW leaflet.[82]

Bennett's systematic use of violence at River Rouge and the assembly plants had brought a halt to the UAW's Ford organizing drive by early 1938. But by the fall of 1940, when the UAW resumed the campaign, it was a battle-tested organization much better prepared for Bennett. It had won at least partial recognition from every major auto manufacturer and parts supplier. It had beaten Ford's two leading rivals, GM and Chrysler, in dramatic sit-down strikes. By 1940 several Detroit-area locals had formed defense forces known as "flying squadrons" trained to protect pickets from assault. They also had established field hospital units, with volunteer doctors and nurses, to care for their wounded during a strike.[83]

Detroit's Federal Screw strike in 1938 had highlighted the UAW's new fighting capabilities. UAW members armed only with bricks and bottles had fought in the streets for hours against hordes of mounted police in what came to be known as the "Battle of Bloody Run."[84] So brave and proficient were the unionists that "more scabs and police went to the hospital that day than pickets." Teamsters' leader Jimmy Hoffa, who was already known as a tough streetbrawler, told Walter Reuther after he witnessed the battle, "I liked the way your boys handled themselves." He was allegedly so impressed with their fighting prowess that he asked Reuther if he could bring his Teamsters' local into the UAW.[85]

Bennett was nonetheless so confident his huge mercenary army could beat back the UAW-CIO's second challenge to Ford that he all but forced a strike. Expressing his disdain for both the union and the NLRB, he announced that Ford would "bargain" if the NLRB decreed it had to, but added, "We will bargain until hell freezes over and give the union nothing."[86] Two weeks later, when Bennett discharged eight UAW-CIO leaders at the Rouge, causing a spontaneous walkout of 50,000 workers, the union leadership officially declared a strike. One of the union's principal demands was the abolition of the Ford Service Department.

Both Bennett and the union leadership knew that neither a sit-down strike nor a strike relying on conventional picket lines could succeed at River Rouge. Only two buildings in the vast complex were near public streets where strikers could receive food and necessary supplies from sympathizers on the outside. And Bennett had made sure that in those buildings, heavy fencing barred the windows facing the streets. To prevent strikers from picketing, he had positioned groups of armed Servicemen at the gates, and placed machine guns on nearby roofs. But the union, by barricading the incoming highways with cars at key intersections away from the Rouge, nonetheless succeeded in shutting down the plant.[87]

The prospects for bloodshed were greater than ever at the Rouge because Bennett made a concerted effort to provoke interracial violence. His purpose was not only to undermine labor solidarity but to force the governor to intervene and break the strike with state troops. The potential for interracial conflict was very real, because Ford was widely admired in Detroit's African American community for providing it with vastly more job opportunities than any other auto manufacturer. Ford's Detroit-area plants employed almost half the blacks in the entire industry.[88] The high esteem Ford enjoyed among African Americans was enhanced by its donations to black churches, and its reliance on black preachers to recruit workers. As a result, the great majority of Detroit's black ministers were anti-union.[89] Bennett had even delegated significant managerial responsibility to an African American, Donald Marshall, whom he placed in charge of hiring and disciplining black workers.[90] Bennett distributed propaganda to black workers claiming that blacks were not welcome in UAW-CIO plants. He also made an outright appeal to antisemitism by having his Servicemen tell black workers that the UAW-CIO was dominated by nefarious Jews.[91]

The UAW-CIO indeed feared that racial antagonisms might sabotage its organizing campaign and strike, and it placed considerable emphasis on recruiting black workers. The union assigned seven salaried black organizers to the Ford campaign. They argued that Ford ran the Rouge like an "industrial plantation," where most blacks were relegated to the least desirable jobs, and that it maintained a "lily-white" hiring policy in the satellite plants. National NAACP director Walter White came to Detroit to build up support for the strike in the black community. The world-famous singer and black activist Paul Robeson also strongly urged black workers to join the UAW-CIO, and he sang at a mass strike rally.[92]

Bennett's plan to foment a "race war" became apparent on the first day of the strike. While many blacks joined the walkout, between 1,500 and 2,500 remained inside the plant. Most of them appear to have been recent migrants from the South whom Ford had hired to offset the UAW-CIO's gains in the last few months. Some were Detroit Golden Gloves and Diamond Belt boxers, hastily recruited by Bennett. Bennett organized these men into "attack squads" under Sam Taylor's direction. Taylor armed them with iron clubs, crowbars, knives, and razor blades, and several times sent them out to assault the mostly white pickets who had moved close to the plant. Fifty strikers were injured; one was stabbed five times, another had both arms broken. Again, Dearborn police would not intervene to stop the violence.[93]

Bennett soon found himself embroiled in a bitter conflict within top Ford management. Henry Ford from the outset had urged Bennett to fight it out with the union, to arm strikebreakers and to use tear gas. Edsel Ford, however, pleaded for the company to negotiate with the union. Even more important, Henry Ford's wife, fearing that Bennett's handling the strike would produce massive bloodshed and rioting, insisted that Ford agree to the UAW-CIO's terms. One Ford executive claimed that she threatened to leave him if he did not.[94]

Union solidarity, strong public support for the strike, and the disarray within Ford management led Henry Ford to capitulate to the UAW-CIO after only ten days. In the NLRB election that followed, Ford workers chose the UAW-CIO to represent them by an overwhelming margin. The union won the best settlement ever in the auto industry. Ford became the first auto manufacturer to grant the union shop, and the first to grant the dues checkoff. While the company did not abolish the Service Department, it did agree to put Servicemen in uniform, making spying more difficult.[95] Bennett blamed Edsel Ford's weakness for the company's defeat. His angry

*African American strikebreakers, near a gate, battle strikers, River Rouge plant, Ford strike, April 1941. Courtesy of the Walter P. Reuther Library, Wayne State University.*

comment that the outcome "is a great victory for the Communist party" revealed his unwillingness to accept unionism as legitimate.[96]

During World War II, conflict within Ford management intensified as a result of Bennett's unstable approach to labor relations, his personal profiteering at company expense, and the confusion and disorder at the Rouge plant, caused in part by Bennett's firing of key production executives.[97] Walter Reuther declared that Bennett was a "chief stumbling block to honest collective bargaining."[98] One UAW-CIO official described Bennett as a "psychopath." Union representatives entering his office for a meeting might find him hiding behind the door, waiting to scare them with an incendiary device, or leaning back in his chair blasting away at a target with a pistol. Victor Reuther recalled, "If he was in an ugly mood, no matter how just your grievances were, screw it!"[99] Edsel Ford and other executives also knew that Bennett "had a real racket going," stealing parts from the company and selling them on the black market.[100]

Partly blaming Bennett for Edsel Ford's premature death in 1943, and fearing that he might gain effective control of the company after Henry Ford died, Edsel's widow Eleanor Ford and his son Henry Ford II moved against him in 1945. Henry Ford II met secretly with anti-Bennett executives at the downtown Detroit Club; they could not meet in Dearborn because the entire city was honeycombed with Bennett's spies.[101] By threatening to sell her family's stock holdings, 42 percent of the company's total, Eleanor Ford forced an ailing Henry Ford to yield control of the company to his grandson, Henry Ford II. Within ten minutes of assuming the presidency, Henry Ford II fired a stunned Bennett. In a wholesale purge of Bennett's supporters, Henry Ford II in the next nine months fired, demoted, or transferred more than 1,000 employees.[102]

With the departure of Bennett, labor relations at Ford were significantly transformed. Edsel's widow confided to Walter Reuther that she had known that stable labor relations could never exist at Ford until Bennett was removed.[103] Henry Ford II shared his father's view that the company should accept a permanent collective bargaining relationship with the UAW. By 1947 UAW leaders detected some improvement in Ford's labor policy: "While serving no tea and crumpets, [Ford] at least wears no brass knuckles."[104] In 1949 Ford became the first auto company to agree to a pension plan for its production workers, and by the late 1960s the UAW considered its labor relations the least objectionable of the Big Three.[105]

Bennett harbored bitter feelings about the Ford Company for the rest of his life, some of which he devoted to organized crime activity. He never held another position in corporate management. Shortly after he was fired, he moved to Palm Springs, California, where he had long maintained a residence, built for him by workers from the Long Beach, California, Ford plant. In Palm Springs, Bennett gathered together several of his former Servicemen, including Dallas's "Fats" Perry, and seized control of the local gambling syndicate, which he ran for many years.[106] In 1951 he told a UAW organizer he encountered in Detroit that "he never knew how good Chevrolet cars were," and that he kept seven of them on his California ranch.[107] Twenty years later, Bennett was still engaging in the tough-guy posturing he had used at Ford to mask his feelings of insecurity. A visitor asked Bennett about a story that John Bugas, the ex-FBI agent whom Henry Ford II had appointed to direct labor relations after firing Bennett, had wrested a gun from him in 1945. Bennett angrily denied it, and boasted, "I'll meet him any place today and give him or anyone else $1000 if he can take a gun from me."[108] Increasingly isolated, he spent his declining years in a California nursing home, where a nurse recalled "once in a while he would sing old songs of the sea."[109]

Harry Bennett's career dramatically illustrates the centrality of violence and espionage to management's campaign to disrupt union organizing and break strikes in America's most "modern" industry in the decades before World War II. The Bull Connors and Sheriff Jim Clarks, who relied on massive physical intimidation to protect the South's Jim Crow system, had their counterpart in Bennett, who used similar methods to preserve the nonunion shop at Ford. His vast mercenary army guarded the world's largest industrial complex, and one of its most technologically advanced, and it ran Dearborn as dictatorially as any company mining town or southern lumber camp. It unleashed bloody assaults in broad daylight on the streets of major American cities. When Bennett died in 1979, the *Detroit News* called him a "feared and hated man"; the UAW's Emil Mazey described him as "without compassion or human understanding."[110] He stood at the pinnacle of power in one of America's leading industrial enterprises; his actions always enjoyed Henry Ford's enthusiastic support. His methods differed only in degree from those of the other auto manufacturers who also engaged in widespread labor espionage, relying on municipal police, rather than private armies, to physically intimidate workers. Looking back in 1993 on the UAW's organizing efforts of the 1930s, Victor Reuther observed, "It's amazing and it never ceases to astound me, that despite all of the violence, espionage, [and] the enormity of the forces that were allied against us, that we prevailed."[111]

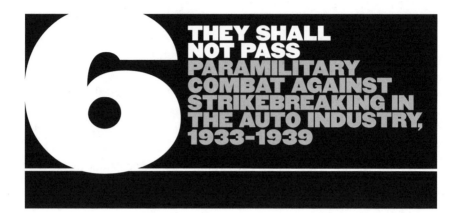

# 6 THEY SHALL NOT PASS PARAMILITARY COMBAT AGAINST STRIKEBREAKING IN THE AUTO INDUSTRY, 1933-1939

In February 1937 during the sit-down strike at General Motors (GM) in Flint, Michigan, auto unionists presented a "living newspaper" pageant before thousands of enthusiastic spectators, highlighting the formidable obstacles they overcame in their struggle to organize. In one scene, a woman dramatically exposed a stool pigeon. In another, the police and company vigilantes attacked the men occupying the Chevy 9 plant with tear gas, while outside members of the union's Women's Emergency Brigade rushed to protect the sit-downers by breaking windows to let in air. The battle of Chevy 4, the climactic event of the strike, in which unionists seized a key engine plant, was depicted in two mass scenes showing men storming the gates as members of the Women's Emergency Brigade locked arms behind them to slow the police advance.[1]

Fiercely determined to prevent unionization, the auto manufacturers and their parts suppliers developed sophisticated and extensive espionage systems and assembled formidable arsenals of tear gas and firearms, which they shared with municipal police departments in the Detroit area and Flint, active agents in the anti-union campaign. Management's commitment to use violence to derail the union effort, its ability to employ the police as an anti-union instrument, and GM's mobilization of vigilante armies in Flint and Anderson, Indiana, precipitated a seemingly endless series of physical confrontations with those attempting to organize the industry.

Auto unionists responded by elaborating a dramatic new strike technique, the sit-down, which had recently been introduced by their Committee for Industrial Organization (CIO) colleagues in the rubber tire industry, and by forming paramilitary groups called Flying Squadrons, of which the Women's Emergency Brigade was the best known.[2] Many early leaders of the United Automobile Workers union (UAW-CIO), including the Reuther brothers, Walter, Victor, and Roy, gained the trust and respect of auto workers by assuming a prominent role in streetfighting against company forces.

The UAW-CIO could not organize auto workers without developing means to combat effectively the police and vigilante violence inspired by management and overcome the pervasive fear engendered by espionage in the plants. When he joined a union in the auto industry, a worker risked not only his job but often his physical safety, even after the passage of the Wagner Act. As a result, the success of an organizing campaign or strike usually depended on a small minority of committed activists. Most workers remained on the sideline until they determined that the union's chances were highly favorable. Even during the 1936–37 GM sit-down strike, only a small percentage of workers occupied the plants, while most—in Flint and across the country—continued to go to work each morning. When the UAW-CIO began its sit-down strike at Chrysler in March 1937, Dodge Local 3 had recruited only 800 out of a work force of 24,000.[3] With most workers sitting on the fence, the collapse of a picket line and a panicky retreat under a police charge, the failure to position sufficient forces at the right plant gates to discourage the entry of strikebreakers, or significant desertions by men sitting down in a plant could easily doom the union's chances.

The auto companies' labor recruitment policy was designed to discourage unionization. They deliberately drew much of their labor force from the South, which was almost entirely nonunion, believing that workers from that region were more docile. The South's rigid caste barriers and limited opportunity for upward mobility encouraged deference toward employers, and management also benefited from the southern worker's lack of familiarity with unions. The proportion of southerners in auto was probably the highest of any major industry. Beginning in the 1920s, the auto manufacturers sent labor agents into the South in a quest for "safe workers" and also advertised extensively on the radio and in newspapers in the southern coal regions and textile towns. These efforts drew large numbers of "gawky mountaineers . . . and stolid plough hands" to Detroit, many arriving on company-chartered buses, with the result that by the 1930s "the southern drawl [was] as common [there] as in Arkansas." No one had a better chance of being hired in auto in Detroit or Flint than "a Southerner with an unsophisticated mien." Labor writer Louis Adamic told of a man he knew who, determined to obtain a job in an auto plant, "practiced up on the Southern dialect and drawl," appeared at the factory gate, and "was hired as soon as he opened his mouth."[4]

Auto unionists did benefit, however, from the industry-wide policy of refusing to hire men over forty years of age, who they believed were physically incapable of keeping up with the assembly line. The labor force remained overwhelmingly young because of the temporary suspension of production for annual model changes; when plants resumed operations, younger men had priority over older in rehiring. Older men in auto often applied shoe polish to conceal gray hair, but anyone still employed over the age of forty was likely to be a stool pigeon or to have performed some favor for the company.[5] Yet auto's youthful labor force provided the union with men eager and strong enough to fight vigorously with police and vigilantes on the picket lines and in the streets, allowing it to engage in effective paramilitary actions during strikes.

The large population of white southern migrants in the Michigan and northern Ohio auto manufacturing centers provided the basis for the emergence of the Black Legion, an anti-labor terrorist organization of 60,000 to 100,000 members, which helped create a climate of fear that inhibited organizing between 1933 and 1936. The Black Legion was the largest and most formidable domestic fascist group in the 1930s. Founded in Bellaire, Ohio, in late 1924 or early 1925 by men hoping to revitalize the local Ku Klux Klan (KKK) chapter, it soon evolved into a movement in its own right that supplanted the KKK in four contiguous states of the Midwest: Michigan, Ohio, Indiana, and Illinois.[6] The Black Legion substituted black robes for white and added a skull and crossbones to the hood, but it shared with the KKK a hatred of Jews, Catholics, and African Americans. Even though its members were largely of rural southern origin, because it emerged in midwestern centers of heavy industry, the Black Legion developed a more strongly anti-labor orientation than the KKK. The Black Legion was organized along semimilitary lines, with armed members grouped into divisions led by colonels and captains, reflecting a commitment to violence that surpassed even that of the KKK.[7]

During the Depression years of the early 1930s the Black Legion greatly expanded its membership, recruiting tens of thousands of southern migrants thrown into competition with workers of southern and eastern European background and African Americans for the diminishing number of jobs in auto. From 1932 to 1935, the Black Legion's new leader, Virgil H. Effinger, a former KKK Grand Titan from Ohio, supervised a massive recruiting effort. The Black Legion was able to establish sizable chapters in nearly all of the major auto manufacturing centers in Michigan and northern Ohio, including Detroit (about 6,400 members), Pontiac (3,200 members), Flint (more than 2,000 members), and Toledo (3,000 members).[8]

But it was not the Black Legion's size so much as its propensity for violence and its ability to gain recruits among police officers and city and county politicians that made it a significant menace to union organizing efforts. Its members also cooperated closely with the espionage systems of the auto companies. The chief of the espionage staff at Hudson, for example, belonged to the Black Legion, as did many of the plant informers. Some Black Legion members also worked for Dawn Patrol, a leading labor spy firm in Detroit. The Michigan state director of Private Employment Agencies was a Black Legion sympathizer, who placed members of the group in auto factories as labor spies.[9]

The sympathy it enjoyed among both police chiefs and ordinary patrolmen greatly facilitated the Black Legion's extensive campaign of violence against auto union organizers and strikers. The police rarely bothered to investigate Black Legion atrocities. A considerable number, perhaps 100, of Detroit's policemen were members of the Black Legion, including possibly Detroit's fiercely anti-labor police chief, Heinrich Pickert. In the fall of 1936 it was revealed that the police chief of Pontiac, Michigan, a major GM production center, along with thirteen of his patrolmen, belonged to the Black Legion, as did the sergeant in charge of the police arsenal in Toledo. The prosecutor of Oakland County, where Pontiac was located, along with his entire staff, had joined the Black Legion, as had dozens of other county and municipal officials in Michigan and northern Ohio.[10]

The Black Legion also drew recruits from the supervisory staff in the auto plants, providing a further obstacle to workers attempting to organize. At GM's Fisher Body 1 plant in Flint a worker, late on a Saturday afternoon, stumbled on a group of foremen putting on their black robes and hoods. Plant management handed the worker a long layoff as a warning to keep silent.[11]

The police never made any arrests in the Black Legion murders of auto unionists George Marchuk of the Communist-led Automobile Workers Union, shot in the head and dumped in a vacant lot in December 1933, and John Bielak, a young American Federation of Labor (AFL) organizer at Hudson, who was "taken for a ride," beaten, and then shot five times the day after he led a work stoppage in the metal finishing department. There was no mistaking that Bielak had been murdered as a warning to other

*Persons model Black Legion robes and display Black Legion weaponry, May 23, 1936. Courtesy of the Walter P. Reuther Library, Wayne State University.*

labor organizers—the killers placed a stack of union membership applications under his head. Isaac White, a Black Legion brigadier general and former Detroit police officer, had twice warned Bielak to desist from his union organizing activities at Hudson. Nor did the police ever seriously investigate the Black Legion's flogging of three Automobile Workers Union activists in Pontiac in 1931.[12]

During the 1935 Motor Products strike in Detroit, the Black Legion bombed the headquarters of United Automobile Workers Local 89, one of the three participating unions, and the homes of six strikers. Local 89's secretary had left the headquarters only fifteen minutes before it was blown up. Black Legion members also threatened strikers with beatings unless they stayed away from the picket lines. Some strikers dared not go home at night "without a bodyguard, or a fast car and a good gun."[13]

The Black Legion collapsed in the wake of the sensational revelations about its terrorist activities that grew out of the highly publicized trials and convictions of some fifty of its members in 1936 and 1937. The men were put on trial as a result of information provided to the police by a Black Legion triggerman named Dayton J. Dean, whom they had linked to the murder of an unemployed auto worker named Charles Poole in May 1936. Like the KKK, the Black Legion considered itself an enforcer of proper moral conduct, and Dean and several other members had whipped and then murdered Poole, a Catholic, allegedly because he was rumored to have beaten his pregnant Protestant wife. Because Poole was not, and had never been, a union organizer or activist, the police made a serious attempt to solve the crime. Their investigation led them to Dean, who implicated the Black Legion in various murders, bombings, and floggings directed against unionists and minorities. Most of the sixteen men indicted for Poole's murder were from the Tennessee and Kentucky hills or the Deep South. When legal proceedings had finally ended in 1939, thirteen members of the Black Legion had received life imprisonment for murder, including Dean, and thirty-seven more were serving prison sentences up to twenty years.[14]

Dean, who had put five bullets into Poole, confessed that in 1935 he had, on the order of Black Legion commanders, plotted the assassination of Maurice Sugar, a Detroit lawyer heavily involved in the early auto organizing efforts, who became the UAW-CIO's leading attorney in 1936. For four and a half months, Dean had rented an apartment in the building where Sugar had lived, waiting for the proper opportunity to strike. Dean's superiors had directed him to explode a bomb at the door of Sugar's apartment, but he claimed to have ultimately rejected the idea for fear of killing others in the building. Dean instead attempted to lure Sugar to a remote location to discuss a case and kill him there, but the plan failed because Sugar made it a practice to see prospective clients only in his office.[15]

The numerous anti-labor atrocities revealed in the Black Legion terrorism trials of 1936 generated greater public sympathy for the campaign to organize the auto industry, convincing many that labor was being unfairly victimized by sinister, anti-democratic forces. Newspaper coverage was largely unfavorable to the Black Legion, as was Hollywood, which condemned the "murderous cult" in a motion picture starring Humphrey Bogart and Ann Sheridan.[16] The unfavorable media publicity surrounding the Black Legion during the trials in the summer and fall of 1936 undoubtedly contributed to the election of a strongly pro-labor governor, Frank Murphy, in November 1936, which was critical to the success of the UAW-CIO's sit-down strikes against GM and Chrysler in early 1937.[17]

The Black Legion's sharp decline after the terrorism trials of 1936 hardly eliminated the threat of physical reprisal against those organizing or joining the UAW-CIO, and a climate of fear persisted at least until American entry into World War II, keeping many auto workers out of the union ranks. Even the UAW-CIO expressed concern that the Black Legion was not yet dead and might reemerge as a dangerous anti-union force, a view shared by leading civil libertarians in Michigan. The head cook for the UAW-CIO at the Fisher Body 1 plant during the 1937 GM sit-down strike recalled that: "What really scared my gals in the kitchen was that the Black Legion would march on Flint."[18]

That GM management itself had drawn lessons from the Black Legion about the efficacy of violence in combating unionism became evident in 1939 during the La Follette Committee hearings in the U.S. Senate on unfair labor practices. The committee uncovered correspondence in which Harry Anderson, GM's vice president in charge of personnel, advised a leading executive of the DuPont corporation concerned about CIO organizing: "Maybe you could use a little Black Legion down in your country. It might help."[19]

In Detroit, Police Commissioner Heinrich Pickert, a Black Legion sympathizer who was widely believed to be a member, was determined to disrupt the UAW-CIO organizing campaign, which began in earnest in 1936. When the 1936 trials focused national attention on the Black Legion, Pickert hastily promoted any police officer who might implicate him as having been associated with it. A former army brigadier general, Pickert assumed charge of Detroit's police force in 1934 and immediately reorganized it along military lines. Civil libertarians expressed alarm over the "military character" of the Detroit Police Department under Commissioner Pickert, and its "brutality and partisanship [to management]." They decried police "interference with the showing of films and distribution of literature sympathetic to labor."[20]

The UAW-CIO and its supporters continually accused the Detroit police of using excessive force against pickets, of illegally seizing and impounding union sound cars, and refusing to investigate the bombings of union halls and union activists' homes, as had been the case in the 1935 Motor Products strike. Leonard Woodcock recalled that "violence on the picket lines was endemic" in Detroit, and the "use of mounted police [against strikers] was routine and expected."[21] When UAW-CIO West Side Local 174 acquired a sound truck, it could not find a garage for it, because it was widely assumed it would be a bombing target. As a result, various members had to guard it in round the clock shifts. One very cold night a shivering Bob Kanter, who was guarding the sound truck, decided to leave it briefly to get a cup of coffee. He had taken just a few steps when a concealed time bomb exploded, totally destroying the truck. Kanter recalled that had he been inside the truck he would have been decapitated, because "a chunk of the transmission case came through the floor board and out the roof." The next day the police arrested Kanter, claiming he had planted the bomb to gain publicity for the union.[22]

UAW-CIO activists and civil libertarians accused Commissioner Pickert of harboring fascist sympathies. They cited two occasions when he ordered his men to disperse pickets at the German consulate as they peacefully protested Nazi persecution of Jews. In December 1934 two of Pickert's patrolmen baited a young Jewish butcher with antisemitic and pro-Hitler remarks, and then shot him to death when, brandishing a plunger, he ordered them out of his shop. Further evidence of Pickert's fascist leanings was provided when his censors prevented the showing of the pro-Loyalist Spanish Civil War movie *Blockade*. Detroit was the only major American city whose theaters did not present it. (Police censorship also resulted in *Blockade*'s withdrawal from Flint after its opening performance.) Pickert's friend Charles Coughlin, the fiercely anti–New Deal, antisemitic radio priest, praised him as the "strong man" Detroit needed to keep it free of radicalism.[23]

The Detroit Police Department and the auto companies openly cooperated during strikes, and provided reciprocal services. For example, during the 1935 Motor Products strike, the company stabled mounted policemen's horses within its gates for three weeks, set up a dining room for the police, and replated 1,300 policemen's badges and 1,300 pairs of police handcuffs. The police afforded strikebreakers protection by driving them home. The police, or company thugs, killed a striker and fractured another's skull, and the police seriously injured twenty-four. Police disrupted the funeral procession of the slain striker, driving alongside it in a car with machine guns sticking out and making it move at thirty-five miles per hour.[24]

The Conference for the Protection of Civil Rights, a coalition that included Michigan AFL unions, the Detroit Building Trades Council, and the American Civil Liberties Union, declared that the Detroit police department had employed "strong arm tactics worthy of Hitler" against the strikers. It accused the police of clubbing and tear gassing without provocation, and breaking up the picket line, "abolish[ing] the civil rights guaranteed by the First Amendment."[25]

Detroit's press devoted little attention to police brutality against auto union organizers and strikers, because the city's major newspapers—the *Detroit Free Press*, the evening *Detroit News*, and Hearst's *Detroit Times*—were, like those in the smaller Michigan towns, strongly anti-union. Union activists compared the *Free Press* with the *Los Angeles Times*, a "vicious, labor-hating sheet."[26] Leonard Woodcock recalled that his family was so disgusted with the *Free Press* that it terminated its subscription. When the *Free Press* subscription agent came to the Woodcocks' home to inquire why the family had stopped taking the newspaper, the Woodcocks told him, "Well, 'cause you don't tell the news." The *Free Press* had made no mention of the Motor Products strike in which Woodcock's father had participated. The subscription agent replied, "We can't print such things, because it'll spread. That sort of thing will spread."[27]

The *Free Press*, *News*, and *Times* similarly neglected to cover the 1933 strike against Briggs, which produced auto bodies for Ford, until the resulting interruption in supply forced the closure of the latter's massive River Rouge complex. Then the three newspapers printed front-page articles designed to undermine the strikers' morale. They implied that the strikers were drifting back to work, highlighted Communist involvement in the strike, and referred to the union's demands as "pleas." On a day when a picket line of 2,500 held fast under repeated police charges, the *Detroit Times* reported, "Briggs Pickets Routed." When a policeman wrested an American flag from a picket, tearing it from its staff as he did so, no headline read "Police Tear Down American Flag." Unionists' frequent visits to the editorial offices to request press coverage of strikes or more balanced treatment were ineffectual.[28]

Pervasive espionage in the plants constituted a formidable obstacle to unionization. Ford established its own spy organization, the Service Department, directed by Harry Bennett, discussed in the previous chapter.

But GM, Chrysler, and the parts suppliers also became extensively involved in espionage, especially after the passage of the National Industrial Recovery Act in 1933, whose Section 7A granted workers the right to organize, stimulated interest in unionism. GM was the most important industrial client of the Pinkerton Detective Agency, the largest labor spying contractor in the country, and had as many as 200 of its agents working for it at various times between 1933 and 1936. Supplementing them were hirelings from at least thirteen other detective agencies. The La Follette Committee concluded that GM's spy system had wrecked the AFL federal unions that tried to gain a foothold before the UAW-CIO was formed, and had forced organizing efforts underground.[29]

According to Genora Dollinger, leader of the Women's Emergency Brigade during the 1936–37 GM sit-down strike, "real terror" gripped Flint because of the corporation's espionage system. UAW-CIO organizing meetings were often held in the pitch dark in workers' homes, so that spies could not identify those in attendance. Poker parties were also sometimes used as a cover. A UAW-CIO member seeking to recruit a man who seemed interested in the union never knew whether he was a company spy, just drawing him out in order to report him. Plant police "were always circling around watching the men suspected of unionism and anyone coming to their homes." Those whom spies identified as unionists were often beaten up or had "accidents" happen to them.[30]

Unionists charged that Chrysler Corporation, which replaced Ford in 1936 as second in national automobile sales, behind GM, maintained "one of the most vicious and unspeakable spy systems ever employed in industry." Chrysler relied almost entirely on the Corporations Auxiliary Service, one of the nation's largest and oldest labor espionage agencies. Originally headquartered in Cleveland, Corporations Auxiliary had infiltrated union ranks in the auto and rubber tire industries since the early 1910s. Unlike Waddell and Mahon, Bergoff Brothers, or Baldwin-Felts, also active during the 1910s, Corporations Auxiliary never furnished gunmen or strikebreakers but concentrated exclusively on spying. Labor journalist John Kenneth Turner credited it with breaking the Akron rubber strike in 1913. Even though the Akron Rubber Workers Union, which led the strike, deliberately held its organizational meeting outside Akron, in Barberton, Ohio, to protect against labor spies, half of its charter members were Corporations Auxiliary agents. From the day it was chartered until after the strike, Corporations Auxiliary agents held all but one of the union's offices, including president, vice president, and secretary. These men deliberately stimulated racial antagonism in the union ranks to undermine strike solidarity and turned over the names of union members to management.[31]

Between 1933 and 1936 Chrysler Corporation was one of the leading corporate spenders for labor spying, paying Corporations Auxiliary over $275,000. Walter Chrysler, Chrysler Corporation's chief executive, had hired Corporations Auxiliary to conduct labor espionage as early as 1911 or 1912, when he was president of Buick. Corporations Auxiliary concentrated on placing its agents in union secretarial positions in order to gain access to the meeting minutes; it managed to do so in Chrysler's key Local 7, UAW-CIO, in Detroit.[32]

That Corporations Auxiliary had penetrated the ranks of the top union leadership from the very beginning of the effort to organize Chrysler's Dodge workers in Detroit in 1933 was dramatically revealed in November 1936, when the La Follette Committee identified Johnny Andrews as a company spy. Andrews was one of the closest friends of Richard Frankensteen, leader of Dodge Local 3, UAW-CIO. Andrews worked in the paint department at Dodge Main and attended all of Local 3's meetings when it first organized as an AFL federal union. Because of fear of company spies, the local met in a "deserted blind pig," where it was so cold the men had to deliberate in overcoats. When the local's officers were first selected, Andrews wrote the names of those nominated on a blackboard, so that he could remember them. Andrews himself was elected vice president. As a result, Chrysler immediately learned the identities of the leading activists, and the next day fired several of the officers. Andrews was among the local's most militant members, "hot all the time about not taking anything from the company." Like many company spies, he acted as a provocateur, often calling for a strike at union meetings. Frankensteen asked him "to cool off, because his inflammatory statements weren't helping the union."[33]

Andrews's wife also became a close friend of Frankensteen's wife, and the two couples became inseparable, even sharing a lake cottage together when they vacationed. All the while, Andrews turned in a daily written report to Corporations Auxiliary, detailing "where [Frankensteen] went, who [he] spoke to, what [he] said [and] everything [he] did." Andrews invited his uncle and his aunt to the vacation cottage the couples rented to meet Frankensteen. Frankensteen recalled that they "just feted us and treated us royally," taking him and his wife to dinner every night. He was very impressed with the uncle's knowledge of the labor movement. But Frankensteen was later stunned to learn that the man Andrews had introduced as his uncle was in reality the head of Corporations Auxiliary, who had come to investigate personally organizing efforts at Chrysler; nor was his wife his friend's aunt.[34]

Frankensteen was amazed when he came to Washington, D.C., to testify before the La Follette Committee about unfair labor practices in the auto industry, and investigators asked him to identify Andrews's spy reports to Chrysler. Andrews and his wife promptly disappeared and were never heard from again. Frankensteen figured, however, that they moved elsewhere and "did the same work for Corporations Auxiliary in another plant."[35]

Labor espionage was a serious impediment to organizing not only at the Big Three but with Detroit's parts suppliers as well. On the eve of the UAW-CIO's first sit-down in Detroit at Midland Steel, which made steel body frames for Chrysler and Ford, secretary-treasurer George Addes learned from the La Follette Committee that the plant's chief steward and leading union recruiter was a company spy. Doug Fraser recalled that labor spies had him fired from his first two jobs in the auto industry, at Bryant Motors and Everhot Heating Company. At Bryant, Fraser "asked the wrong person to sign a [union] membership card" in the very early stages of an organizing campaign. Company spies at Everhot, suspecting he was involved in organizing, actually broke into his tool box and found union membership cards he was planning to distribute.[36]

The UAW-CIO also had to contend with the auto companies' use of "missionaries," spies assigned to workers' neighborhoods rather than the plants, where they spread anti-strike propaganda, with the particular intention of undermining morale among unionists' wives. Missionaries, who were used in numerous industries, sometimes posed as sales agents for household appliances, furniture, vacuum cleaners, or anything that a man on strike could not afford to purchase for his wife. The wife might then blame the union for her inability to acquire the desired commodity. Women missionaries tried to frighten the wives of union members into thinking that the strike would destroy the family's ability to survive. They pretended to sell face cream door to door, claiming they had to eke out a living that way because their husbands had lost their jobs by participating in a strike.[37]

Auto companies not only hired spies from detective agencies like Pinkerton and Corporations Auxiliary but engaged the services of many of their own workers, for a much lesser sum. Some auto workers were driven to espionage by financial distress; others believed it would enhance their chances of promotion, or of avoiding a layoff. Management often preferred to approach the worker at home, in the presence of a wife, who, "tired of scrimping and doing without," would favor the opportunity for extra income. "Hooked men," as these spies were called, were usually more difficult to detect than agents of the professional spy agencies because they seldom made their reports in writing. Management could force a man to continue spying, even when he wanted to quit, by threatening him with exposure. The company often demanded a receipt from him when he was paid, and held that as evidence they employed him as a spy.[38]

The UAW-CIO leadership was well aware that the 1937 sit-down strikes against GM and Chrysler could succeed only if it neutralized the labor spies that had penetrated it. Only a very small group of leaders knew in advance of the plan to seize Chevy 4 in Flint, which proved the critical turning point in the strike. These few men did not discuss the plan in the regular leadership councils, which they knew had been "totally infiltrated" by Pinkerton agents. The plant targeted in these councils was Chevy 9, which was, sure enough, where GM concentrated its security forces, permitting a handful of unionists to seize Chevy 4, which made the engines for all Chevrolet plants in the United States.[39]

In the middle of the Flint strike, when the morale of the sit-downers and those on the picket line and doing kitchen work had sagged considerably, Roy Reuther energized the union rank and file by publicly unmasking a member of the strike committee as a Pinkerton spy, dramatically illustrating the perfidious tactics GM was using against them. Unionists considered the stool pigeon "worse than a cobra," and to emphasize his criminality the UAW-CIO took mug shots of anyone it discovered and mailed them to all affiliated locals around the country. Reuther led the spy to believe he was to receive a public tribute at the mass strike meeting for his union service and sat next to him on the stage. Before a packed hall, Reuther spoke of GM's efforts to undermine the UAW-CIO by sending infiltrators to sow discord in its ranks. He described the stool pigeon as the "lowest creature in the world" and then announced that there was one present at the meeting. Roy's brother Victor recalled that the crowd reacted with "almost the lynch spirit," and when the spy was clearly identified, "there was a move to rush him." The angry crowd was held back only by the trusted lieutenants Roy Reuther had placed on the stage. Reuther informed the spy that he would be escorted from the hall, under the union's protection, but was ordered to leave Flint "if you know what is best for you." Roy Reuther's dramatic exposure of the Pinkerton "built a spirit of determination and solidarity such as we hadn't experienced before," recalled Victor Reuther. But GM was undeterred in its commitment to use espionage as a strikebreaking weapon. The corporation sent the spy, under a new name, to Anderson, Indiana, where the UAW-CIO was also engaged in a sit-down.[40]

As in Flint, the leadership of the 1937 Chrysler sit-down strike had been infiltrated by company spies, and the UAW-CIO warned that they were spreading rumors designed to undermine the participants' morale. Local 3's *Dodge Main News* told the sit-downers to believe nothing they heard, unless it came directly from that newspaper or their chief shop stewards. But it became clear late in the strike that not even the latter could be trusted, when *Dodge Main News* reported that a chief shop steward who had acted as security chief for the sit-downers at Dodge Main was a company stool pigeon. During the strike, the union conducted all of its telephone communication from the occupied plants in a code that it changed daily, to ensure that company spies did not learn its plans.[41]

Perhaps the most dramatic development in the Chrysler sit-down strike was the union's discovery that the corporation's files contained extensive stool pigeon reports. Determined to publicly expose Chrysler's violation of the Wagner Act, UAW-CIO activists visited Governor Frank Murphy in Lansing, and dumped on his desk a bushel basket full of cards marked "Active in union; do not rehire," each with a worker's name and badge number.[42]

The UAW-CIO's success in organizing the auto industry was based in part on its effective use in 1936 and 1937 of the sit-down, which was designed to prevent the importation of strikebreakers, effectively shut down production, and neutralize the police as an anti-union weapon. Conventional strikes often collapsed when police charged picket lines, clubbing and arresting unionists. The sit-down reduced the prospects for violence, because the strikers were inside the plant, not outside where the police could attack them. It was also difficult for the union to marshal a sufficient number of strikers for twenty-four-hour picket duty, often in the cold and rain, enabling management to slip strikebreakers into plants at night. Many auto plants, like GM's Fisher Body 1 and Chevy 4 in Flint, or Dodge Main and Briggs-Mack in Detroit, were so large it required huge numbers of pickets to surround them. Morale was also generally highest in a sit-down, because close bonds developed among men living together twenty-four hours a day. In a conventional strike, by contrast, solidarity was somewhat interrupted when the participants went home each day. They were also more exposed to anti-strike rumors and propaganda outside the plant.[43]

An outraged management denounced the sit-down as an illegal interference in the rights of private property, but the UAW-CIO rejected the claim, insisting that the striker was merely protecting his own property, his job, from seizure by a strikebreaker and had no intention of taking any of the company's property. The union leadership warned sit-downers that anyone caught stealing or damaging company property would be brought before a special trial board and punished. In any event, the UAW-CIO believed that the sit-down was justified by company tactics, which included espionage, blacklisting, the use of municipal police as a strikebreaking weapon, and the spending of huge sums on anti-strike advertisements in the newspapers. Employers in the auto industry refused to bargain collectively and maintained that the Wagner Act was unconstitutional. Management was engaged in "warfare" against the union, and labor had to fight "fire with fire."[44]

A sit-down, in fact, required almost military organization and discipline, because the participants were in a state of siege, surrounded by police and sometimes vigilante forces who might try to oust them from the plants at any time. Doug Fraser recalled that during sit-downs "there were always rumors that they were going to attack the plant," and "we had all sorts of equipment on the roof to defend ourselves."[45]

The UAW-CIO sit-downers identified their struggle with that of the embattled Spanish Loyalists, courageously defending democracy against formidable fascist armies. In 1937 sit-down strikers at Chrysler, defying corporate threats to evict them, mounted "rudely constructed cannons" on the roof of an occupied Dodge factory in Detroit, and displayed a sign with the Spanish Loyalist slogan "They Shall Not Pass." To identify further the union's struggle with that of the Spanish Loyalists, the UAW-CIO's *West Side Conveyor* told of a former member of Detroit's Local 174 and veteran of its 1936 sit-down strike at Kelsey-Hayes Wheel, who was fighting with the Abraham Lincoln Battalion in northern Spain, and reported that shop stewards were raising contributions to purchase cigarettes for the Battalion's soldiers. Local 174's Joint Council also unanimously passed a resolution calling on the UAW-CIO to send ambulances to the Spanish Loyalist armies. In announcing the resolution to the press, the local's president, Walter Reuther, explained that Detroit's auto workers were engaged in the same struggle as the Spanish Loyalists, because "the threat of fascism is real in this country," and reactionary forces were mobilizing in Michigan, as they had in Germany and Italy, to destroy the trade unions.[46]

Viewing any sit-down as illegal and illegitimate, the auto companies amassed huge arsenals of tear gas guns and shells to dislodge the strikers, placing them in considerable danger. Chevrolet's personnel chief, Alfred

Marshall, disclosed at the La Follette Committee hearings in February 1937 that he had ordered $4,000 to $5,000 worth of tear gas and equipment to fire it prior to the GM sit-down, which police used against strikers in the fighting at Flint's Chevy 9 plant. Sit-downers at Dodge Main in March 1937, examining office files, discovered that the corporation had ordered tear gas, gas masks, rifles, pistols, ammunition, and steel helmets in anticipation of the strike, and located the arsenal in the plant.[47]

Against the guns and tear gas of the police and company vigilantes, sit-downers held fire hoses in readiness, with nozzle displayed in window, and assembled large supplies of metal parts—hinges, belts, and nuts—that could be thrown down at attackers from roofs. Paint guns could also be used as easily against police or vigilantes as on car bodies.[48]

However, the UAW-CIO's development of effective paramilitary techniques for use outside the plants, combined with the mobilization of mass picket lines and a sympathetic governor, protected sit-downers from violence in the larger strikes. Success still required a high level of planning and organization, and tight discipline from those on the inside. The UAW-CIO leadership carefully studied the sit-down strikes that occurred in France during May and June 1936 and discussed them with the rank and file in workers' education classes. The union assigned sit-downers to groups with specific duties, like security patrol, kitchen help, coal passing, and maintenance of buildings' heat, electrical, and water equipment. The leaders also organized entertainment and educational workshops for the sit-downers when they were not engaged in those tasks. At Dodge Main during the March 1937 Chrysler strike, union leaders mounted a military-style map of the occupied plant, with pin flags placed to show the numbers sitting down in each department, which they used in planning the building's defense and rotating men to various duties.[49]

In its early sit-downs in late 1936, particularly at Kelsey-Hayes Wheel, the UAW-CIO perfected its ability to organize men inside occupied plants and, just as important, learned how to coordinate their efforts with those of members outside, which was essential if such strikes were to succeed. The union had to maintain contact between strike leaders inside and outside the plant to warn sit-downers of impending police attacks, to provide them with food and necessary supplies, and to permit communication between sit-downers and their families, without which morale might collapse. During the Kelsey-Hayes Wheel strike, for example, management attempted to lure sit-downers out of the plant by sending them phony telegrams reporting that their wives or children had fallen sick. Food often had to be hauled over high fences and then hoisted up to plant windows, while hundreds of women toiled endless hours preparing meals for an "army of occupation." Because only a small proportion of the work force actually remained in the plants during any of the sit-downs, the union also needed to mount impressive demonstrations of support outside the buildings, to refute claims by management and the press that the overwhelming majority of workers rejected the union.[50]

In the Kelsey-Hayes Wheel sit-down of December 1936, the UAW-CIO frustrated management's effort to break the strike by expertly using its forces inside and outside the plant to transform it into an impregnable fortress. It protected the sit-downers by rapidly mobilizing massive numbers of pickets across a wide area, and built a formidable barricade to thwart Ford management's attempt to resume production by seizing key brake dies and removing them to another plant. Kelsey-Hayes Wheel, on Detroit's West Side, manufactured most of Ford's brake drums and shoes.[51]

The sit-down exposed the vulnerability of any of the Big 3 to a work stoppage at a key parts supplier. Shutting down an auto assembly plant had no impact, because the company could just shift the work elsewhere; however, an engine plant shutdown would paralyze all production. It was unusual for Ford, or GM or Chrysler, to rely solely on one supplier for a key part. Until the previous month, Bendix in South Bend, Indiana, had been a co-supplier of brake shoes with Kelsey-Hayes Wheel. But, angered by the UAW-CIO's sit-down strike there, Ford had removed all the dies from the Bendix plant and placed them in Kelsey-Hayes's, thereby putting all "its eggs in one basket."[52]

When Kelsey-Hayes management, whose instructions came from Ford, shipped about a dozen strikebreakers, or thugs, "who looked like underworld characters," into the plant to provoke a fight with the sit-downers and provide the police an excuse to expel them, the UAW-CIO sent out an "SOS call" to all its locals in the Detroit area, and within half an hour 5,000 pickets had assembled in front of the building. Union leaders gave the thugs fifteen minutes to leave the building, an ultimatum underlined by chants of "fifteen minutes" and "throw the scabs out." Police Commissioner Pickert was prevented from using his patrolmen to protect the thugs by Detroit mayor Frank Couzens, who hesitated to support strikebreaking openly in the immediate aftermath of the landslide election victories of President Roosevelt and Governor Murphy, strong supporters of labor's right to organize. When union leaders promised that the crowd would not harm the strikebreakers, management evacuated them, although pickets spat on them.[53]

The dramatic climax of the strike occurred when the UAW-CIO blocked the attempt of Ford trucks to carry away the dies from the plant. To prevent the moving of dies to the trucks, the strikers erected a three-foot-high wall, with a dozen steel containers loaded with two tons of hub castings. Behind it they set up a dolly load of eighteen-inch T-irons. The union then sent out another call for help to its Detroit-area locals, and, as Victor Reuther recalled, "they came from the east side, the north, all sections—even volunteers from Windsor, Ontario, came across to join the picket line," in a "massive show of strength." The UAW-CIO also received the support of the unionized railwaymen and teamsters, who refused to move anything out of the plant. As Victor Reuther put it, the strikers "had 'em by the balls," and Ford, desperately in need of parts with the production of new models about to begin, decided to settle.[54]

The UAW-CIO formed mobile paramilitary groups called Flying Squadrons, whose members wore army-style overseas caps, leather jackets, and armbands. Their purpose was to protect picket lines and hold a strike together during police attacks or when management was bringing in strikebreakers. They moved rapidly to any trouble spot in a city where the union needed to display force. The Flying Squadrons demonstrated "that acts of aggression" against the union "would be met with retaliation." Locals like Dodge 3 and Briggs 212 set up their own Flying Squadrons, "ready to fight cops at the slightest provocation." Leaders of these locals, like Emil Mazey at Briggs 212 and Richard Frankensteen at Dodge 3, joined their Flying Squadrons in the streets; they "neither asked nor expected anything of [their] followers that [they were] not personally willing to take part in [themselves]." The Flying Squadrons sometimes linked together to form union caravans, lines of cars that traveled vast distances and sometimes across state lines to reinforce outnumbered pickets and provide "a lesson in solidarity [the strikers] would not soon forget," as in the 1937 Flint and Anderson, Indiana, sit-downs. In fact, as labor reporter F. Raymond Daniell commented, the prospects for physical confrontation between Flying Squadrons and pro-company vigilantes were high in Michigan, because it had the highest per capita ownership of automobiles in the world, allowing both "armies" to bring their members quickly to trouble points.[55]

Richard Frankensteen claimed that the auto companies were "scared stiff" of the Flying Squadrons, which proved highly effective in rallying pickets and boosting morale at critical stages in both sit-downs and conventional strikes. But the Flying Squadrons' reliance on numbers, their members' fists, and sturdy picket signs was sometimes not sufficient when they confronted the guns and brass knuckles of organized crime thugs hired by management or rival AFL unions. It was UAW-CIO policy for its members not to carry firearms. Leonard Woodcock recalled a morning in 1938 when he was out with a UAW-CIO Flying Squadron in Detroit trying to recruit AFL bakers into the CIO Bakery Workers Union. The Flying Squadron was distributing a leaflet that boldly proclaimed, "Join a Fighting Union!" But Jimmy Hoffa, supporting the AFL, appeared with nine thugs from Detroit's infamous Purple Gang, and they quickly terminated the handbill distribution by roughing up the auto unionists. At headquarters, angry union leaders told the Flying Squadron: "They can't do this to us! You've got to go back!" So the Flying Squadron resumed leafleting the next morning at the same location. Before long nine Fords pulled up, from which eighteen Purple Gang thugs emerged, led by Hoffa, each of whom wore brass knuckles under his gloves and had a blackjack hanging out of his pocket. Hoffa approached the police lieutenant on duty, backed by four thugs in a wedge formation, shoved him in the chest, and barked, "Beat it copper! We'll take care of this!"[56]

Well aware that they could not match the thugs' firepower, the Flying Squadron's members obeyed Hoffa's order to leave quickly. A "big goon" accompanying Hoffa approached Woodcock as he was getting into his car, patted him on the shoulder, and told him, "Kid, you're not going to get to grow very much older if you keep this sort of thing up." He warned him not to start his car without checking the motor each morning. For the next several months, Woodcock slept in a different place each night.[57]

Nonetheless, during the epic Flint sit-down strike the Flying Squadrons did not shrink from "murderous bullet and gas attack[s]" by the GM-dominated municipal police, or from confrontation with the corporation-inspired vigilante movement, the Flint Alliance, led by former Flint mayor and Buick paymaster George Boysen. GM hoped that the Flint Alliance would stimulate a back-to-work movement, but most workers resisted pressure from foremen and superintendents to join. Still, GM mobilized against the strikers several hundred armed men from Safety Committees it had established shortly before the sit-down in each of its Flint plants. For service on the committees, they were promised shorter layoffs than other workers.[58]

Anticipating violent assault by police and vigilantes against the sit-downers, women relatives of the strikers prepared to assume a central role in their defense, organizing their own Flying Squadron, called the Women's Emergency Brigade. Genora Johnson [Dollinger], the brigade's captain, recalled, "We wanted to set up a military formation that could be thrown in the battle lines." To emphasize the brigade's military character, its leaders held army ranks; there was a captain and five lieutenants, and its members wore red berets and armbands. The Flint Alliance immediately sought to discredit the brigade by claiming that Genora Johnson's involvement required her to abandon her two young children. But Johnson and the brigade won praise from the UAW-CIO newspaper for defying police bullets and tear gas, fighting "in the front ranks" in battles at Fisher 2 and Chevy 4.[59]

Flint's Women's Emergency Brigade served as the model for others that female UAW-CIO supporters established elsewhere after the strike. These brigades were composed of women on call twenty-four hours a day, who donned berets and wore armbands marked "EB." Each brigade was identified by its own color; while Flint's wore red berets, Detroit's wore green, Lansing's white, and Ohio's blue.[60]

Genora Johnson was among several Flint UAW-CIO activists who placed themselves in serious danger, driving to Saginaw during the strike to assist in organizing its GM auto workers, terrorized by corporation-inspired violence. GM vigilantes in Saginaw were "beating people up every day." Johnson noticed at the union meeting in Saginaw that many of the forty or fifty people in attendance "had bandages on their eyes and heads or arms from being beaten up." When the organizers left Saginaw, two cars filled with union men armed with clubs escorted them to the city limits. But two big limousines carrying vigilantes nonetheless slipped in ahead of and behind the Flint activists' car. Shutting off their headlights, zooming ahead at speeds up to eighty miles an hour, weaving in and out of cars on the road, the Flint activists managed to escape. According to Johnson, GM's vigilantes had hoped, by causing the death or serious injury of the union organizers in an "accident," to give Saginaw's auto workers "something to think about."[61]

UAW-CIO activists in Flint were similarly at great physical risk throughout the strike, despite strong support from the Flying Squadrons. When rumors reached Detroit one night that GM vigilantes were preparing "to dig the sit-downers out of the plants," union leaders at the three Hudson plants distributed fliers to each worker telling him "to get in his car and pick up his buddies and go to Flint." As a result, the UAW-CIO assembled

30,000 members and supporters in Flint, a display of strength sufficiently impressive to cause the vigilantes to reconsider their plans.[62] But Victor Reuther recalled Flint police firing on him from nearby plant windows as he led union forces in the Battle of Bulls' Run. GM had provided the police with access to any building not occupied by sit-downers. In fact, the UAW-CIO leadership insisted that Victor Reuther leave Flint after the Battle of Bulls' Run for his own personal safety, even though union bodyguards protected him while he slept. Two days after Victor Reuther left Flint for Anderson, Indiana, GM vigilantes dragged his brother Roy from his sound car, beat him, and smashed his loudspeaker.[63]

The UAW-CIO's ability to mobilize massive numbers of members and supporters in picket lines at the occupied plants during the Chrysler sit-down, which began soon after the Flint strike was settled, prevented the enforcement of a circuit court injunction to vacate them. As in Flint, local Flying Squadrons were supplemented by CIO "shock troops" from as far away as Ohio and Pennsylvania. The *New York Times* observed that the buildings would "be as hard to capture as fortresses." When the "zero hour" for the ordered evacuation arrived, crowds of 10,000 auto unionists and strike sympathizers each surrounded Dodge Main and Chrysler Jefferson, while smaller groups assembled at the other six occupied Chrysler, Dodge, Plymouth, and DeSoto plants. At Dodge Main, a mass picket line completely encircled the huge plant, which normally employed 25,000, a distance of two miles.[64]

The union demonstrations were accompanied by military-style display, reflecting fierce determination to prevent the breaking of the strike. Strikers placed two mock cannon made of wood and stovepipe on Dodge Main's roof, beneath a sign proclaiming, "We Want Wilcox, the Army, and the Navy," Wilcox being the county sheriff charged with carrying out the sit-downers' eviction. Pickets carried a huge sign reading, "Give Us Liberty or Give Us Death," and ran the union banner up the plant's flagpole to a position just beneath the American flag, as though Dodge Main were, indeed, a fort defended by soldiers. The strikers impugned the masculinity and character of workers who had chosen to leave the plant rather than join the sit-in, as they would deserters from the army, hanging up an effigy bearing a sign "Rat No. 1 Fence-Jumper." The Kelsey-Hayes sit-downers had referred to such men as "weaklings." Sit-downers in Dodge Main could be seen "waving their homemade blackjacks in jubilation."[65]

As in Flint, the Chrysler sit-down's success was in great part due to

Governor Murphy's refusal to use state police or National Guardsmen to break it, but the mass picket lines had a significant impact on the outcome. As the *New York Times* noted, the sheriff dared not risk "the inevitable large amount of bloodshed and the state of armed insurrection" that undoubtedly would have resulted from any attempt to evict the sit-downers.[66]

The most violent of the auto sit-down strikes occurred in Anderson, Indiana, where the UAW-CIO rushed in Flying Squadrons from Michigan and Ohio to support a small group of unionists menaced by a GM vigilante army and corporation-controlled police. Anderson, a city of 40,000 residents, was one of the nation's most important auto production centers outside the Detroit area and Flint. The Anderson sit-down was boldly initiated shortly after Flint's by the 400 UAW-CIO unionists in a GM labor force that numbered over 11,000. GM employed nearly all of Anderson's 14,000 wage-earners at two of its major parts suppliers, Guide Lamp Division, which manufactured headlights, and Delco-Remy Division, which produced distributors, generators, and other automobile electrical equipment. The sit-down was staged at Guide Lamp; GM then locked out the workers at Delco-Remy.[67]

As in Flint, GM controlled Anderson's municipal officials, police, and newspapers. Victor Reuther, whom the UAW-CIO leadership sent to Anderson from Flint to lead the strike during its fourth week, called the city "an isolated medieval duchy." He noted that "the whole town was silenced by the enormous power and pressure and dominating presence of General Motors. . . . [N]o ministers spoke out [for the union], no educator."[68]

Anderson's strikers needed union support from outside the state, because there was no CIO presence in the region. Moreover, major Indiana cities like Indianapolis, Kokomo, Muncie, and New Castle were unorganized. The nearest UAW-CIO local was 130 miles away, in South Bend, Indiana. Anderson was also a "very Southern town," populated by migrants from that region, with a tradition of Ku Klux Klan activism that undoubtedly facilitated GM's mobilization of a vigilante army.[69]

The prospects for violence quickly escalated as GM formed the Citizens League for Industrial Security, a vigilante force similar to the Flint Alliance. GM denounced the "alien leadership" of the UAW-CIO but promoted the league as a cross section of Anderson's population. Headed by realtor Homer Lambert but largely led by GM supervisory personnel, the Citizens League claimed a membership of 18,500. Financed by GM, it bought up all the available time on Anderson's only radio station to broadcast anti-strike messages, which it also presented in full-page newspaper advertisements. Fearing a vigilante assault, sit-downers prepared to defend themselves by hooking a fire hose to a water line.[70]

Anderson's police permitted GM's vigilantes to ransack union headquarters. The assault badly demoralized the strikers, who had already ended their occupation of Guide Lamp. At the urging of GM's personnel director, who had provided it with free liquor, a mob of more than 1,000, including Citizens League members, marched on union headquarters, determined to expel the "outside agitators" from Anderson. A group that included GM supervisory personnel badly beat three unionists it encountered in the street. The UAW-CIO identified the plant managers of Delco-Remy and Guide Lamp, Fred Kroeger and Frank L. Burke, as having stood by during the beatings "laughing and applauding."[71]

UAW-CIO organizer Hugh Thompson, who had charge of the strike, believed that the mob planned to lynch him and frantically appealed to Indiana's governor, M. Clifford Townshend, for protection. He recalled seeing the mob display "the rope by which [he] was to be hung." As rocks smashed through the headquarters windows, he called the governor to request the sending of state police but was refused. Thompson had barely hung up the phone when Anderson police entered and arrested the twenty unionists in the office, taking them off to jail. UAW-CIO organizer Sophie Reuther, wife of Victor, escaped by climbing out a rear window of the building. As the police chief and several patrolmen looked on, the mob proceeded to wreck the union office, hurling typewriters and the local's records out the window and breaking up the furniture. Company officials obtained some of the local's records and inspected them. Four hundred members of the mob then advanced on the Guide Lamp plant, drove off the pickets, and burned down their picket shack. Confirmation of GM's control of the police was contained in the summation of the night's activities on the station house blotter: "Nothing to report."[72]

The UAW-CIO leadership sent Victor Reuther to assume leadership of the Anderson strike because it believed it was too dangerous for him to remain in Flint after directing its forces in the Battle of Bulls' Run, but when he arrived at his new post the night after the ransacking of union headquarters, his life was still at risk. He could not even rent a hotel room in Anderson, because proprietors feared vigilantes might wreck or burn any building housing him. His own safety required that he stay with friends he could trust, and he moved to different quarters each night to escape detection. An Anderson unionist recalled, "If Victor Reuther had been staying in a hotel . . . they would have got him." It took Reuther several days to locate the key union activists in Anderson, including his wife Sophie, because they were also in hiding. Reuther later learned that one of them, the treasurer of the Anderson UAW-CIO local, was a Pinkerton agent.[73]

With Anderson "virtually taken over by vigilantes," Reuther had to hold his first union meetings twenty-five miles away, in Alexandria. He described the vigilante movement in Anderson as "almost . . . Klan-like," employing "open terror" against the union leaders. Vigilantes circled union activists' homes in cars at night to intimidate them and waylaid them individually when they went out, beating them up.[74]

But Reuther did not shy away from confrontation, and during his second week in Anderson he led a union automobile caravan into the city, had it circle the Guide Lamp plant, and then reestablished the picket line. The caravan's lead car displayed the American flag, appropriated by the union as its war colors, and defining the strike as a struggle for liberty against corporate tyranny. That interpretation was reinforced when "big burly plug uglies," newly deputized by Anderson's police chief, cursed and spat at the pickets in an attempt to provoke a fight and provide the police with an excuse to drive the unionists out of town. One of them slugged Victor Reuther, but Reuther persuaded the pickets that retaliation would only play into the corporation's hands. Guide Lamp also openly filmed the pickets, in an unsuccessful attempt to intimidate them into desisting. Having used a sound truck with great effect in Flint's Battle of Bulls' Run, Reuther obtained one in an effort to present the strikers' case to the large group of undecided workers. But the Anderson police immediately confiscated it. When Reuther procured another, GM had the municipal government pass an ordinance prohibiting the use of any sound equipment on the city's streets. The strikers' difficulties were compounded by GM spies inside Anderson's UAW-CIO local, whose reports identifying new union recruits to management caused their immediate discharge.[75]

When the Flint strike was settled, the UAW-CIO in Anderson assumed it would be able to meet freely to discuss the terms of settlement, but a mob estimated at anywhere from 200 to 1,500 GM vigilantes, including some GM supervisory personnel, terrorized those who assembled, disrupting the proceedings and putting at risk the lives of 800 to 1,000 unionists and sympathizers. Victor Reuther believed this attack on the union meeting was designed to rob the UAW-CIO "of the euphoria of the moment and to prevent . . . further recruitment." Reuther had great difficulty finding a meeting place, because municipal authorities prevented the UAW-CIO from gathering in the city armory or any of the schools, and Anderson's churches denied the union the use of their facilities. A pro-labor state legislator finally turned over to the union the rundown Crystal Theater, of which he was part owner, vacant for several years. The building had no heat, so the union procured kerosene stoves.[76]

But no sooner had the meeting begun than a mob of vigilantes wielding pitchforks, shotguns, and clubs began pelting the building with rocks, and unionists alleged they then fired into the building. Anderson police chief Joseph Carney and his men made no effort to stop the rock-throwing, although they did not allow the vigilantes to enter the building. Carney then entered the theater and told Reuther the mob would disperse if Reuther would submit to protective arrest. But Reuther was sure that the minute he stepped out of the building "there would be a lynching party" and refused. Fearing that the vigilantes might storm the theater at any moment, listening to the screams of hysterical children, Reuther "aged ten years that night." Not until 4:00 A.M., when the mob had dissipated, could the unionists safely leave the building. While police had fired tear gas freely against strikers in Flint, in Anderson they rejected the unionists' pleas to use it, or fire hoses, to disperse the mob.[77]

When the UAW-CIO in Michigan and northern Ohio learned of the mob assault on the Crystal Theater meeting, "a wave of anger swept through the ranks," and within hours of the building's evacuation, several hundred cars carrying Flying Squadrons from Flint (where the sit-down had ended), Detroit, Pontiac, Lansing, and Toledo were headed toward the Indiana border to reinforce the Anderson strikers against the vigilantes. The union caravan included members of Flint's Women's Emergency Brigade, wearing their red berets and armbands. Many of the men were veterans of the Flint sit-down, easily identifiable because they sported several weeks growth of beard. Victor Reuther had traveled to Indianapolis immediately after leaving the Crystal Theater to ask the governor to declare martial law and send troops to Anderson to protect the strikers against the vigilantes, but he had refused. Only when an Indiana state police reconnaissance plane spotted the union caravans on the roads did the governor declare martial law in Madison County, where Anderson was situated.[78]

Tracking the union caravans with radio-equipped planes, Indiana National Guardsmen and state police halted many of the cars and forced them to turn back. The Flint police collaborated in the effort to turn back the caravans, alerting the Indiana state police whenever auto unionists left that city for Anderson. At Alexandria, National Guardsmen mounted machine guns at a highway intersection and turned back seventy carloads from Michigan. None of the unionists had firearms, although some carried lengths of gas pipe. State police were instructed to halt and question the occupants of all cars in north central Indiana with Michigan license plates.[79]

The arrival of Flying Squadrons, many of which managed to slip through the state police blockades, energized the Anderson strikers. Many of the cars stopped twenty-five miles from Anderson, and the "rescuers" walked through the fields to the city. A mystique was already developing about the Flint sit-downers, who had emerged from the occupied GM plants just days before. "Flint Is Coming" became an inspirational slogan for beleaguered UAW-CIO pickets. Because the Flint strikers had defeated the world's largest corporation, auto unionists everywhere believed "they could lick lions."[80]

During the next weeks, the Flying Squadrons' presence contributed to a steady growth in Anderson's UAW-CIO membership, as auto workers' fears of brutality lessened. The governor's declaration of martial law, which the union had sought as a means of curbing vigilante power, initially hampered organizing activity but worked to the union's advantage in the long run. The National Guard forbade any public gathering of over three people, including union meetings, and refused to allow press conferences at union headquarters. But the governor pressured state police to suppress vigilante activity, and the union benefited as the restrictions on public assembly were gradually removed.[81]

Still, the UAW-CIO remained weaker in Anderson than in Flint. It easily won an NLRB election in April 1940 at Guide Lamp but lost at Delco-Remy. The union did, however, win on its second try in the fall, sealing its triumph over the most violent management-inspired strikebreaking effort outside the Ford Motor Company.[82]

Not long after the Anderson strike, in an assault that was the "most brutal yet" in a sit-down, Detroit police in April 1937 evicted 150 UAW-CIO strikers, mostly young women, from the Yale & Towne Lock Company plant, which manufactured car door locks, seized a union sound truck, and arrested numerous Flying Squadron members, along with Walter and Victor Reuther, after fierce fighting outside. It was the first defeat the UAW-CIO had suffered in a sit-down. The entire work force was discharged, and the plant permanently shut down. Because of a public backlash against sit-down strikes, Governor Murphy allowed a court injunction against the sit-down to stand, permitting the police, led by Commissioner Pickert, to unleash a half hour tear gas barrage and storm the plant. Detroit had experienced scores of sit-downs in recent months as hotel workers, department and drug store clerks, laundry workers, warehousemen, meat packers, and others had followed the auto workers' example, resulting in middle-class citizens and state legislators clamoring for the police to apply even greater force. Four sit-downers were hospitalized as a result of the police attack.[83]

Although their strike had been defeated, the young women sit-downers, who had held their plant, with a handful of men, for thirty-six days, displayed the fighting qualities of their predecessors at GM and Chrysler. They donned military-style white berets, with "Y & T," for Yale & Towne, embroidered on them in red. They proudly called themselves the "tear gas eaters." No sooner were they released from jail than they were on the picket line, joined by 5,000 UAW-CIO members from a dozen Detroit auto plants, in a massive protest against police brutality.[84]

Worse even than the tear gas attacks against the sit-downers were the mounted police charges at Federal Screw, a Ford and GM parts supplier, and American Brass in 1938, conventional strikes that were the most violent in Detroit's history. The intensity of the street fighting and extensive neighborhood involvement in it were reminiscent of the urban transit strikes earlier in the century. Working-class strike sympathizers, including many women and children, accumulated arsenals of rocks, bottles, and tin cans on porches and rooftops, while mounted police clubbed, trampled, and pursued them on to porches and into backyards, causing severe injury to many. The strikes occurred at a time when the Roosevelt recession and diminishing federal sympathy for labor had placed the UAW-CIO on the defensive, desperately trying to retain its organization and resist wage cuts and layoffs.[85]

UAW-CIO leaders believed that if the union did not successfully challenge the enactment of a wage cut at Federal Screw, the other auto manufacturers and parts suppliers would also slash wages. It therefore viewed the strike as a critical test of strength: "No peanut manufacturer in a shop employing 300 workers would dare take this attitude if it stood alone. Federal Screw is representing the auto manufacturers of this city."[86]

Local 174, UAW-CIO, led by Walter Reuther, which joined together workers from a multitude of shops on Detroit's West Side, expected that its pickets would be drawn into physical confrontation with the police, assigned to escort strikebreakers into the Federal Screw Works, and secured the services of physicians friendly to labor to treat its casualties. The local's

*Detroit police fire tear gas to dislodge Yale & Towne sit-down strikers, 1937.*
*Courtesy of the Walter P. Reuther Library, Wayne State University.*

newspaper, the *West Side Conveyor*, rallied the rank and file on the eve of the strike as though it were a military engagement, announcing that "the battle field for all West Siders is in front of the Federal Screw plant," and that "[e]very West Sider in fighting trim will be there."[87]

The strike reached a "bloody climax" on its third day, as mounted and foot police, moving in military wedge formation, escorted strikebreakers toward the plant, precipitating a violent confrontation with about 150 pickets, many of whom were wearing bandages to cover wounds received in earlier skirmishes. According to Victor Reuther, who helped to lead the Federal Screw strike, the police's purpose was "to really break the morale of the strike," and "to serve notice on the whole neighborhood 'This we ain't gonna win, boys.'" About 600 policemen were stationed in the immediate vicinity of the plant, including a tear gas squad. But thousands of residents of the working-class neighborhood surrounding the plant had massed in nearby windows, doorways, streets, and alleys. During the previous few days, UAW-CIO activists had fanned out through the neighborhood, encouraging its residents to gather bricks and bottles, and pile them at strategic intersections, near the strikebreakers' line of march. Flying Squadrons

*Detroit policemen escort arrested striker or strike sympathizer, Federal Screw strike, 1938. Courtesy of the Walter P. Reuther Library, Wayne State University.*

from Kelsey-Hayes Wheel, Dodge, and other Detroit-area shops were also present to support the pickets. The UAW-CIO had posted lookouts along the route it expected the police and strikebreakers to follow, who signaled to the pickets at the main gate as the procession approached. As the cry "Here Come the Rats!" went up along the picket line, the mounted police charged, swinging their clubs and riding directly at the strikers.[88]

Strikers who faced the prospect of being ridden down and clubbed by mounted police used two principal means of defense. Many converted their picket signs into clubs, and swung them at the rider's kneecaps, dismounting him. Daniel Gallagher, a veteran of the Federal Screw strike, remarked in 1960 that "there are policemen still crippled from it." Strikers also rolled ball bearings under the mounted policemen's horses, knocking them down on the streets.[89]

In what came to be known as the "Battle of Bloody Run," mounted police, in repeated charges, clubbed and trampled unionists and neighborhood residents in streets, alleys, and yards, including, according to the UAW-CIO, "little girls" and "unarmed women." Walter Reuther, president

*Street fighting breaks out during Detroit's Federal Screw strike, 1938.*
*Courtesy of the Walter P. Reuther Library, Wayne State University.*

of Local 174, charged that a police officer had pulled a gun on school-children who booed him when he beat a woman on her porch.[90]

Five policemen cornered Percy Keyes, a thirty-eight-year-old African American auto unionist, in a yard a block from the plant and nearly killed him. Keyes raised his hands to surrender, but the police yelled, "Give it to the nigger!" and clubbed and stomped him unconscious. After a time his body began to twitch, and they "club[bed] him all over again." The beating left Keyes with a fractured skull, a broken back, a fractured kneecap, and internal injuries. The police also clubbed a union doctor as he bent over Keyes, yelling, "Get outta here, you lousy Communist!" Walter Reuther declared, "If Keyes dies, it will be direct murder by the police." When unionists brought Keyes to Detroit's Women's Hospital, he was refused treatment because he was African American. He did not recover from the beating for several months. The police also fractured the skull of a Flying Squadron member from Pontiac while he was leaning down to pick up a thirteen-year-old girl whose ribs they had broken. The police had injured so many unionists, recalled Daniel Gallagher, that the floor of Local

*Detroit police charge and club strikers and strike sympathizers, Federal Screw strike, 1938. Courtesy of the Walter P. Reuther Library, Wayne State University.*

174's headquarters "was so bloody that you slipped down on it taking people in there."[91]

The UAW-CIO prevailed in the Federal Screw strike, preventing a pay cut that probably would have opened the way for wage reductions throughout the entire auto industry, but the very next month it was drawn into another "out and out war" against the Detroit police in the American Brass strike. The Flying Squadrons came to the aid of their "CIO brothers" in the Mine, Mill, and Smelter Workers Union after their sit-down at American Brass, a subsidiary of Anaconda Copper, was terminated by Detroit police. Viewing the American Brass strike as another "showdown fight" to determine whether management could impose wage reductions in a multitude of industries, hundreds of UAW-CIO members joined the picket line.[92]

Fighting broke out over a four-block area near the plant when police fired a tear gas bomb at a UAW-CIO sound truck. As at Federal Screw, mounted police with night sticks charged unionists armed with picket signs. Unionists erected a barricade across West Jefferson Avenue, which was under repair, hurling paving stones at cars carrying strikebreakers. The first of these cars to arrive at the barricade was forced to halt, and pickets pulled out the strikebreakers and pummeled them. The police caused the pickets to retreat by firing tear gas. More than sixty-seven people were injured in the street fighting, including twenty policemen—one with a fractured skull—and Flying Squadron members from the UAW-CIO's West Side 174, Dodge, Plymouth, and Chevy Forge locals. A picket picked up a tear gas bomb fired by police and hurled it back, where it exploded in a policeman's face, blinding him. Police arrested many of the injured unionists and shackled them to their hospital beds.[93]

Hundreds of UAW-CIO members jammed Detroit's City Hall to protest alleged Detroit police "savagery" and collaboration with management in strikebreaking, as well as Police Commissioner Pickert's order prohibiting pickets from carrying signs, which he claimed they used as clubs. UAW-CIO attorney Larry Davidow argued that Pickert's ban on picket signs violated a citizen's constitutional right to bear arms, guaranteed by the Second Amendment. Walter Reuther declared that union members would not surrender their right as American citizens to "defend themselves against the lawless violence of the police." UAW-CIO members also sharply criticized management's practice of feeding the police hot dogs, pies, and coffee inside the plant. Reuther noted, "Companies do not do these things without service in return."[94]

Anti-union violence in auto strikes, endemic in the 1930s, diminished greatly in the immediate postwar years, a key transition period in the history of the industry's labor conflict. Union recognition had been achieved, and as a result the UAW-CIO enjoyed strong backing from the overwhelming majority of auto workers when it began a strike, in sharp contrast to the 1930s, when most workers remained uncommitted until they became convinced the union had a highly favorable chance of winning. Reporting on the 1950 Chrysler strike, Mary Heaton Vorse commented, "These auto workers can't imagine themselves without their union. You hear men say, 'You might as well take away a man's religion as his union.'" By the postwar period collective bargaining had achieved much wider acceptance and was endorsed by the federal government, whereas the Flint and Chrysler sit-downs in 1937 had been waged before the Supreme Court had validated the constitutionality of the Wagner Act. Nonetheless, as Irving Bluestone noted, bargaining was "damn tough" in the 113-day 1945–46 national GM strike, the CIO's first major postwar challenge to corporate power, because collective bargaining was still in its infancy, and management "obviously [still] didn't want [it]."[95]

Bluestone, a regional leader in the 1945–46 GM strike who later headed the UAW's GM Department, noted that the atmosphere at GM had already changed significantly when he began work in 1941 at its Harrison, New Jersey, plant, which manufactured ball bearings for aircraft engines. Although management clearly expressed anti-union sentiment, there was no espionage in the plant. When Bluestone, head of the plant bargaining committee, organized a wildcat strike against management's sudden extension of the workday to twelve hours, he was fired, but "[t]here were no threats of violence by management." He commented that ten years before "there would have been wholesale discharges and very serious efforts to hire scabs," but "nothing like that was done." Of course, the federal government during the war had an interest in maintaining armaments production and could sympathize with the union's argument that worker fatigue, caused by an excessively long workday, might undermine the safety of military personnel flying aircraft, because product quality would suffer. A defective ball bearing in a plane's engine could result in a crash and the deaths of those on board. In this case management, pressured by the NLRB, called Bluestone in and negotiated a settlement that restored an eight-hour day.[96]

In neither the 1945–46 GM walkout, which involved 320,000 workers, nor the 1950 Chrysler strike, did the UAW-CIO set up mass picket lines, because the corporations made no attempt to import strikebreakers. In fact, during the GM strike the UAW-CIO leadership, fearing that violent confrontation outside the plant might antagonize public opinion and the White House, ordered the locals to permit white-collar employees and foremen to enter the workplace.[97]

Mary Heaton Vorse, who had chronicled the birth of the CIO, emphasized the "tremendous contrast" between the 1937 and 1950 strikes at Chrysler. In 1937, "mass picket lines surrounded the plants and hundreds of flying squadron cars filled the streets." The entire Detroit police force was on strike duty, while "[union] halls boiled with activity around the clock, seven days a week." Before the settlement, the UAW-CIO staged a "monster mass meeting" in Detroit's Cadillac Square. Police expected a riot, and advised employers in the neighborhood to send their office workers home. They stationed Black Marias around the square to transport to jail those they arrested, while ambulances were positioned nearby, prepared to take away any dead or wounded. To Vorse, the 1950 strike, by contrast, appeared "strange." Instead of instituting mass picketing to maintain morale, the UAW-CIO relied on radio broadcasts to the strikers (it had much greater access to radio than during the 1930s), union-sponsored recreation and entertainment, and a newly instituted union counseling service. The counselors made home visits to determine strikers' needs, helped them forestall eviction, and persuaded finance companies to accept deferred payment on loans.[98]

The returning World War II veterans who joined the UAW-CIO picket lines during the 1945–46 GM strike did extend the union's tough, paramilitary posture into the postwar period, although they did not actually engage in physical conflict with the police. The UAW-CIO leadership had been "scared stiff" about the attitude of these men, many of whom had left the plants before the union had much of a chance to establish itself. But Leonard Woodcock recalled that "one of the great wonders at that time was the positive attitude these veterans brought back. They were for the most part very pro-union." At GM's Linden, New Jersey, plant, demobilized soldiers and sailors wearing their uniforms and battle ribbons walked the picket line, carrying signs that defined the strike as a continuation of the World War II struggle for democracy against fascism. The signs displayed such slogans as "We Fought the Axis. Now We Fight GM for a Living Wage," "Mussolini Tojo Hitler Learned We Were Tough. Soon GM Will Say They Had Enough," and "We Fought Guadalcanal, Munda, New Guinea, Philippines, Africa. Now It's GM." Exuding confidence because of their war combat experience, battle-hardened veterans at Linden proclaimed, "We Licked GM in '37 and We Can Do It Again." At Fisher Body in Flint, uniformed army and navy veterans displayed "30% or Fight" badges, referring to their demand for a 30 percent wage increase.[99]

By maintaining an aggressive posture and remaining "solid as hell all the way through," the participants in the 1945–46 GM strike convinced management they enthusiastically backed their union and firmly established the UAW-CIO's credibility as a collective bargaining presence, even though the wage increase they gained, which fell short of their demand, was erased by inflation that followed the removal of price controls in 1946. The strong rank-and-file commitment to the strike, which convinced management not to import strikebreakers and that using violence would be counterproductive, helped make possible the UAW-CIO's progress during the next several decades.[100]

# EPILOGUE
# ANTI-UNIONISM
# IN AMERICA,
# 1945-2000

Obituaries noting the death of Pearl Bergoff in August 1947 identified him as the last professional anti-unionist and strikebreaker, a once common breed now vanished from the American landscape. The "tough, unlettered Michigan boy" had risen from rags to riches, earning $10 million disrupting union organizing campaigns and breaking strikes. He had defeated unions using armed mercenaries, who kept businesses operating during strikes "with pate-cracking and machine gun fire" until the workers surrendered. New Deal reforms guaranteeing labor the right to organize and bargain collectively, and prohibiting the interstate transportation of strikebreakers, had allegedly rendered Bergoff obsolete and "driven [him] out of business" by the late 1930s. *Time* portrayed him in old age as a lonely relic of a more primitive environment, guilt-stricken and tormented in a more enlightened time by the violent abuse he had inflicted on labor. It even quoted him as announcing a year before he died: "If I had my life to live over . . . I'd be for labor, I'd be another John L. Lewis."[1]

After World War II, the increasingly bureaucratized workplace required individuals to suppress their intense feelings in the interest of group harmony. This led to a new managerial emphasis on restraining anger on the job, an objective many workers now also found desirable. Not only Bergoff, the "Red Demon" who had terrorized labor before the war, but his union adversary Lewis, a physically imposing and hot-tempered man who had punched down an opponent at an AFL convention, seemed out of place in the new postwar emotional climate. While efforts to delegitimate anger were more pronounced and effective in the white-collar sector, they made significant inroads in mass production. The labor turmoil of the 1930s had caused management to seek new methods of defusing worker protest and had alarmed many workers, who feared recurring workplace conflict jeopardized job security. Corporate executives advised foremen and supervisors to control their tempers and maintain an outwardly friendly demeanor toward workers, in order to manipulate them more effectively. To chastise a worker openly might provoke resentment, and spark protest. Presenting itself as teammate rather than adversary, management sometimes even actively solicited employee input on improving the production process. And whereas corporations in the prewar period relied heavily on aptitude testing in hiring and assigning personnel, they now increasingly turned to personality testing to screen out the anger-prone, whom they assumed were more likely to challenge authority on the job.[2]

By the 1960s the conflation of masculinity with physicality and aggression was less pronounced than in the early twentieth century, even in the working class. This held significant implications for both corporate anti-unionism, which came to rely less heavily on brute force, and men's labor militancy, which declined considerably. School authorities increasingly stigmatized boys' aggressive behavior, redefining as delinquent acts previously dismissed as merely annoying. The Western, a highly popular form of print and film entertainment since the 1920s, which glamorized male courage and righteous anger, and climaxed in a dramatic walk-down confrontation, nearly disappeared after the early 1960s.[3] Martial valor, highly regarded in World War II, associated with both the professional strikebreaker and the labor militant, was devalued in the aftermath of Vietnam, a long drawn out, seemingly purposeless, and unsuccessful war of attrition that provided no opportunity for heroism. With the end of the draft in 1973, a far smaller proportion of youth entered the military, the most important remaining social arena in which male combativeness was encouraged.

The increasing suburbanization of the working class, along with the declining age at which men married during the 1950s, undermined the all-male leisure institutions, like the pool hall and the boxing club, that had encouraged male combativeness. Suburbanization also undermined the boisterous urban street corner society that had celebrated male physicality and aggressiveness, isolating the working-class man in the female-controlled home. The movement toward androgyny that began in the middle class in the 1960s resulted in a further softening of working-class masculinity. Even in many working-class neighborhoods the unisex hair style salon replaced the barber shop, formerly one of the principal centers of male sociability. Many working-class men even began wearing their hair long, or in a pony tail, and donned colorful clothes and buckled shoes, and later earrings, practices they would earlier have disdained as effeminate.[4]

In the period immediately following World War II, organized labor was more solidly entrenched than it had ever been, and it expected to extend its influence significantly during the next several years. Union membership had expanded enormously, from 3.8 million in 1935 to 7.2 million in 1940, and to over 14 million by the end of the war. Key mass production industries, like auto, steel, rubber, meat-packing, electrical machinery, agricultural equipment, aircraft, shipbuilding, and mining were 80 to 100 percent organized. Even the most intransigent opponents of unionization during the 1930s, Ford and the "Little Steel" companies, had been unionized during 1941. During 1945 unions won an overwhelming majority, 82.9 percent, of the 5,000 National Labor Relations Board (NLRB) union representation elections held. Management and police directed far less violence at labor during the massive 1945–46 strike wave than during the organizing drives and walkouts of the 1930s. Parallels that labor drew between corporate business's use of armed mercenaries and spies and the "storm troop armies of the Fascist nations" undoubtedly inhibited employers from using them in the immediate aftermath of America's triumph over Nazi Germany.[5]

Yet organized labor's position was far more precarious than it appeared. The sole legislation a New Deal Congress had passed to undermine the power of professional strikebreaking agencies, the Byrnes Act of 1936, proved entirely ineffectual. The bill made it a felony "knowingly" to transport a person across state lines "with intent to employ" him to "interfere with the right of peaceful picketing." But strikebreaking firms easily circumvented the law by recruiting within the state where the strike occurred. Nor did the bill define "intent" or "knowingly," or provide for any punishment for the strikebreakers themselves. Only one indictment was ever made by a federal grand jury under the Byrnes Act, against Pearl Bergoff and James Rand Jr. of the Remington-Rand corporation of New Haven, Connecticut, in 1936, and both defendants were acquitted. Although labor activists hoped the Byrnes Act would lead Congress to enact more effective legislation to combat strikebreaking, none was ever passed. Some states passed so-called Pinkerton laws, which forbade the importation of armed guards from outside their boundaries, but these were easily evaded by shipping the guards and the weapons separately, or hiring the men within the state.[6]

While the proportion of the nonagricultural labor force organized in unions continued to increase until the mid-1950s, political and legal developments during that period significantly increased labor's vulnerability during strikes and management's ability to disrupt organizing campaigns. Organized labor suffered a devastating defeat in the November 1946 elections, when the Republicans assumed control of both houses of Congress for the first time since 1930. Determined to make it more difficult for labor to organize and to win strikes, the new Eightieth Congress passed the Taft-Hartley Act over President Truman's veto, despite labor's desperate lobbying against what it branded a "slave labor" bill. Taft-Hartley dispensed with the "card check" system of determining union representation, still used in Canada, whereby a union was certified if a certain percentage of workers signed authorization cards. Instead, NLRB-supervised secret ballot elections were required, resulting often in lengthy, expensive campaigns, during which union activists were vulnerable to discharge. The act allowed employers to require employees to attend "captive audience" meetings prior to these elections, where they could present their anti-union message in a setting they completely controlled. It also permitted states to pass "right to work" laws banning the union shop, which spread particularly throughout the South and Southwest, significantly weakening labor's prospects in areas it sorely needed to organize.[7]

With the election of Dwight Eisenhower as president in 1952, it also became clear that the NLRB, initially assumed to be a firm guarantor of labor's rights, might, in a Republican administration, not adequately support them. By 1954 a Republican president's appointees to the NLRB, who tended to side with management, constituted a majority on it for the first time since it had been established in 1935. This contributed to labor's increasing lack of success in winning NLRB elections during the 1950s and in protecting union activists from discharge. In 1981, President Reagan even appointed to chair the NLRB an individual openly associated with combating unions in representation campaigns—John Van de Water, a management consultant who once bragged of helping an employer defeat the union in 125 of 130 elections. Reagan also drastically reduced the NLRB's budget, seriously inhibiting its agents' ability to fully investigate unions' charges of unfair labor practices.[8]

In the South, management during the late 1940s and early 1950s continued to employ violent tactics previously associated with Pearl Bergoff and Harry Bennett. Industrialization lagged behind the North, and the workplace remained less bureaucratized. The legacy of slavery and race had shaped a more authoritarian culture, and the new approaches to anger and violence were slower to take hold. Management's repressive tactics contributed significantly to the collapse of the CIO's Operation Dixie of 1948–53, organized labor's last full-scale effort to organize the region. Although the CIO made a major financial commitment to the drive, it failed to make any headway in industries it targeted, like textiles, furniture, and lumber. In fact, by 1951 membership of the CIO textile affiliate had even declined to 15 percent from 20 percent a few years before. As in Anderson, Indiana, in 1937, pro-company vigilantes during Operation Dixie ransacked the CIO office in Gadsden, Alabama, hurling furniture and typewriters out of an upstairs window on to the sidewalk. During the first five months of the CIO's campaign, seventeen union organizers and members were "severely assaulted." In Avondale, Alabama, a company police chief visited a textile workers' union organizer confined to a hospital bed, whom his men had beaten almost to death, and warned him that he would be killed if he ever returned to the town. In Florence, South Carolina, a pro-company mob informed another organizer it would tar and feather him if he did not leave. Local police invariably refused to intervene when union organizers and supporters were beaten.[9]

From the mid-1950s to the present, the proportion of the American labor force organized in unions has declined precipitously, from 34 percent in 1954 to around 20 percent in 1979, to 12 percent today, and less than 10 percent in the private sector. The proportion of unionized workers in the labor force today is less than it was before passage of the Wagner Act. During the 1970s even the total number of union members began to fall. Labor's ability to win strikes has also declined significantly. For decades, the labor movement has been on the defensive. This can be attributed in part to structural changes in the U.S. and global economies; to foreign competition resulting in the erosion of America's manufacturing base, where unions were most strongly entrenched; and to the migration of blue-collar jobs abroad. Technological developments, including the emergence of computers, eliminated large numbers of jobs in unionized crafts, like printing, and in semiskilled occupations like telephone operating, which faced near obliteration. The proportion of lower white-collar and service jobs in the labor force, traditionally less organized, increased significantly. Industry also migrated from the more unionized Northeast and North Central regions to the South and Southwest, "an old, but [by the 1970s] ominously increasing threat to organized labor." Employers also tended to rely more on part-time and temporary workers, traditionally very difficult to unionize.[10]

The labor movement, considered the principal progressive force in the

1930s, was overshadowed during the 1960s and early 1970s by other, more dynamic grass-roots campaigns for social change. The civil rights, antiwar, and women's movements all perceived organized labor as largely indifferent or even hostile to their goals, an obstacle to progress. The mass media, sensitive to the importance of "the latest" in a rapidly changing society, considered these emerging mass movements far more worthy of attention than the unions, even if their coverage was often condescending and unfriendly. Lacking the new movements' youthful activists, innovative tactics, and flair for publicity, organized labor seemed torpid, played out, no longer relevant. Television portrayed the working man as a buffoon, a troglodyte—Archie Bunker, in the 1970s, or Al Bundy in the 1990s—crude and prejudiced, the opposite of the social idealist.

To be sure, as Victor Reuther noted, the steady diminution of organized labor's strength is partly due to the fact that "[i]t has lost a lot of the crusading spirit which made possible the growth of the CIO and the revitalization of the old AFL unions." George Meany, president of the AFL-CIO from 1955 to 1980, a period when union membership dropped from 34 percent of the labor force to 19 percent, once even boasted that he had never walked a picket line. Certainly the AFL-CIO and most unions during the last three decades placed considerably less emphasis on organizing than before, a reality John Sweeney acknowledged when he assumed the AFL-CIO presidency as an insurgent in 1996. Victor Reuther observed that "[a] leadership has come to power in many unions which is no longer really dedicated to the principle of helping the guy in the workplace. . . . [The union leader] measures everything in terms of whether his salary matches that of the corporate leaders. And whether his paneled office matches that of the boss."[11]

After 1960 management increasingly exploited diminished but often still significant employee anxiety over masculinity to discredit union leaders who, unlike their 1930s counterparts, had never engaged in production or service work and had grown distant from the rank and file. Employers benefited from the mass media's portrayal of union leaders as overweight, self-interested pencil pushers, bureaucrats unworthy of respect from men who dirtied their hands in physical toil. Only a tiny handful of unions permitted their members to vote directly for the top union offices. Rather than stand shoulder to shoulder with workers on the picket line, by the 1980s union officials, when they did confront management, preferred to wage a "corporate campaign" centered around a lawsuit or proxy fight. Lawyers eliminated much of the rank and file's opportunity for activism.[12]

Nissan Motor Company handily defeated a UAW organizing drive in 1989 in Smyrna, Tennessee, in part by suggesting that union membership restricted personal freedom and thus threatened workers' manhood. It convinced a large majority of its heavily male labor force that a UAW victory meant subordination to authoritarian labor "bosses" uninvolved in production, concerned only with squeezing dues out of their hard-earned paychecks. Elaborate contractual regulations would allegedly undermine employee initiative on the job and eliminate opportunities for male-bonding during breaks at basketball hoops and volleyball nets management had installed near work stations. Nissan employees eagerly donned T-shirts bearing the slogan "Union Free and Proud"; one worker remarked, "I don't think we need people coming in here telling us what to do."[13]

The consumer culture allowed workers to maintain their image of masculinity even as their real autonomy diminished in the nonunion workplace. Driving a pickup truck or a "man's car"—defined by length of hood in relation to chassis—provided the illusion of power. By controlling such a machine, designed for speed and rapid acceleration, often distinctively marked, capable of forcing other vehicles to move aside on the highway, a worker acquired feelings of strength, mastery, and individuality. A worker's purchase of home power tools or hunting rifles stimulated similar fantasies of rugged independence.

Management also benefited from a widening generational divide among male workers, as youth increasingly derided the masculinity of their middle-aged counterparts, who were far more strongly committed to unionism. Younger workers considered the traditional union concerns like pensions, health insurance, workplace safety, and employment security less relevant, because they displayed less job persistence, found it easier to secure alternate employment, and often enjoyed taking risks. Union seniority rules protected older workers, requiring that the young be discharged first in a layoff. Labor's remote, middle-aged leadership lacked the energy and dynamism that might inspire working-class youth. Production work often accelerated the aging process, quickly robbing a man of the strength and vitality the working class associates with masculinity. In the eyes of the young, a man is emasculated by middle age, transformed into an object of ridicule. At the same time younger workers resent the middle-aged man's independence, because they lack the earning power to live outside their parental household, rarely attend residential colleges, and, in the postdraft era, are far less likely to break away through the military. In the 1992

Ravenswood Aluminum strike, young workers expressed open contempt for the locked-out union members, whose average age was fifty-two. As they crossed the picket line, flaunting their paychecks, they sneered, "Thanks for the job, Grandpa."[14]

Also contributing significantly to the steep, long-term decline in the proportion of workers organized, and in labor's prospects for winning strikes, was a "recovery of nerve" by management during the late 1940s and 1950s, and the elaboration of new, sophisticated union-busting techniques. The increasingly conservative political climate after the election of the Eightieth Congress in late 1946 encouraged business to adopt a tougher stance toward organized labor. Corporations migrating to the South were usually deliberately seeking an environment less hospitable to unionization. And even those like GM and Ford that had long accepted a permanent collective bargaining arrangement with their blue-collar employees firmly opposed any attempt to extend organization to their office or laboratory personnel.[15]

Although many of the largest and most influential corporations had extended union recognition by the early postwar period, they remained committed to at least containing, if not reducing, labor's influence. In the more conservative, post–New Deal climate, corporate business became increasingly aware it could rely often on the federal government to achieve this objective, as demonstrated by the passage of the Taft-Hartley Act and the actions of a Republican-dominated NLRB during most of the Eisenhower administration. And the fiercely intransigent anti-unionism prevalent among corporations during the 1920s still remained significant in what in the late 1940s and 1950s could be described as the "industrializing fringes of the South and West," a sector that steadily grew in importance in subsequent decades.[16]

After World War II, many major corporations placed renewed emphasis on paternalism in their labor relations, in an effort to diminish union influence in the workplace. This approach also influenced the new anti-union consulting firms that became increasingly significant after 1970. Underlying it was the assumption that labor and management shared a common interest, and unions became necessary only when the employer failed, because of inadequate communication, to inculcate in the worker a sense of trust and belonging in the company.[17]

Corporations relied increasingly on foremen and supervisors, whose ranks were considerably expanded, as "a first line of defense against unionism." These were, after all, the managerial officials in closest contact with the workers and thus able to communicate most easily with them. They were to compete openly with shop stewards in an effort to shift the employee's primary loyalty from the union to the company. Foremen were expected to personalize their relationships with those they supervised by greeting them by name each day and listening to their complaints. Suggestion boxes in the workplace and telephone "hot lines" to management encouraged employees to believe that their employer cared about their input.[18]

The corporation also sought to convince employees that they were recognized and appreciated as individuals. It provided merit prizes for achievements at work and awards for length of service, often with elaborate ceremony, and sent employees greetings on their birthdays. Management also designated an "employee of the month," whom it honored with a plaque or special parking place. It enhanced employees' sense of prestige, which it hoped might compensate for inadequate wages or benefits, by upgrading their job titles. In retail stores, sales "clerks" became sales "associates"; Nissan called its American assembly line workers "production technicians."[19]

Corporate executives attempted to reduce union officials' influence with their work force by speaking directly to the employees through letters, company publications, and bulletin boards. Such communication provided no role or acknowledgment of the union, implying its marginality or irrelevance in employees' lives. Starting in 1946, for example, Henry Ford II each year sent a letter extending Christmas greetings to every Ford employee. Larger corporations revived the employee magazine, a staple of the Progressive Era, to promote the concept that the entire work force—executives, managers, foremen, office personnel, and factory hands alike—constituted one harmonious family, in which all shared a common interest and outlook. To reinforce a sense of family, the larger corporations also placed renewed emphasis on sports and recreational activities like company picnics. Corporate athletic programs intensified employees' identification with the company, for whose teams the worker rooted, and blurred the distinction between labor and management.[20]

During the 1970s union-busting consultants, who were generally either lawyers or industrial psychologists, emerged as highly significant in combating labor organizing, forming special firms for this purpose. "Union avoidance" was the "hot business of the decade." By 1981 corporations hired these "preventive labor relations" consulting firms to advise them in nearly two-thirds of union campaigns. Many established lavish headquarters, resembling those of leading corporate law firms. Instead of using violence to intimidate workers, these consultants instructed employers how to pressure them psychologically to oppose the union, and on both legal and illegal methods they could use to undermine an organizing drive.[21]

These anti-union consultants often assumed near total control in a company during an organizing drive. The employer assigned his executive secretaries to the consultant and instructed all other employees at headquarters to obey the consultant's orders. Often the consultant even assumed the power of hiring and firing company employees. He also had charge of company propaganda during the campaign.[22]

The "union avoidance" business expanded enormously over the past three decades, from only a few firms specializing in combating unionization in 1970 to 1,000 already by the early 1980s. By 1993 this was a billion dollar industry involving over 7,000 practitioners.[23]

The consulting firms also conducted seminars, often lasting several days, on how to prevent a union organizing campaign from even starting. Indicative of union busting's increasing respectability is the willingness of universities to host and sponsor such seminars.[24]

The pioneer in the "preventive labor relations" consulting business, who elaborated many of the tactics used today, was Nathan Shefferman, who founded Labor Relations Associates of Chicago in 1939. The fiercely anti-union Sears, Roebuck, and Company, for which he had been employee relations director since 1935, provided him financing to set up the firm, which disbanded in 1959. Shefferman assisted clients in forming "loyal workers" committees during organizing drives, whose members often received ample financial reward and time off work to campaign against the union. Shefferman also introduced employee surveys on workplace issues, whose real purpose, which management concealed, was to determine the identities of union sympathizers. Labor Relations Associates grossed $2.4 million between 1949 and 1955. Shefferman's clients included major New York department stores, American Express, Allstate Insurance, United Parcel Service, Morton Frozen Foods, and Schaeffer Brewing Company.[25]

Anti-union consulting firms during the past three decades have developed a multitude of other techniques designed to eliminate potential union sympathizers in hiring and to identify them during campaigns, to defame the labor movement and union organizers, and to instill fear and anxiety in workers and their families. They have contributed significantly to a dramatic drop in organized labor's success rate in NLRB union representation elections—from 82.9 percent in 1945, to 60.7 percent in 1967, to 46 percent in 1978.[26]

The consultants advise their clients that union organizing campaigns can be avoided entirely by properly screening those who apply for work, using personal interviews and specially designed questionnaires. Today consultants consider African Americans, viewed in the early twentieth century as disproportionately hostile to organized labor and prone to strike-breaking, as especially sympathetic to unionism. They therefore sometimes recommend against hiring them.[27] As early as 1961 Nathan Shefferman asserted that "the Negro worker . . . is an easy target for unions." He ascribed this to a greater awareness of oppression stimulated by the civil rights conflict. Shefferman also noted that organized labor's commitment to protecting job security appealed to African Americans, traditionally the first to be laid off in slow seasons or economic downturns.[28] Contemporary anti-union consultants similarly stereotype Hispanics, except for Cubans, as more anger-prone and thus receptive to unionism, and advise their clients against employing them in significant numbers.[29]

Recently, African American anti-union consultants have emerged, who specialize in advising corporations targeted in organizing campaigns on how to persuade their black workers to oppose the union. They also promise that they can elevate the corporation's overall image in the black community.[30]

The "preventive labor relations" firms also devise questions for job interviews designed specifically to uncover potential union supporters among all ethnic and racial groups. Such questions will reveal, for example, any tendency to sympathize with the underdog or any involvement in consumer rights or tenant rights organizations.[31]

During union organizing drives, consultants instruct management on how to propagandize against the union, instilling anxiety in the work force by associating it with violence, plant relocations and closings, and strikes that result in long-term loss of income or permanent job loss. The law permits management to present its views in the workplace, while prohibiting workers from campaigning for the union on work time. Consultants draft letters for management to send to workers' homes, designed to inculcate anxiety in wives already worried that loss of a husband's income in a strike would be injurious to their children's welfare. Even in working-class families with wives employed outside the home, the combined incomes of both spouses are generally necessary to meet basic expenses. Supervisors also hand deliver letters stating the employer's position to the worker in the plant and ask to discuss them. The supervisors then funnel any questions they find difficult back to the consultant, who explains how to answer them. Such encounters between supervisor and worker, which might occur as many as thirty times during the course of an organizing campaign, "can easily develop into intimidation, harassment, and even victimization."[32]

Consultants often create horrifying, even apocalyptic, images depicting the union as an agent of economic devastation and social chaos. Such propaganda was often very effective in the postwar period, as society increasingly devalued anger-based aggression. A partner in Chicago's Imberman and DeForest firm explained to textile and furniture executives, at an anti-union seminar sponsored by Wake Forest University, how to "scare the beejesus" out of female employees, allegedly more easily frightened by visions of picket line violence. Days before an NLRB union representation election, a North Carolina textile company mailed to each of its employees a record in the form of a fictional radio news broadcast of a strike at this plant, punctuated with sounds of gunshots, and speeches by local ministers blaming the union for undermining community harmony. J. P. Stevens textile company brought a one-legged man into its High Point, North Carolina, plant one day before an NLRB representation election, informing the workers that he had lost his leg in a strike.[33]

Consultants also advised employers to assemble employees in special meetings during work time, at which management representatives would present anti-union arguments, often using films and videos. Sometimes workers are forbidden to ask questions. In 1973 an NLRB trial examiner ruled against twenty-two J. P. Stevens employees, who had protested being fired en masse for trying to ask questions during an anti-union speech at a captive audience meeting. The examiner stated that they were guilty of insubordination serious enough to justify discharge, because their employer was paying them during the time they were at the meeting. In 80 percent of NLRB union representation election campaigns today, employers force workers to attend such "captive-audience meetings," permissible under the Taft-Hartley Act.[34]

The anti-union consultants benefit enormously from a provision of the Landrum-Griffin Act of 1959, which requires unions to make public their annual financial reports. Union officers also had to disclose any financial transactions involving themselves or their relatives that could constitute a conflict of interest. The consultants therefore had access to highly detailed financial information about the unions they opposed, which they made every effort to exploit, and often distort, in order to depict them as wasteful, irresponsible, and overly bureaucratized.[35]

Marty Levitt, an anti-union consultant from 1969 to 1987, who worked for two of the largest firms in the business, John Sheridan Associates and Modern Management Methods, recalled that they placed heavy emphasis in their "prevention" campaigns on defaming union activists. Levitt and those who worked under him "routinely pried into workers' police records, personnel files, credit histories, medical records, and family lives" in an effort to uncover anything that could damage the activists' reputations and drive the uncommitted employees away from them. Levitt often fabricated charges that activists were homosexuals or adulterers, which he noted could be very damaging to a union trying to organize in a blue-collar town.[36]

The consultants train managerial personnel to react immediately to an organizing effort, with a high level of coordination. In Glens Falls, New York, for example, supervisors at C. R. Bard, one of the world's largest manufacturers of medical supplies, were already calling workers at home on Saturday morning, instructing employees not to speak with union organizers who had begun home visits on Friday afternoon. On Monday morning at 7:00 A.M. the plant manager began captive-audience meetings, fifteen of which were held, where supervisors warned employees that the corporation might shut the plant down if it were unionized. The supervisors had been taught how to run these meetings at special seminars, including what they should say at them, and how to identify the most pro-company workers. By Monday, a "loyal workers" committee had formed and was distributing anti-union bumper stickers and signs.[37]

Consultants have prepared the essential materials to be distributed in an anti-union campaign—videos, leaflets, posters, letters—long in advance. Their basic message is interchangeable, differing little from one industry or location to another, with often only the company's name having to be altered. Scenes of a factory can be removed from an anti-union video, and footage of a nursing home substituted, if that is currently the consultant's client.[38]

Anti-union consultants also advise employers how to design the physical layout of a workplace so as to inhibit union organizing. They recommend that buildings contain numerous points of entry, which makes the distribution of union handbills more difficult. The scattering of employee rest rooms, water fountains, and coffee machines around a plant makes it unlikely that any significant number of employees will concentrate at one point, as does scheduling workers to eat lunch at different times. Consultants also recommend that employers stagger employee working hours, to reduce the likelihood of car pooling, another means by which union sympathizers can come into contact with the uncommitted.[39]

While the anti-union consulting firms today for the most part rely on methods that do not involve physical force, there are still areas of the country, particularly in the South, where corporations employ violence to discourage unionization and to break strikes. The South has traditionally been the region most inhospitable to unionization, in part because of employers' greater ability to exploit racism to divide the labor force, particularly up through the 1960s. For example, the International Union of Electrical, Radio, and Machine Workers (IUE) narrowly lost an NLRB union representation election at the Neco Company in Bay Springs, Mississippi, in the mid-1950s after management circulated a photograph of IUE president James Carey dancing with a black woman, an African delegate to an International Labor Organization meeting.[40] Also significant were the South's more rigid caste barriers, dampening workers' sense that they could improve their conditions, and the more paternalistic social relations, delegitimating challenges to the ruling strata. Fundamentalist Protestantism was also more strongly entrenched among southern working people, which placed greater emphasis on seeking solutions as an individual, rather than within a collective framework. The proportion of the southern labor force that is organized is only about half that of the North.[41]

In the South, politicians, local employers, and the police work in concert to disrupt union organizing drives. Labor leaders refer to this coalition of forces as the "southern conspiracy." During a United Textile Workers union drive in 1976 at the Milledgeville, Georgia, plant of J. P. Stevens, the nation's second largest textile manufacturer, the town's mayor, "who always took a leadership role in such matters," summoned J. P. Stevens management, officials of local companies, and town officials, to plan how to prevent organization of the plant. Milledgeville policemen were assigned to observe union meetings and note down the license plate numbers of workers who attended, just as Harry Bennett's Servicemen had done in the Ford drives of the 1930s and 1940–41. Using the police computer in Atlanta, they then determined the names and addresses of the union sympathizers and distributed them to J. P. Stevens and other local employers, who could discharge and blacklist them. Management of the local Holiday Inn, where the organizing local usually met, provided police with a room directly above that the union rented, allowing them to observe any worker who entered.[42]

The *Economist* noted in 1979 that "[v]iolence is never far from the surface of labor organizing drives in the South." Police shadowed union organizer Mel Tate from the time he arrived in Milledgeville to organize J. P. Stevens in June 1976 until 1979. Fearing beatings and worse, Tate always drove to union meetings using a different route. He told a reporter that he did not dare fall sick, because he could not be sure anyone would take him to a hospital. A female union sympathizer driving home one night was followed by a tailgating police car that began repeatedly bumping her vehicle. When she accelerated to escape the bumping, unaware it was a police car, the police officer stopped her for speeding. A Milledgeville police detective who informed the *Economist* that his chief had ordered him to conduct illegal surveillance on the textile workers' union during this organizing drive was mysteriously killed by a car on a lonely road late in the campaign. In Florida, five bullets were fired into the car of Arthur Riffe, a United Steelworkers Union organizer during campaigns. Riffe noted that company security men or police badly beat up many of his colleagues.[43]

The South's relative inhospitality to unions even caused corporations that had long been unionized, like GM, in the 1970s to oppose organization of new plants it opened in the region, in locations like Clinton and Brookhaven, Mississippi, and Fitzgerald, Georgia. By the late 1970s, Japanese and European auto companies were deliberately setting up plants there because they wanted them to operate nonunion. Leonard Woodcock recalled that when he served as president of the UAW, from 1970 to 1977, he urged Japanese auto corporations, along with Volkswagen and Volvo, to build plants in the United States. When these corporations sent feasibility teams here, they usually started their investigations at the UAW's Solidarity House in Detroit, and "it was taken for granted" that the new plants they opened would be union. That assumption changed after 1977.[44]

During the 1980s, management was increasingly willing to break strikes with "permanent replacement workers," using them in nearly one-fifth of strikes between 1985 and 1989. A House of Representatives committee in 1989 estimated that around 21,000 strikers had lost their jobs to permanent replacements that year. Because this meant the strikers would never be reemployed, it constituted a "virtual declaration of open warfare" on unions. In the late 1980s, some companies upped the ante by advertising for permanent replacements, and even hiring them, during contract negotiations, a highly intimidating tactic that made clear to workers that a strike could result in their termination.[45]

Corporations began relying more heavily on professional security services specializing in combating unions to protect their "replacement workers." Vance International, for example, directed by former U.S. Secret Service agent Charles Vance, which was hired to protect strikebreakers in the Pittston coal strike in 1989 and the Caterpillar tractor strike in 1992, provides armed guards "dressed in combat gear," who employ film cameras to identify pickets. Vance guards have "become fixtures wherever a major strike occurs." Vance International advertises for what unions call "mercenaries" in *Soldier of Fortune* magazine. During strikes, these security firms sometimes also erect elaborate barbed wire fences around plants to inhibit picket line activity.[46]

Most companies had refrained from using permanent replacements during the post–World War II period until 1981, when President Reagan fired 13,000 striking air traffic controllers, who were federal employees, banning them from federal reemployment for life, and filling their positions with nonunion trainees. Reagan's action destroyed the strikers' union, the Professional Air Traffic Controllers Organization (PATCO), encouraging private corporations to pursue a similar approach. Corporations that subsequently employed permanent replacements for strikers included Greyhound Bus, International Paper, Caterpillar Tractor, Pittston Coal, and Eastern Airlines. Phelps Dodge and Continental Airlines both broke their unions in the early 1980s by filling strikers' positions with permanent replacements.[47]

The bitterly fought eight-month Pittston coal strike in 1989, waged largely to preserve medical benefits, involving 6,000 active, retired, and laid off UMW members, mostly in southwestern Virginia and southern West Virginia, was marked by the Vance guards' and state police's rough tactics against nonviolent strikers, along with the Connecticut-headquartered conglomerate's attempt to employ permanent replacements. The UMW possessed far less leverage in a strike than in the early part of the century, because coal was now much less important as a fuel source. The percentage of bituminous coal that was mined by UMW members had fallen drastically from the World War II period, from 80 percent to one-third by 1989.[48]

To supplement the Vance guards, Virginia's governor stationed 350 state troopers armed with shot guns in the coal fields, "like an occupying army," at a cost to the taxpayers of over $1 million a month. The state police joined with Vance guards to harass and intimidate strikers and their supporters. A state police helicopter followed the sixteen-year-old daughter of a disabled UMW member, who was president of her high school UMW auxiliary, when she walked home from school, while Vance guards forced her brother's car off the road. Vance guards in five jeeps surrounded a strike rally, and shot videos of the participants to intimidate them. They also conspicuously photographed the houses of union activists, as though they were criminal suspects. A woman protested the state police's practice of photographing arrested strikers after forcing them to their knees, handcuffed and in a "subjugated position," comparing the troopers to "guards overseeing a road gang."[49]

Shaped by a long tradition of violent labor conflict and used to risking their lives underground, the miners were more likely than most workers to confront state police and company guards aggressively. Although the Pittston strikers refrained from the violence often employed by union miners in the early twentieth century, they vigorously applied tactics of nonviolent civil disobedience inspired by the 1960s civil rights movement. They dressed in military-style camouflage uniforms to convey the feeling that they were at war and to make it more difficult for the police to identify them as individuals. Miners and their supporters set up mile-long rolling roadblocks with vehicles, to interfere with the delivery of strikebreakers, sat down en masse on the road with the same intent, and placed knots of welded nails on the roads, called jack rocks, designed to shred the tires of state police cars, Vance security vans, and coal trucks driven by strikebreakers. Women strike supporters proudly wore miniature versions as earrings. In April and May 1989 alone state police arrested 3,000 people for blocking mine entrances, many of whom they treated roughly. The UMW's journal published a photograph showing a striker, smiling defiantly, his arm in a sling, wearing "the decoration he received from the Virginia state police for participating in a non-violent civil protest": a sprained wrist and a dislocated thumb. One miner's wife complained that state police had kept her and others they had arrested on a bus for seven hours without permitting them to go to the bathroom, or even have a drink of water.[50]

Like their counterparts in the early twentieth century, the strikers referred to southern West Virginia as a miniature, corporate-run autocracy, in which union miners' protest was suppressed with massive armed force. To illustrate this claim, the UMW journal ran a photograph of Pittston strikers posing with a sign "This Is South West Virginia, Not South Africa."[51]

The Dallas-based Greyhound Bus Corporation, which had promoted an image of paternalism in labor relations, nonetheless "felt not a moment's . . . doubt" in 1990 about hiring permanent replacements for their drivers as soon as they indicated they might strike. Greyhound CEO Fred Currey had sought to enhance employee prestige and sense of belonging by honoring its drivers for individual achievement at company banquets and by soliciting employee opinion on certain business decisions. Yet less than a week into the strike, he had hired 700 permanent replacements for his drivers, and Greyhound ridership had risen already to 38 percent of normal levels. In desperation, fearing permanent loss of employment, some of the striking drivers resorted to "old-fashioned bare-knuckle violence." Striker violence escalated after a newly hired "replacement worker" lost control of his bus and ran over a union picket, crushing him to death. In nine states, snipers fired at Greyhound buses driven by strikebreakers; in one Florida shooting, flying shrapnel injured seven passengers. The gunfire further contributed to Greyhound's problem in recruiting strikebreakers, already difficult because relatively low unemployment had caused "the tightest labor market in years," allowing the union in this instance to survive.[52]

Caterpillar Tractor, the world's largest manufacturer of earth-moving and construction equipment, had considerably more success employing the permanent replacement strategy against the UAW in 1991–92, when the economic situation had become much worse. The five-month strike marked the first time in decades that management had confronted the UAW, perhaps the nation's strongest union, with the threat of permanently replacing large numbers of striking members. The press described the strike, in which 13,000 workers participated, as the biggest showdown between labor and management since President Reagan broke PATCO in 1981. Caterpillar hired Vance International, denounced by the UAW as a "rent-a-thug service," to guard its plants during the strike. Vance guards, dressed in black, stood on building rooftops, videotaping union pickets.[53]

Unfortunately for the UAW, because of the level of underemployment and unemployment Caterpillar was deluged with applications from persons willing to replace permanently the strikers, who earned an average of $17 an hour. As in the Ravenswood lockout, youth eagerly took jobs away from middle-aged men they considered pampered; the strikers, protected from layoffs by union commitment to seniority, averaged twenty-four years on the job. In Peoria, Illinois, where Caterpillar's flagship plant was located, the unemployment rate was 9 percent. There were 56,000 calls placed to a special telephone number providing job information to potential striker replacements within one three-hour period. A worker recently laid off from a $6.30 an hour job at a rubber parts factory, preparing to cross the picket line, exclaimed, "$17 an hour and they don't want to work?"[54]

The flood of job applications caused the union to collapse "like a house of cards," only eight days after Caterpillar announced that it would permanently replace any striker who did not return to work. The corporation imposed a settlement on its terms, which "ha[d] ominous implications for unions across the United States." A Canadian magazine noted that "the humbling of one of America's most powerful trade unions sent shock waves through Canadian labor circles as well."[55]

In the aftermath of Caterpillar's defeat of the UAW, organized labor made the passage of a federal law banning the permanent replacement of strikers its top legislative priority. The U.S. Supreme Court in 1938 had formally upheld an employer's right to replace strikers permanently in the case of *NLRB v. McKay Radio*. Doug Fraser and Irving Bluestone both stated that organized labor never considered overturning that decision a priority because postwar business made little effort to break strikes with permanent replacements before 1981. It was the PATCO strike of that year, and corporate business's subsequent decision to start using permanent replacements "on a massive scale," that "really . . . triggered the labor movement" into pushing for legislation to bar this practice. "The PATCO strike . . . was followed by Eastern [Airlines], which was followed by Greyhound, which got great public notice."[56]

But the bill banning the use of permanent replacements in strikes, introduced in Congress after the Caterpillar strike, failed to pass, yet another indication that organized labor's political clout was much diminished. Although President Clinton endorsed the bill, *Newsweek* noted in 1993 that "all signs are that the White House would be happy to see the issue fade away."[57]

Organized labor now had genuine cause to fear that its ability to strike, which it considered a fundamental right in a democratic society, was seriously jeopardized, at least in periods when unemployment and underemployment were significant. Management had demonstrated time and again during the 1980s and early 1990s its willingness to replace strikers permanently. Not since the early 1920s, when many large corporations eliminated existing trade unions, in an anti-labor offensive whose very name, the American Plan, implied trade unionism's illegitimacy, had antiunionism appeared so publicly acceptable. The permanent replacement of strikers, highly publicized by the mass media, seriously inhibited union organizing, because many workers feared that if they belonged to a union, labor leaders would draw them out on strike. Anti-labor consultants began producing videos to use during NLRB election campaigns, which emphasized that a yes vote for the union might well lead to the worker's being permanently replaced during a strike.[58]

The National Labor Relations Act of 1935 was still on the books in the year 2000, but the AFL-CIO's deputy organizing director spoke of the right to organize in the United States as a "legal fiction." Anti-union consultants advised employers how to delay NLRB representation elections for lengthy periods, often two or three years, using such tactics as refusing to agree on which workers should be allowed to vote in it. This allows management to discharge the leading union activists, intimidating the rest of the work force. The prospects for leading activists to be fired are exceedingly high; in 1980 at least one of every twenty workers who voted for a union in an NLRB election was dismissed. To be sure, firing a worker for joining or supporting a union is against the law, but the procedure a worker must follow in challenging a discharge is unusually "long [and] tortuous," often lasting years, by which time the organizing drive often has already fizzled out. As a result there is no union to prevent the activist from being fired again. The discharged employee is not permitted to return to his or her old job and collect back pay until all appeals have been exhausted. Even when a worker wins reinstatement with back pay, the cost to the employer is minuscule, far less than it would be were the workers to win a union contract. The worker cannot recover attorneys' fees, and the company can subtract from a back pay award whatever sum the worker has earned from any other employment after being discharged. The company is also entitled to deduct any NLRB back pay awards from its taxes as a legitimate business expense. For this reason, many corporate executives refer to NLRB back pay awards as their "hunting license," allowing them to employ an illegal, but highly effective, tactic against union organizing campaigns. AFL-CIO secretary-treasurer Richard Trumka, who had led the UMW in the Pittston strike, sadly observed in 1999 that "intimidation and interference by employers is such standard practice in today's workplaces that the freedom to form a union doesn't really exist at all."[59]

# NOTES

INTRODUCTION

1. *San Francisco Chronicle*, 20, 25–26, 30 April 1902; *San Francisco Examiner*, 27–28 April 1902.
2. *San Francisco Chronicle*, 25 April 1902.
3. *San Francisco Examiner*, 28 April 1902.
4. *San Francisco Chronicle*, 18, 20–24 April 1902.
5. Interchurch World Movement, *Public Opinion and the Steel Strike* (New York: Harcourt Brace, 1921), 1, 4–5; J. P. Shalloo, *Private Police: With Special Reference to Pennsylvania* (Philadelphia: American Academy of Political and Social Science, 1933), 142; *Coast Seamen's Journal*, 29 December 1915, 12.
6. Jerold S. Auerbach, *Labor and Liberty: The La Follette Committee and the New Deal* (Indianapolis: Bobbs-Merrill, 1966), 97.
7. Harold A. Cranefield, interview by Jack W. Skeels, 17 May 1963, 9, Oral History Collection, Archives of Labor and Urban Affairs, Walter P. Reuther Library, Wayne State University, Detroit, Mich.
8. Robert Hunter, *Violence and the Labor Movement* (New York: Macmillan, 1919), 280; H. M. Gitelman, "Perspectives on American Industrial Violence," *Business History Review* 47 (Spring 1973): 21–22.
9. Interchurch World Movement, *Public Opinion and the Steel Strike*, 4; Sidney Howard, *The Labor Spy* (New York: Republic Publishing, 1924), 19, 40. On Farley's earnings, see chapter 2.
10. J. Bernard Hogg, "Public Reaction to Pinkertonism and the Labor Question," *Pennsylvania History* 11 (1944): 177.
11. Ibid., 177–78.
12. James D. Horan, *The Pinkertons: The Detective Dynasty That Made History* (New York: Crown Publishers, 1967), 343–44, 358. Several Pinkerton agents and strike supporters were killed in the gun battle.
13. John Mackay, *Allan Pinkerton: The First Private Eye* (New York: John Wiley & Sons, 1996), 212, 214–15; Wayne G. Bruel, *The Molly Maguires* (New York: Vintage, 1964), 352.
14. *United Mine Workers Journal* (hereafter, *UMWJ*), 17 October 1901; John A. Fitch, *The Causes of Industrial Unrest* (New York: Harper & Brothers, 1924), 184.
15. F. B. McQuiston, "The Strike Breaker," *Independent*, 17 October 1901, 2456–57.
16. Ibid., 2456–58; Harry Laidler, *Boycotts and the Labor Struggle: Economic and Legal Aspects* (New York: John Lane, 1913), 304.
17. McQuiston, "Strike Breaker," 2457.
18. Nels Anderson, *The Hobo: The Sociology of the Homeless Man* (Chicago: Univer-

sity of Chicago Press, 1923), 57; Alexander Keyssar, *Out of Work: The First Century of Unemployment in Massachusetts* (New York: Cambridge University Press, 1986), 59; U.S. Senate, *Industrial Relations: Final Report and Testimony Submitted to Congress by the Commission on Industrial Relations*, vol. 1, 64th Cong., 1st sess., 1916, S. Doc. 415, 103–5; David Montgomery, *The Fall of the House of Labor* (New York: Cambridge University Press, 1987), 59–60.

19. Keyssar, *Out of Work*, 91, 94.

20. Ibid., 43.

21. Ibid., 152.

22. Stephan Thernstrom, *The Other Bostonians: Poverty and Progress in the American Metropolis, 1880–1970* (Cambridge, Mass.: Harvard University Press, 1973), 225, 227; U.S. Senate, *Industrial Relations*, 1:101, 110.

23. "The Unemployed in New York," *Public Opinion*, 31 March 1906, 399; Anderson, *The Hobo*, 3.

24. Jack London, *War of the Classes* (New York: Macmillan, 1905), 61–64.

25. *UMWJ*, 16 April 1914; U.S. Senate, *Report of the Committee on Education and Labor Pursuant to S. Res. 266: Strikebreaking Services*, 76th Cong., 1st sess., 1939, 73; Alan W. Elkins to Lester Levin, n.d., box 85, Violations of Free Speech and Rights of Labor, Record Group 46, National Archives, Washington, D.C.; Anderson, *The Hobo*, 5.

26. *Labor News* (Worcester, Mass.), 28 August 1909; *UMWJ*, 6 January 1916; Hunter, *Violence and the Labor Movement*, 320.

27. *California Social-Democrat*, 11 March 1916; *International Brotherhood of Teamsters, Chauffeurs, Stablemen, and Helpers*, April 1914, 13.

28. Jack London, *The Iron Heel* (1907; reprint, New York: Sagamore Press, 1957), 70.

29. *Miners' Magazine*, 15 February 1912; *UMWJ*, 7 July 1913.

30. Felix Yates to Boy Scouts of America, 13 January 1913, reel 28, John Mitchell Papers, Catholic University of America Archives, Washington, D.C.; *UMWJ*, 7 July 1913; *Des Moines Register and Leader*, 11 September and 28 August 1911; *California Social-Democrat*, 16 September 1912; *Chicago Daily Socialist*, 15 March 1912.

31. Victor Reuther, interview by Stephen H. Norwood, Washington, D.C., 26 August 1993.

32. Stephen H. Norwood, *Labor's Flaming Youth: Telephone Operators and Worker Militancy, 1878–1923* (Urbana: University of Illinois Press, 1990), 110–21.

CHAPTER ONE

1. *New York Journal*, 7 March 1905; *New York Evening Post*, 7 March 1905; *Daily People*, 8 March 1905.

2. *New York Herald*, 8 March 1905; *New York World*, 8 March 1905; *New York Journal*, 8 March 1905.

3. *New York Evening Post*, 7 March 1905; *New York Sun*, 8 March 1905. During the

strike, the "brawny" Whitwell, who worked as a conductor, talked of how he "enjoyed the excitement of hauling . . . muckers out of the [subway] car, and of suppressing strike sympathizers [with force]." Eager to fight with his fists, he also carried a Colt .45 revolver in his pocket. *New York Journal*, 11 March 1905.

4. *Brooklyn Daily Eagle*, 9 March 1905.

5. *New York Journal*, 7 March 1905.

6. *Lumberjack* (Alexandria, La.), 30 January 1913.

7. *Brooklyn Daily Eagle*, 7 March 1905.

8. Median parental income for the 1920s at private colleges was about $5,000 and at state universities about $3,000, far more than even skilled workers earned in a year. Colin B. Burke, *American Collegiate Populations: A Test of the Traditional View* (New York: New York University Press, 1982), 228; Paula Fass, *The Damned and the Beautiful: American Youth in the 1920s* (New York: Oxford University Press, 1977), 134–35.

   By the 1890s the state universities were shifting their focus to training businessmen and professionals, rather than plain farmers and mechanics, leading many to charge that they had become "dude factories." Oscar Handlin and Mary F. Handlin, *Facing Life: Youth and the Family in American History* (Boston: Little Brown, 1971), 189.

9. Robert Wiebe, *The Search for Order, 1877–1920* (New York: Hill and Wang, 1967), 121; James Hulme Canfield, *The College Student and His Problems* (New York: Macmillan, 1902), 83.

10. Fass, *Damned and Beautiful*, 172; Seymour Deming, *The Pillar of Fire: A Profane Baccalaureate* (Boston: Small, Maynard, 1915), 28.

11. Christopher Jencks and David Riesman, *The Academic Revolution* (Garden City, N.Y.: Doubleday, 1968), 49.

12. *California Social-Democrat*, 30 March 1912; *Worker*, 14 February 1904; *Call Magazine* (*New York Call*), 24 August 1919.

13. Samuel Eliot Morison, *Three Centuries of Harvard, 1636–1936* (Cambridge, Mass.: Harvard University Press, 1946), 401; *New York Herald*, 30 May 1903. The United Mine Workers union newspaper expressed its contempt for collegians' frivolity, noting facetiously that "workmen do not exercise alone the prerogative of the strike." It reported that 4,000 University of Pennsylvania students had just walked out of classes because the administration had refused them permission to stage a celebration of their school's football victory over Michigan. *United Mine Workers Journal*, 12 December 1912.

14. The University of Chicago, for example, was established largely as result of a $34 million gift from John D. Rockefeller, founder of the Standard Oil Company; Stanford University received $24 million from the estate of the Southern Pacific Railroad head. Walter P. Metzger, *Academic Freedom in the Age of the University* (New York: Columbia University Press, 1955), 139, 141. See also J. E. Kirkpatrick, *The American College and Its Rulers* (New York: New Republic, 1926), 96, 99–100.

15. Metzger, *Academic Freedom*, 213; Maurice Caullery, *Universities and Scientific Life in the United States* (Cambridge, Mass.: Harvard University Press, 1922), 53.

16. Metzger, *Academic Freedom*, 153.

17. Bud Schultz and Ruth Schultz, *It Did Happen Here: Recollections of Political Repression in America* (Berkeley: University of California Press, 1989), 8–9; *Labor News* (Worcester, Mass.), 10 July 1915.

18. Isaac Kramnick, "The Professor and the Police," *Harvard Magazine*, September–October 1989, 42, 44; *Harvard Lampoon*, 16 January 1920.

19. *International Brotherhood of Teamsters, Chauffeurs, Stablemen, and Helpers*, November 1914, 8; Henry James, *Charles W. Eliot: President of Harvard University, 1869–1909* (Boston: Houghton Mifflin, 1930), 2:154–56; Hugh Hawkins, *Between Harvard and America: The Educational Leadership of Charles W. Eliot* (New York: Oxford University Press, 1972), 151; "President Eliot's Latest," *Weekly Bulletin of the Clothing Trades*, 12 February 1904, 11, in box 298, Charles W. Eliot Papers, Harvard University Archives, Pusey Library, Harvard University, Cambridge, Mass.; Samuel Gompers, "President Eliot's Mental Decadence," *American Federationist*, February 1906, 94.

20. Morison, *Three Centuries*, 466; Nicholas Murray Butler, *Across the Busy Years: Recollections and Reflections* (New York: Charles Scribner's Sons, 1940), 2:365–66; Arthur Twining Hadley to Paul Kennaday, 23 February 1905, Box 107, Arthur Twining Hadley Papers, Sterling Library, Yale University, New Haven, Conn.

21. Henry Seidel Canby, *American Memoir* (Boston: Houghton Mifflin, 1947), 144–45.

22. Malcolm Ross, *Death of a Yale Man* (New York: Farrar and Rinehart, 1939), 377; "Diary of Algernon Lee," 17 May 1916, reel 58, Socialist Party of America Papers, microfilm, Duke University Library, Durham, N.C. Lee, while expecting college students to be "pretty ignorant," expressed shock at hearing students make this complaint when he lectured at New York University.

23. Fass, *Damned and Beautiful*, 343–44; "College Women Not Radical but Highly Conservative," *New Student*, 1 November 1924, 1–2.

24. Harold Laski, "Why Don't Your Young Men Care? The Political Indifference of the American Undergraduate," *Harper's Magazine*, July 1931, 129, 133.

25. Albert Edwards, "The Spirit of the Russian Student," *Intercollegiate Socialist*, October–November 1913, 14, 25.

26. Samuel Gompers, "Editorial: The Students' Debasement," *American Federationist*, April 1905, 217–18.

27. At its peak in 1917, the ISS boasted no more than 60–70 undergraduate chapters. Morris Hillquit, *Loose Leaves from a Busy Life* (New York: Macmillan, 1934), 61; Lewis S. Feuer, *The Conflict of Generations* (New York: Basic Books, 1969), 342–44. Some delegates at the 1912 ISS convention even objected to putting the organization on record as condemning strikebreaking by college students, because it was "primarily a study group," and passing such a resolution might antagonize prospective members "who were not Socialists." *New York Call*, 29 December 1912.

28. John Chalberg, *Emma Goldman: American Individualist* (New York: Harper Collins, 1991), 170.

29. Charles Denby, "Mere Man and Student," *New Student*, 30 December 1922, 1; William Ross, "Student and Worker," *New Student*, 2 February 1924, 7; "College Women Not Radical but Highly Conservative," 1; Feuer, *Conflict*, 351.

30. Elliot J. Gorn, *The Manly Art: Bare-Knuckle Prize Fighting in America* (Ithaca, N.Y.: Cornell University Press, 1986), 185–91; Michael C. C. Adams, *The Great Adventure: Male Desire and the Coming of World War I* (Bloomington: Indiana University Press, 1990), 36–37, 43.

31. Gorn, *Manly Art*, 192; C. Wright Mills, *White Collar: The American Middle Classes* (New York: Oxford University Press, 1951), 75, 98–99.

32. Gorn, *Manly Art*, 180; Benjamin Rader, *American Sports: From the Age of Folk Games to the Age of Televised Sport* (Englewood Cliffs, N.J.: Prentice-Hall, 1990), 24–25, 215.

33. Peter N. Stearns, *Be a Man! Males in Modern Society* (New York: Holmes and Meier, 1979), 59, 77.

34. William Brown Meloney, "Strikebreaking as a Profession," *Public Opinion*, 25 March 1905, 440–41; B. T. Fredericks, "James Farley, Strikebreaker," *Leslie's Monthly Magazine*, May 1905, 108; *San Francisco Chronicle*, 15 May 1907.

35. Morris Joseph Clurman, "The American Game of Football: Is It a Factor for Good or for Evil?," *Medical Record* 79 (7 January 1911): 19.

36. E. Anthony Rotundo, *American Manhood: Transformations of Masculinity from the Revolution to the Modern Era* (New York: Basic Books, 1993), 240; Roberta J. Park, "Physiology and Anatomy Are Destiny?! Brains, Bodies, and Exercise in Nineteenth Century American Thought," *Journal of Sport History* 18 (Spring 1991): 32.

37. Malcolm Townshend, "A Cane Rush," in Norman W. Bingham Jr., ed., *The Book of Athletics and Out-of-Door Sports* (Boston: Lothrop Publishing, 1895), 226.

38. Ibid., 226–36.

39. *New York Herald*, 25 October 1896; *New York Tribune*, 25 October 1896.

40. *Triangle*, 19 December 1901, University Archives, Bobst Library, New York University, New York.

41. Arthur Twining Hadley to Henry Parks Wright, 9 May 1900, box 1, Henry Parks Wright Papers, Sterling Library, Yale University, New Haven, Conn.; *Yale Daily News*, 18 May 1903.

42. *San Francisco Examiner*, 21 and 22 August 1901; "President Wheeler Dodges," *Coast Seamen's Journal*, 11 September 1901, 2.

43. "Labor to the University," *Coast Seamen's Journal*, 28 August 1901, 10; "President Wheeler Dodges," 2.

44. *Chicago Tribune*, 11, 13, 14, 17, and 18 April 1903; *Chicago Socialist*, 11 April 1903.

45. *Minnesota Daily*, 26 and 29 September 1903; *Minneapolis Journal*, 26 September 1903.

46. *Minneapolis Journal*, 28 September 1903; *Minnesota Daily*, 1 October 1903.

47. *New Haven Evening Register*, 11 May 1903.

48. *New York Herald*, 17 May 1903; *New York Tribune*, 19 February 1905; *Worker*, 26 February 1905; "Capitalistic Hadley," *Social Democratic Herald*, 27 June 1903; Arthur Twining Hadley to H. G. Nicholls, 9 May 1903, box 104, and Hadley to

Paul Kennaday, 23 February 1905, box 107, Arthur Twining Hadley Papers, Sterling Library, Yale University, New Haven, Conn. During the 1905 Chicago teamsters' strike, Marshall Field & Company, a leading department store, hired Northwestern University football players to drive its horse-drawn North Shore suburban delivery wagons. *Chicago Tribune*, 2 May 1905.

49. *New York Call*, 31 January 1912; *Labor News*, 10 February 1912; *Tech*, 2 February 1912, MIT Museum Collection, Massachusetts Institute of Technology, Cambridge, Mass. That same year, a union spokesperson denounced Wesleyan College students as "thugs" for "the methods [they] employed . . . in quelling the strike" of weavers at the Russell Manufacturing Company in Middletown, Connecticut. Many Wesleyan students, including most of the football team, had signed on as sheriff's deputies to guard the mill during the strike. The union spokesperson claimed that when the collegians were not "breaking bones" on the gridiron, they "enjoyed . . . beating women [strikers] over the heads with baseball bats." *Newark (N.J.) Evening News*, 11 June 1912.

50. Stephen H. Norwood, *Labor's Flaming Youth: Telephone Operators and Worker Militancy, 1878–1923* (Urbana: University of Illinois Press, 1990), 189–90.

51. Ibid., 189, 285.

52. "Announcement of A. Lawrence Lowell," 9 September 1919, folder 1087, A. Lawrence Lowell Papers, Harvard University Archives, Pusey Library, Harvard University, Cambridge, Mass.; "Harvard Men in the Boston Police Strike," *School and Society*, 11 October 1919, 425.

53. *Boston Evening Globe*, 9 September 1919. Even more students would have volunteered, but Harvard's fall term did not begin for another week. The football team arrived early. Francis Russell, *A City in Terror: The 1919 Boston Police Strike* (New York: Penguin, 1975), 142–43.

54. *Boston Evening Transcript*, 12 September 1919.

55. *Wellesley College News*, 9 October 1907.

56. The phrase "'neath the oaks" is from Mary Barnett Gilson, *What's Past Is Prologue* (New York: Harper and Brothers, 1940), 10; Melvyn Dubofsky, *When Workers Organize: New York City in the Progressive Era* (Amherst: University of Massachusetts Press, 1968), 55, 83; Graham Adams Jr., *Age of Industrial Violence: The Activities and Findings of the United States Commission on Industrial Relations* (New York: Columbia University Press, 1966), 109; *Indianapolis News*, 20 January 1910, clipping in Wellesley College Archives, Margaret Clapp Library, Wellesley College, Wellesley, Mass.; *Wellesley College News*, 26 January 1910.

57. *Harvard Crimson*, 13 June 1912; *Christian Science Monitor*, 6 and 10 June 1912; *New York Times*, 10 June 1912.

58. *Wellesley College News*, 15 February 1911; "College Women Not Radical but Highly Conservative," 1.

59. Norwood, *Labor's Flaming Youth*, 283–84.

60. Adams, *Industrial Violence*, 109; *New York Times*, 16 January 1910.

61. Untitled play, n.d., 4, in New York Women's Trade Union League Papers, New York State Department of Labor Library, New York, N.Y.

62. Christopher Lasch, foreword to David Noble, *America by Design: Science, Technology, and the Rise of Corporate Capitalism* (New York: Alfred A. Knopf, 1977), xii; David Montgomery, *Workers' Control in America: Studies in the History of Work, Technology, and Labor Struggles* (New York: Cambridge University Press, 1979), 26–27; Daniel Rodgers, *The Work Ethic in Industrial America, 1850–1920* (Chicago: University of Chicago Press, 1978), 55.

63. Noble, *America by Design*, 41.

64. Ibid., 139, 144.

65. Ibid., 39, 51.

66. *Detroit Free Press*, 15 June 1901.

67. *New York Herald*, 3 June 1901; *Worker*, 27 October 1901; *Detroit Free Press*, 15 June 1901.

68. *Detroit Free Press*, 16 June 1901; *Columbia Spectator*, 10 March 1905. An editorial in New York University's student weekly noted that the collegians' strike-breaking for the IRT disproved the frequently heard claim that "a college education makes a man unfit for hard, practical work." *Triangle*, 14 March 1905.

69. *San Francisco Chronicle*, 12 May 1913; Upton Sinclair, *The Goose-Step: A Study of Academic Education* (Pasadena, Calif.: published by the author, 1922), 135. The *California Social-Democrat* reported that a delegation of Berkeley socialists planned to visit President Wheeler and the Board of Regents to determine whether professors or administrators were requiring students to become strikebreakers in order to receive academic credit. The newspaper declared, "It is stated that in the past [University of California] students have been given their regular credits while away helping to break the strikes of the carmen's union along with Farley's criminals and thugs, of the dock workers, of the lumbermen, and of the laundry workers." *California Social-Democrat*, 17 May 1913.

70. *Stute* (Stevens Institute of Technology), 5 May 1920; *New York Tribune*, 14 April 1920; *Philadelphia Inquirer*, 14 April 1920.

71. *New York Tribune*, 14 April 1920; *Daily Princetonian*, 14 and 15 April 1920; *Columbia Spectator*, 15 April 1920.

72. *Stute*, 5 May 1920. Collegians from Lehigh (an engineering school), Lafayette, Franklin and Marshall, Swarthmore, University of Pennsylvania, and Rutgers, especially engineering students and athletes, joined those from MIT, Stevens Institute, Princeton, and Columbia in helping to break the strike. *Philadelphia Inquirer*, 14–16 April 1920; *New York Tribune*, 14 April 1920.

73. "The Institute and the Railroad Strike," *Technology Review* 23 (November 1921): 585; *Tech*, 28 October 1921, MIT Museum Collection, Massachusetts Institute of Technology, Cambridge, Mass.

74. *Harvard Crimson*, 24 October 1921; *New York Times*, 19 and 26 October 1921; *Baltimore Sun*, 18 October 1921. The *New York Times* noted that Johns Hopkins students had "volunteered and performed efficient service" during a railroad strike in the autumn of 1919. They held down every job on the regular runs from Baltimore to New York, Philadelphia, Harrisburg, and Washington except that of engineer. *New York Times*, 19 October 1921.

75. *Williams Record*, 22 October 1921; *North Adams (Mass.) Evening Transcript*, 25 October 1921.

76. Bruce Nelson, *Workers on the Waterfront: Seamen, Longshoremen, and Unionism in the 1930s* (Urbana: University of Illinois Press, 1988), 133, 169; Lloyd Morris, *Not So Long Ago* (New York: Random House, 1949), 361; John McCarten, "The Little Man in Henry Ford's Basement," *American Mercury*, May 1940, 8–10.

77. Feuer, *Conflict*, 353.

78. Fass, *Damned and Beautiful*, 130, 205; Mary Ryan, *Womanhood in America: From Colonial Times to the Present* (New York: Franklin Watts, 1983), 220.

CHAPTER TWO

1. Richard Harding Davis, *Real Soldiers of Fortune* (New York: Charles Scribner's Sons, 1906), 86.

2. Gail Bederman, *Manliness and Civilization: A Cultural History of Gender and Race in the United States, 1880–1917* (Chicago: University of Chicago Press, 1995), 17–19.

3. *Chicago Tribune*, 26 January 1904.

4. *St. Louis Globe-Democrat*, 11 June 1900.

5. *San Francisco Chronicle*, 10 May 1907; *San Francisco Examiner*, 8 May 1907.

6. *Chicago Chronicle*, 21 November 1903.

7. *Richmond Times-Dispatch*, 1 August and 3 July 1903; *Washington Post*, 24 June 1903.

8. *Chicago Inter-Ocean*, 13 November 1903; *New York Sun*, 24 July 1904.

9. Sarah Henry, "The Strikers and Their Sympathizers: Brooklyn in the Trolley Strike of 1895," *Labor History* 32 (Summer 1991): 337–38; *Chicago Tribune*, 6 June 1915.

10. *San Francisco Examiner*, 6 May 1907.

11. Jon C. Teaford, *The Twentieth Century American City: Problem, Promise, and Reality* (Baltimore: Johns Hopkins University Press, 1986), 8–9; *New York American*, 24 October 1906.

12. *New York American*, 10 November and 23 and 24 October 1906.

13. Robert H. Babcock, "'Will You Walk? Yes We'll Walk!' Popular Support for a Street Railway Strike in Portland, Maine," *Labor History* 35 (Summer 1994): 381; "Responsibility of Instructors," *Motorman and Conductor*, May 1904, 13.

14. *New Orleans Daily Picayune*, 9 October 1902.

15. "The Cleveland Strike," *Motorman and Conductor*, August 1899, 2.

16. *St. Louis Post-Dispatch*, 13 May 1900; *Motorman and Conductor*, June 1900, 1; *St. Louis Globe-Democrat*, 12 June 1900.

17. *Report of the Bureau of Statistics of Labor for the State of Louisiana, 1902–3* (Baton Rouge: Advocate, Official Journal of Louisiana, 1904), 33; *New Orleans Daily Picayune*, 30 September 1902; *New York Herald*, 6 March 1905.

18. *New York Tribune*, 24 February 1910; *New Orleans Item*, 5 July 1929.

19. *San Francisco Examiner*, 8 May 1907.

20. "The St. Louis Strike," *Collier's Weekly*, 30 June 1900, 18.

21. *New York Tribune*, 3 and 4 June 1909.

22. *Cleveland Plain-Dealer*, 24, 25, and 29 July and 9 and 12 August 1899; *Cleveland Citizen*, 5 August 1899; *St. Louis Post-Dispatch*, 20 June 1900; *St. Louis Globe-Democrat*, 21 June 1900.

23. *St. Louis Globe-Democrat*, 11 June 1900; *San Francisco Chronicle*, 14 and 15 May 1907; *Philadelphia Inquirer*, 30 May 1909; *Cleveland Plain-Dealer*, 21 July 1899. In Bay City, Michigan, in 1905, strike sympathizers blocked streetcar tracks with 800-pound waterpipes. *Detroit Free Press*, 8 June 1905.

24. *Chicago Tribune*, 12 and 13 November 1903; Howard B. Myers, "The Policing of Labor Disputes in Chicago: A Case Study," pt. 1 (Ph.D. dissertation, University of Chicago, 1929), 405, 407.

25. *Richmond Times-Dispatch*, 4 July 1903.

26. *St. Louis Globe-Democrat*, 26 May 1900.

27. *St. Louis Post-Dispatch*, 28 May 1900.

28. *St. Louis Globe-Democrat*, 23 May 1900.

29. Ibid., 11 May 1900.

30. *Cleveland Plain-Dealer*, 13 August 1899.

31. *New Orleans Daily Picayune*, 9 October 1902.

32. A. J. Scopino Jr., "Community, Class, and Conflict: The Waterbury Trolley Strike of 1903," *Connecticut History* 24 (1983): 36–37; *Chicago Tribune*, 13 November 1903.

33. *San Francisco Examiner*, 8 May 1907.

34. Ibid., 5, 6, and 7 May 1907.

35. Myers, "Policing," 406–7.

36. Scott Compton Osborn and Robert L. Phillips Jr., *Richard Harding Davis* (Boston: Twayne Publishers, 1978), 87.

37. Michael Rosenthal, *The Character Factory: Baden-Powell's Boy Scouts and the Imperatives of Empire* (New York: Pantheon Books, 1984), 3; Theodore Ropp, *War in the Modern World* (New York: Collier Books, 1959), 231, 232; Modris Eksteins, *Rites of Spring: The Great War and the Birth of the Modern Age* (New York: Anchor Books, 1989), 160; Byron Farwell, "Taking Sides in the Boer War," *American Heritage* 27 (April 1976): 22.

38. *New Orleans Daily Picayune*, 8 October 1902; *Richmond Times-Dispatch*, 3 July 1902.

39. *Cleveland Plain-Dealer*, 21 July 1899.

40. *Richmond Times-Dispatch*, 28 and 30 June 1903.

41. Ibid., 27 June 1903.

42. *Detroit Free Press*, 23 June 1905; "Report of Selig Perlman," 10 March 1914, 5, box 18, Records Relating to Commission on Industrial Relations Studies, 1912–15, Department of Labor Records, Record Group (hereafter, RG) 174, National Archives (hereafter, NA), College Park, Md.

43. *San Francisco Examiner*, 8 May 1907.

44. *St. Louis Post-Dispatch*, 10 May 1900.

45. Elliot J. Gorn, *The Manly Art: Bare-Knuckle Prize Fighting in America* (Ithaca,

N.Y.: Cornell University Press, 1986), 192–93; Michael Isenberg, *John L. Sullivan and His America* (Urbana: University of Illinois Press, 1988), 11–12.

46. Bederman, *Manliness and Civilization*, 15.

47. *Chicago Chronicle*, 14 November 1903.

48. Roderick Nash, *The Nervous Generation: American Thought, 1917–1930* (Chicago: Rand, McNally, 1970), 140; Jane Tomkins, *West of Everything: The Inner Life of Westerns* (New York: Oxford University Press, 1992), 143–44.

49. William Brown Meloney, "Strikebreaking as a Profession," *Public Opinion*, 25 March 1905, 440.

50. Leroy Scott, "'Strike-Breaking' as a New Occupation," *World's Work*, May 1905, 6203.

51. *Philadelphia Inquirer*, 10 March 1910; *St. Louis Post-Dispatch*, 18 May 1900.

52. John H. Craige, "The Violent Art of Strike-Breaking," *Collier's*, 7 January 1911, 29.

53. *Philadelphia Inquirer*, 25 February 1910; Richard Slotkin, *The Fatal Environment: The Myth of the Frontier in the Age of Industrialization* (New York: Atheneum, 1985), 480; Richard Slotkin, *Gunfighter Nation: The Myth of the Frontier in Twentieth Century America* (New York: Harper Collins, 1992), 107.

54. On strikebreakers as prisoners of war, see, for example, *New Orleans Daily Picayune*, 8 October 1902. The newspaper reported that strikers captured four strikebreakers and held them prisoner at a location the union refused to disclose. The strikers claimed the men were defectors.

55. *Chicago Tribune*, 14 November 1903; *Chicago Inter-Ocean*, 14 and 15 November 1903.

56. *San Francisco Chronicle*, 14 May 1907.

57. *Detroit Free Press*, 28 June 1905; *New York Tribune*, 17 September 1916.

58. *Cleveland Plain-Dealer*, 22 July 1899; *St. Louis Post-Dispatch*, 20 May 1900.

59. *San Francisco Chronicle*, 14 May 1907; *New Orleans Item*, 5 July 1929.

60. *Philadelphia Inquirer*, 21 and 22 February 1910; *New York Tribune*, 22 February 1910.

61. "What the World Is Doing: A Record of Current Events," *Collier's*, 12 March 1910, 12; *New York Tribune*, 23 February 1910; *Pennsylvania State Police*, Public Information Bulletin No. 1, July 1961, 4, Historical Publications, box 33, Samuel W. Pennypacker Papers, Manuscript Group 171, Pennsylvania State Archives, Harrisburg, Pa.

62. *Chicago Record-Herald*, 14 November 1903.

63. Ibid.; Myers, "Policing," pt. 1, 400; *Chicago Inter-Ocean*, 13 November 1903; *Chicago Tribune*, 14 November 1903.

64. *Chicago Tribune*, 15 November 1903.

65. Fairfax Downey, *Richard Harding Davis: His Day* (New York: Charles Scribner's Sons, 1933), 182; Davis, *Soldiers*, 30–31, 75; *California Social-Democrat*, 9 September 1911.

66. Slotkin, *Gunfighter Nation*, 202; Edgar Rice Burroughs, *The Warlord of Mars* (1913; reprint, New York: Ballantine Books, 1985), 110.

67. *New York Times*, 8 March 1905.

68. Meloney, "Strikebreaking as a Profession," 440; B. T. Fredericks, "James Farley, Strikebreaker," *Leslie's Monthly Magazine*, May 1905, 106; *Social Democratic Herald*, 24 September 1904, 3.

69. *United Mine Workers Journal*, 15 December 1904, 2; "New Methods of Self-Preservation," *American Industries*, 1 April 1905, 3; *Social Democratic Herald*, 24 September 1904, 3.

70. On Farley's intervention in the Lodi, New Jersey, dye works strike, see, for example, *New York Tribune*, 5 October 1905, and *Newark Evening News*, 4 and 5 October 1905; Meloney, "Strikebreaking as a Profession," 441.

71. *United Mine Workers Journal*, 15 December 1904, 2; Fredericks, "Farley," 108; Meloney, "Strikebreaking as a Profession," 441; Scott, "Strikebreaking as a New Occupation," 6200. Farley was reputed to smoke fifty to sixty black Havana cigars a day.

72. John Kenneth Turner, "Gunman Profession First Founded by James Farley," *Appeal to Reason*, 6 June 1914, 1 (Farley's IRT profit was $184,000); Fredericks, "Farley," 108; Scott, "Strikebreaking as a New Occupation," 6201; *Social Democratic Herald*, 24 September 1904, 3; *New York Journal*, 6 March 1905.

73. Scott, "Strikebreaking as a New Occupation," 6200; Meloney, "Strikebreaking as a Profession," 440; obituary of James Farley, *Plattsburgh (N.Y.) Sentinel*, 16 September 1913.

74. Fredericks, "Farley," 109; Scott, "Strikebreaking as a New Occupation," 6200; *Chicago Tribune*, 8 November 1903.

75. Scott, "Strikebreaking as a New Occupation," 6200; Turner, "Gunman," 1.

76. The *Chicago Record-Herald*, 9 November 1903, reported that Farley "first became prominent in street car strikes last winter in Connecticut." Leroy Scott stated in 1905 that Farley "first attained his present rank as a strikebreaking general with absolute power" in Providence in 1902, but there is no mention of him in the newspaper accounts of the strike. Scott, "Strikebreaking as a New Occupation," 6200. The *Social Democratic Herald* stated that Farley was involved in breaking the 1901 Scranton and the 1902 Providence streetcar strikes but does not indicate whether he had complete charge of the situation, as he did in Richmond. It did imply that he was in full command in Waterbury in 1903. *Social Democratic Herald*, 23 May and 24 September 1904.

77. Obituary of Farley, *Plattsburgh Sentinel*, 16 September 1913; Fredericks, "Farley," 108; *Washington Post*, 24 June and 3 July 1903; *Richmond Times-Dispatch*, 27 June 1903.

78. *Richmond Times-Dispatch*, 19 and 20 June and 4 July 1903; *Baltimore Sun*, 21 June 1903; "New Methods of Self Preservation," 3.

79. *New York Tribune*, 29 November 1903; *Chicago Tribune*, 8 November 1903; *Chicago Record-Herald*, 13 November 1903.

80. David Montgomery, *The Fall of the House of Labor* (New York: Cambridge University Press, 1987), 269; Myers, "Policing," pt. 1, 385; *Chicago Tribune*, 13 November 1903; *New York Tribune*, 29 November 1903.

81. Myers, "Policing," pt. 1, 401–2; *Chicago Tribune*, 13 November 1903.

82. *Chicago Tribune*, 16 November 1903.

83. Ibid., 11 and 13 November 1903; *Chicago Chronicle*, 13, 15, and 21 November 1903; "Chicago Strike Ended," *Street Railway Journal*, 28 November 1903, 935; *Chicago Inter-Ocean*, 13 November 1903.

84. *New York Tribune*, 29 November 1903.

85. Myers, "Policing," pt. 1, 402, 418–19, 420; *Chicago Record-Herald*, 12 November 1903; *Chicago Tribune*, 16 November 1903; Sidney Harring, *Policing a Class Society: The Experience of American Cities, 1865–1915* (New Brunswick, N.J.: Rutgers University Press, 1983), 228. Herman Schuettler had helped over-power and arrest the Haymarket anarchist Louis Lingg in a fierce fight in 1887. Paul Avrich, *The Haymarket Tragedy* (Princeton, N.J.: Princeton University Press, 1984), 232.

86. Harring, *Policing a Class Society*, 28–29, 49–50, 53, 55; Myers, "Policing," pt. 1, 419.

87. "Chicago Street Railway Strike," *Street Railway Journal*, 21 November 1903, 921; *Philadelphia Inquirer*, 23 February 1910.

88. *New York Sun*, 24 July 1904.

89. Ibid.; Fredericks, "Farley," 107.

90. "New Methods," 3; Fredericks, "Farley," 106, 107; *New York Times*, 8 March 1905.

91. *New York American*, 6 March 1905; *New York Times*, 3, 7, 8, and 10 March 1905; *New York Evening Post*, 7 March 1905; *New York Herald*, 6, 7, 8, and 9 March 1905; *Chicago Tribune*, 7 March 1905.

92. *New York Herald*, 7 and 8 March 1905; Fredericks, "Farley," 108; *New York American*, 6 March 1905.

93. *New York Herald*, 8 March 1905; *New York Times*, 8 March 1905; *New York Journal*, 8 and 13 March 1905; *New York American*, 7 March 1905.

94. *New York American*, 6 and 8 March 1905; *New York Herald*, 6 and 8 March 1905.

95. John H. Craige, "The Professional Strike-Breaker," *Collier's*, 3 December 1910, 31.

96. *St. Louis Globe-Democrat*, 31 May 1900; *New Orleans Daily Picayune*, 9 October 1902.

97. *New York Journal*, 7 March 1905; *New York Herald*, 8 March 1905; *Chicago Tribune*, 7 March 1905.

98. *New York Tribune*, 29 October 1906; *New York American*, 27 and 28 October and 5 November 1906.

99. *New York Tribune*, 29 October 1906.

100. Turner, "Gunman," 1; *San Francisco Chronicle*, 7 May 1907.

101. Henry K. Brent, "The Strike Situation in San Francisco," *Street Railway Journal*, 21 September 1907, 416; *San Francisco Examiner*, 6 and 7 May 1907.

102. *San Francisco Chronicle*, 7 May 1907; *San Francisco Examiner*, 6 and 7 May 1907.

103. Brent, "Strike Situation," 416.

104. *San Francisco Examiner*, 7 May 1907; *San Francisco Chronicle*, 6 May 1907.

105. *San Francisco Examiner*, 8 May 1907.

106. *Motorman and Conductor*, June 1907, n.p.; James B. Morrow, "The Story of the Great Strikes," *Collier's Weekly*, 12 August 1899, 3.

107. *Social Democratic Herald*, 25 November 1905.

108. *New York Tribune*, 2 May 1905.

109. Jack London, *The Iron Heel* (1907; reprint, New York: Sagamore Press, 1957), 70, 191.

110. Obituary of Farley, *New York Times*, 11 September 1913; obituary of Farley, *Plattsburgh Sentinel*, 16 September 1913.

111. Obituary of Farley, *Labor News* (Worcester, Mass.), 13 September 1913; obituary of Farley, *New York Times*, 11 September 1913; Turner, "Gunman," 1.

112. Craige, "Professional Strike-Breaker," 20.

113. Turner, "Gunman," 1.

114. *New Orleans Daily Picayune*, 10 October 1902.

115. Ibid., 27 September 1902; *San Francisco Chronicle*, 23 April 1902.

116. *St. Louis Post-Dispatch*, 9 May and 14 June 1900; *St. Louis Globe-Democrat*, 11 May 1900.

117. Ibid., 8 May 1900; *New York Times*, 7 March 1905; *San Francisco Chronicle*, 23 April 1902.

118. John Kenneth Turner, "Posing as Alexander Craige, Turner Gets Damning Facts from Bergoff, Gunman Chief," *Appeal to Reason*, 13 June 1914, 1; Edward Levinson, *I Break Strikes! The Technique of Pearl L. Bergoff* (New York: Robert M. McBride, 1935), 61.

119. "Strikebreaking," *Fortune*, January 1935, 57; John Kenneth Turner, "Guggenheims' Favorite Gun Crew," *Appeal to Reason*, 8 August 1914, 2.

120. Turner, "Guggenheims' Favorite Gun Crew"; *New York Times*, 5 June 1914.

121. "Strikebreaking," 57, 58. Famed Western novelist Zane Grey, another proponent of exaggerated masculinity, dropped his original first name Pearl when he overheard a young woman on a train refer to him as "she" while discussing his work. Tomkins, *West of Everything*, 158.

122. "Strikebreaking," 57, 59.

123. Ibid., 57, 59–60; Jack Lait, "How a Big Strikebreaker Works," *American Magazine*, January 1917, 51.

124. *New York Post*, 24 October 1934.

125. *New York Tribune*, 12 September 1916; *New York Times*, 12 September 1916; "Strikebreaking," 89.

126. Levinson, *I Break Strikes!*, 63, 64. In the 1907 San Francisco streetcar strike, Farley's conductors developed the trick of palming a half dollar in one hand and giving back only 45 cents in change for the nickel fare after receiving a silver dollar from the passenger. When the passenger protested, the conductor showed the passenger the palmed half dollar and told the passenger he had given him that coin, not a dollar. Brent, "Strike Situation," 417.

127. *New York Times*, 12 September 1916, 5 and 7 September 1920.

128. Ibid., 7 and 8 September 1916; *New York Tribune*, 2 September 1920.

129. Lait, "How a Big Strikebreaker Works," 51; *New York Tribune*, 8 September 1916.

130. Obituary of Bergoff, *New York Times*, 13 August 1947; Turner, "Posing as Alexander Craige," 1; obituary of Mahon, *New York Times*, 5 June 1914; "Strikebreaking," 57.

131. "Strikebreaking," 57, 60–61.

132. *San Francisco Examiner*, 7 May 1905; *New York Times*, 7 March 1902.

133. Teaford, *Twentieth Century American City*, 62; *Chicago Tribune*, 14 June 1915.

134. *New Orleans Item*, 3 July 1929.

135. Myers, "Policing," pt. 1, 421; *New Orleans Daily Picayune*, 8 October 1902.

136. "Providence and Pawtucket Railway Strike," *Street Railway Journal*, 21 June 1902, 776; Scott Molloy, *Trolley Wars: Streetcar Workers on the Line* (Washington, D.C.: Smithsonian Institution Press, 1996), 141; *New Orleans Daily Picayune*, 8–9 October 1902.

137. *Washington Post*, 24 June 1903; *Richmond Times-Dispatch*, 15 July 1903; *San Francisco Chronicle*, 14 May 1907.

138. "Report of Selig Perlman," 1, RG 174, NA; *Indianapolis Star*, 14 November 1913.

139. *New York Times*, 9 September 1916; *New York Tribune*, 22 February 1910.

140. *New Orleans Item*, 7 July 1929.

141. *Richmond Times-Dispatch*, 28 June and 5 July 1903.

142. Ibid., 28 and 29 July and 1 and 2 August 1903.

143. *Washington Post*, 30 July 1903; *Richmond Times-Dispatch*, 1 August 1903.

144. Robert M. Fogelson, *America's Armories: Architecture, Society, and Public Order* (Cambridge, Mass.: Harvard University Press, 1989), xiii, 42, 45–46.

145. *Cleveland Plain-Dealer*, 21 and 26 July 1899.

146. *New York Tribune*, 16 June 1902; *Providence Journal*, 14 June 1902.

147. *Richmond Times-Dispatch*, 24 and 26 June 1903.

148. John Ellis, *The Social History of the Machine Gun* (1975; reprint, New York: Arno Press, 1981), 42.

149. *Providence Journal*, 15 and 17 June 1902; *New York Times*, 25 June 1903; Scorpino, "Waterbury," 37.

150. *New Orleans Daily Picayune*, 10 October 1902.

151. *New York Herald*, 3–4 and 6 February 1903.

152. Samuel Walker, *A Critical History of Police Reform: The Emergence of Professionalism* (Lexington, Mass.: D. C. Heath, 1977), 76; Gerda Ray, "'We Can Stay until Hell Freezes Over': Strike Control and the State Police in New York, 1919–1923," *Labor History* 36 (Summer 1995): 404, 417; "Pennsylvania's Mounted Police," *Public Opinion*, 12 May 1906, 583; Inis Weed, "Drafts of Reports on Violence and Suppression in Industrial Disputes," 45, reel 7, U.S. Commission on Industrial Relations Papers, Department of Labor Records, RG 174, NA.

153. Walker, *Police Reform*, 76; *New York Tribune*, 24 February 1910; "Pennsylvania's Mounted Police," 584; Frank Morn, *"The Eye That Never Sleeps": A History of the Pinkerton National Detective Agency* (Bloomington: Indiana University Press, 1982), 168; Ray, "'We Can Stay,'" 404, 417.

154. Katherine Mayo, *Justice to All: The Story of the Pennsylvania State Police* (Boston: Houghton Mifflin, 1920), 175–76.

155. *Philadelphia Inquirer*, 25 February 1910; *New York Tribune*, 25 February 1910.

156. Mayo, *Justice to All*, 176–77; *New York Herald*, 25 February 1910.

157. "What the World Is Doing: A Record of Current Events," 10; *Philadelphia Inquirer*, 25 February 1910.

158. *Philadelphia Inquirer*, 10 March 1910; Ken Fones-Wolf, "The Philadelphia General Strike of 1910," in Ronald Filippelli, ed., *Labor Conflict in the United States: An Encyclopedia* (New York: Garland Press, 1990), 415–16; *Pennsylvania State Police*, 4, box 33, Samuel W. Pennypacker Papers, Pennsylvania State Archives, Harrisburg, Pa.

159. Richard Harding Davis, "The Reporter Who Made Himself King," in Grant Overton, ed., *The World's One Hundred Best Short Stories* (New York: Funk & Wagnalls, 1927), 1:33.

CHAPTER THREE

1. F. E. Wolfe, *Admission to American Trade Unions* (Baltimore: Johns Hopkins University Press, 1912), 117, 119, 125; "Organizing Negro Workers," n.d., and "Organized Labor and the Negro Worker," n.d., series 6, box 89, National Urban League Papers, Library of Congress, Washington, D.C.; Peter Gottlieb, *Making Their Own Way: Southern Blacks' Migration to Pittsburgh, 1916–1930* (Urbana: University of Illinois Press, 1987), 152. Research for this chapter was supported in part by a grant from the Oklahoma Foundation for the Humanities and the National Endowment for the Humanities. Findings, opinions, and conclusions do not necessarily represent the views of the foundation or the NEH.

2. Kenneth Kusmer, *A Ghetto Takes Shape: Black Cleveland, 1870–1930* (Urbana: University of Illinois Press, 1978), 153.

3. Booker T. Washington, "The Negro and the Labor Unions," *Atlantic Monthly*, June 1913, 757; August Meier and Elliott Rudwick, "Attitudes of Negro Leaders toward the American Labor Movement from the Civil War to World War I," in Julius Jacobson, ed., *The Negro and the American Labor Movement* (Garden City, N.Y.: Doubleday, 1968), 39–41.

4. Meier and Rudwick, "Attitudes of Negro Leaders," 41; Kusmer, *Ghetto*, 152–53; "Springfield," *Horizon: A Journal of the Color Line*, August 1908, 10. According to August Meier and Elliott Rudwick, even most members of the militant Niagara Movement "showed little interest either in attracting the Negro masses or in demonstrating how much they had in common with white laborers." Meier and Rudwick, "Attitudes of Negro Leaders," 43.

5. E. Franklin Frazier, *Black Bourgeoisie: The Rise of a New Middle Class in the United States* (New York: Collier Books, 1962 [1957]), 27–28.

6. G. David Houston, "Weaknesses of the Negro College," *Crisis*, July 1920, 122. The absence of academic freedom in the southern black colleges persisted

until the 1960s. Staughton Lynd and Roberta Yancy, "Southern Negro Students: The College and the Movement," *Dissent*, Winter 1964, 41.

7. Frazier, *Black Bourgeoisie*, 74. During the 1920s, African American college students did stage rebellions on campus, some of which forced the resignations of the college president, and challenged white racism, but none appeared motivated by a desire to express solidarity with African American labor organizing or militancy. Raymond Wolters's book on black college rebellions in the 1920s does not include "labor" or "union" in the index. After 1920, black students protested the vocational orientation of their education and demanded more of a voice in managing their schools. They challenged restrictive dress codes and prohibitions against dancing. They sometimes also demanded more emphasis on fraternities and sororities and on college sports. But Wolters mentions no campus demonstrations in support of striking African American workers or involvement in labor organizing, as, for example, in the Brotherhood of Sleeping Car Porters campaign, which began in earnest in 1925. Raymond Wolters, *The New Negro on Campus: Black College Rebellions of the 1920s* (Princeton, N.J.: Princeton University Press, 1975), vii–viii, 13, 28, 31, 37, 45, 56–57, 63, 198, 254.

8. Frazier, *Black Bourgeoisie*, 63.

9. "Negroes to Break Strikes?," *Worker*, 18 May 1902.

10. *New York Age*, 18 May 1905.

11. Sidney Harring, *Policing a Class Society: The Experience of American Cities* (New Brunswick, N.J.: Rutgers University Press, 1983), 123; Allan H. Spear, *Black Chicago: The Making of a Negro Ghetto, 1890–1920* (Chicago: University of Chicago Press, 1967), 39; Howard B. Myers, "The Policing of Labor Disputes in Chicago: A Case Study," pt. 2 (Ph.D. dissertation, University of Chicago, 1929), 557.

12. *St. Louis Post-Dispatch*, 7 May 1905. William M. Tuttle Jr. has emphasized black strikebreakers' "determin[ation] to defend themselves" against strikers and strike sympathizers during the 1905 Chicago teamsters' strike. However, he states that in the previous year's packinghouse strike they "generally fled." William M. Tuttle Jr., *Race Riot: Chicago in the Red Summer of 1919* (New York: Atheneum, 1970), 121–22.

13. Joel Williamson, *The Crucible of Race: Black-White Relations in the American South since Emancipation* (New York: Oxford University Press, 1984), 117; Leon F. Litwack, *Trouble in Mind: Black Southerners in the Age of Jim Crow* (New York: Alfred A. Knopf, 1998), 157–58.

14. Williamson, *Crucible*, 189.

15. Ibid., 189, 221; Litwack, *Trouble in Mind*, 315.

16. Williamson, *Crucible*, 205–6, 217; Charles Crowe, "Racial Massacre in Atlanta, September 22, 1906," *Journal of Negro History* 54 (April 1969): 150, 157.

17. Ray Stannard Baker, "The Riddle of the Negro," 520, and "The Color Line in the North," 350, 352, *American Magazine*, 1907, box 17, Office Files of Ethelbert Stewart, Bureau of Labor Statistics (hereafter, BLS) Records, Record Group (hereafter, RG) 257, National Archives (hereafter, NA), College Park, Md.

18. "Alleged Discrimination against Colored Students," *Outlook*, 18 October 1902, 383.

19. "Springfield," *Moon Illustrated Weekly* (Memphis), 17 March 1906, 3, 4; "Springfield," *Horizon: A Journal of the Color Line*, August 1908, 9; Louis Harlan, *Booker T. Washington: The Wizard of Tuskegee* (Oxford University Press, 1983), 360.

20. Kelly Miller, *Race Adjustment: Essays on the Negro in America* (New York: Neale Publishing, 1908), 293–94.

21. Marvin Fletcher, *The Black Soldier and Officer in the United States Army, 1891–1917* (Columbia: University of Missouri Press, 1974), 153, 159; J. Anthony Lukas, *Big Trouble* (Simon & Schuster, 1997), 123.

22. Fletcher, *Black Soldier*, 67; Harlan, *Booker T. Washington: The Wizard of Tuskegee*, 316.

23. "The Negro in the Navy," *Horizon: A Journal of the Color Line*, November 1909, 7.

24. Fletcher, *Black Soldier*, 31, 153–54; Litwack, *Trouble in Mind*, 466.

25. Ann J. Lane, *The Brownsville Affair: The National Crisis and Black Reaction* (Port Washington, N.Y.: National University Publications, Kennikat Press, 1971), 5, 39; Francis Butler Simkins, *Pitchfork Ben Tillman: South Carolinian* (Baton Rouge: Louisiana State University Press, 1944), 441; Lukas, *Big Trouble*, 131; *Companies B, C, D, Twenty-fifth United States Infantry Report on the Proceedings of the Court of Inquiry Relative to the Shooting Affray at Brownsville, Texas, August 13–14, 1906* (Washington, D.C.: Government Printing Office, 1911), 4:896, 1287; 11:2316.

26. *Companies B, C, D*, 4:990; 6:1406, 1475, 1479–80; *Affray at Brownsville, Tex., August 13 and 14, 1906: Proceedings of a General Court-Martial Convened at Headquarters Department of Texas, San Antonio, Tex., February 4, 1907, in the Case of Maj. Charles W. Penrose, Twenty-fifth United States Infantry* (Washington, D.C.: Government Printing Office, 1907), 239, 243, 264, 541–42, 1243, 1485; Lane, *Brownsville Affair*, 5.

  R. B. Creager, an attorney and U.S. commissioner and deputy clerk of the U.S. circuit and district courts of the southern district of Texas testified at the court-martial of Major Charles W. Penrose, a white officer of the Twenty-fifth Infantry Regiment, that the major had told him that his black troops "had as much right upon the streets and sidewalks of the town of Brownsville as any white man, and that the people of Brownsville must recognize that fact." Creager had responded that "as long as he was in the South they would find that as a matter of practice that when a negro and white man met on the sidewalk the negro would have to step aside." *Affray at Brownsville*, 264.

27. Lane, *Brownsville Affair*, 13. In July 1906, the Twenty-fifth Infantry Regiment's white commanding officer, Colonel Hoyt, had urged the War Department not to transfer it to Texas because of the race prejudice there, and "many of his officers expressed fear that discord would result from a contact of the soldiers with the Texas Militia." The regimental chaplain, the Twenty-fifth's only African American officer, predicted that the black soldiers would become involved in "an armed conflict" with white Texans. *Companies B, C, D*, 1475.

28. "The Race Press," *Horizon: A Journal of the Color Line*, January 1907, 18; "Talk Number Three," *Horizon: A Journal of the Color Line*, August 1908, 7.

29. Warren C. Whatley, "African-American Strikebreaking from the Civil War to the New Deal," *Social Science History* 17 (Winter 1993): 542; Lukas, *Big Trouble*, 118, 150–51; Fletcher, *Black Soldier*, 89.

30. *New York Tribune*, 29 June 1902.

31. Alma Herbst, *The Negro in the Slaughtering and Meat-Packing Industry in Chicago* (Boston: Houghton Mifflin, 1932), 24; R. R. Wright Jr., "The Negro in Times of Industrial Unrest," *Charities*, 7 October 1905, 71; William M. Tuttle Jr., *Race Riot: Chicago in the Red Summer of 1919* (New York: Atheneum, 1970), 117; Sterling Spero and Abram Harris, *The Black Worker: The Negro and the Labor Movement* (New York: Columbia University Press, 1931), 267. The stockyards industries constituted the largest industrial sector in Chicago, paying 10 percent of the city's total manufacturing wages in 1900. "Harry Rosenberg on Packing Industry and the Stockyards," n.d., 3, box 3, Mary McDowell Papers, Chicago Historical Society (hereafter, CHS), Chicago, Ill.

32. *Chicago Record-Herald*, 8 August 1904; James R. Barrett, *Work and Community in the Jungle: Chicago Packinghouse Workers, 1894–1922* (Urbana: University of Illinois Press, 1987), 44–45.

33. William Hard, "Labor in the Chicago Stockyards," *Outlook*, 16 June 1906, 371.

34. Ernest Poole, *The Bridge; My Own Story* (New York: Macmillan, 1940), 93; *Chicago Record-Herald*, 8 August 1904.

35. *Chicago Inter-Ocean*, 15 August 1904.

36. Charles J. Bushnell, *The Social Problem at the Chicago Stockyards* (Chicago: University of Chicago Press, 1902), 45; Barrett, *Work and Community*, 171; Poole, *The Bridge*, 93; Tuttle, *Race Riot*, 119; *Chicago Tribune*, 1 August 1904.

37. Bushnell, *Social Problem*, 45; "Rosenberg on Packing Industry," 14, box 3, Mary McDowell Papers, CHS; *Chicago Daily News*, 26 July 1904.

38. *Chicago Tribune*, 18 July and 16 August 1904.

39. *Chicago Chronicle*, 18 July 1904; *Chicago Inter-Ocean*, 18 July 1904; *Kansas City Star*, 29 July 1904.

40. *Chicago Daily News*, 27 July 1904; *Chicago Inter-Ocean*, 28 July 1904.

41. *Chicago Chronicle*, 13 August 1904.

42. *Chicago Tribune*, 21 August 1904; *Chicago Inter-Ocean*, 22 August 1904.

43. See, for example, *Chicago Chronicle*, 18 July 1904, on "cowardly" whites.

44. *Chicago Inter-Ocean*, 18 July 1904.

45. *Chicago Daily News*, 20 July 1904; *Chicago Tribune*, 23 July 1904.

46. *Omaha World-Herald*, 20 and 27 July 1904.

47. *Dallas Morning News*, 28, 29, and 30 July 1904.

48. *Omaha World-Herald*, 24 August 1904.

49. *Kansas City Star*, 1 August 1904.

50. Ibid., 18 August 1904.

51. *Chicago Tribune*, 7 August 1904. Mary McDowell, who had lived above a day nursery in the stockyards, recalled being wakened each morning when it was "barely light" by "the cry of the little children in protest against their mothers' enforced desertion." Mary McDowell, "Labor—The Great Strike," 3, n.d., box 3, Mary McDowell Papers, CHS.

52. *Chicago Chronicle*, 25 July 1904; *Chicago Tribune*, 25 July 1904. Members of these ethnic groups did not ordinarily bring presents to the wedding feast. Instead, guests tried to break a plate by throwing silver coins at it. The man who broke the plate was the first to dance with the bride, and no woman was allowed to dance until the plate was broken. *Chicago Tribune*, 14 August 1904.

53. *Chicago Tribune*, 11 August 1904; *Chicago Daily News*, 28 and 29 July 1904.

54. *Chicago Inter-Ocean*, 29 July 1904; *Chicago Tribune*, 29 July 1904.

55. *Chicago Inter-Ocean*, 17 and 19 August 1904.

56. *Chicago Tribune*, 17 August 1904; A. M. Simons, "The Battle of the Meat Makers," *Chicago Socialist*, 27 August 1904. The *Chicago Inter-Ocean* claimed that a "railway track almost devoid of lights" in the stockyards had "been named Lovers' Lane" and was "well patronized." *Chicago Inter-Ocean*, 15 August 1904. Some strike supporters of northern and western European ancestry depicted strikebreakers from southern and eastern Europe as similar to African Americans. Mary McDowell, for example, visited the Chicago packinghouses during the strike and observed two groups of Macedonian strikebreakers "trying to be gay." She noted that one group was dancing to the music "of Pan's own pipe," suggesting sexual debauchery. The other was singing to the accompaniment of a "primitive bagpipe" made from a "kid's skin with its baby hoof still hanging on," reflecting a cruelty to animals associated with savages. Mary McDowell, "Labor—The Great Strike," 7, Mary McDowell Papers, CHS.

57. *Chicago Chronicle*, 1 August 1904; *Chicago Record-Herald*, 1 August 1904.

58. *Chicago Daily News*, 29 July 1904.

59. Simons, "Battle," *Chicago Socialist*, 27 August 1904.

60. Poole, *The Bridge*, 94; *Chicago Tribune*, 14 August 1904.

61. *Chicago Tribune*, 22 August 1904; *Chicago Inter-Ocean*, 29 July 1904.

62. *Chicago Tribune*, 24 and 26 August 1904; *Chicago Inter-Ocean*, 24 August 1904.

63. John Roach, "Packingtown Conditions," *American Federationist*, August 1906, 534; Spear, *Black Chicago*, 38.

64. *Chicago Inter-Ocean*, 28 April 1905; Myers, "Policing," pt. 2, 557, 581; Spear, *Black Chicago*, 40. William M. Tuttle Jr. has noted that after the 1904 strike many packinghouse workers equated "Negro" with "scab" and that "the bloody teamsters' strike of 1905 . . . made more indelible the image of blacks as a 'scab race.'" Tuttle, *Race Riot*, 120.

65. "Teamsters' Side of the Strike," *Literary Digest*, 20 May 1905, 732.

66. *Chicago Daily News*, 5 May 1905; *St. Louis Globe-Democrat*, 6 May 1905.

67. Palmer M. Stewart, "Manuscript Report on Strike of International Teamsters' Union against Montgomery Ward & Company, April 6, 1905," 220, box 15, Office Files of Ethelbert Stewart, BLS Records, RG 257, NA; Myers, "Policing," pt. 2, 599.

68. Rhodri Jeffrey-Jones, *Violence and Reform in American History* (New York: New Viewpoints, 1978), 82; *St. Louis Globe-Democrat*, 29 April 1905; *St. Louis Post-Dispatch*, 7 May 1905; Myers, "Policing," pt. 2, 589.

69. David Montgomery, *The Fall of the House of Labor* (New York: Cambridge University Press, 1987), 269; Myers, "Policing," pt. 2, 561.

70. *New York Age*, 18 May 1905; John Cummings, "The Chicago Teamsters' Strike— A Study in Industrial Democracy," *Journal of Political Economy* 13 (September 1905): 551–52.

71. *St. Louis Globe-Democrat*, 1 May 1905; *Chicago Inter-Ocean*, 4 May 1905.

72. *Chicago Record-Herald*, 2 May 1905.

73. Ibid.; *Chicago Inter-Ocean*, 2 and 3 May 1905.

74. *Chicago Inter-Ocean*, 4 May 1905.

75. Ibid.

76. *Chicago Tribune*, 2 May 1905; *Chicago Record-Herald*, 2 May 1905.

77. *Chicago Tribune*, 3 May 1905; *Chicago Record-Herald*, 3 May 1905; *St. Louis Globe-Democrat*, 3 May 1905; *Chicago Daily News*, 3 May 1905.

78. *Chicago Inter-Ocean*, 3 May 1905; *Chicago Tribune*, 3 May 1905; *St. Louis Globe-Democrat*, 3 and 4 May 1905; Ethelbert Stewart to Commissioner of Labor, 15 May 1905, box 14, Office Files of Ethelbert Stewart, BLS Records, RG 257, NA.

79. *Chicago Tribune*, 4 May 1905; *St. Louis Post-Dispatch*, 3 May 1905; *Kansas City Star*, 2 May 1905.

80. *Chicago Record-Herald*, 2 May 1905; *St. Louis Post-Dispatch*, 7 and 10 May 1905.

81. Randy Roberts, *Papa Jack: Jack Johnson and the Era of White Hopes* (New York: Free Press, 1983), 26. Roberts notes that the leading white heavyweight fighters of the late nineteenth and early twentieth centuries had a much higher percentage of bouts won by knockout—"a yardstick for aggression"—than the leading African American fighters.

82. *St. Louis Post-Dispatch*, 7 May 1905.

83. *Chicago Record-Herald*, 3 May 1905; *New Orleans Times-Democrat*, 2 May 1905.

84. Myers, "Policing," pt. 2, 608–9.

85. *Chicago Record-Herald*, 20 May 1905; Stewart, "Manuscript Report," 171, box 15, Office Files of Ethelbert Stewart, BLS Records, RG 257, NA.

86. *New Orleans Times-Democrat*, 6 May 1905.

87. *Commercial Appeal* (Memphis), 7 May 1905. See also the editorial in the *Atlanta Journal*, 5 May 1905.

88. *St. Louis Post-Dispatch*, 7 May 1905.

89. *Chicago Tribune*, 11 May 1905.

90. Stewart, "Manuscript Report," 251–52, box 15, Office Files of Ethelbert Stewart, BLS Records, RG 257, NA; *Chicago Tribune*, 13 and 16 May 1905.

91. *Kansas City Star*, 16 May 1905; *Chicago Inter-Ocean*, 17 and 18 May 1905; Ethelbert Stewart to Commissioner of Labor, 15 May 1905, box 14, Office Files of Ethelbert Stewart, BLS Records, RG 257, NA; *Chicago Tribune*, 18 May 1905.

92. *Chicago Inter-Ocean*, 2 May 1905; *Chicago Record-Herald*, 2 and 9 May 1905.

93. *New York Age*, 25 May 1905.

94. *Chicago Record-Herald*, 15 May 1905.

95. Ibid., 9 and 10 May 1905; *Chicago Tribune*, 10 May 1905.

96. *New York Age*, 18 May 1905; *Freeman* (Indianapolis), 20 May 1905.

97. *Broad Ax* (Chicago), 6 May 1905; *Chicago Daily News*, 6 May 1905.

98. *Chicago Tribune*, 8 May 1905.

99. Cummings, "Chicago Teamsters' Strike," 560; Wright, "Negro in Times of Indus-

trial Unrest," 71; *Chicago Inter-Ocean*, 2 June 1905; *Chicago Record-Herald*, 26 and 27 May 1905; Ethelbert Stewart to Commissioner of Labor, 27 May 1905, box 14, Office Files of Ethelbert Stewart, BLS Records, RG 257, NA; *Chicago Daily News*, 29 May 1905.

100. *Chicago Inter-Ocean*, 4 May 1905; Ethelbert Stewart to Commissioner of Labor, 23 May 1905, box 14, Office Files of Ethelbert Stewart, BLS Records, RG 257, NA; *Chicago Tribune*, 1 May 1905.

101. Harring, *Policing a Class Society*, 125; *Chicago Tribune*, 6 May 1905; Walter Palmer, special agent Chicago, 13 June 1905, box 14, Office Files of Ethelbert Stewart, BLS Records, RG 257, NA; Myers, "Policing," pt. 2, 608, 609. The Employers' Association claimed several young women it employed as undercover detectives had become International Brotherhood of Teamsters (IBT) president Cornelius Shea's "most intimate associates in his nocturnal experiences," implying they had provided it with a full record of the union's plans and financial situation during the strike. *Chicago Inter-Ocean*, 18 June 1905.

102. Stewart, "Manuscript Report," 373, 377, 384, box 15, Office Files of Ethelbert Stewart, BLS Records, RG 257, NA.

103. Wright, "Negro in Times of Industrial Unrest," 73.

104. Spear, *Black Chicago*, 40.

105. Eric Arnesen, *Waterfront Workers of New Orleans: Race, Class, and Politics, 1863–1923* (New York: Oxford University Press, 1991); Daniel Letwin, *The Challenge of Interracial Unionism: Alabama Coal Miners, 1878–1921* (Chapel Hill: University of North Carolina Press, 1998); James R. Green, "The Brotherhood of Timber Workers, 1910–1913: A Radical Response to Industrial Capitalism in the Southern U.S.A.," *Past and Present* 60 (August 1973); Stephen H. Norwood, "Bogalusa Burning: The War against Biracial Unionism in the Deep South, 1919," *Journal of Southern History* 63 (August 1997). Biracial organizing—recruiting blacks and whites into racially separate locals of the same union—was the practice in nearly every case in which whites and blacks in the same trade organized together before the 1930s. Eric Arnesen, "Following the Color Line of Labor: Black Workers and the Labor Movement before 1930," *Radical History Review* 55 (Winter 1993): 58.

106. David Roediger, *Towards the Abolition of Whiteness: Essays on Race, Politics, and Working-Class History* (London: Verso, 1994), 133.

107. Norwood, "Bogalusa Burning," 592–93, 603; Roediger, *Towards Abolition*, 133.

108. Norwood, "Bogalusa Burning," 603–5.

109. Ibid., 591–93, 601, 614–15, 617, 619–20.

110. Ibid., 597–600, 628.

111. Gottlieb, *Making Their Own Way*, 161–62; Whatley, "African-American Strikebreaking," 527, 545. Similarly in the 1921 national packinghouse strike, also defeated largely by the use of African American strikebreakers, Morris & Company, one of Chicago's leading packinghouses, opened a recruiting office for strikebreakers in the middle of Chicago's black ghetto. In addition, the employment office at the stockyards was opened and "deluged with applicants . . . with the colored . . . given preference on account of their non-union

activities." Chicago's African American population grew, largely as a result of the Great Migration, by 148 percent between 1910 and 1920, and other northern cities also experienced substantial gains. Whatley, "African-American Strikebreaking," 545; "Negroes in the Packing House Strike in Chicago," n.d., box C-320, National Association for the Advancement of Colored People (hereafter, NAACP) Papers, Library of Congress (hereafter, LC), Washington, D.C.; Kusmer, *A Ghetto Takes Shape*, 157.

112. Henry M. McKiven, *Iron and Steel: Class, Race, and Community in Birmingham, Alabama, 1875–1920* (Chapel Hill: University of North Carolina Press, 1995), 123.

113. "Synopsis of Interview with Mr. K," 20 November 1919, 3, 5, box 4, Heber Blankenhorn Papers, Archives of Labor and Urban Affairs (hereafter, ALUA), Walter P. Reuther Library, Wayne State University (hereafter, WSU), Detroit, Mich.

114. Eugene Kincle Jones to John R. Shillady, 19 November 1918, box C-319, NAACP Papers, LC.

115. Minutes of Meeting of Order of Sleeping Car Conductors' Local No. 15, n.d., box 25, Chicago Federation of Labor Records, John Fitzpatrick Papers, CHS.

116. David Brody, *Steelworkers in America: The Nonunion Era* (1960; reprint, New York: Harper & Row, 1969), 266; Cliff Brown, "Racial Conflict and Split Labor Markets: The AFL Campaign to Organize Steel Workers, 1918–19," *Social Science History* 22 (Fall 1998): 331, 342.

117. Spear, *Black Chicago*, 163; "Synopsis," 2, box 4, Heber Blankenhorn Papers, ALUA, WSU. In January 1919, the Supervisor of Negro Economics in Illinois expressed grave concern over rising tension between white and black workers "due to the fact that while whites in large proportion are joining unions, only a small percentage of Negroes have done so." Forrester B. Washington to John Fitzpatrick, 25 January 1919, box 25, Chicago Federation of Labor Records, John Fitzpatrick Papers, CHS.

118. Spero and Harris, *The Black Worker*, 258, 259; Gottlieb, *Making Their Own Way*, 147; "Synopsis," 1, box 4, Heber Blankenhorn Papers, ALUA, WSU.

119. "The Failure of the Negro Church," *Messenger*, October 1919, 6.

120. Chandler Owen, "The Failure of the Negro Leaders," *Messenger*, January 1918, 23.

121. Gottlieb, *Making Their Own Way*, 173.

122. Ibid., 172; Frazier, *Black Bourgeoisie*, 87.

123. Frazier, *Black Bourgeoisie*, 147; *Chicago Defender*, 15 July 1919. The *Defender's* anti-unionism was at times so pronounced that until the end of 1927 it aggressively opposed African American attempts to organize the black sleeping car porters into a union. A labor reporter identified the *Defender* as "the mouthpiece of the Pullman Company in southside Chicago, the Negro district." Harry Kletzky, "Porter Brotherhood's Power Forces Negro Paper to Change Front," Federated Press, Chicago Bureau, 28 December 1927, box 25, Chicago Federation of Labor Records, John Fitzpatrick Papers, CHS.

124. Brody, *Steelworkers*, 254–55.

125. Gottlieb, *Making Their Own Way*, 160, 163; Brody, *Steelworkers*, 255.
126. Spero and Harris, *The Black Worker*, 262–63.
127. Jervis Anderson, *A. Philip Randolph: A Biographical Portrait* (New York: Harcourt Brace Jovanovich, 1972), 178–79, 184–85, 215; William Harris, *Keeping the Faith: A. Philip Randolph, Milton Webster, and the Brotherhood of Sleeping Car Porters, 1925–37* (Urbana: University of Illinois Press, 1977), 98–99, and cartoons following 116; Velma Murphy Hill and David Evanier, "Cracking the Rock of Segregation," *Forward*, 20 April 2001.
128. Robert H. Zieger, *The CIO, 1935–1955* (Chapel Hill: University of North Carolina Press, 1995), 83–85; August Meier and Elliott Rudwick, *Black Detroit and the Rise of the UAW* (New York: Oxford University Press, 1979), 4, 21–22.

CHAPTER FOUR

1. *Fort Smith Times-Record*, 20 January 1915.
2. *United Mine Workers Journal* (hereafter, *UMWJ*), 3 October 1901; Charles Maurer, *The Constabulary of Pennsylvania* (Reading, Pa.: Charles Maurer, n.d.), 8; Samuel Gompers, "Russianized West Virginia," *American Federationist*, October 1913, 825, 828–30, 835.
3. Kate Richards O'Hare, "War in the Copper Country," *National Rip-Saw*, December 1913, 3; *Miners' Magazine*, 28 August 1913.
4. "Militarism: What it Costs the Taxpayers," n.d., 4, box 738, Gifford Pinchot Papers, Library of Congress (hereafter, LC), Washington, D.C.
5. On the emergence of a new heterosocial youth culture in the big cities and the impact of the new consumerism on gender relations, see Kathy Peiss, *Cheap Amusements: Working Women and Leisure in Turn-of-the-Century New York* (Philadelphia: Temple University Press, 1986); Lewis A. Erenberg, *Steppin' Out: New York Nightlife and the Transformation of American Culture, 1890–1930* (Westport, Conn.: Greenwood Press, 1981); Stephen H. Norwood, *Labor's Flaming Youth: Telephone Operators and Worker Militancy, 1878–1923* (Urbana: University of Illinois Press, 1990); Nan Enstad, *Ladies of Labor, Girls of Adventure: Working Women, Popular Culture, and Labor Politics at the Turn of the Twentieth Century* (New York: Columbia University Press, 1999); and William Leach, "Transformations in a Culture of Consumption: Women and Department Stores, 1890–1925," *Journal of American History* 71 (September 1984).
6. On separate spheres in mining communities, see, for example, Elizabeth Jameson, "Imperfect Unions: Class and Gender in Cripple Creek, 1894–1904," in Milton Cantor and Bruce Laurie, eds., *Class, Sex, and the Woman Worker* (Westport, Conn.: Greenwood Press, 1977), 166, 169–75.
7. Mary E. Odem, "Teenage Girls, Sexuality, and Working-Class Parents in Early Twentieth Century California," in Joe Austin and Michael Nevin Willard, eds., *Generations of Youth: Youth Cultures and History in Twentieth-Century America* (New York: New York University Press, 1998), 52.
8. "The Coal Strike: A Near-by View," *Outlook*, 18 October 1902, 399; George

McGovern and Leonard F. Guttridge, *The Great Coal Field War* (Boston: Houghton Mifflin, 1972), 222. Colorado National Guard officers also accused the strikers of firing poisoned bullets at militiamen. "Van Cise Exhibit No. 1," in U.S. Senate, *Industrial Relations: Final Report and Testimony Submitted to Congress by the Commission on Industrial Relations*, vol. 8, 64th Cong., 1st sess., 1916, S. Doc. 415, 7328.

9. G. P. West, "Report on Ludlow," 15 May 1914, 10–11, 18, box 17, Records Relating to Commission on Industrial Relations, Department of Labor Records, Record Group (hereafter, RG) 174, National Archives (hereafter, NA), College Park, Md.

10. Reports of Agent No. 607, Republic, Pa., 26 April and 7 and 8 May 1922, and Agent No. 414, 29 April 1922, box 1, Office of Commissioner, Strike Reports, Pennsylvania State Police Records, RG 30, Pennsylvania State Archives (hereafter, PSA), Harrisburg, Pa. Corporate leaders also complained of "black hand" intimidation of strikebreakers in a 1906 strike. Robert Mitchell to Governor Samuel W. Pennypacker, Executive Correspondence, box 20, Samuel W. Pennypacker Papers, Manuscript Group (hereafter, MG) 171, PSA.

11. George Wolfe to Justus Collins, 30 April 1917, box 15, Justus Collins Papers, West Virginia Archives, West Virginia University Library (hereafter, WVUL), Morgantown, W.Va.; "Militarism: What It Costs the Taxpayer," Gifford Pinchot Papers, LC.

12. *Parkersburg (W.Va.) Dispatch-News*, 21 August 1913, clipping in box 32, William E. Glasscock Papers, WVUL; Harold E. West, "Civil War in the West Virginia Coal Mines," *Survey*, 5 April 1913, 50; *UMWJ*, 22 May 1913.

13. Dale Fetherling, *Mother Jones, the Miners' Angel: A Portrait* (Carbondale: Southern Illinois University Press, 1974), 123, 135–36.

14. "Testimony of Henry Batter," in U.S. House of Representatives, *Conditions in the Copper Mines of Michigan: Hearings before a Subcommittee of the Committee on Mines and Mining*, 63rd Cong., 2nd sess., 1914, pt. 6, 2194.

15. "Testimony of Lowell F. Limpus," 938, and "Statement of Philip Murray," 16, 19, in U.S. Senate, *Conditions in the Coal Fields of Pennsylvania, West Virginia, and Ohio*, 70th Cong., 1st sess., 1928; Hugh Graham and Ted Gurr, eds., *Violence in America: Historical and Comparative Perspectives* (Beverly Hills, Calif.: Sage Publications, 1979), 204; "Eddie's Draft" [of Governor Gifford Pinchot's speech], 4, box 926, Gifford Pinchot Papers, LC; Robert V. Bruce, *1877: Year of Violence* (Chicago: Quadrangle Books, 1959), 18–19; J. P. Shalloo, *Private Police: With Special Reference to Pennsylvania* (Philadelphia: American Academy of Political and Social Science, 1933), 128. In 1925, the Pennsylvania state legislature passed a bill that extended the right to hire private police to water companies, electric light and power companies, express companies, and quarries. "Notes on coal and iron police," 1929, box 4, Harold J. Ruttenberg Papers, Historical Collections and Labor Archives (hereafter, HCLA), Pattee Library, Pennsylvania State University (hereafter, PSU), University Park, Pa.

16. "Eddie's Draft," 6; *Carlisle (Pa.) Evening Sentinel*, 1 February 1928, clipping in box 738, Gifford Pinchot Papers, LC.

17. "Testimony of Edward McGrory," 8387–88, "Testimony of David Wilson," 8391,

"Testimony of Abraham Cunningham," 8396, "Testimony of W. H. Jenkins," 9130A–B, box 4, Proceedings of the Anthracite Coal Strike Commission, Michael J. Kosik Collection, HCLA, PSU; *UMWJ*, 25 September 1902.

18. "Argument of John T. Lenahan," 9328–30, and "Argument of Ira H. Burns," 9559, box 5, Proceedings of Anthracite Coal Strike Commission, Kosik Collection, HCLA, PSU.

19. James H. Maurer, *It Can Be Done: The Autobiography of James Hudson Maurer* (New York: Rand School Press, 1938), 143; "Testimony of John Mitchell," 422, box 1, Proceedings of Anthracite Strike Commission, Michael J. Kosik Collection, HCLA, PSU.

20. Frank Julian Warne, *The Slav Invasion and the Mine Workers* (Philadelphia: J. B. Lippincott, 1904), 143; "The Coal Strike," *Outlook*, 18 October 1902, 398; John Mitchell statement, 18 June 1902, reel 4, John Mitchell Papers, Catholic University of America Archives (hereafter, CUA), Washington, D.C.; *Philadelphia Press*, 9 and 14 June 1902.

21. "Testimony of Charles M. Brumm," 9287, box 4, Proceedings of Anthracite Strike Commission, Michael J. Kosik Collection, HCLA, PSU; John Mitchell statement, 18 June 1902, reel 4, John Mitchell Papers, CUA.

22. Warne, *Slav Invasion*, 150–51; Graham and Gurr, *Violence*, 199; "Testimony of R. J. Beamish," 8366–67, and "Testimony of William McLaughlin," 8484–86, box 4, Proceedings of Anthracite Strike Commission, Michael J. Kosik Collection, HCLA, PSU; *UMWJ*, 21 August 1902.

23. Powers Hapgood, *In Non-Union Mines: The Diary of a Coal Digger in Central Pennsylvania, August–September 1921* (New York: Bureau of Industrial Research, 1922), 28–30, 46–47.

24. Entries for 26 March and 12 May 1927, Diary of George Medrick, 1927, box 1, George Medrick Papers, HCLA, PSU.

25. "Testimony of Lowell F. Limpus," in U.S. Senate, *Conditions in Coal Fields of Pennsylvania, West Virginia, and Ohio*, 973.

26. *Pennsylvania State Police*, Public Information Bulletin No. 1, July 1961, 1, 3–4, Historical Publications, box 33, and John C. Groome to Hon. Samuel W. Pennypacker, Reports, box 1, Samuel W. Pennypacker Papers, MG 171, PSA; Samuel Whitaker Pennypacker, *The Autobiography of a Pennsylvanian* (Philadelphia: John C. Winston, 1918), 349; Annual Report of Department of State Police of Commonwealth of Pennsylvania 1906 (Pittsburgh, Pa.: State Printer, 1907), 3, Series Reports, box 3, RG 30, Pennsylvania State Police Records, PSA.

27. "Proceedings of Tri-District Convention, Districts 1, 7, and 9, United Mine Workers of America, Shamokin, Pa., 14 December 1905, box 5, Michael J. Kosik Collection, HCLA, PSU; "Statement of Horace F. Baker," in U.S. Senate, *Conditions in the Coal Fields of Pennsylvania, West Virginia, and Ohio*, 192.

28. *Biennial Report of the Pennsylvania State Police for the Years 1922–23* (Harrisburg, Pa.: J. L. L. Kuhn, 1924), 7, and *Annual Report of the Department of State Police of the Commonwealth of Pennsylvania 1910* (Harrisburg, Pa.: C. E. Aughinbaugh, 1911), 4–5, Series Reports, box 4, Pennsylvania State Police Records, RG 30, PSA.

29. *Philadelphia North American*, n.d., Series: News Clippings, box 1, Pennsylvania State Police Records, RG 30, PSA.

30. *Pittsburgh Gazette Times*, 4 April 1909, Series: News Clippings, box 1, Pennsylvania State Police Records, RG 30, PSA.

31. "Strikes," *Proceedings of the Twenty-second Annual Convention of the United Mine Workers of America, District No. 5*, Pittsburgh, Pa., 27 March–1 April 1911, 68, HCLA, PSU; "History of the Pennsylvania State Federation of Labor," *Pennsylvania Federation of Labor Yearbook*, 1910, 41, HCLA, PSU.

32. *Chicago Inter-Ocean*, 25 June 1905; *Topeka Daily Capital*, 5 May 1905.

33. "Annual Report, Troop 'C,' Pennsylvania State Police Force 1906," Troop Reports, box 4, Pennsylvania State Police Records, RG 30, PSA. The Constabulary claimed the crowd fired on it first.

34. J. B. Cheyney to Hon. Samuel W. Pennypacker, 5 April 1906, Samuel W. Pennypacker Papers, MG 171, PSA.

35. "Strikes," 41, 71.

36. Ibid., 41, 68; Maurer, *Constabulary*, 13, 17, 21.

37. "Address by Mrs. George Morton," in *Report of Proceedings of the Eighteenth Consecutive and Third Biennial Convention of District No. 1, United Mine Workers of America*, Scranton, Pa., 21 July 1919, 101–8, HCLA, PSU.

38. Ibid., 112, 116; *Proceedings of the Tri-District Convention of Districts 1-7-9, United Mine Workers of America*, Wilkes-Barre, Pa., 19–23 August 1919, 45–46, HCLA, PSU.

39. *New York Call*, 6, 10, and 13 May 1922, roll 27, American Civil Liberties Union (hereafter, ACLU) Papers, microfilm; Mildred Allen Beik, *The Miners of Windber: The Struggles of New Immigrants for Unionization, 1890s–1930s* (University Park: Pennsylvania State University Press, 1996), 278–79.

40. "Statement of Miss Anna Jupin," 180–81, "Testimony of H. T. Brundidge," 874, and "Statement of Mrs. Myrtle Spurlock," 251, in U.S. Senate, *Conditions in the Coal Fields of Pennsylvania, West Virginia, and Ohio*.

41. P. S. Stahlnecker to Capt. George F. Lumb, 29 January 1931, and Richard Heagy to Capt. George F. Lumb, 26 January 1931, box 1723; *Altoona Mirror*, 1 February 1928, box 738; and "Eddie's Draft," box 926, Gifford Pinchot Papers, LC.

42. *Carlisle Evening Sentinel*, 1 February 1928, and *Pittsburgh Post-Gazette*, 2 February 1928, box 738, Gifford Pinchot Papers, LC.

43. Vern Smith, "The Armed Thugs of the Coal Barons," *Solidarity*, August 1931, box 2525, Gifford Pinchot Papers, LC; State Police Reports, Ebensburg, Pa., 15 February, 21 March, and 4 and 15 June 1932, and Greensburg, Pa., 4 October 1933 (all from Commanding Officer, Troop "A," State Police to Superintendent, Pennsylvania State Police), boxes 2520–21, Gifford Pinchot Papers, LC.

44. Gompers, "Russianized West Virginia," 825–26, 829.

45. Howard B. Lee, *Bloodletting in Appalachia* (Morgantown: West Virginia University Press, 1969), 11, 19; *UMWJ*, 3 July 1913; West, "Civil War," 43.

46. *UMWJ*, 18 June and 30 July 1903; David Alan Corbin, *Life, Work, and Rebellion in the Coal Fields: The Southern West Virginia Miners, 1880–1922* (Urbana: University of Illinois Press, 1981), 8.

47. Evelyn L. K. Harris and Frank J. Krebs, *From Humble Beginnings: West Virginia State Federation of Labor, 1903–1957* (Charleston: West Virginia Labor History Publishing Fund, 1960), 150; Helen G. Norton, "Feudalism in West Virginia," *Nation*, 12 August 1931, 155; West, "Civil War," 46.

48. *UMWJ*, 3 July 1913; Corbin, *Life, Work, and Rebellion*, 51.

49. W. B. Northrup, "Mine Slaves of West Virginia," *New York Call*, 9 March 1913, 10; *UMWJ*, 18 June and 30 July 1903; Anna Rochester, *Labor and Coal* (New York: International Publishers, 1931), 94–96.

50. *UMWJ*, 18 June 1903.

51. Delos Walker, interview by John Laing, 15 April 1923, and Walker, "Mingo County," n.d., box 203, U.S. Coal Commission Records, RG 68, NA.

52. Corbin, *Life, Work, and Rebellion*, 50; Richard M. Hadsell and William E. Coffey, "From Law and Order to Class Warfare: Baldwin-Felts Detectives in the Southern West Virginia Coal Fields," *West Virginia History* 40 (Spring 1979): 269–70; "Baldwin-Felts Detectives, Inc.," in *Mercer County History 1984* (Princeton, W.Va.: Mercer County Historical Society, 1984), 36; "Thomas J. Felts," in *Mercer County History 1987*, n.p. Baldwin-Felts guards had protected the company payroll and work crews during the construction of the Norfolk & Western. William G. Baldwin ran a general store as a young man in Tazewell, Virginia, and then joined the Eureka Detective Agency of Charleston, West Virginia, in 1889. He established Baldwin's Railroad Detectives two years later, and shortly afterward entered into partnership with Thomas Felts. "W. G. Baldwin Dies in Roanoke," *Bluefield (W.Va.) Daily Telegraph*, 1 April 1936, and "Baldwin Funeral This Morning," *Bluefield Daily Telegraph*, 2 April 1936.

53. *Huntington (W.Va.) Herald-Dispatch*, 11 September 1937.

54. Obituary, *Bluefield Daily Telegraph*, 11 September 1937; "Thomas J. Felts"; "Thomas J. Felts," in *West Virginians of 1934–35* (Wheeling, W.Va.: Wheeling Intelligencer, n.d.), 85.

55. Corbin, *Life, Work, and Rebellion*, 48; *UMWJ*, 19 March 1903.

56. *UMWJ*, 18 September 1902.

57. Ibid., 3 October 1901. T. L. Lewis, another UMW organizer, stated shortly before the strike that when he was in Fairmont, West Virginia, "I was followed by 1 to 3 [thugs] every place I went." T. L. Lewis to W. R. Fairley, 5 May 1902, reel 4, John Mitchell Papers, CUA.

58. *UMWJ*, 4 and 18 September 1902.

59. Ibid., 18 September 1902; Corbin, *Life, Work, and Rebellion*, 33–34, 89.

60. *UMWJ*, 3 July and 18 September 1902.

61. T. L. Felts to Justus Collins, 18 January 1910, series 1, box 6, Justus Collins Papers, WVUL.

62. T. L. Felts to P. J. Riley, 19 March 1907, series 1, box 2, Justus Collins Papers, WVUL.

63. *The United Mine Workers in West Virginia*, Submitted by the Bituminous Operators' Special Committee to the United States Coal Commission, August 1923, 109; Ronald D. Eller, *Miners, Millhands, and Mountaineers: Industrialization of the Appalachian South, 1880–1930* (Knoxville: University of Tennessee Press,

1982), 215. Don Chafin during the 1920s served as a bodyguard for heavyweight boxing champion Jack Dempsey, who had lived in Logan County as a child. G. T. Swain, *History of Logan County, West Virginia* (Logan, W.Va.: G. T. Swain, 1927), 180, 182; Don Chafin, interview by Walker, 16 May 1923, box 203, U.S. Coal Commission Records, RG 68, NA.

64. Corbin, *Life, Work, and Rebellion*, 87; West, "Civil War," 43; H. G. Creel, "The Story of West Virginia," *National Rip-Saw*, September 1913, 12.

65. *UMWJ*, 12 June 1913.

66. M. Michelson, "Sweet Land of Liberty!," *Everybody's Magazine*, May 1913, 617–18; Lawrence R. Lynch, "The West Virginia Coal Strike," *Political Science Quarterly* 29 (December 1914): 628–31; *Parkersburg Dispatch-News*, 21 August 1912, clipping in box 32, William E. Glasscock Papers, WVUL.

67. Lynch, "West Virginia Coal Strike," 644; Michelson, "Sweet Land," 622–23.

68. *Charleston Gazette*, 14 June 1912, clipping in box 32, William E. Glasscock Papers, WVUL.

69. John Kenneth Turner, "A Military Commission," *Appeal to Reason*, 7 June 1913, 2; John Kenneth Turner, "The Private, Labor-Hunting Army," *Appeal to Reason*, 17 May 1913, 1; *UMWJ*, 26 June 1913.

70. *Huntington Herald-Dispatch*, 8 January 1913.

71. Turner, "The Private, Labor-Hunting Army," 1; *Appeal to Reason*, 26 April 1913, 5.

72. *UMWJ*, 26 September 1912; *Report of West Virginia Mining Investigation, 1912, Appointed by Governor Glasscock, August 28, 1912* (Charleston, W.Va., 27 November 1912), 19.

73. *UMWJ*, 17 April 1913; John Kenneth Turner, "Crimes of a Private Army," *Appeal to Reason*, 31 May 1913, 1; Michelson, "Sweet Land," 623.

74. *New York Call*, 21 July 1912.

75. John Kenneth Turner, "Battles Ere Martial Law," *Appeal to Reason*, 7 June 1913, 1; H. G. Creel, "The Story of West Virginia," *National Rip-Saw*, September 1913, 12.

76. *UMWJ*, 13 February 1913.

77. Michelson, "Sweet Land," 625–27; *New York Call*, 28 July 1912.

78. Walter B. Palmer, "An Account of the Strike of Bituminous Coal Miners in the Kanawha Valley of West Virginia, April 1912 to March 1913 Compiled from Periodicals," n.p., box 23, file 16/13, Chief Clerk's File, Department of Labor Records, RG 174, NA; *In the Circuit Court of Marshall County, W.Va. In re R. E. Shanklin Habeas Corpus*, 79, 84.

79. Corbin, *Life, Work, and Rebellion*, 95; Palmer, "Account," 10–11, RG 174, NA; Gompers, "Russianized West Virginia," 829.

80. Turner, "The Private, Labor-Hunting Army," 1.

81. *UMWJ*, 13 February 1913.

82. Creel, "Story of West Virginia," 12; Lynch, "West Virginia Coal Strike," 639; *UMWJ*, 13 February 1913.

83. *UMWJ*, 19 June 1913.

84. Corbin, *Life, Work, and Rebellion*, 90; *Huntington Herald-Dispatch*, 11 February 1913.

85. W. H. Thompson, "Strike Settlements in West Virginia," *International Socialist Review* (hereafter, *ISR*), August 1913, 89; *Appeal to Reason*, 13 May 1913, 1; *UMWJ*, 12 June 1913; Palmer, "Account," RG 174, NA.

86. *Huntington Herald-Dispatch*, 12 February 1913; Creel, "Story of West Virginia," 12; *UMWJ*, 27 February 1913.

87. Creel, "Story of West Virginia," 12; Gompers, "Russianized West Virginia," 830; Palmer, "Account," 18, 23, RG 174, NA.

88. Lynch, "West Virginia Coal Strike," 640–41; *UMWJ*, 24 June 1915 and 31 December 1914; Corbin, *Life, Work, and Rebellion*, 100.

89. Gompers, "Russianized West Virginia," 835; Corbin, *Life, Work, and Rebellion*, 117.

90. John Kenneth Turner, "Under the Iron Heel," *Appeal to Reason*, 21 February 1914, 1; Sidney Howard, *The Labor Spy* (New York: Republic Publishing, 1924), 187; "The Massacre of the Innocents," *Appeal to Reason*, 2 May 1914, 1; Inis Weed, "The Colorado Strike and the Fight in Butte," box 17, Department of Labor Records, RG 174, NA.

91. Corbin, *Life, Work, and Rebellion*, 51; Priscilla Long, "The Voice of the Gun: Colorado's Great Coalfield War of 1913–1914," *Labor's Heritage* 1 (October 1989): 7; Weed, "Colorado Strike," 8, RG 174, NA; *UMWJ*, 1 January 1914; M. McCuster, "Report on Colorado Situation," February 1915, 8, *Records Relating to Commission on Industrial Relations Studies, 1912–1915*, Department of Labor Records, RG 174, NA; Turner, "Under Iron Heel," 1.
    A mine official testified before the Commission on Industrial Relations, when asked whether a democratic form of government existed in Huerfano County: "There is no form of government in Huerfano County. They call it the Kingdom of Farr [after Sheriff Jeff Farr]." "Testimony of Joseph H. Patterson," in U.S. Senate, *Industrial Relations: Final Report and Testimony Submitted by Commission on Industrial Relations*, 6784.

92. McGovern and Guttridge, *Great Coalfield War*, 117–18; Weed, "Colorado Strike," 17, RG 174, NA; Turner, "Under Iron Heel," 1; "Loss of Life in the Colorado Strike," *Miner's Magazine*, 3 September 1914, clipping in box 2, Mother Jones Papers, Catholic University of America Archives (hereafter, CUA).

93. *UMWJ*, 25 September 1913 and 1 January 1914.

94. Weed, "Colorado Strike," 13, 15, RG 174, NA; Long, "Voice of the Gun," 7, 13; McGovern and Guttridge, *Great Coalfield War*, 109–10.

95. McGovern and Guttridge, *Great Coalfield War*, 103, 120; Long, "Voice of the Gun," 12.

96. George Falconer, "Machine Guns and Coal Miners," *ISR*, December 1913, 329; McGovern and Guttridge, *Great Coalfield War*, 122; Turner, "Under Iron Heel," 1; Weed, "Colorado Strike," 17, RG 174, NA.

97. McGovern and Guttridge, *Great Coalfield War*, 128, 134, 158; "Militarism: What It Costs the Taxpayers," 2, Gifford Pinchot Papers, LC; John Kenneth Turner,

"Thieves and Robbers," *Appeal to Reason*, 28 February 1914, 2; John Kenneth Turner, "Czar Chase Is Real Colorado Governor," *Appeal to Reason*, 14 March 1914, 2; *New York Call*, 12 August 1914.

98. "Militarism: What It Costs the Taxpayer," 9, 10, 11, Gifford Pinchot Papers, LC; M. McCuster, "Reports on Colorado Situation," 9, box 16, Department of Labor Records, RG 174, NA.

99. John Kenneth Turner, "Soldiers Attack Helpless Women," *Appeal to Reason*, 4 April 1914, 1; John Kenneth Turner, "Cossacks Outdone by Colorado Militiamen," *Appeal to Reason*, 21 March 1914.

100. "Militarism: What It Costs the Taxpayer," 4, 15, Gifford Pinchot Papers, LC; McGovern and Guttridge, *Great Coalfield War*, 171, 173–74; Long, "Voice of the Gun," 16–17; Fethering, *Mother Jones*, 119–20; "Mother Jones Parade," *ISR*, March 1914, 518.

101. McCuster, "Colorado Situation," 13–17. The Ludlow tent colony included mostly Greeks, Montenegrans, Bulgarians, Serbs, Croats, Italians, Mexicans, and Austrians. U.S. Senate, *Industrial Relations: Final Report and Testimony Submitted by the Commission on Industrial Relations*, 7314.

102. McGovern and Guttridge, *Great Coalfield War*, 186, 205, 211, 213; West, "Report on Ludlow," 9–10.

103. Turner, "Czar Chase," 2; McGovern and Guttridge, *Great Coalfield War*, 167; West, "Report on Ludlow," 10–11.

104. Frank Bohn, "The Colorado War," *National Rip-Saw*, June 1914, 5; West, "Report on Ludlow," 11–12; McGovern and Guttridge, *Great Coalfield War*, 212.

105. West, "Report on Ludlow," 1, 2; Leslie H. Marcy, "The Class War in Colorado," *ISR*, June 1914, 715, 717; McCuster, "Colorado Situation," 9, RG 174, NA.

106. "Militia Began to Fight, Says Colorado Woman," *Appeal to Reason*, 23 May 1914, 2; West, "Report on Ludlow," 16–17; *UMW et al. v. Pennsylvania Mining Company*, Transcript of Record, U.S. Circuit Court of Appeals, 1:276–77, Special Collections, University of Arkansas Library, Fayetteville, Ark.

107. Fetherling, *Mother Jones*, 126; "The Massacre of the Innocents," *Appeal to Reason*, 2 May 1914, 2; *Rocky Mountain News* (Denver), 22 April 1914.

108. Marcy, "Class War," 714; McGovern and Guttridge, *Great Coalfield War*, 286.

109. Marcy, "Class War," 720; West, "Report on Ludlow," 2–5.

110. Fetherling, *Mother Jones*, 132–33; Long, "Voice of the Gun," 20–21.

111. William B. Gates Jr., *Michigan Copper and Boston Dollars* (Cambridge, Mass.: Harvard University Press, 1951), 133; Arthur W. Thurner, *Rebels on the Range: The Michigan Copper Miners' Strike of 1913–14* (Lake Linden, Mich.: John H. Forster Press, 1984), 141–57.

112. Graham Romeyn Taylor, "The Clash in the Copper Country," *Survey*, 1 November 1913, 135, 146; O'Hare, "War in Copper Country," 3; Inis Weed, "The Reasons Why the Copper Miners Struck," *Outlook*, 31 January 1914, 247.

113. Peter Clark MacFarlane, "The Issues at Calumet," *Collier's*, 7 February 1914, 6; "Testimony of James A. Cruse," in U.S. House of Representatives, *Conditions in the Copper Mines of Michigan: Hearings before a Subcommittee of the Committee on Mines and Mining*, 63rd Cong., 2nd sess., 1914, pt. 5, 2022.

114. "Testimony of James A. Cruse," 2022, 2025; Phil Wagner, "Worse than Huerta's Savagery in Mexico," *National Rip-Saw*, November 1913, 13; U.S. Senate, *Strike in the Copper Mining District of Michigan*, 63rd Cong., 2nd sess., 1914, S. Doc. 381, 8:56, 58, 60.

115. U.S. Senate, *Strike in the Copper Mining District*, 56; MacFarlane, "Issues at Calumet," 23.

116. "Testimony of Edward Collins," pt. 6, 2227–29, pt. 4, 1349, and "Testimony of Victor Berger," pt. 2, 684, in U.S. House of Representatives, *Conditions in the Copper Mines*; O'Hare, "War in Copper Country," 2–3.

117. Edward J. McGurty, "The Copper Miners' Strike," *ISR*, September 1913, 151; "The Copper Strike," *ISR*, November 1913, 271; "Testimony of Fred Aladalo," in U.S. House of Representatives, *Conditions in Copper Mines*, pt. 3, 1080, 1082.

118. O'Hare, "War in Copper Country," 16; Kate Richards O'Hare, "Creed of Capitalism and the Copper Strike," *National Rip-Saw*, December 1913, 20.

119. U.S. House of Representatives, *Conditions in the Copper Mines*, 1103; O'Hare, "War in the Copper Country," 16; *UMWJ*, 12 March 1914.

120. Thurner, *Rebels*, 75.

121. U.S. Senate, *Strike in the Copper Mining District*, 8:44–45; *Miner's Magazine*, 28 August 1913.

122. "Testimony of Frank King," in U.S. House of Representatives, *Conditions in Copper Mines*, pt. 2, 1085, 1088–89.

123. Thurner, *Rebels*, 122, 130–31; Leslie H. Marcy, "Calumet," *ISR*, February 1914, 455; O'Hare, "War in the Copper Country," 16.

124. "Testimony of Judge O. N. Hilton," in U.S. House of Representatives, *Conditions in Copper Mines*, pt. 1, 153; Thurner, *Rebels*, 151, 157; "Murder Will Out," *National Rip-Saw*, February 1914, 11.

125. U.S. House of Representatives, *Conditions in Copper Mines*, pt. 6, 2256–60; Thurner, *Rebels*, 160–62; Graham Romeyn Taylor, "Moyer's Story of Why He Left the Copper Country," *Survey*, 10 January 1914, 433–35.

126. U.S. House of Representatives, *Conditions in Copper Mines*, pt. 6, 2260–62; Marcy, "Calumet," 456; MacFarlane, "Issues," 24.

127. U.S. Senate, *Strike in the Copper Mining District*, 8:62–64; Thurner, *Rebels*, 229–30, 252; Charles Moyer, "Gunmen Defeated Copper Strikers, Says Moyer," *Appeal to Reason*, 25 April 1914, 2; Gates, *Michigan Copper*, 134.

128. Frederick Lynne Ryan, *The Rehabilitation of Oklahoma Coal Mining Communities* (Norman: University of Oklahoma Press, 1935), 108; James R. Green, *Grass-Roots Socialism: Radical Movements in the Southwest, 1895–1943* (Baton Rouge: Louisiana State University Press, 1978), 203.

129. Green, *Grass-Roots Socialism*, 201; *Fort Smith Times-Record*, 22 June 1915; *Newark (N.J.) Evening News*, 16 November 1914.

130. *Newark Evening News*, 16 November 1914; Report of R. L. O'D, 15 October 1914; Report of Joe Gallucci, 9 October 1914; Reports of J. G., 3, 7, and 8 October 1914, Reports of Agents to Bureau of Investigation, Department of Justice microfilm, University of Arkansas Library, Fayetteville, Ark.

131. *Fort Smith Times-Record*, 6 April 1914; Officers of UMW District 21 to the

District and Local Organizations Affiliated with UMW of Am., 30 November 1914, reel 6, Department of Justice Strike Files (hereafter, DJSF), Department of Justice Records, RG 60, NA; Samuel A. Sizer, "This Is Union Man's Country: Sebastian County 1914," *Arkansas Historical Quarterly* 27 (1968): 314, 316–17; *United Mine Workers of America* (hereafter, UMWA) *et al. v. Coronado Coal Company* (hereafter, CCC) *et al.*, 1203–4, 1225, University of Arkansas Library; Commissioner of Labor to Gov. George W. Hays, n.d., reel 5, DJSF, RG 60, NA.

132. Commissioner of Labor to Gov. George W. Hays, n.d., DJSF, RG 60, NA.

133. Sizer, "This Is Union Man's Country," 317; *Tulsa World*, 7 April 1914; *CCC v. UMWA—Briefs*, 1:73–74, University of Arkansas Library; *Fort Smith Times-Record*, 18 May 1914.

134. Sizer, "This Is Union Man's Country," 317–18, 320; *Fort Smith Times-Record*, 19 April 1914; John W. Goolsby to Ethelbert Stewart, 11 December 1914, box 2, Office Files of Ethelbert Stewart, Bureau of Labor Statistics (hereafter, BLS) Records, RG 257, NA.

135. *Fort Smith Times-Record*, 19 May 1914; Read McDonough to Hon. J. V. Bourland, 21 May 1914, reel 5, DJSF, RG 60, NA.

136. *Second Biennial Report of Bureau of Labor and Statistics of the State of Arkansas, 1915–1916* (Little Rock: Democrat P. & L., 1917), 13; *New York Call*, 16 August 1914, clipping in box 8, Office Files of Ethelbert Stewart, BLS Records, RG 257, NA.

137. *UMWA v. CCC*, 2584–89, 2592–94, 2610–11; Transcript of Record, U.S. Circuit Court of Appeals, 1:261–62, University of Arkansas Library.

138. *CCC v. UMWA—Briefs*, 1:79–80.

139. Ibid., 81.

140. *Fort Smith Times-Record*, 13 June and 1 and 2 July 1914.

141. Notes [apparently of Ethelbert Stewart], n.d., box 3, Office Files of Ethelbert Stewart, BLS Records, RG 257, NA; *Fort Smith Times-Record*, 16 July 1914; *McAlester (Okla.) News-Capital*, 18 July 1914.

142. James McDonough to U.S. Attorney-General, 21 July 1914, reel 6, DJSF, RG 60, NA; *Fort Smith Times-Record*, 17 July 1914.

143. *Fort Smith Times-Record*, 17 July 1914; *CCC v. UMWA—Briefs*, 1:89, 94, 95; Franklin Bache to Hon. Attorney-General, 6 November 1914, reel 6, DJSF, RG 60, NA.

144. UMW District 21 to the District and Local Organizations Affiliated with UMW of Am., 30 November 1914, reel 6, DJSF, RG 60, NA; *Newark Evening News*, 16 November 1914; *Fort Smith Times-Record*, 17 July 1914.

145. *Tulsa World*, 18 and 19 July 1914; *Fort Smith Times-Record*, 19 July 1914.

146. *New York Call*, 16 August 1914, clipping in box 8, Office Files of Ethelbert Stewart, BLS Records, RG 257, NA.

147. *Fort Smith Times-Record*, 29 October 1914; J. H. Porter, U.S. Marshal, to Attorney-General, 29 October 1914, reel 6, DJSF, RG 60, NA.

148. J. H. Porter, U.S. Marshal, to Attorney-General, 2 November 1914, and Hull to Attorney-General, 2 November 1914, reel 6, DJSF, RG 60, NA.

149. *Tulsa World*, 4–6 November 1914; *Fort Smith Times-Record*, 4–6, 8 November 1914.

150. William C. Fites, "Result of Prosecutions at Fort Smith, Arkansas," 25 January 1915, and UMW District 21 to the District and Local Organizations, reel 6, DJSF, RG 60, NA; *UMWJ*, 3 December 1914.

151. "From Comrade Holt in Jail at Fort Smith for Fidelity to the Working Class," *National Rip-Saw*, March 1915; *Fort Smith Times-Record*, 20 January 1915.

152. William C. Fites, "Result of Prosecutions at Fort Smith, Arkansas," 25 January 1915, reel 6, DJSF, RG 60, NA.

153. "From Comrade Holt."

154. *Fort Smith Times-Record*, 13, 15, and 20 January 1915.

155. Sizer, "This Is Union Man's Country," 326–29; *CCC v. UMW—Briefs*, 1:108.

156. Corbin, *Life, Work, and Rebellion*, 195, 219, 224; Lon Savage, *Thunder in the Mountains: The West Virginia Mine War, 1920–21* (Pittsburgh: University of Pittsburgh Press, 1990), xvi, 33, 65–66, 120.

157. Savage, *Thunder*, 14–16, 18; *UMWJ*, 1 June 1920.

158. Savage, *Thunder*, 19–26; Lee, *Bloodletting*, 52–57; *UMWJ*, 1 June 1920.

159. T. L. Felts to Gov. John J. Cornwell, 28 May 1920, and T. L. Felts to Hon. John J. Cornwell, 10 June 1920, box 46, John J. Cornwell Papers, WVUL; Lee, *Bloodletting*, 55–56; *Bluefield Daily Telegraph*, 21 May 1920; "Resolution Passed by Rotary Club of Bluefield, West Virginia," 31 May 1920, box 46, John J. Cornwell Papers, WVUL; *Huntington Herald-Dispatch*, 20 May 1920.

160. *UMWJ*, 1 June and 1 July 1920; Mrs. Jessie Hayden to Gov. Cornwell, 1 June 1920, box 46, John J. Cornwell Papers, WVUL.

161. Savage, *Thunder*, 33, 45; Charlie Lively as told to William K. Wilbur, "The Killing of Sid Hatfield and Ed Chambers," box 2, T. R. Johns Papers, HCLA, PSU.

162. Lively, "Killing."

163. Ibid.

164. Ibid.; Lee, *Bloodletting*, 65.

165. Lee, *Bloodletting*, 67; Lively, "Killing."

166. Lee, *Bloodletting*, 67–68, 70; Lively, "Killing."

167. Savage, *Thunder*, 76–77, 82–83, 114–16, 119–20; Corbin, *Life, Work, and Rebellion*, 236.

168. Savage, *Thunder*, 120, 125, 128, 136; Art Shields, "The Battle of Logan County," *Liberator*, 1 October 1921, 107–8, roll 127, ACLU Papers.

169. Savage, *Thunder*, 112, 143, 146, 160–61.

170. Ibid., 164–66; Rochester, *Labor and Coal*, 198.

171. "A State Constabulary," clipping in box 145, John J. Cornwell Papers, WVUL; *The United Mine Workers in West Virginia*, Submitted by the Bituminous Operators' Special Committee to the United States Coal Commission, August 1923, 113–15.

172. "Labor Spies Operating Here," *Independent Observer* (Beckley, W.Va.), 10 December 1937; "McKee's Life Threatened," *Independent Observer*, 17 December 1937; "Hooked Spy Confesses Bombing," *Independent Observer*, 4 March 1938.

173. "Labor Spies"; "McKee's Life"; Hadsell and Coffey, "From Law and Order," 285.
174. Obituary of T. L. Felts, *Bluefield Daily Telegraph*, 11 September 1937; obituary of W. G. Baldwin, *Bluefield Daily Telegraph*, 2 April 1936; "Baldwin-Felts Detectives, Inc.," in *Mercer County History*, 36; *West Virginians of 1934–35*, 85.
175. Carl Haessler, "Arrest 73 UAW Distributors at Ford Gates in Test Case," 9 December 1937, box 1, UAW Public Relations Department—Ford Papers, Archives of Labor and Urban Affairs, Walter P. Reuther Library, Wayne State University, Detroit, Mich.


CHAPTER FIVE

1. "NLRB Calls Ford Lawbreaker for Sixth Time," 9 August 1940, box 1, UAW Public Relations Department—Ford Papers, Archives of Labor and Urban Affairs (hereafter, ALUA), Walter P. Reuther Library, Wayne State University (hereafter, WSU), Detroit, Mich.; United States of America before the National Labor Relations Board, Cases C-1554–58, Formal and Informal Unfair Labor Practices and Representation Case Files, box 1952, National Labor Relations Board (hereafter, NLRB) Papers, Record Group (hereafter, RG) 25, National Archives (hereafter, NA), College Park, Md.
2. USA before NLRB, Cases XVI-C-509, 542, 544, 545, 550, pp. 15–16, 81, Formal and Informal Unfair Labor Practices and Representation Case Files, box 1953, NLRB Papers, RG 25, NA. An NLRB examiner later asked Perry what "persuaders" were, and he replied, "Persuade them to talk. . . . The boys we would catch that wouldn't talk, we applied the rubber to them." Ibid., 17.
3. George Lambert to American Civil Liberties Union and Workers Defense League, 19 August 1937, box 40, Workers Defense League (hereafter, WDL) Papers, ALUA, WSU.
4. USA before NLRB, Cases XVI-C-509 et al., p. 35, box 1953, NLRB Papers, RG 25, NA.
5. Ibid., 35–36; *United Automobile Worker*, 13 March 1940.
6. Carl Brannin to Comrade Burt, 10 August 1937, Box 40, WDL Papers, ALUA, WSU; USA before NLRB, Cases C-1554–58, box 1952, NLRB Papers, RG 25, NA.
7. USA before NLRB, Cases C-1554–58, box 1952, NLRB Papers, RG 25, NA.
8. "$1 Million Suit Filed by Ford," box 2, UAW Public Relations Department—Ford Papers, ALUA, WSU.
9. NLRB Press Release, "Ford Motor Company Ordered to Cease Unfair Labor Practices," 9 August 1940, box 54, Maurice Sugar Papers, ALUA, WSU.
10. USA before NLRB, Cases C-1554–58, p. 59, box 1952, NLRB Papers, RG 25, NA.
11. Victor Reuther, interview by Stephen H. Norwood, Washington, D.C., 26 August 1993.
12. Sidney Fine, *Sit-Down: The General Motors Strike of 1936–1937* (Ann Arbor: University of Michigan Press, 1969), 38, 213–15.
13. *Dodge Main News*, 25 March 1937, box 9, John Zaremba Papers, ALUA, WSU.
14. Allen Nevins and Frank Ernest Hill, *Ford: Decline and Rebirth, 1933–1962* (New

York: Charles Scribner's Sons, 1963), 232; John McCarten, "The Little Man in Henry Ford's Basement," *American Mercury*, May 1940, 9.

15. "The Little Giant Goes," *Time*, 8 October 1945, 81; Nevins and Hill, *Decline and Rebirth*, 236; Harry Bennett, *We Never Called Him Henry* (New York: Gold Medal Books, 1951), 5.

16. Bennett, *We Never*, 13; *Detroit News*, 29 September 1945, Clip Book 135, Ford Motor Company Archives, Henry Ford Museum and Greenfield Village Research Center (hereafter, HFMGVRC), Dearborn, Mich.; "The Ford Heritage," *Fortune*, June 1944, 143; Nevins and Hill, *Decline and Rebirth*, 115; Booten Herndon, *Ford: An Unconventional Biography of the Men and Their Times* (New York: Weybright and Talley, 1969), 157.

17. Irving Bernstein, *The Turbulent Years* (Boston: Houghton Mifflin, 1970), 735.

18. Victor Reuther, interview by Norwood.

19. Nevins and Hill, *Decline and Rebirth*, 240.

20. "The Ford Heritage," 143.

21. *Detroit News*, 29 September 1945, Clip Book 135, Ford Motor Company Archives, HFMGVRC.

22. Ibid.; Sam Andre and Nat Fleischer, *A Pictorial History of Boxing* (New York: Bonanza Books, 1989), 77, 184.

23. David L. Lewis, "Harry Bennett, Ford's Tough Guy, Breaks 30 Years of Silence and Tells His Side of the Story," *Detroit Magazine* (*Detroit Free Press*), 20 January 1974, 14.

24. *Detroit Free Press*, 8 February 1942.

25. *Detroit News*, 29 September 1945, Clip Book 135, Ford Motor Company Archives, HFMGVRC; *Detroit Free Press*, 8 February 1942; William C. Richards, *The Last Billionaire: Henry Ford* (New York: Charles Scribner's Sons, 1948), 231.

26. Bennett, *We Never*, 6–7; *Detroit News*, 30 September 1945, Clip Book 135, Ford Motor Company Archives, HFMGVRC.

27. Keith Sward, *The Legend of Henry Ford* (New York: Rinehart, 1948), 338; *Detroit Saturday Night, the Ford Industries Number*, 15 June 1935, 20, box 32, Mary Van Kleeck Papers, ALUA, WSU.

28. Stephen Meyer III, *The Five Dollar Day: Labor Management and Social Control in the Ford Motor Company, 1908–1921* (Albany: State University of New York Press, 1981), 6, 196–98.

29. Charles Sorensen, *My Forty Years with Ford* (New York: W. W. Norton, 1956), 256; Reminiscences of Irving R. Bacon, September 1952, 39, Oral History Section (hereafter, OHS), Accession 65, Ford Motor Company Archives, HFMGVRC; Richards, *Last Billionaire*, 232.

30. Reminiscences of Harry Hanson, 20 March 1956, 238, 310, OHS, Accession 65, Ford Motor Company Archives, HFMGVRC; Testimony of Clifford E. Sheldon, "Official Report of Proceedings before NLRB," Case VII-C-61, pp. 1148–49, NLRB Transcripts and Exhibits, box 2993, NLRB Papers, RG 25, NA.

31. Allen Nevins and Frank Ernest Hill, *Ford: Expansion and Challenge, 1915–1933* (New York: Charles Scribner's Sons, 1957), 524; Bernstein, *Turbulent*, 735; Sorensen, *My Forty Years with Ford*, 258.

32. Donald F. Davis, "The Price of Conspicuous Production: The Detroit Elite and the Automobile Industry, 1900–1933," *Journal of Social History* 16 (Fall 1982): 24, 29. Leadership includes mainly senior executives, along with some principal stockholders.

33. Reminiscences of Willis F. Ward, May 1955, 13, OHS, Accession 65, Ford Motor Company Archives, HFMGVRC. On Henry Ford's hostility to college-educated men, see also Reminiscences of John Wandersee, 31 January 1952, 33–34.

34. Nevins and Hill, *Decline and Rebirth*, 236–37.

35. Richards, *Last Billionaire*, 232–33.

36. Henry S. Thompson to Henry Ford, 6 December 1929, box 1, Accession 23, Henry Ford Office Papers, Ford Motor Company Archives, HFMGVRC; Dan Gillmor, "Ford's Fascism, Proof," pt. 2, *Friday*, 31 January 1941, 5, box 1, UAW Public Relations Department—Ford Papers, ALUA, WSU.

37. Joe McCarthy, "The Ford Family," pt. 2, *Holiday*, July 1957, 97–98.

38. Lloyd Morris, *Not So Long Ago* (New York: Random House, 1949), 362; Nevins and Hill, *Decline and Rebirth*, 238; Sward, *Legend*, 300.

39. Steve Babson, *Working Detroit: The Making of a Union Town* (New York: Adama Books, 1984), 149.

40. Sward, *Legend*, 299; *Ford Facts*, 18 November 1940, box 15, Unbound Newspaper Collection, ALUA, WSU; Richards, *Last Billionaire*, 233.

41. Bennett, *We Never*, 109; Fine, *Sit-Down*, 60; Nevins and Hill, *Expansion and Challenge*, 534.

42. Doug Fraser, interview by Stephen H. Norwood, Detroit, Mich., 8 October 1993.

43. Orry Barrule [Leslie McDonnell], "Life with Uncle Henry," 31, box 46, Accession 65, Ford Motor Company Archives, HFMGVRC.

44. "What's This about 'Labor Trouble' in Ford Plants?," United Automobile Workers, CIO, box 6, Harry Ross Papers, ALUA, WSU; Harry Ross, interview by Jack W. Skeels, 26 January 1960, 46, Oral History Collection (hereafter, OHC), ALUA, WSU.

45. Reminiscences of W. Griffith, April 1951, 31, OHS, Accession 65, Ford Motor Company Archives, HFMGVRC.

46. "He Laughed in a Ford Plant," *Ford Facts*, 19 February 1941, box 15, Unbound Newspaper Collection, ALUA, WSU; Bernstein, *Turbulent*, 738.

47. Ken Bannon, interview by Jack W. Skeels, 28 February 1963, 3, OHC, ALUA, WSU; "Radio Talk," 5 August 1940, box 1, Edward Levinson Papers, ALUA, WSU; *United Automobile Worker*, 30 June 1937.

48. Christopher H. Johnson, *Maurice Sugar: Law, Labor, and the Left in Detroit, 1912–1950* (Detroit: Wayne State University Press, 1988), 120; Sidney Fine, *Frank Murphy: The Detroit Years* (Ann Arbor: University of Michigan Press, 1975), 403–4.

49. Nevins and Hill, *Decline and Rebirth*, 33; Reminiscences of Irving Bacon, September 1952, 92–93, OHS, Accession 65, Ford Motor Company Archives, HFMGVRC; Fine, *Murphy*, 404.

50. *Detroit Times*, 8 March 1932, box 3, Robert Dunn Papers, ALUA, WSU.

51. Bernstein, *Turbulent*, 737.

52. Eleanor R. Hunter, "The Labor Policy of the Ford Motor Company" (M.A. thesis, Wayne University, 1942), 47.

53. "Outline of Status of Investigation," NLRB, Case VII-C-148, 8 March 1941, p. 20, box 2, Heber Blankenhorn Papers, ALUA, WSU; Carl Haessler, memorandum on Upton Sinclair's *The Flivver*, n.d., box 19, Carl Haessler Papers, ALUA, WSU; Gillmor, "Ford's Fascism, Proof," pt. 2, *Friday*, 31 January 1941, box 1, UAW Public Relations Department—Ford Papers, ALUA, WSU.

54. Bill Reich, "Henry Ford, No. 1 Fascist," box 2, and Gillmor, "Ford's Fascism, Proof," pt. 2, *Friday*, 31 January 1941, box 1, UAW Public Relations Department—Ford Papers, ALUA, WSU.

55. "Outline," NLRB Case VII-C-148, p. 87, box 2, Heber Blankenhorn Papers, ALUA, WSU; Doug Fraser, interview by Norwood.

56. Victor Reuther, interview by Norwood.

57. Gillmor, "Ford's Fascism, Proof," pt. 2, *Friday*, 31 January 1941, box 1, UAW Public Relations Department—Ford Papers, ALUA, WSU; H. C. Tuedke to Harry Bennett, 7 October 1932, box 30, Accession 572, Ford Motor Company Archives, HFMGVRC.

58. *United Automobile Worker*, 7 May 1938.

59. "Detroit Labor, 1900 to 1916," box 1, Accession 958, George Heliker Papers, and unidentified clipping, 27 September 1951, box 16, Accession 940, Frank Hill Research Collection, Ford Motor Company Archives, HFMGVRC.

60. Babson, *Working Detroit*, 92; "A Payroll of Criminals Paroled to Ford from Michigan Jails," box 2, UAW Public Relations Department—Ford Papers, ALUA, WSU.

61. Victor Reuther, interview by Norwood.

62. Gillmor, "Ford's Fascism, Proof," pt. 2, *Friday*, 31 January 1941, box 1, UAW Public Relations Department—Ford Papers, ALUA, WSU.

63. *Dearborn Press*, 23 September 1943, Clip Book 129, Ford Motor Company Archives, HFMGVRC; *Detroit News*, 21 July 1932; "Official Report of Proceedings before the National Labor Relations Board," Case VII-C-148, 26 May 1941, p. 524, box 2799, NLRB Papers, RG 25, NA.

64. "J. R. Davis Discussed the Ford Lunch Tables," box 1, Accession 975, Ford Motor Company Archives, HFMGVRC.

65. Ibid.

66. Harry Ross, interview by Jack W. Skeels, 65, OHC, ALUA, WSU.

67. McCarthy, "Ford Family," pt. 2, *Holiday*, July 1957, 98; Sward, *Legend*, 341.

68. Nevins and Hill, *Decline and Rebirth*, 140.

69. "Transcripts and Exhibits," Case VII-C-61, 7 July 1937, pp. 111–12, 126–33, 216, box 2993, NLRB Papers, RG 25, NA; "Statement Concerning Riot at Gate 5, Ford Motor Co., River Rouge Plant," 10 June 1937, box 6, Victor Reuther Papers, ALUA, WSU; Carl Raushenbush, *Fordism* (New York: League for Industrial Democracy, 1937), 3–4, box 10, Joe Brown Papers, ALUA, WSU; Victor Reuther, *The Brothers Reuther and the Story of the UAW* (Boston: Houghton Mifflin, 1976), 203; obituary of Oscar Young, *Detroit Free Press*, 18 October 1982.

70. Gillmor, "Ford's Fascism, Proof," pt. 4, *Friday*, 14 February 1941, box 1, UAW

Public Relations Department—Ford Papers, ALUA, WSU; Alfred E. Kahn, *High Treason: The Plot against the People* (New York: Lear Publishers, 1950), 173.

71. Doug Fraser, interview by Norwood.

72. "Statement Concerning Riot at Gate 5," box 6, Victor Reuther Papers, ALUA, WSU; Raushenbush, *Fordism*, 26, box 10, Joe Brown Papers, ALUA, WSU.

73. Manuscript on history of Ford organizing campaign, n.d., Percy Llewellyn Papers, ALUA, WSU; David L. Lewis, *The Public Image of Henry Ford: An American Folk Hero and His Company* (Detroit: Wayne State University Press, 1976), 252–53; *Ford Facts*, 19 January and 18 November 1940, box 15, Unbound Newspaper Collection, ALUA, WSU.

74. George Lambert, "Memphis Is Safe for Ford," *Nation*, 22 January 1938, 93.

75. USA before NLRB, Cases XVI-C-509 et al., p. 48, box 1953, NLRB Papers, RG 25, NA; George N. Green, "Discord in Dallas," *Labor's Heritage* 1 (July 1989): 24, 26, 28; Nevins and Hill, *Decline and Rebirth*, 142–43; George Lambert, "Dallas Tries Terror," *Nation*, 9 October 1937, 377.

76. Michael K. Honey, *Southern Labor and Black Civil Rights: Organizing Memphis Workers* (Urbana: University of Illinois Press, 1993), 87–89; Lambert, "Memphis," 93.

77. Reuther, *Brothers Reuther*, 206–8; "Blankenhorn Confidential Memo—Summary of Facts on Reuther Shootings Presented to Senate Committee on Crime, Senator Kefauver, Chairman," June 1950, 28–30, box 3, Heber Blankenhorn Papers, ALUA, WSU.

There is no question that Bennett ordered Walter Reuther's kidnapping. Reuther received an anonymous telephone call from a man who offered to meet him at a bar at midnight and identify his assailants. This man told Reuther that Bennett had arranged the attempt, and named his two assailants, both "known Bennett men," whom police had to arrest. Nineteen persons who had been in Reuther's apartment that evening separately identified the two in the police lineup. According to Victor Reuther, the trial was a "farce," in which the defense viciously red-baited the Reuthers; even the judge was surprised by the acquittal. Reuther, *Brothers Reuther*, 209.

78. "Statement of UAW Publicity Department," 5 June 1937, box 2, UAW Public Relations Department—Ford Papers ALUA, WSU; *United Automobile Worker*, 15 March 1941.

79. See, for example, "What's This about 'Labor Trouble' in Ford Plants?," box 6, Harry Ross Papers, ALUA, WSU.

80. Edward Levinson to Raymond Daniell, 17 January 1944, box 7, Edward Levinson Papers, ALUA, WSU; Nevins and Hill, *Decline and Rebirth*, 181; "Blankenhorn Confidential Memo," 31, box 3, Heber Blankenhorn Papers, ALUA, WSU; Albert Lee, *Henry Ford and the Jews* (New York: Stein and Day, 1980), 110.

In 1941, Harvard professor Gaetano Salvemini, a refugee from Mussolini's Italy and one of the world's leading academic authorities on fascism, declared that "[t]he automobile plant of Henry Ford at River Rouge is organized along almost purely fascist lines." He noted that the methods Ford used to combat union organizing were "similar to those used by Italian industry to crush the workers' strike . . . on the eve of Mussolini's rise to power." *Harvard Crimson*, 22 April 1941.

81. Doug Fraser, interview by Norwood.

82. *Detroit News*, 24 December 1937 and 3 January 1938, box 14, Joe Brown Papers, ALUA, WSU; *Ford Facts*, 19 February 1941, box 15, Unbound Newspaper Collection, ALUA, WSU; "Uncle Sam Cracks Down on Ford: Labor Board Orders Ford Motor Company at St. Louis to Obey Wagner Act," 6 May 1940, box 2, and "Judge Kills Bennett Gag Law," box 1, UAW Public Relations Department—Ford Papers, ALUA, WSU.

83. Doug Fraser, interview by Norwood.

84. Daniel Gallagher, interview by Jack W. Skeels, 26 January 1960, 45, OHC, ALUA, WSU.

85. Victor Reuther, interview by Norwood.

86. *PM* (New York), 3 April 1941.

87. Raushenbush, *Fordism*, 36, box 10, Joe Brown Papers, ALUA, WSU; Harry Ross, interview by Skeels, 57–60, OHC, ALUA, WSU; Bernstein, *Turbulent*, 744.

88. August Meier and Elliot Rudwick, *Black Detroit and the Rise of the UAW* (New York: Oxford University Press, 1979), 5, 88.

89. Horace White, "Who Owns the Negro Churches?," *Christian Century*, 9 February 1938, 176; Walter White to A. Philip Randolph, 7 April 1941, Group 2, box A334, National Association for the Advancement of Colored People Papers, Library of Congress, Washington, D.C.

90. Reminiscences of Willis F. Ward, 13–14, OHS, Accession 65, Ford Motor Company Archives, HFMGVRC.

91. "Suggested Policy on Negro Problem in Ford Drive," box 8, UAW President's Office—Walter Reuther Papers, ALUA, WSU; "The Truth about American Big Business; Gestapo Terrorism Confessed by Ford Spy," *In Fact*, 21 July 1941, box 12, Joe Brown Papers, ALUA, WSU.

92. *United Automobile Worker*, 1 January 1938; *Ford Facts*, 19 April 1941, box 15, Unbound Newspaper Collection, ALUA, WSU.

93. Meier and Rudwick, *Black Detroit*, 87; *Ford Facts*, 5 April 1941, box 15, Unbound Newspaper Collection, ALUA, WSU; Harry Ross, interview by Skeels, 60, OHC, ALUA, WSU; *PM*, 3 April 1941.

94. Bernstein, *Turbulent*, 745, 751; Reminiscences of Irving Bacon, 204, OHS, Accession 65, Ford Motor Company Archives, HFMGVRC.

95. Doug Fraser, interview by Norwood.

96. Bennett, *We Never*, 136; Nevins and Hill, *Decline and Rebirth*, 164.

97. Nevins and Hill, *Decline and Rebirth*, 244, 255; *PM*, 9 March 1944, clipping in box 10, Joe Brown Papers, ALUA, WSU.

98. "Blankenhorn Confidential Memo," 31, box 3, Heber Blankenhorn Papers, ALUA, WSU.

99. Harry Ross, interview by Skeels, 64, 67, OHC, ALUA, WSU; Victor Reuther, interview by Norwood.

100. "Blankenhorn Confidential Memo," 31, box 3, Heber Blankenhorn Papers, ALUA, WSU; Reminiscences of E. G. Liebold, 1212, OHS, Accession 65, Ford

Motor Company Archives, HFMGVRC; Ken Bannon, interview by Jack W. Skeels, 28 February 1963, 15, OHC, ALUA, WSU. Edsel Ford's son, Henry Ford II, stated, "I don't have any idea how much [Bennett] pilfered. . . . But I'm positive . . . that he could not have lived the way he did on the salary he had." Reminiscences of Henry Ford II, 14 April 1980, 29, OHS, Accession 1606, Ford Motor Company Archives, HFMGVRC.

101. McCarthy, "Ford Family," pt. 3, *Holiday*, August 1957, 78.
102. Lewis, *Public Image*, 404. Henry Ford II admitted in 1980 that he was "physically . . . and mentally scared" when he fired Bennett and was also "frightened to death that it wouldn't stick." He called Bennett "the dirtiest, lousiest son-of-a-bitch I ever met in my life save one . . . [Lee] Iacocca." Reminiscences of Henry Ford II, 14 April 1980, 27–31, OHS, Accession 1606, Ford Motor Company Archives, HFMGVRC.
103. Victor Reuther, interview by Norwood.
104. Lewis, *Public Image*, 436–37.
105. Nevins and Hill, *Decline and Rebirth*, 338; Herndon, *Ford*, 197–98.
106. Ralph Winstead, "New Developments in the Harry Bennett Story," box 3, Heber Blankenhorn Papers, ALUA, WSU.
107. Harry Ross, interview by Skeels, 67, OHC, ALUA, WSU. Ken Bannon, former head of the UAW's Ford Department, stated that Bennett lived for a time in Las Vegas, where he owned and operated a gas station and auto repair shop. Ken Bannon, telephone interview by Stephen H. Norwood, 6 April 1995.
108. Lewis, "Harry Bennett," 6.
109. *Detroit Free Press*, 14 January 1979.
110. Ibid.; *Detroit News*, 13 and 17 January 1979.
111. Victor Reuther, interview by Norwood.

CHAPTER SIX

1. *United Automobile Worker*, 25 February 1937.
2. Nelson Lichtenstein, *The Most Dangerous Man in Detroit: Walter Reuther and the Fate of American Labor* (New York: Basic Books, 1995), 75.
3. Ibid., 75–76; Robert Zieger, *The CIO, 1935–1955* (Chapel Hill: University of North Carolina Press, 1995), 43–45; John Zaremba, interview by Jack W. Skeels, 11 August, 29 September, and 6 October 1961, 13, Oral History Collection (hereafter, OHC), Archives of Labor and Urban Affairs (hereafter, ALUA), Walter P. Reuther Library, Wayne State University (hereafter, WSU), Detroit, Mich.
4. Victor Reuther, interview by Stephen H. Norwood, Washington, D.C., 26 August 1993; "The Labor Market in the Auto Industry," 1, 4–5, n.d., and Blanche Bernstein, "Hiring Policies in the Auto Industry," 1, 3, 5, box 2, Edward Levinson Papers, ALUA, WSU.
5. Harry Ross, interview by Jack W. Skeels, 10 July 1961, 13–14, OHC, ALUA, WSU; Frank Marquart, *An Auto Worker's Journal: The UAW from Crusade to*

One-Party Union (University Park: Pennsylvania State University Press, 1975), 138.

6. Peter Amann, "Vigilante Fascism: The Black Legion as an American Hybrid," *Comparative Studies in Society and History* 25 (1983): 491; Christopher Johnson, *Maurice Sugar: Law, Labor, and the Left in Detroit, 1912–1950* (Detroit: Wayne State University Press, 1988), 182.

7. A. B. Magil and Henry Stevens, *The Peril of Fascism: The Crisis of American Democracy* (New York: International Publishers, 1938), 207–8; Albert E. Kahn, *High Treason: The Plot against the People* (New York: Lear Publishers, 1950), 204.

8. Amann, "Vigilante Fascism," 502–3, 505–7.

9. Edward Wieck to Joe Brown, 6 February 1937, box 10, Edward Wieck Papers, ALUA, WSU; Magil and Stevens, *The Peril of Fascism*, 207; "Black Legion," n.d., box 3, UAW Research Department Papers, ALUA, WSU; Johnson, *Maurice Sugar*, 182; George Morris, *The Black Legion Rides* (New York: Workers Library Publishers, 1936), 9.

10. Morris, *The Black Legion Rides*, 24; "The Cult of Violence," *Christian Century*, 17 June 1936, 864; "Stamp Out the Black Legion," box 2, Office of the President—Walter Reuther Papers, ALUA, WSU; *Detroit Free Press*, 30 June 1936; Johnson, *Maurice Sugar*, 182; Henry Kraus, *The Many and the Few: A Chronicle of the Dynamic Auto Workers* (1947; reprint, Urbana: University of Illinois Press, 1985), 36; *Daily Worker*, 3 and 7 December 1936. The Pontiac city administration permitted policemen to remain on active duty even after they publicly admitted to membership in the Black Legion. *Detroit Free Press*, 2 July 1936, clipping in box 9, Peter Amann Collection, ALUA, WSU.

11. Kraus, *The Many and the Few*, 37–38.

12. Morris, *The Black Legion Rides*, 12–13; *United Automobile Worker*, 7 July 1936; Forrest Davis, "Labor Spies and the Black Legion," *New Republic*, 17 June 1936, 170; Johnson, *Maurice Sugar*, 182; Homer Martin and George Addes to Officers and Members of All Local Unions Affiliated with the International Union, United Automobile Workers of America, 2 June 1936, box 13, Peter Amann Collection, ALUA, WSU.

13. "History of Motor Products Strike at Detroit Michigan," box 1, and "Stamp Out the Black Legion," box 2, Series I, Office of the President—Walter Reuther Papers, ALUA, WSU; *United Automobile Worker*, 7 July 1936.

14. Amann, "Vigilante Fascism," 520–21; obituary of Dayton J. Dean, *Detroit Free Press*, 20 January 1960, box 1, Maurice Sugar Papers, ALUA, WSU; Magil and Stevens, *Peril of Fascism*, 209; Morris Janowitz, "Black Legions on the March," in Daniel Aaron, ed., *America in Crisis* (New York: Alfred A. Knopf, 1952), 305.

15. "The True Story of the Black Legion Plot to Murder Maurice Sugar," box 1, Maurice Sugar Papers, ALUA, WSU; Johnson, *Maurice Sugar*, 185.

16. *Indianapolis Star*, 22 January 1937; Amann, "Vigilante Fascism," 521.

17. Kraus, *Many and Few*, 36.

18. *United Automobile Worker*, September 1936; Press Release by Conference for the Protection of Civil Rights, 23 April 1937, box 58, Workers Defense League

Papers, ALUA, WSU; *Detroit Free Press*, 9 January 1972, clipping in box 9, Peter Amann Collection, ALUA, WSU.

19. Kraus, *Many and Few*, 36–37; "Statement by Walter Reuther, Vice-President and Director, GM Dept.," 19 January 1944, box 3, Edward Levinson Papers, ALUA, WSU.

20. Amann, "Vigilante Fascism," 515–16; "Statement of Civil Rights Federation," 11 June 1938, box 6, John Zaremba Papers, ALUA, WSU.

21. Leonard Woodcock, interview by Stephen H. Norwood, Ann Arbor, Mich., 15 December 1993.

22. May Reuther, interview by Jack W. Skeels, 29 May 1963, 12–13; Bob Kanter, interview by Jack W. Skeels, 31 August 1961, 20–21, OHC, ALUA, WSU.

23. American Civil Liberties Union, "Local Civil Liberties Committees Reports, 1937–38," June 1938, 15–16; "Resolutions of the Civil Rights Federation," n.d., box 79, Civil Rights Congress of Michigan Collection, ALUA, WSU; *Daily Worker*, 12 January 1935, clipping on roll 122, and *Washington (D.C.) News*, 22 May 1936, clipping on roll 135, American Civil Liberties Union (hereafter, ACLU) Papers, microfilm; *United Automobile Worker*, 9 July 1938.

In May 1945, the Detroit Police Department censored the documentary film *Maidanek*, requiring Detroit movie theaters to delete the section of the film that showed the execution of Nazi SS officers convicted of committing atrocities against inmates of the Maidanek annihilation camp near Lublin, Poland. The Nazis murdered 1,380,000 people there, most of them Jews. A Detroit Police Department spokesman stated that "the bitterness caused by seeing pictures of this kind, is not in keeping with . . . American policy." Jack Raskin to John F. Ballenger, 4 and 7 August 1945, and Charles W. Snyder to Charles Garner, 22 August 1945, box 80, Civil Rights Congress of Michigan Collection, ALUA, WSU; Lucy S. Dawidowicz, *The War against the Jews, 1933–1945* (New York: Bantam Books, 1975), 148–49.

24. "History of the Motor Products Strike at Detroit, Michigan," 26–27, box 1, Series I, UAW President's Office—Walter Reuther Papers, ALUA, WSU.

25. Conference for the Protection of Civil Rights, "Statement on Motor Products Strike," 6 December 1935, box 55, Civil Rights Congress of Michigan Collection, ALUA, WSU.

26. Joe Brown to Edward Wieck, 11 January 1938, box 10, Edward Wieck Papers, ALUA, WSU.

27. Leonard Woodcock, interview by Norwood; Leonard Woodcock, interview by Jack W. Skeels, 30 April 1963, 5, 24, OHC, ALUA/WSU.

28. "Briggs Strike Detroit," n.d., and "Attitude of Detroit Newspapers toward Auto Strikes of 1933," n.d., box 19, Joe Brown Papers, ALUA, WSU.

29. Sidney Fine, *Sit-Down: The General Motors Strike of 1936–37* (Ann Arbor: University of Michigan Press, 1969), 37–38, 41.

30. Genora Dollinger, interview by Jack W. Skeels, 31 July 1960, 4–5, OHC, ALUA, WSU; "Talk by Maurice Sugar on the Legality and Ethics of the Sit-Down Strike before the Cuyohoga County Bar Association," 4 April 1937, box 32, Mary Van Kleeck Papers, ALUA, WSU.

31. *New York Times*, 21 March 1937; John Kenneth Turner, "Labor Union and Socialist Local Infested with Corporate Spies," *Appeal to Reason*, 25 July 1914, 2. Turner learned this from John W. Reid, a Corporations Auxiliary spy in Akron for more than five years and a former soldier of James Farley, after he left the agency early in 1914.

32. Irving Bernstein, *The Turbulent Years* (Boston: Houghton Mifflin, 1970), 551–53; Doug Fraser, interview by Stephen H. Norwood, Detroit, Mich., 8 October 1993.

33. Harry Ross, interview by Skeels, 10 July 1961, 8–9, OHC, ALUA, WSU; Richard Frankensteen, interview by Jack W. Skeels, 10 and 23 October and 6 November 1959 and 7 December 1961, 12, 13; *New York American*, 28 January 1937, clipping on roll 149, ACLU Papers.

34. Richard Frankensteen, interview by Skeels, OHC, ALUA, WSU, 13–14, 16, 18.

35. Ibid., 16–17; "Testimony of Richard Frankensteen," in U.S. Senate, *Violations of Free Speech and Rights of Labor: Hearings before a Subcommittee of the Committee on Education and Labor*, 75th Cong., 1st sess., 1937, pt. 4, *Corporations Auxiliary Company, Chrysler Corporation*, 1271.

36. Kraus, *Many and Few*, 62; Doug Fraser, interview by Norwood.

37. Sidney Howard, *The Labor Spy* (New York: Republic Publishing, 1924), 63; "Oppressive Labor Practices Bill S. 1970—Press Comments," *Union Leader*, 17 June 1939, Oversized Materials and "Glossary," box 114, Violations of Free Speech and Rights of Labor Records, Record Group (hereafter, RG) 46, National Archives (hereafter, NA), Washington, D.C.

38. Robert W. Dunn, *Spying on Workers* (New York: Labor Research Association, 1932), 5 in box 1, Maurice Sugar Papers, ALUA, WSU; *Austin (Minn.) Unionist*, 1 October 1937, roll 146, ACLU Papers.

39. Leonard Woodcock, interview by Norwood.

40. Victor Reuther, interview by Norwood; John Zaremba, interview by Skeels, 19–20, OHC, ALUA, WSU.

41. *Dodge Main News*, 11 and 24 March 1937, and "Minutes of Executive Committee," 23 March 1937, box 9, John Zaremba Papers, ALUA, WSU; Zaremba, interview by Skeels, 16.

42. Frank Tuttle, interview by William A. Sullivan, 27 April 1959, 18, OHC, ALUA, WSU; *Detroit Free Press*, 23 March 1937, clipping in box 8, Edward Levinson Papers, ALUA, WSU.

43. Doug Fraser, interview by Norwood; *Daily Worker*, 4 March 1937, roll 148, ACLU Papers; Johnson, *Maurice Sugar*, 191; *United Automobile Worker*, 5 June 1937.

44. Mary Van Kleeck to Board of Directors, American Civil Liberties Union, 11 January 1937, roll 152, ACLU Papers; Clarence Tschippert, "May I Sit Down?," *St. Francis Home Journal*, March 1937, 68, and "Sit-Downs Result of Lawless Employers, Murphy Says," Federated Press, 13 January 1939, box 19, Carl Haessler Papers, ALUA, WSU; "Company Property to Be Left Alone!!!," *Dodge Main News*, 9 March 1937, box 9, John Zaremba Papers, ALUA, WSU; Richard Frankensteen interview by Skeels, 36, OHC, ALUA, WSU.

45. Doug Fraser, interview by Norwood.

46. *New York Times*, 19 March 1937; *West Side Conveyor* (Detroit), 25 January 1938; *Daily Worker*, 6 August 1937.

47. *United Automobile Worker*, 25 February 1937; "Punch Press," Official Strike Bulletin No. 11, box 21, Joe Brown Papers, ALUA, WSU; Harry Ross, interview by Skeels, 21–22, OHC, ALUA, WSU; *Daily Worker*, 23 November 1936.

48. *Daily Worker*, 4 March 1937, clipping on roll 148, ACLU Papers.

49. Harry Ross, interview by Skeels, 19, OHC, ALUA, WSU; Fine, *Sit-Down*, 128; "The Story of Dodge Local 3," *Dodge Main News*, 10 May 1952.

50. *Detroit News*, 28 November 1936; *Daily Worker*, 30 November 1936 and 4 March 1937; "The Kelsey-Hayes Sit-In Strike," box 1, Series I, UAW President's Office—Walter Reuther Papers, ALUA, WSU.

51. Fine, *Sit-Down*, 131–32; Victor Reuther, interview by Norwood.

52. Fine, *Sit-Down*, 132; Leonard Woodcock, interview by Norwood; Richard Frankensteen, interview by Skeels, 32, OHC, ALUA, WSU.

53. Melvin Bishop, interview by Jack W. Skeels, 29 March 1963, 16–18, OHC, ALUA, WSU; *United Automobile Worker*, December 1936; Lichtenstein, *Most Dangerous Man*, 70; "The Kelsey-Hayes Sit-In Strike."

54. Victor Reuther, interview by Norwood; *United Automobile Worker*, 22 January 1937.

55. Doug Fraser, interview by Norwood; Lichtenstein, *Most Dangerous Man*, 100; John R. Coyne, "Emil Mazey . . . Father of Local 212" [3rd installment], box 4, Emil Mazey Papers, ALUA, WSU; Ronald Edsforth, *Class Conflict and Cultural Consensus: The Making of a Mass Consumer Society in Flint, Michigan* (New Brunswick, N.J.: Rutgers University Press, 1987), 174; *New York Times*, 29 June 1937, box 2, UAW Public Relations Department—Ford Papers, ALUA, WSU.

56. Richard Frankensteen, interview by Skeels, 29, OHC, ALUA, WSU; Leonard Woodcock, interview by Norwood.

57. Leonard Woodcock, interview by Norwood.

58. *United Automobile Worker*, November 1936 and 19 and 22 January 1937; Edsforth, *Class Conflict and Cultural Consensus*, 172.

59. Genora Dollinger, interview by Skeels, 18, 19, 23, OHC, ALUA, WSU; *United Automobile Worker*, 22 January 1937.

60. Catherine Geller, interview by Jack W. Skeels, 7 July 1961, 4–5, OHC, ALUA, WSU.

61. Genora Dollinger, interview by Skeels, 38–40, OHC, ALUA, WSU.

62. Tracy Doll, interview by Jack W. Skeels, 21 April 1961, 19, OHC, ALUA, WSU.

63. Victor Reuther, interview by Norwood.

64. *New York Times*, 17–19 March 1937.

65. Ibid., 18 March 1937; "The Kelsey-Hayes Sit-In Strike," box 1, UAW President's Office—Walter Reuther Papers, Series I, ALUA, WSU.

66. *New York Times*, 19 March 1937.

67. Fine, *Sit-Down*, 210; *United Automobile Worker*, October 1936; Victor Reuther, *The Brothers Reuther and the Story of the UAW* (Boston: Houghton Mifflin, 1976), 172–73.

68. Reuther, *Brothers Reuther*, 180; Victor Reuther, interview by R. T. King, 26

September 1980, 22, Indiana University Oral History Research Project, ALUA, WSU.

69. Claude Hoffman, *Sit-Down in Anderson: UAW Local 663, Anderson, Indiana* (Detroit: Wayne State University Press, 1968), 45; Victor Reuther, interview by Norwood; Johnson, *Maurice Sugar*, 198; *Socialist Call*, 20 February 1937, roll 148, ACLU Papers.

70. Fine, *Sit-Down*, 212; *Indianapolis Times*, 1 February 1937; *United Automobile Worker*, 4 June 1938; Hoffman, *Sit-Down in Anderson*, 40.

71. Fine, *Sit-Down*, 213–14; Hoffman, *Sit-Down in Anderson*, 47–49; Kraus, *Many and Few*, 184; *Anderson Auto Workers Daily News*, 11 February 1937, box 94, Mary Heaton Vorse Papers, ALUA, WSU.

72. Hugh Thompson, interview by Jack W. Skeels, 28 March 1963, 23, OHC, ALUA, WSU; Fine, *Sit-Down*, 213–14; Kraus, *Many and Few*, 184; *Indianapolis Times*, 26 January 1937; Reuther, *Brothers Reuther*, 175; Mary Heaton Vorse, "Reasons for an Investigation in Anderson, Ind.," n.d., box 94, Mary Heaton Vorse Papers, ALUA, WSU.

73. Jack Jourdan, interview by R. T. King, 14 August 1979, 27, and Victor Reuther, interview by R. T. King, 26 September 1980, 8, Indiana University Oral History Research Project, ALUA, WSU; Fine, *Sit-Down*, 214.

74. Victor Reuther, interview by Skeels, 18, OHC, ALUA, WSU; Victor Reuther, interview by King, 10, 11, Indiana University Oral History Research Project, ALUA, WSU.

75. Victor Reuther, interview by Skeels, 19, OHC, ALUA, WSU; Reuther, *Brothers Reuther*, 177.

76. Fine, *Sit-Down*, 313; Victor Reuther, interview by Skeels, 20–21, OHC, ALUA, WSU; Victor Reuther, interview by King, 19, Indiana University Oral History Research Project, ALUA, WSU; Reuther, *Brothers Reuther*, 178.

77. Reuther, *Brothers Reuther*, 178–79; Fine, *Sit-Down*, 313–14; Victor Reuther, interview by Skeels, 22–23, OHC, ALUA, WSU.

78. Victor Reuther, interview by Skeels, 24, OHC, ALUA, WSU; Reuther, *Brothers Reuther*, 180; *Detroit News*, 14 February 1937, clipping in box 21, Joe Brown Papers, ALUA, WSU.

79. *Detroit News*, 14 February 1937; *New York World-Telegram*, 13 and 15 February 1937, on roll 148, ACLU Papers; *Indianapolis Star*, 16 February 1937.

80. Reuther, *Brothers Reuther*, 181; Victor Reuther, interview by Skeels, 24, OHC, ALUA, WSU; Genora Dollinger, interview by Skeels, 40, OHC, ALUA, WSU.

81. Fine, *Sit-Down*, 316–17; Hoffman, *Sit-Down in Anderson*, 68; Reuther, *Brothers Reuther*, 181; Victor Reuther, interview by Skeels, 24, OHC, ALUA, WSU; *Indianapolis Star*, 15 February 1937.

82. Fine, *Sit-Down*, 316–17; Hoffman, *Sit-Down in Anderson*, 68, 85; Reuther, *Brothers Reuther*, 181; Victor Reuther, interview by Skeels, 24, OHC, ALUA, WSU; *Indianapolis Star*, 15 February 1937; *United Automobile Worker*, 25 February 1937 and 1 November 1940.

83. "Press Release by Conference for Protection of Civil Rights," 16 April 1937, box 58, Workers Defense League Papers, ALUA, WSU; *Kenosha (Wis.) Labor*, 16

April 1937, roll 149, ACLU Papers; Lichtenstein, *Most Dangerous Man*, 81; Telegram to Roger Baldwin, 16 April 1937, roll 153, ACLU Archives; *Indianapolis Times*, 23 May 1937.

84. *Austin (Minn.) Unionist*, 30 April 1937, roll 149, ACLU Papers; *Daily Worker*, 19 April 1937, clipping on roll 149, ACLU Papers; *Detroit Times*, 6 March 1938.

85. Daniel Gallagher, interview by Jack W. Skeels, 26 January 1960, 45–46, OHC, ALUA, WSU; Blankenhorn Confidential Memo, "Summary of Facts on Reuther Shooting Presented to Senate Committee on Crime, Senator Kefauver, Chairman," Detroit, Mich., June 1950, box 3, Heber Blankenhorn Papers, ALUA, WSU; Lichtenstein, *Most Dangerous Man*, 91, 98; Margaret Collingwood Nowak, *Two Who Were There: A Biography of Stanley Nowak* (Detroit: Wayne State University Press, 1989), 124–25.

86. "Statement on Federal Screw," n.d., box 11, George Clifton Edwards Sr. Papers, ALUA, WSU.

87. Lichtenstein, *Most Dangerous Man*, 98–100.

88. *United Automobile Worker*, 2 April 1938; Victor Reuther, interview by Norwood; *Detroit News*, 30 March 1938; Lichtenstein, *Most Dangerous Man*, 98–100; Daniel Gallagher, interview by Skeels, 45–46, OHC, ALUA, WSU; *West Side Conveyor*, 5 April 1938; Catherine Geller, interview by Skeels, 13, OHC, ALUA, WSU.

89. Daniel Gallagher, interview by Skeels, 46, OHC, ALUA, WSU; Doug Fraser, interview by Norwood.

90. *West Side Conveyor*, 5 April 1938; Walter Reuther, "Background of Federal Screw Works Strike," 30 March 1938, box 55, Civil Rights Congress of Michigan Collection, ALUA, WSU.

91. *West Side Conveyor*, 5 April 1938; Carl Haessler, "Police Brutality Fails to Bust Picket Lines; Federal Screw Closed," Federated Press, 31 March 1938, box 8, Edward Levinson Papers, ALUA, WSU; *United Automobile Worker*, 2 April 1938; Daniel Gallagher, interview by Skeels, 45, OHC, ALUA, WSU.

92. Daniel Gallagher, interview by Skeels, 47, OHC, ALUA, WSU; *West Side Conveyor*, 28 May 1938.

93. *West Side Conveyor*, 28 May 1938; *United Automobile Worker*, 28 May 1938; *Detroit News*, 27 May 1938, clipping in box 79, Civil Rights Congress of Michigan Collection, ALUA, WSU; *Detroit Times*, 27 May 1938. Daniel Gallagher stated in 1960 that the policeman was still blind, tending a cigar stand in downtown Detroit. Daniel Gallagher, interview by Skeels, 47, OHC, ALUA, WSU.

94. Haessler, "Police Brutality Fails to Bust Picket Lines"; *Detroit Times*, 31 March and 3 and 5 June 1938; *Detroit News*, 1 April 1938.

95. Lichtenstein, *Most Dangerous Man*, 235; Zieger, *CIO*, 214; Mary Heaton Vorse, "Low-Pitched Strike at Chrysler," *Reporter*, 25 April 1950, 28; Irving Bluestone, interview by Stephen H. Norwood, Detroit, Mich., 13 October 1993.

96. Irving Bluestone, interview by Norwood.

97. Lichtenstein, *Most Dangerous Man*, 236; Irving Bluestone, interview by Norwood.

98. Vorse, "Low-Pitched Strike," 27–28; Mary Heaton Vorse, "Chrysler Strike Report #1," 17 February 1950," box 95, Mary Heaton Vorse Papers, ALUA, WSU.

99. *United Automobile Worker*, December 1945. The UAW-CIO was also worried about the returning veterans because after World War I demobilized soldiers, sailors, and marines had constituted a significant source of strikebreakers. John Fitzpatrick, president of the Chicago Federation of Labor, noted in 1919 that private and federal government employment offices were doing "a big business in furnishing returned soldiers, sailors, and marines in strikes, and where employers are trying to force wages back to 1914 standards." He cited as examples the Excelsior Motorcycle and Columbian Bank Note Company strikes, both broken by demobilized veterans. The Red Cross furnished soldiers maimed in France to replace gardeners and florists in Chicago's residential suburbs, who had demanded higher wages. Fitzpatrick noted that many citizens considered it "decidedly unpatriotic" for workers to picket strikebreaking soldiers and sailors. John Fitzpatrick to Frank Morrison, 1 May 1919, box 8, Chicago Federation of Labor Records, John Fitzpatrick Papers, Chicago Historical Society, Chicago, Ill.

100. Doug Fraser, interview by Norwood; Barton Bernstein, "Walter Reuther and the General Motors Strike of 1945–46," *Michigan History* 49 (September 1965): 276–77.

EPILOGUE

1. Obituary, *New York Times*, 13 August 1947; obituary, *Time*, 25 August 1947, 66.

2. Carol Zisowitz Stearns and Peter Stearns, *Anger: The Struggle for Emotional Control in America's History* (Chicago: University of Chicago Press, 1986), 111, 113, 116–18, 120, 122–23, 156, 211, 215, 224, 241.

3. Ibid., 167, 221.

4. Ned Polsky, *Hustlers, Beats, and Others* (1967; reprint, New York: Lyons Press, 1998), 20–23.

5. Hervey A. Juris and Myson Roomkin, eds., *The Shrinking Perimeter: Unionism and Labor Relations in the Manufacturing Sector* (Lexington, Mass.: D. C. Heath, 1980), ix; Michael Goldfield, *The Decline of Organized Labor in the United States* (Chicago: University of Chicago Press, 1987), p. xiii; Howell John Harris, *The Right to Manage: Industrial Relations Policies of American Business in the 1940s* (Madison: University of Wisconsin Press, 1982), 43; David Brody, *Workers in Industrial America* (New York: Oxford University Press, 1980), 173; *Labor Record*, 16 June 1939, clipping in "Oversized Materials," Violations of Free Speech and Rights of Labor Records, Record Group (hereafter, RG) 46, National Archives (hereafter, NA), Washington, D.C.

6. Carroll R. Daugherty, *Labor Problems in American Industry* (Boston: Houghton Mifflin, 1938), 943–44; *Washington Daily News*, 26 January 1939, clipping in "Oversized Materials," RG 46, NA; Jerold S. Auerbach, *Labor and Liberty:*

The La Follette Committee and the New Deal (Indianapolis: Bobbs-Merrill, 1966), 7–8, 102–3; Irving Bernstein, *The Lean Years* (Baltimore: Penguin, 1960), 205; Robert M. Smith, "From Blackjacks to Briefcases: Commercial Anti-Union Agencies, 1865–1985" (Ph.D. dissertation, University of Toledo, 1989), 65–67; *United Automobile Worker*, 29 May 1937, 6; *New York World-Telegram*, 24 November 1937, clipping on roll 131, American Civil Liberties Union Papers, microfilm.

7. Robert H. Zieger, *The CIO, 1935–1955* (Chapel Hill: University of North Carolina Press, 1995), 245–46; Thomas Geoghegan, *Which Side Are You On? Trying to Be for Labor When It's Flat on Its Back* (New York: Penguin, 1992), 52; Richard B. Freeman, "Why Are Unions Faring Poorly in NLRB Representation Elections?," in Thomas A. Kochan, ed., *Challenges and Choices Facing American Labor* (Cambridge, Mass.: MIT Press, 1985), 61.

8. Janice A. Klein and E. David Wanger, "The Legal Setting for the Emergence of the Union Avoidance Strategy," in Kochan, *Challenges*, 78–79; Steve Lagerfeld, "The Pop Psychologist as Union Buster," *American Federationist*, November 1981, 6; Martin Jay Levitt, *Confessions of a Union Buster* (New York: Crown Publishers, 1993), 223.

9. Bert Cochran, "American Labor in Mid-Passage" in Bert Cochran, ed., *American Labor in Mid-Passage* (New York: Monthly Review Press, 1959), 46; Barbara Griffith, *The Crisis of American Labor: Operation Dixie and the Defeat of the CIO* (Philadelphia: Temple University Press, 1988), 98–99, 103, 104.

10. Robert H. Zieger, *American Workers, American Unions* (1986; reprint, Baltimore: Johns Hopkins University Press, 1994), 194–95; Thomas A. Kochan, Harry C. Katz, and Robert B. McKersie, *The Transformation of American Industrial Relations* (New York: Basic Books, 1986), 249; "No Welcome Mat for Unions in the Sunbelt," *Business Week*, 17 May 1976, 108; Brody, *Workers in Industrial America*, 248.

11. Victor Reuther, interview by Stephen H. Norwood, Washington, D.C., 26 August 1993; "American Union-Busting," *Economist*, 17 November 1979, 39.

12. Geoghegan, *Which Side*, 14, 242–43.

13. Zieger, *American Workers*, 197; *Christian Science Monitor*, 11 August 1989; *Washington Post*, 30 July 1989.

14. Tom Juravich and Kate Brofenbrenner, *Ravenswood: The Steelworkers' Victory and the Revival of American Labor* (Ithaca, N.Y.: ILR Press, 1999), 35; *Los Angeles Times*, 26 November 1991; Zieger, *American Workers*, 198.

15. Freeman, "Why Are Unions Faring Poorly," 54–61; Klein and Wanger, "Legal Setting," 76; Kochan et al., *Transformation*, 61.

16. Harris, *Right to Manage*, 154.

17. Fred K. Foulkes, *Personnel Policies in Large Nonunion Companies* (Englewood Cliffs, N.J.: Prentice-Hall, 1980), 259–60.

18. Elizabeth Fones-Wolf, *Selling Free Enterprise: The Business Assault on Labor and Liberalism, 1945–60* (Urbana: University of Illinois Press, 1994), 75–76; Harris, *Right to Manage*, 171; Foulkes, *Personnel Policies*, 296.

19. Fones-Wolf, *Selling Free Enterprise*, 77; Chris Woods, interview by Stephen H.

Norwood, Washington, D.C., 13 August 1997; David Pauly, "Nissan Takes on the UAW," *Newsweek*, 21 February 1983, 64.

20. Fones-Wolf, *Selling Free Enterprise*, 80–81, 91; Robert F. Wheeler, "Organized Sport and Organized Labour: The Workers' Sports Movement," *Journal of Contemporary History* 13 (April 1978): 194–95.

21. Levitt, *Confessions*, 150; Kinsey Wilson and Steve Askin, "Secrets of a Union Buster," *Nation*, 13 June 1981, 726.

22. Charles McDonald and Dick Wilson, "Peddling the 'Union-Free' Guarantee," *American Federationist*, April 1979, 13; Levitt, *Confessions*, 21; Steven Lagerfeld, "To Break a Union: Goons Give Way to Consultants," *Harper's*, May 1981, 18–19.

23. Lagerfeld, "Pop Psychologist," 6; Levitt, *Confessions*, 5, 12.

24. Jerry Flint, "A New Breed—Professional Union Breakers," *Forbes*, 25 June 1979, 29; McDonald and Wilson, "Peddling," 12; Levitt, *Confessions*, 150.

25. Leo Huberman, "No More Class War?," in Cochran, *American Labor in Mid-Passage*, 90; Smith, "Blackjacks," 204–06.

26. Brody, *Workers in Industrial America*, 248; Kochan et al., *Transformation*, 77; "Labor Fights Back against Union Busters," *U.S. News and World Report*, 10 December 1979, 96; Flint, "New Breed," 29.

27. "Labor Fights Back," 97; Smith, "Blackjacks," 227–28.

28. Nathan Shefferman, *The Man in the Middle* (Garden City, N.Y.: Doubleday, 1961), 270–71.

29. Lagerfeld, "To Break a Union," 18.

30. Tony Dunbar and Bob Hall, "Union Busters: Who, Where, When, How, and Why," *Southern Exposure*, Summer 1980, 30, 32.

31. Lagerfeld, "To Break a Union," 18; McDonald and Wilson, "Peddling," 17; Smith, "Blackjacks," 227–28.

32. Wilson and Askin, "Secrets of a Union Buster," 727; Phillis Payne, "The Consultants Who Coach the Violators," *American Federationist*, September 1977, 27–28; "American Union-Busting," 50.

33. Dunbar and Hall, "Union Busters," 34, 37; Ron Chernow, "Grey Flannel Goons: The Latest in Union Busting," *Working Papers for a New Society*, January–February 1981, 21. Two films that management frequently showed to employees during NLRB representation campaigns, *And Women Must Weep* and *Springfield Gun*, associated unions with violence and the destruction of property. Alfred T. Demaria, *How Management Wins Union Organizing Campaigns* (New York: Executive Enterprise Publications, 1980), 121.

34. Ed McConville, "How 7,041 Got Fired," *Nation*, 25 October 1975, 393; James B. Parks, "Down and Dirty and Legal," *America @ Work*, July 1998, 16; Mike Hall, "7 Days in June," *America @ Work*, August 1999, 13.

35. Levitt, *Confessions*, 40–41.

36. Ibid., 1–3.

37. Chris Woods, interview by Norwood.

38. Ibid.

39. Payne, "Consultants Who Coach the Violators," 27.

40. Cochran, "American Labor in Mid-Passage," 49.

41. Ibid., 49; Huberman, "No More Class War?," 88; "American Union-Busting," 49; "No Welcome Mats for Unions in the Sunbelt," 111.

42. "No Welcome Mats for Unions in the Sunbelt," 108; Ed McConville, "Dirty Tricks Down South," *Nation*, 9 February 1980, 143–44; "American Union-Busting," 46.

43. "American Union-Busting," 46; McConville, "Dirty Tricks," 143–44.

44. Kochan et al., *Transformation*, 60; Leonard Woodcock, interview by Stephen H. Norwood, Ann Arbor, Mich., 15 December 1993.

45. Zieger, *American Workers, American Unions*, 198–99; Marc Levinson, "One for the Rank and File," *Newsweek*, 19 July 1993, 38; "Wrong Time for Scare Tactics?," *Business Week*, 16 April 1990, 28.

46. *Washington Post*, 27 May 1996; "Caterpillar's Ploys Won't Play in Peoria," *Solidarity*, March 1992, 17; Doug Fraser, interview by Stephen H. Norwood, Detroit, Mich., 8 October 1993.

47. "Wrong Time for Scare Tactics?," 27; Janice Castro, "Labor Draws an Empty Gun," *Time*, 26 March 1990, 56; Zieger, *American Workers, American Unions*, 198.

48. "Why a Coal Strike Isn't What It Used to Be," *U.S. News and World Report*, 19 December 1977, 86; "Twilight for the UMW?," *Business Week*, 3 July 1989, 32.

49. Geoghegan, *Which Side Are You On?*, 242; Alexander Cockburn, "Their Miners and Ours," *Nation*, 21–28 August 1989, 195; Tom Johnson, "Work, Family, and Union: Pittston Attacks a Way of Life," *United Mine Workers Journal* (hereafter, *UMWJ*), July–August 1989, 9; Damon Hale, "The Rank and File Speaks," *UMWJ*, July–August 1989, 12; letter from Jennifer Rose, *UMWJ*, June 1989, 2; letter from Bobby L. Bragg, *UMWJ*, July–August 1989, 2.

50. James R. Green, "'Tying the Knot of Solidarity': The Pittston Strike of 1989–1990," in John H. M. Laslett, ed., *The United Mine Workers of America: A Model of Industrial Solidarity?* (University Park: Pennsylvania State University Press, 1996), 520; "Coal Country's War with Itself," *U.S. News and World Report*, 24 July 1989, 45; William Lowther, "A Bitter Deadlock," *Maclean's*, 20 November 1989, 72; "John L., You'd Be Amazed," *Time*, 15 May 1989, 38; *UMWJ*, July–August 1989, 1–2.

51. *UMWJ*, June 1989, 8.

52. "Wrong Time for Scare Tactics?," 27; Kevin Kelley, "Greyhound May Be Coming to the End of the Line," *Business Week*, 21 May 1990, 45; Castro, "Labor Draws an Empty Gun," 56; Zieger, *American Workers, American Unions*, 198.

53. "The Cat and the Mice," *Newsweek*, 20 April 1992, 56; "Showdown on Labor's Front Line," *Time*, 20 April 1992, 32; "Caterpillar's Ploys Won't Play in Peoria," 17; "Moving Mountains on a Picket Line," *U.S. News and World Report*, 20 April 1992, 20; "Cat Gets Its Back Up. Way Up," *Business Week*, 20 April 1992, 40.

54. "Cat Gets Its Back Up," 40; "The Cat and the Mice," 56; "Showdown on Labor's Front Line," 32.

55. "After Cat: What Does the Right to Strike Mean Now?," *Business Week*, 4 May 1992, 36; Kevin Kelly, "Labor's Metamorphosis? The High Stakes at Caterpillar,"

*Commonweal*, 15 January 1993, 7; Brenda Dalglish, "Caterpillar's Showdown," *Maclean's*, 27 April 1992, 37.

56. Levinson, "One for the Rank and File," 38; Daniel Seligman, "Unions and Strikers: A Huge Nonproblem," *Fortune*, 31 May 1993, 175; Irving Bluestone, interview by Stephen H. Norwood, Detroit, Mich., 13 October 1993; Doug Fraser, interview by Norwood.

57. Castro, "Labor Draws an Empty Gun," 56; Levinson, "One for the Rank and File," 39.

58. Kochan, *Transformation*, 9; Doug Fraser, interview by Norwood.

59. Chris Woods, interview by Stephen H. Norwood, Washington, D.C., 14 August 1997; Anne Field, " 'Pinkertons' in Pin Stripes Wage War on Women," *Working Woman*, December 1980, 70; Freeman, "Why Unions Are Faring Poorly," in Kochan et al., *Challenges*, 53–54; Geoghegan, *Which Side Are You On?*, 253–54; Hendrik Hertzberg, "Labor's China Syndrome," *New Yorker*, 5 June 2000, 31; McConville, "How 7,041 Got Fired," 393; Hall, "7 Days in June," 14.

# BIBLIOGRAPHY

MANUSCRIPT COLLECTIONS

Archives of Labor and Urban Affairs, Walter P. Reuther Library, Wayne State
    University, Detroit, Michigan
    Peter Amann Collection
    John Nicholas Beffel Papers
    Heber Blankenhorn Papers
    Joe Brown Papers
    Civil Rights Congress of Michigan Collection
    Robert Dunn Papers
    George Clifton Edwards Sr. Papers
    Carl Haessler Papers
    Edward Levinson Papers
    Percy Llewellyn Papers
    Emil Mazey Papers
    Victor Reuther Papers
    Harry Ross Papers
    Maurice Sugar Papers
    UAW President's Office—Walter Reuther Papers
    UAW Public Relations Department—Ford Papers
    UAW Research Department Papers
    Mary Van Kleeck Papers
    Mary Heaton Vorse Papers
    Edward Wieck Papers
    Workers Defense League Papers
    John Zaremba Papers
Catholic University of America Archives, Washington, D.C.
    Mother Jones Papers
    John Mitchell Papers
Chicago Historical Society, Chicago, Illinois
    John Fitzpatrick Papers
    Mary McDowell Papers
Ford Motor Company Archives, Henry Ford Museum and Greenfield Village
    Research Center, Dearborn, Michigan
    Accessions 23, 65, 572, 940, 958, 975, 1606
    Clip Books 129 and 135
Harvard University Archives, Pusey Library, Harvard University, Cambridge,
    Massachusetts
    Charles W. Eliot Papers
    A. Lawrence Lowell Papers

Historical Collections and Labor Archives, Pattee Library, Pennsylvania State
  University, University Park, Pennsylvania
    T. R. Johns Papers
    Michael J. Kosik Collection
    George Medrick Papers
    Harold J. Ruttenberg Papers
Library of Congress, Washington, D.C.
    National Association for the Advancement of Colored People Papers
    National Urban League Papers
    Gifford Pinchot Papers
Microfilm Editions
    American Civil Liberties Union Papers
    Socialist Party of America Papers
National Archives, Washington, D.C., and College Park, Maryland
    Bureau of Labor Statistics Records
    Department of Justice Records
    Department of Labor Records
    Federal Bureau of Investigation Records
    Federal Mediation and Conciliation Service Records
    National Labor Relations Board Papers
    U.S. Coal Commission Records
    Violations of Free Speech and Rights of Labor Records
New York State Department of Labor Library, New York, New York
    New York Women's Trade Union League Papers
Pennsylvania State Archives, Harrisburg, Pennsylvania
    Pennsylvania State Police Records
    Samuel W. Pennypacker Papers
Special Collections, University of Arkansas Library, Fayetteville, Arkansas
    *UMW et al. v. Pennsylvania Mining Company*, U.S. Circuit Court of Appeals
    *United Mine Workers of America et al. v. Coronado Coal Company et al.*
Sterling Library, Yale University, New Haven, Connecticut
    Arthur Twining Hadley Papers
    Henry Parks Wright Papers
West Virginia Archives, West Virginia University Library, Morgantown, West
  Virginia
    Justus Collins Papers
    John J. Cornwell Papers
    William E. Glasscock Papers

GOVERNMENT DOCUMENTS

*Affray at Brownsville, Texas, August 13 and 14, 1906: Proceedings of a General Court-*
  *Martial Convened at Headquarters Department of Texas, San Antonio, Tex.,*

February 4, 1907, in the Case of Maj. Charles W. Penrose, Twenty-fifth United States Infantry. Washington, D.C.: Government Printing Office, 1907.

Companies B, C, D, Twenty-fifth United States Infantry Report on the Proceedings of the Court of Inquiry Relative to the Shooting Affray at Brownsville, Texas, August 13–14, 1906. Vols. 4, 6, and 11. Washington, D.C.: Government Printing Office, 1911.

Report of the Bureau of Statistics of Labor for the State of Louisiana, 1902–3. Baton Rouge: Advocate, Official Journal of Louisiana, 1904.

Report of West Virginia Mining Investigation, 1912, Appointed by Governor Glasscock, August 28, 1912. Charleston, W.Va., 11 November 1912.

Second Biennial Report of Bureau of Labor and Statistics of the State of Arkansas, 1915–1916. Little Rock: Democrat P8-L, 1917.

U.S. House of Representatives. Conditions in the Copper Mines of Michigan: Hearings before a Subcommittee of the Committee on Mines and Mining. 63rd Cong., 2nd sess., 1914.

U.S. Senate. Conditions in the Coal Fields of Pennsylvania, West Virginia, and Ohio. 70th Cong., 1st sess., 1928.

——. Industrial Relations: Final Report and Testimony Submitted to Congress by the Commission on Industrial Relations. 64th Cong., 1st sess., 1916, S. Doc. 415.

——. Report of the Committee on Education and Labor Pursuant to S. Res. 266: Strikebreaking Services. 76th Cong., 1st sess., 1939.

——. Strike in the Copper Mining District of Michigan. 63rd Cong., 2nd sess., 1914, S. Doc. 381.

——. Violations of Free Speech and Rights of Labor: Hearings before a Subcommittee of the Committee on Education and Labor. 75th Cong., 1st sess., 1937.


NEWSPAPERS


Appeal to Reason, 1914
Atlanta Journal, 1905
Baltimore Sun, 1903, 1921
Bluefield (W.Va.) Daily Telegraph, 1936, 1937
Boston Evening Transcript, 1919
Boston Globe, 1919
Broad Ax (Chicago), 1905
Brooklyn Daily Eagle, 1905
California Social-Democrat, 1911, 1912, 1913, 1916
Chicago Chronicle, 1903, 1904
Chicago Daily News, 1904, 1905
Chicago Defender, 1919
Chicago Inter-Ocean, 1903, 1904, 1905
Chicago Record-Herald, 1903, 1904, 1905
Chicago Socialist, 1903, 1904, 1912

*Chicago Tribune*, 1903, 1904, 1905, 1915
*Christian Science Monitor*, 1912, 1989
*Cleveland Citizen*, 1899
*Cleveland Plain-Dealer*, 1899
*Coast Seamen's Journal*, 1901, 1915
*Columbia Spectator*, 1905, 1920
*Commercial Appeal* (Memphis), 1905
*Daily People*, 1905
*Daily Princetonian*, 1920
*Daily Worker*, 1936, 1937
*Dallas Morning News*, 1904
*Des Moines Register and Leader*, 1911
*Detroit Free Press*, 1901, 1905, 1936, 1942, 1979
*Detroit News*, 1932, 1936, 1938, 1945, 1979
*Detroit Times*, 1938
*Dodge Main News*, 1952
*Ford Facts*, 1940, 1941
*Fort Smith Times-Record*, 1914, 1915
*Forward*, 2001
*Freeman* (Indianapolis), 1905
*Harvard Crimson*, 1912, 1921, 1941
*Huntington (W.Va.) Herald-Dispatch*, 1913, 1920
*Independent Observer* (Beckley, W.Va.), 1937, 1938
*Indianapolis News*, 1910
*Indianapolis Star*, 1913, 1937
*Indianapolis Times*, 1937
*International Brotherhood of Teamsters, Chauffeurs, Stablemen, and Helpers*, 1914
*Kansas City Star*, 1904, 1905
*Labor News* (Worcester, Mass.), 1909, 1912, 1913
*Los Angeles Times*, 1991
*Lumberjack* (Alexandria, La.), 1913
*Machinists' Monthly Journal*, 1909
*McAlester (Okla.) News-Capital*, 1914
*Miner's Magazine*, 1912, 1913
*Minneapolis Journal*, 1903
*Minnesota Daily* (University of Minnesota), 1903
*Motorman and Conductor*, 1899, 1900, 1904, 1907
*National Rip-Saw*, 1913, 1914, 1915
*Newark (N.J.) Evening News*, 1905, 1912, 1914
*New Haven Evening Register*, 1903
*New Orleans Daily Picayune*, 1902
*New Orleans Item*, 1911, 1929
*New Orleans Times-Democrat*, 1905
*New Orleans Times-Picayune*, 1919, 1921, 1925, 1938
*New York Age*, 1905

*New York American*, 1905, 1906
*New York Call*, 1912, 1913, 1914, 1919
*New York Evening Post*, 1905, 1934
*New York Herald*, 1896, 1901, 1903, 1905
*New York Journal*, 1905
• *New York Sun*, 1904, 1905
*New York Times*, 1902, 1903, 1905, 1912, 1913, 1914, 1916, 1919, 1920, 1921, 1937, 1947
*New York Tribune*, 1896, 1902, 1903, 1905, 1906, 1909, 1910, 1916, 1920
*New York World*, 1905
*North Adams (Mass.) Evening Transcript*, 1921
*Omaha World-Herald*, 1904
*Philadelphia Inquirer*, 1909, 1910, 1920
*Philadelphia Press*, 1902
*Plattsburgh (N.Y.) Sentinel*, 1913
*PM* (New York, N.Y.), 1941, 1944
*Providence Journal*, 1902
*Richmond Times-Dispatch*, 1902, 1903
*Rocky Mountain News* (Denver), 1914
*San Francisco Chronicle*, 1902, 1907, 1913
*San Francisco Examiner*, 1901, 1902, 1905, 1907
*Social Democratic Herald*, 1904, 1905
*St. Louis Globe-Democrat*, 1900, 1905
*St. Louis Post-Dispatch*, 1900, 1905
*Stute* (Stevens Institute of Technology), 1920
*Tech* (Massachusetts Institute of Technology), 1912, 1921
*Topeka Daily Capital*, 1905
*Triangle* (New York University), 1905
*Tulsa World*, 1914
*United Automobile Worker*, 1936, 1937, 1938, 1940, 1941, 1945
*United Mine Workers Journal*, 1901, 1902, 1903, 1904, 1913, 1914, 1916, 1920, 1989
*Washington Post*, 1903, 1989, 1996
*Wellesley College News*, 1907, 1910, 1911
*West Side Conveyor* (Detroit, Mich.), 1938
*Williams Record* (Williams College), 1921
*Worker*, 1901, 1902, 1904
*Yale Daily News*, 1903

ORAL HISTORY INTERVIEWS

Ford Motor Company Archives, Henry Ford Museum and Greenfield Village
    Research Center
    Reminiscences of Irving Bacon, September 1952
    Reminiscences of Henry Ford II, interview by David L. Lewis, 14 April 1980

Reminiscences of John Wandersee, 31 January 1952
Reminiscences of Willis F. Ward, May 1955
Indiana University Oral History Research Project, Interviews by R. T. King,
    Transcripts in Archives of Labor and Urban Affairs
    Jack Jourdan, 14 August 1979
    Victor Reuther, 26 September 1980
By Stephen H. Norwood
    Ken Bannon, telephone interview, 6 April 1995
    Irving Bluestone, Detroit, Mich., 13 October 1993
    Doug Fraser, Detroit, Mich., 8 October 1993
    Victor Reuther, Washington, D.C., 26 August 1993
    Leonard Woodcock, Ann Arbor, Mich., 15 December 1993
    Chris Woods, Washington, D.C., 13 and 14 August 1997
By Jack W. Skeels, Transcripts in Oral History Collection, Archives of Labor and
    Urban Affairs
    Ken Bannon, 28 February 1963
    Melvin Bishop, 29 March 1963
    Harold A. Cranefield, 17 May 1963
    Tracy Doll, 21 April 1961
    Genora Dollinger, 31 July 1960
    Richard Frankensteen, 10 and 23 October, 6 November 1959, and 7 December
        1961
    Daniel Gallagher, 26 January 1960
    Catherine Geller, 7 July 1961
    Bob Kanter, 31 August 1961
    May Reuther, 29 May 1963
    Harry Ross, 10 July 1961
    Hugh Thompson, 28 March 1963
    Leonard Woodcock, 30 April 1963
    John Zaremba, 11 August, 29 September, and 6 October 1961

BOOKS

Aaron, Daniel, ed. *America in Crisis*. New York: Alfred A. Knopf, 1952.
Adams, Graham, Jr. *Age of Industrial Violence: The Activities and Findings of the
    United States Commission on Industrial Relations*. New York: Columbia
    University Press, 1966.
Adams, Michael C. C. *The Great Adventure: Male Desire and the Coming of World
    War I*. Bloomington: Indiana University Press, 1990.
Anderson, Jervis. *A. Philip Randolph: A Biographical Portrait*. New York: Harcourt
    Brace Jovanovich, 1972.
Anderson, Nels. *The Hobo: The Sociology of the Homeless Man*. Chicago: University
    of Chicago Press, 1923.

Andre, Sam, and Nat Fleischer. *A Pictorial History of Boxing*. New York: Bonanza Books, 1989.

Arnesen, Eric. *Waterfront Workers of New Orleans: Race, Class, and Politics, 1863–1923*. New York: Oxford University Press, 1991.

Auerbach, Jerold S. *Labor and Liberty: The La Follette Committee and the New Deal*. Indianapolis: Bobbs-Merrill, 1966.

Austin, Joe, and Michael Nevin Willard, eds. *Generations of Youth: Youth Cultures and History in Twentieth-Century America*. New York: New York University Press, 1998.

Avrich, Paul. *The Haymarket Tragedy*. Princeton, N.J.: Princeton University Press, 1984.

Babson, Steve. *Working Detroit: The Making of a Union Town*. New York: Adama Books, 1984.

Barrett, James. *Work and Community in the Jungle: Chicago's Packinghouse Workers, 1894–1922*. Urbana: University of Illinois Press, 1987.

Bederman, Gail. *Manliness and Civilization: A Cultural History of Gender and Race in the United States, 1880–1917*. Chicago: University of Chicago Press, 1995.

Beik, Mildred Allen. *The Miners of Windber: The Struggles of New Immigrants for Unionization, 1890s–1930s*. University Park: Pennsylvania State University Press, 1996.

Bennett, Harry. *We Never Called Him Henry*. New York: Gold Medal Books, 1951.

Bernstein, Irving. *The Lean Years*. Baltimore: Penguin, 1960.

———. *The Turbulent Years*. Boston: Houghton Mifflin, 1970.

Bing, Alexander M. *War-Time Strikes and Their Adjustment*. New York: E. P. Dutton, 1921.

Bingham, Norman W. *The Book of Athletics and Out-of-Door Sports*. Boston: Lothrop Publishing, 1895.

Brody, David. *Steelworkers in America: The Nonunion Era*. 1960. Reprint, New York: Harper & Row, 1969.

———. *Workers in Industrial America*. New York: Oxford University Press, 1980.

Bruce, Robert V. *1877: Year of Violence*. Chicago: Quadrangle Books, 1959.

Bruel, Wayne G. *The Molly Maguires*. New York: Vintage, 1964.

Burke, Colin B. *American Collegiate Populations: A Test of the Traditional View*. New York: New York University Press, 1982.

Burroughs, Edgar Rice. *The Warlord of Mars*. 1913. Reprint, New York: Ballantine Books, 1985.

Bushnell, Charles. *The Social Problem of the Chicago Stockyards*. Chicago: University of Chicago Press, 1902.

Butler, Nicholas Murray. *Across the Busy Years: Recollections and Reflections*. Vol. 2. New York: Charles Scribner's Sons, 1940.

Canby, Henry Seidel. *American Memoir*. Boston: Houghton Mifflin, 1947.

Canfield, James Hulme. *The College Student and His Problems*. New York: Macmillan, 1902.

Cantor, Milton, and Bruce Laurie, eds. *Class, Sex, and the Woman Worker*. Westport, Conn.: Greenwood Press, 1977.

Caullery, Maurice. *Universities and Scientific Life in the United States*. Cambridge, Mass.: Harvard University Press, 1922.

Chalberg, John. *Emma Goldman: American Individualist*. New York: Harper Collins, 1991.

Cochran, Bert, ed. *American Labor in Mid-Passage*. New York: Monthly Review Press, 1959.

Corbin, David Alan. *Life, Work, and Rebellion in the Coal Fields: The Southern West Virginia Miners, 1880–1922*. Urbana: University of Illinois Press, 1981.

Cronin, James, and Sirianni, Carmen, eds. *Work, Community, and Power*. Philadelphia: Temple University Press, 1983.

Daugherty, Carroll R. *Labor Problems in American Industry*. Boston: Houghton Mifflin, 1938.

Davis, Richard Harding. *Real Soldiers of Fortune*. New York: Charles Scribner's Sons, 1906.

Dawidowicz, Lucy S. *The War against the Jews, 1933–1945*. New York: Bantam Books, 1975.

Demaria, Alfred T. *How Management Wins Union Organizing Campaigns*. New York: Executive Enterprise Publications, 1980.

Deming, Seymour. *The Pillar of Fire: A Profane Baccalaureate*. Boston: Small, Maynard, 1915.

Downey, Fairfax. *Richard Harding Davis: His Day*. New York: Charles Scribner's Sons, 1933.

Draper, Alan. *Conflict of Interests: Organized Labor and the Civil Rights Movement in the South, 1954–1968*. Ithaca, N.Y.: ILR Press, 1994.

Dubofsky, Melvyn. *When Workers Organize: New York City in the Progressive Era*. Amherst: University of Massachusetts Press, 1968.

Dunn, Robert W. *Spying on Workers*. New York: Labor Research Association, 1932.

Edsforth, Ronald. *Class Conflict and Cultural Consensus: The Making of a Mass Consumer Society in Flint, Michigan*. New Brunswick, N.J.: Rutgers University Press, 1987.

Eksteins, Modris. *Rites of Spring: The Great War and the Birth of the Modern Age*. New York: Anchor Books, 1989.

Eller, Ronald D. *Miners, Millhands, and Mountaineers: Industrialization of the Appalachian South, 1880–1930*. Knoxville: University of Tennessee Press, 1982.

Ellis, John. *The Social History of the Machine Gun*. 1975. Reprint, New York: Arno Press, 1981.

Enstad, Nan. *Ladies of Labor, Girls of Adventure: Working Women, Popular Culture, and Labor Politics at the Turn of the Twentieth Century*. New York: Columbia University Press, 1999.

Erenberg, Lewis A. *Steppin' Out: New York Nightlife and the Transformation of American Culture, 1890–1930*. Westport, Conn.: Greenwood Press, 1981.

Fass, Paula. *The Damned and the Beautiful: American Youth in the 1920s*. New York: Oxford University Press, 1977.

Fetherling, Dale. *Mother Jones, the Miners' Angel: A Portrait*. Carbondale: Southern Illinois University Press, 1974.

Feuer, Lewis S. *The Conflict of Generations*. New York: Basic Books, 1969.

Filippelli, Ronald, ed. *Labor Conflict in the United States: An Encyclopedia*. New York: Garland, 1991.

Fine, Sidney. *Frank Murphy: The Detroit Years*. Ann Arbor: University of Michigan Press, 1975.

——. *Sit-Down: The General Motors Strike of 1936–1937*. Ann Arbor: University of Michigan Press, 1969.

Fink, Gary, ed. *Labor Unions*. Westport, Conn.: Greenwood Press, 1977.

Fitch, John A. *The Causes of Industrial Unrest*. New York: Harper & Brothers, 1924.

Fletcher, Marvin. *The Black Soldier and Officer in the United States Army, 1891–1917*. Columbia: University of Missouri Press, 1974.

Fogelson, Robert M. *America's Armories: Architecture, Society, and Public Order*. Cambridge, Mass.: Harvard University Press, 1989.

Fones-Wolf, Elizabeth. *Selling Free Enterprise: The Business Assault on Labor and Liberalism, 1945–60*. Urbana: University of Illinois Press, 1994.

Foulkes, Fred K. *Personnel Policies in Large Nonunion Companies*. Englewood Cliffs, N.J.: Prentice-Hall, 1980.

Frazier, E. Franklin, *Black Bourgeoisie: The Rise of a New Middle Class in the United States*. 1957. Reprint, New York: Collier Books, 1962.

Gates, William B., Jr. *Michigan Copper and Boston Dollars*. Cambridge, Mass.: Harvard University Press, 1951.

Geoghegan, Thomas. *Which Side Are You On?: Trying to Be for Labor When It's Flat on Its Back*. New York: Penguin, 1992.

Gilson, Mary Barnett. *What's Past Is Prologue*. New York: Harper and Brothers, 1940.

Goldfield, Michael. *The Decline of Organized Labor in the United States*. Chicago: University of Chicago Press, 1987.

Gorn, Elliott J. *The Manly Art: Bare-Knuckle Prize Fighting in America*. Ithaca, N.Y.: Cornell University Press, 1986.

Gottlieb, Peter. *Making Their Own Way: Southern Blacks' Migration to Pittsburgh, 1916–1930*. Urbana: University of Illinois Press, 1987.

Graham, Hugh, and Ted Gurr, eds. *Violence in America: Historical and Comparative Perspectives*. Beverly Hills, Calif.: Sage Publications, 1979.

Green, James R. *Grass-Roots Socialism: Radical Movements in the Southwest, 1895–1943*. Baton Rouge: Louisiana State University Press, 1978.

Griffith, Barbara. *The Crisis of American Labor: Operation Dixie and the Defeat of the CIO*. Philadelphia: Temple University Press, 1988.

Grossman, James R. *Land of Hope: Chicago, Black Southerners, and the Great Migration*. Chicago: University of Chicago Press, 1989.

Handlin, Oscar, and Mary F. Handlin. *Facing Life: Youth and the Family in American History*. Boston: Little Brown, 1971.

Hapgood, Powers, *In Non-Union Mines: The Diary of a Coal Digger in Central Pennsylvania, August–September 1921*. New York: Bureau of Industrial Research, 1922.

Harlan, Louis. *Booker T. Washington: The Wizard of Tuskegee*. New York: Oxford University Press, 1983.

Harring, Sidney. *Policing a Class Society: The Experience of American Cities, 1865–1915*. New Brunswick, N.J.: Rutgers University Press, 1983.

Harris, Evelyn, and Frank J. Krebs. *From Humble Beginnings: West Virginia State Federation of Labor, 1903–1957*. Charleston: West Virginia Labor History Publishing Fund, 1960.

Harris, Howell John. *The Right to Manage: Industrial Relations Policies of American Business in the 1940s*. Madison: University of Wisconsin Press, 1982.

Harris, William. *Keeping the Faith: A. Philip Randolph, Milton Webster, and the Brotherhood of Sleeping Car Porters, 1925–37*. Urbana: University of Illinois Press, 1977.

Hawkins, Hugh. *Between Harvard and America: The Educational Leadership of Charles W. Eliot*. New York: Oxford University Press, 1972.

Herbst, Alma. *The Negro in the Slaughtering and Meat-Packing Industry in Chicago*. Boston: Houghton Mifflin, 1932.

Herndon, Booton. *Ford: An Unconventional Biography of the Men and Their Times*. New York: Weybright and Talley, 1969.

Higham, John. *Strangers in the Land: Patterns of American Nativism, 1860–1925*. New York: Atheneum, 1970.

Hillquit, Morris. *Loose Leaves from a Busy Life*. New York: Macmillan, 1934.

Hoffman, Claude. *Sit-Down in Anderson: UAW Local 663, Anderson, Indiana*. Detroit: Wayne State University Press, 1968.

Honey, Michael K. *Southern Labor and Black Civil Rights: Organizing Memphis Workers*. Urbana: University of Illinois Press, 1993.

Horan, James. *The Pinkertons: The Detective Dynasty That Made History*. New York: Crown Publishers, 1967.

Howard, Sidney. *The Labor Spy*. New York: Republic Publishing, 1924.

Hunter, Robert. *Violence and the Labor Movement*. New York: Macmillan, 1919.

Interchurch World Movement. *Public Opinion and the Steel Strike*. New York: Harcourt Brace, 1921.

Isenberg, Michael. *John L. Sullivan and His America*. Urbana: University of Illinois Press, 1988.

Jacobson, Julius, ed. *The Negro and the American Labor Movement*. Garden City, N.Y.: Doubleday, 1968.

James, Henry. *Charles W. Eliot: President of Harvard University, 1689–1909*. Vol. 2. Boston: Houghton Mifflin, 1930.

Jeffrey-Jones, Rhodri. *Violence and Reform in American History*. New York: New Viewpoints, 1978.

Jencks, Christopher, and Riesman, David. *The Academic Revolution*. Garden City, N.Y.: Doubleday, 1968.

Johnson, Christopher. *Maurice Sugar: Law, Labor, and the Left in Detroit, 1912–1950*. Detroit: Wayne State University Press, 1988.

Juravich, Tom, and Kate Bronfenbrenner. *Ravenswood: The Steelworkers' Victory and the Revival of American Labor*. Ithaca, N.Y.: ILR Press, 1999.

Juris, Hervey A., and Myson Roomkin, eds. *The Shrinking Perimeter: Unionism and Labor Relations in the Manufacturing Sector*. Lexington, Mass.: D. C. Heath, 1980.

Kahn, Alfred E. *High Treason: The Plot against the People*. New York: Lear Publishers, 1950.

Keyssar, Alexander. *Out of Work: The First Century of Unemployment in Massachusetts*. New York: Cambridge University Press, 1986.

Kirkpatrick, J. E. *The American College and Its Rulers*. New York: New Republic, 1926.

Kochan, Thomas A., ed. *Challenges and Choices Facing American Labor*. Cambridge, Mass.: MIT Press, 1985.

Kochan, Thomas A., Harry C. Katz, and Robert B. McKersie, *The Transformation of American Industrial Relations*. New York: Basic Books, 1986.

Kraus, Henry. *The Many and the Few: A Chronicle of the Dynamic Auto Workers*. 1947. Reprint, Urbana: University of Illinois Press, 1985.

Kusmer, Kenneth. *A Ghetto Takes Shape: Black Cleveland, 1870–1930*. Urbana: University of Illinois Press, 1978.

Laidler, Harry. *Boycotts and the Labor Struggle: Economic and Legal Aspects*. New York: John Lane, 1913.

Lane, Ann J. *The Brownsville Affair: The National Crisis and Black Reaction*. Port Washington, N.Y.: National University Publications, Kennikat Press, 1971.

Laslett, John H. M., ed. *The United Mine Workers of America: A Model of Industrial Solidarity?* University Park: Pennsylvania State University Press, 1996.

Lee, Albert. *Henry Ford and the Jews*. New York: Stein and Day, 1980.

Lee, Howard. *Bloodletting in Appalachia*. Morgantown: West Virginia University, 1969.

Letwin, Daniel. *The Challenge of Interracial Unionism: Alabama Coal Miners, 1878–1921*. Chapel Hill: University of North Carolina Press, 1998.

Levinson, Edward. *I Break Strikes! The Technique of Pearl L. Bergoff*. New York: Robert M. McBride, 1935.

Levitt, Martin Jay. *Confessions of a Union Buster*. New York: Crown Publishers, 1993.

Lewis, David L. *The Public Image of Henry Ford: An American Folk Hero and His Company*. Detroit: Wayne State University Press, 1976.

Lichtenstein, Nelson. *The Most Dangerous Man in Detroit: Walter Reuther and the Fate of American Labor*. New York: Basic Books, 1995.

Lichtenstein, Nelson, and Howell John Harris, eds. *Industrial Democracy in America: The Ambiguous Promise*. New York: Cambridge University Press, 1993.

Litwack, Leon F. *Trouble in Mind: Black Southerners in the Age of Jim Crow*. New York: Knopf, 1998.

London, Jack. *The Iron Heel*. 1907. Reprint, New York: Sagamore Press, 1957.

———. *War of the Classes*. New York: Macmillan, 1905.

Lukas, J. Anthony. *Big Trouble*. New York: Simon & Schuster, 1997.

Mackay, John. *Allan Pinkerton: The First Private Eye*. New York: John Wiley & Sons, 1996.

Magil, A. B., and Henry Stevens. *The Peril of Fascism: The Crisis of American Democracy*. New York: International Publishers, 1938.

Marquart, Frank. *An Auto Worker's Journal: The UAW from Crusade to One-Party Union*. University Park: Pennsylvania State University Press, 1975.

Maurer, Charles. *The Constabulary of Pennsylvania*. Reading, Pa.: Charles Maurer, n.d.

Maurer, James H. *It Can Be Done: The Autobiography of James Hudson Maurer*. New York: Rand School Press, 1938.

Mayo, Katherine. *Justice to All: The Story of the Pennsylvania State Police*. Boston: Houghton Mifflin, 1920.

McGovern, George, and Leonard F. Guttridge. *The Great Coal Field War*. Boston: Houghton Mifflin, 1972.

McKiven, Henry. *Iron & Steel: Class, Race, and Community in Birmingham, Alabama, 1875–1920*. Chapel Hill: University of North Carolina Press, 1995.

McLaurin, Melton A. *The Knights of Labor in the South*. Westport, Conn.: Greenwood Press, 1978.

Meier, August, and Elliott Rudwick. *Black Detroit and the Rise of the UAW*. New York: Oxford University Press, 1979.

Metzger, Walter P. *Academic Freedom in the Age of the University*. New York: Columbia University Press, 1955.

Meyer, Stephen, III. *The Five Dollar Day: Labor Management and Social Control in the Ford Motor Company, 1908–1921*. Albany: State University of New York Press, 1981.

Miller, Kelly. *Race Adjustment: Essays on the Negro in America*. New York: Neale Publishing, 1908.

Mills, C. Wright. *White Collar: The American Middle Classes*. New York: Oxford University Press, 1951.

Molloy, Scott. *Trolley Wars: Streetcar Workers on the Line*. Washington, D.C.: Smithsonian Institution Press, 1996.

Montgomery, David. *The Fall of the House of Labor*. New York: Cambridge University Press, 1987.

———. *Workers' Control in America: Studies in the History of Work, Technology, and Labor Struggles*. New York: Cambridge University Press, 1978.

Morison, Samuel Eliot. *Three Centuries of Harvard, 1636–1936*. Cambridge, Mass.: Harvard University Press, 1946.

Morn, Frank. *"The Eye That Never Sleeps": A History of the Pinkerton National Detective Agency*. Bloomington: Indiana University Press, 1982.

Morris, George. *The Black Legion Rides*. New York: Workers Library Publishers, 1936.

Morris, Lloyd. *Not So Long Ago*. New York: Random House, 1949.

Nash, Roderick. *The Nervous Generation: American Thought, 1917–1930*. Chicago: Rand, McNally, 1970.

Nelson, Bruce. *Workers on the Waterfront: Seamen, Longshoremen, and Unionism in the 1930s*. Urbana: University of Illinois Press, 1988.

Nevins, Allen, and Frank Ernest Hill. *Ford: Decline and Rebirth, 1933–1962*. New York: Charles Scribner's Sons, 1963.

——. *Ford: Expansion and Challenge, 1915–1933*. New York: Charles Scribner's Sons, 1957.

Noble, David. *America by Design: Science, Technology, and the Rise of Corporate Capitalism*. New York: Alfred A. Knopf, 1977.

Norwood, Stephen H. *Labor's Flaming Youth: Telephone Operators and Worker Militancy, 1878–1923*. Urbana: University of Illinois Press, 1990.

Nowak, Margaret Collingwood. *Two Who Were There: A Biography of Stanley Nowak*. Detroit: Wayne State University Press, 1989.

Osborn, Scott Compton, and Robert L. Phillips Jr. *Richard Harding Davis*. Boston: Twayne Publishers, 1978.

Overton, Grant, ed. *The World's Best One Hundred Short Stories*, Vol. 1. New York: Funk & Wagnalls, 1927.

Peiss, Kathy. *Cheap Amusements: Working Women and Leisure in Turn-of-the Century New York*. Philadelphia: Temple University Press, 1986.

Pennypacker, Samuel Whitaker. *The Autobiography of a Pennsylvanian*. Philadelphia: John C. Winston, 1918.

Polsky, Ned. *Hustlers, Beats, and Others*. 1967. Reprint, New York: Lyons Press, 1998.

Poole, Ernest. *The Bridge: My Own Story*. New York: Macmillan, 1940.

Rader, Benjamin. *American Sports: From the Age of Folk Games to the Age of Televised Sport*. Englewood Cliffs, N.J.: Prentice-Hall, 1990.

Reuther, Victor. *The Brothers Reuther and the Story of the UAW*. Boston: Houghton Mifflin, 1976.

Richards, William C. *The Last Billionaire: Henry Ford*. New York: Charles Scribner's Sons, 1948.

Roberts, Randy. *Papa Jack: Jack Johnson and the Era of White Hopes*. New York: Free Press, 1983.

Rochester, Anna. *Labor and Coal*. New York: International Publishers, 1931.

Rodgers, Daniel. *The Work Ethic in Industrial America, 1850–1920*. Chicago: University of Chicago Press, 1978.

Roediger, David. *Towards the Abolition of Whiteness: Essays on Race, Politics, and Working-Class History*. London: Verso, 1994.

Ropp, Theodore. *War in the Modern World*. New York: Collier Books, 1959.

Rosenthal, Michael. *The Character Factory: Baden-Powell's Boy Scouts and the Imperatives of Empire*. New York: Pantheon Books, 1984.

Ross, Malcolm. *Death of a Yale Man*. New York: Farrar and Rinehart, 1939.

Rotundo, Anthony. *American Manhood: Transformations of Masculinity from the Revolution to the Modern Era*. New York: Basic Books, 1993.

Russell, Francis. *A City in Terror: The 1919 Boston Police Strike*. New York: Penguin, 1975.

Ryan, Frederick Lynne. *The Rehabilitation of Oklahoma Coal Mining Communities*. Norman: University of Oklahoma Press, 1935.

Ryan, Mary. *Womanhood in America: From Colonial Times to the Present*. New York: Franklin Watts, 1983.

Savage, Lon. *Thunder in the Mountains: The West Virginia Mine War, 1920–21*. Pittsburgh: University of Pittsburgh Press, 1990.

Schultz, Bud, and Ruth Schultz. *It Did Happen Here: Recollections of Political Repression in America*. Berkeley: University of California Press, 1989.

Shalloo, J. P. *Private Police: With Special Reference to Pennsylvania*. Philadelphia: American Academy of Political and Social Science, 1933.

Shefferman, Nathan. *The Man in the Middle*. Garden City, N.Y.: Doubleday, 1961.

Simkins, Francis Butler. *Pitchfork Ben Tillman: South Carolinian*. Baton Rouge: Louisiana State University Press, 1944.

Sinclair, Upton. *The Goose-Step: A Study of Academic Education*. Pasadena, Calif.: published by the author, 1922.

Slotkin, Richard. *The Fatal Environment: The Myth of the Frontier in the Age of Industrialization*. New York: Atheneum, 1985.

———. *Gunfighter Nation: The Myth of the Frontier in Twentieth Century America*. New York: Harper Collins, 1992.

Sorensen, Charles. *My Forty Years with Ford*. New York: W. W. Norton, 1956.

Spear, Allen H. *Black Chicago: The Making of a Negro Ghetto, 1890–1920*. Chicago: University of Chicago Press, 1967.

Spero, Sterling, and Abram Harris. *The Black Worker: The Negro and the Labor Movement*. New York: Columbia University Press, 1931.

Stearns, Carol Zisowitz, and Peter N. Stearns. *Anger: The Struggle for Emotional Control in America's History*. Chicago: University of Chicago Press, 1986.

Stearns, Peter N. *Be a Man! Males in Modern Society*. New York: Holmes and Meier, 1979.

Swain, G. T. *History of Logan County, West Virginia*. Logan, W.Va.: G. T. Swain, 1927.

Sward, Keith. *The Legend of Henry Ford*. New York: Rinehart, 1948.

Teaford, John. *The Twentieth Century American City: Problem, Promise, and Reality*. Baltimore: Johns Hopkins University Press, 1986.

Thernstrom, Stephan. *The Other Bostonians: Poverty and Progress in the American Metropolis, 1880–1970*. Cambridge, Mass.: Harvard University Press, 1973.

Thurner, Arthur. *Rebels on the Range: The Michigan Copper Miners' Strike of 1913–14*. Lake Linden, Mich.: John H. Forster Press, 1984.

Tomkins, Jane. *West of Everything: The Inner Life of Westerns*. New York: Oxford University Press, 1992.

Tuttle, William, Jr. *Race Riot: Chicago in the Red Summer of 1919*. New York: Atheneum, 1970.

Walker, Samuel. *A Critical History of Police Reform: The Emergence of Professionalism*. Lexington, Mass.: D. C. Heath, 1977.

Warne, Frank Julian. *The Slav Invasion and the Mine Workers*. Philadelphia: J. B. Lippincott, 1904.

Wiebe, Robert. *The Search for Order, 1877–1920*. New York: Hill and Wang, 1967.

Williamson, Joel. *The Crucible of Race: Black-White Relations in the American South since Emancipation*. New York: Oxford University Press, 1984.

Wolfe, F. E. *Admission to American Trade Unions*. Baltimore: Johns Hopkins University Press, 1912.

Wolters, Raymond. *The New Negro on Campus: Black College Rebellions of the 1920s*. Princeton, N.J.: Princeton University Press, 1975.

Zieger, Robert H. *American Workers, American Unions*. 1986. Reprint, Baltimore: Johns Hopkins University Press, 1994.

——. *The CIO, 1935–1955*. Chapel Hill: University of North Carolina Press, 1995.


## ARTICLES IN JOURNALS

Amann, Peter. "Vigilante Fascism: The Black Legion as an American Hybrid." *Comparative Studies in Society and History* 25 (1983): 490–524.

Arnesen, Eric. "Following the Color Line of Labor: Black Workers and the Labor Movement before 1930." *Radical History Review* 55 (Winter 1993): 53–87.

Babcock, Robert H. " 'Will You Walk? Yes We'll Walk!' Popular Support for a Street Railway Strike in Portland, Maine." *Labor History* 35 (Summer 1994): 372–98.

Bernstein, Barton. "Walter Reuther and the General Motors Strike of 1945–46." *Michigan History* 49 (September 1965): 260–77.

Brown, Cliff. "Racial Conflict and Split Labor Markets: The AFL Campaign to Organize Steel Workers, 1918–19." *Social Science History* 22 (Fall 1998): 319–47.

Clurman, Morris Joseph. "The American Game of Football: Is It a Factor for Good or for Evil?" *Medical Record* 79 (7 January 1911): 18–20.

Crowe, Charles. "Racial Massacre in Atlanta, September 22, 1906." *Journal of Negro History* 54 (April 1969): 150–73.

Cummings, John. "The Chicago Teamsters' Strike—A Study in Industrial Democracy." *Journal of Political Economy* 13 (September 1905): 536–73.

Davis, Donald F. "The Price of Conspicuous Production: The Detroit Elite and the Automobile Industry, 1900–1933." *Journal of Social History* 16 (Fall 1982): 21–46.

Farwell, Byron. "Taking Sides in the Boer War." *American Heritage* 27 (April 1976): 20–25, 92–97.

Gitelman, H. M. "Perspectives on American Industrial Violence." *Business History Review* 47 (Spring 1973): 1–23.

Green, George N. "Discord in Dallas." *Labor's Heritage* 1 (July 1989): 20–33.

Green, James R. "The Brotherhood of Timber Workers, 1910–1913: A Radical Response to Industrial Capitalism in the Southern U.S.A." *Past and Present* 60 (August 1973): 161–200.

Hadsell, Richard M., and William E. Coffey, "From Law and Order to Class Warfare: Baldwin-Felts Detectives in the Southern West Virginia Coal Fields." *West Virginia History* 40 (Spring 1979): 268–86.

Henry, Sarah. "The Strikers and Their Sympathizers: Brooklyn in the Trolley Strike of 1895." *Labor History* 32 (Summer 1991): 329–53.

Hogg, J. Bernard. "Public Reaction to Pinkertonism and the Labor Question." *Pennsylvania History* 11 (1944): 171–99.

Leach, William. "Transformations in a Culture of Consumption: Women and Department Stores, 1890–1925." *Journal of American History* 71 (September 1984): 319–42.

Long, Priscilla. "The Voice of the Gun: Colorado's Great Coal Field War of 1913–1914." *Labor's Heritage* 1 (October 1989): 4–23.

Lynch, Lawrence R. "The West Virginia Coal Strike." *Political Science Quarterly* 29 (December 1914): 626–63.

Norwood, Stephen H. "Bogalusa Burning: The War against Biracial Unionism in the Deep South, 1919." *Journal of Southern History* 63 (August 1997): 591–628.

Park, Roberta J. "Physiology and Anatomy Are Destiny?! Brains, Bodies, and Exercise in Nineteenth Century American Thought." *Journal of Sport History* 18 (Spring 1991): 31–63.

Ray, Gerda. " 'We Can Stay until Hell Freezes Over': Strike Control and the State Police in New York, 1919–1923." *Labor History* 36 (Summer 1995): 403–25.

Scopino, A. J. "Community, Class, and Conflict: The Waterbury Trolley Strike of 1903." *Connecticut History* 24 (1983): 29–46.

Sizer, Samuel A. "This Is Union Man's Country: Sebastian County 1914." *Arkansas Historical Quarterly* 27 (Winter 1968): 306–29.

Whatley, Warren C. "African-American Strikebreaking from the Civil War to the New Deal." *Social Science History* 17 (Winter 1993): 525–58.

Wheeler, Robert F. "Organized Sport and Organized Labour: The Workers' Sports Movement." *Journal of Contemporary History* 13 (April 1978): 191–210.


MAGAZINE ARTICLES (SIGNED)

Brent, Henry K. "The Strike Situation in San Francisco." *Street Railway Journal*, 21 September 1907.

Castro, Janice. "Labor Draws an Empty Gun." *Time*, 26 March 1990.

Chernow, Ron. "Gray Flannel Goons: The Latest in Union Busting." *Working Papers for a New Society*, January–February 1981.

Cockburn, Alexander. "Their Miners and Ours." *Nation*, 21–28 August 1989.

Craige, John. "The Professional Strike-Breaker." *Collier's*, 3 December 1910.

——. "The Violent Art of Strike-Breaking." *Collier's*, 7 January 1911.

Dalglish, Brenda. "Caterpillar's Showdown." *Maclean's*, 27 April 1992.

Davis, Forrest. "Labor Spies and the Black Legion." *New Republic*, 17 June 1936.

Denby, Charles. "Mere Man and Student." *New Student*, 30 December 1922.

Dunbar, Tony, and Bob Hall. "Union Busters: Who, Where, When, How, and Why." *Southern Exposure*, Summer 1980.

Edwards, Albert. "The Spirit of the Russian Student." *Intercollegiate Socialist*, October–November 1913.

Falconer, George. "Machine Guns and Coal Miners." *International Socialist Review*, December 1913.

Field, Anne. "'Pinkertons' in Pin Stripes Wage War on Women." *Working Women*, December 1980.

Flint, Jerry. "A New Breed—Professional Union Breakers." *Forbes*, 25 June 1979.

Fredericks, B. T. "James Farley: Strikebreaker." *Leslie's Monthly Magazine*, May 1905.

Gompers, Samuel. "Editorial: The Students' Debasement." *American Federationist*, April 1905.

———. "President Eliot's Mental Decadence." *American Federationist*, February 1906.

———. "Russianized West Virginia." *American Federationist*, October 1913.

Hall, Mike. "7 Days in June." *America @ Work*, August 1999.

Hard, William. "Labor in the Chicago Stockyards." *Outlook*, 16 June 1906.

Hertzberg, Hendrik. "Labor's China Syndrome." *New Yorker*, 5 June 2000.

Houston, G. David. "Weaknesses of the Negro College." *Crisis*, July 1920.

Kelly, Kevin. "Greyhound May Be Coming to the End of the Line." *Business Week*, 21 May 1990.

———. "Labor's Metamorphosis: The High Stakes at Caterpillar." *Commonweal*, 15 January 1993.

Kramnick, Isaac. "The Professor and the Police." *Harvard Magazine*, September–October 1989.

Lagerfeld, Steven. "The Pop Psychologist as Union Buster." *American Federationist*, November 1981.

———. "To Break a Union: Goons Give Way to Consultants." *Harper's*, May 1981.

Lait, Jack. "How a Big Strikebreaker Works." *American Magazine*, January 1917.

Lambert, George. "Dallas Tries Terror." *Nation*, 9 October 1937.

———. "Memphis Is Safe for Ford." *Nation*, 22 January 1938.

Laski, Harold. "Why Don't Your Young Men Care? The Political Indifference of the American Undergraduate." *Harper's Magazine*, July 1931.

Levinson, Marc. "One for the Rank and File." *Newsweek*, 19 July 1993.

Lewis, David L. "Harry Bennett, Ford's Tough Guy, Breaks 30 Years of Silence and Tells His Side of the Story." *Detroit Magazine*, 20 January 1974.

Lowther, William. "A Bitter Deadlock." *Maclean's*, 20 November 1989.

Lynd, Staughton, and Roberta Yancy. "Southern Negro Students: The College and the Movement." *Dissent*, Winter 1964.

MacFarlane, Peter Clark. "The Issues at Calumet." *Collier's*, 7 February 1914.

Marcy, Leslie H. "Calumet." *International Socialist Review*, February 1914.

———. "The Class War in Colorado." *International Socialist Review*, June 1914.

McCarten, John. "The Little Man in Henry Ford's Basement." *American Mercury*, May 1940.

McCarthy, Joe. "The Ford Family." *Holiday*, July and August 1957.

McConville, Ed. "Dirty Tricks Down South." *Nation*, 9 February 1980.

———. "How 7,041 Got Fired." *Nation*, 25 October 1975.

McDonald, Charles, and Dick Wilson. "Peddling the 'Union-Free' Guarantee." *American Federationist*, April 1979.

McGurty, Edward J. "The Copper Miners' Strike." *International Socialist Review*, September 1913.

McQuiston, F. B. "The Strike Breaker." *Independent*, 17 October 1901.

Meloney, William. "Strikebreaking as a Profession." *Public Opinion*, 25 March 1905.

Michelson, M. "Sweet Land of Liberty." *Everybody's Magazine*, May 1913.

Morrow, James B. "The Story of the Great Strikes." *Collier's Weekly*, 12 August 1899.

Norton, Helen G. "Feudalism in West Virginia." *Nation*, 12 August 1931.

Owen, Chandler. "The Failure of the Negro Leaders." *Messenger*, October 1919.

Parks, James B. "Down and Dirty and Legal." *America @ Work*, July 1998.

Pauly, David. "Nissan Takes on the UAW." *Newsweek*, 21 February 1983.

Payne, Phillis. "The Consultants Who Coach the Violators." *American Federationist*, September 1977.

Roach, John. "Packingtown Conditions." *American Federationist*, August 1906.

Ross, William. "Student and Worker." *New Student*, 2 February 1924.

Scott, Leroy. "'Strike-Breaking' as a New Occupation." *World's Work*, May 1905.

Seligman, Daniel. "Unions and Strikers: A Huge Nonproblem." *Fortune*, 31 May 1993.

Taylor, Graham Romeyn. "The Clash in the Copper Country." *Survey*, 1 November 1913.

——. "Moyer's Story of Why He Left the Copper Country." *Survey*, 10 January 1914.

Thompson, W. H. "Strike Settlements in West Virginia." *International Socialist Review*, August 1913.

Vorse, Mary Heaton. "Low-Pitched Strike at Chrysler." *Reporter*, 25 April 1950.

Washington, Booker T. "The Negro and the Labor Unions." *Atlantic Monthly*, June 1913.

Weed, Inis. "The Reasons Why the Copper Miners Struck." *Outlook*, 31 January 1914.

West, Harold E. "Civil War in the West Virginia Coal Mines." *Survey*, 5 April 1913.

White, Horace. "Who Owns the Negro Churches?" *Christian Century*, 9 February 1938.

Wilson, Kinsey, and Steve Askin. "Secrets of a Union Buster." *Nation*, 13 June 1981.

Wright, R. R., Jr. "The Negro in Times of Industrial Unrest." *Charities*, 7 October 1905.

MAGAZINE ARTICLES (UNSIGNED)

"After Cat: What Does the Right to Strike Mean Now?" *Business Week*, 4 May 1992.

"Alleged Discrimination against Colored Students." *Outlook*, 18 October 1902.

"American Union-Busting." *Economist*, 17 November 1979.

"The Cat and the Mice." *Newsweek*, 20 April 1992.

"Caterpillar's Ploys Won't Play in Peoria." *Solidarity*, March 1992.

"Cat Gets Its Back Up. Way Up." *Business Week*, 20 April 1992.

"Chicago Street Railway Strike." *Street Railway Journal*, 21 November 1903.

"Chicago Strike Ended." *Street Railway Journal*, 28 November 1903.

"The Class War in Colorado." *International Socialist Review*, June 1914.

"The Cleveland Strike." *Motorman and Conductor*, August 1899.

"Coal Country's War with Itself." *U.S. News and World Report*, 24 July 1989.

"The Coal Strike: A Near-by View." *Outlook*, 18 October 1902.

"College Women Not Radical but Highly Conservative." *New Student*, 1 November 1924.

"The Copper Strike." *International Socialist Review*, November 1913.

"The Cult of Violence." *Christian Century*, 17 June 1936.

"The Failure of the Negro Church." *Messenger*, October 1919.

"The Ford Heritage." *Fortune*, June 1944.

"Harvard Men in the Boston Police Strike." *School and Society*, 11 October 1919.

"The Institute and the Railroad Strike." *Technology Review*, November 1921.

"John L., You'd Be Amazed." *Time*, 15 May 1989.

"Labor Fights Back against Union Busters." *U.S. News and World Report*, 10 December 1979.

"The Little Giant Goes." *Time*, 8 October 1945.

"Mother Jones Parade." *International Socialist Review*, March 1914.

"Moving Mountains on the Picket Line." *U.S. News and World Report*, 20 April 1992.

"The Negro in the Navy." *Horizon: A Journal of the Color Line*, November 1909.

"New Methods of Self-Preservation." *American Industries*, 1 April 1905.

"No Welcome Mat for Unions in the Sunbelt." *Business Week*, 17 May 1976.

"Pennsylvania's Mounted Police." *Public Opinion*, 12 May 1906.

"President Wheeler Dodges." *Coast Seamen's Journal*, 11 September 1901.

"Providence and Pawtucket Railway Strike." *Street Railway Journal*, 21 June 1902.

"The Race Press." *Horizon: A Journal of the Color Line*, January 1907.

"Responsibility of Instructors." *Motorman and Conductor*, May 1904.

"Showdown on Labor's Front Line." *Time*, 20 April 1992.

"Springfield." *Horizon: A Journal of the Color Line*, August 1908.

"Springfield." *Moon Illustrated Weekly*, 17 March 1906.

"The St. Louis Strike." *Collier's Weekly*, 30 June 1900.

"Strikebreaking." *Fortune*, January 1935.

"Talk Number Three." *Horizon: A Journal of the Color Line*, August 1908.

"Teamsters' Side of the Strike." *Literary Digest*, 20 May 1905.

"Twilight for the UMW?" *Business Week*, 3 July 1989.

"The Unemployed in New York." *Public Opinion*, 31 March 1906.

"What the World Is Doing: A Record of Current Events." *Collier's*, 12 March 1910.

"Why a Coal Strike Isn't What It Used to Be." *U.S. News and World Report*, 19 December 1977.

"Wrong Time for Scare Tactics?" *Business Week*, 16 April 1990.

## DISSERTATIONS AND THESES

Hunter, Eleanor R. "The Labor Policy of the Ford Motor Company." Master's thesis, Wayne University, 1942.

Myers, Howard B. "The Policing of Labor Disputes in Chicago." Ph.D. dissertation, University of Chicago, 1929.

Smith, Robert M. "From Blackjacks to Briefcases: Commercial Anti-Union Agencies, 1865–1985." Ph.D. dissertation, University of Toledo, 1989.

# INDEX

Addams, Jane, 35, 92

Adonis, Joe, 178

Aging, 8; in auto industry, 196; young workers' perception of, 234–35

Airplane use in strikes, 163, 167–68, 218

Amalgamated Meat Cutters and Butcher Workmen's Union, 87, 94

American Brass strike, 220, 224–25

American Federation of Labor (AFL), 11, 115, 197, 228; and African Americans, 79, 109–10, 112; in Bogalusa, La., 108

Ameringer, Oscar, 17

Anderson, Ind., auto strike, 173, 194, 211, 215–19

Andrews, Johnny, 204–5

Androgyny, 229–30

Anger, 14, 228–29, 231, 238–39

Antisemitism: at Harvard, 19; of Ford Motor Company, 187, 189; of Black Legion, 196; of Detroit police, 201, 290 (n. 23)

Armored car use in strikes, 142–43

Armored train use in strikes, 114, 138–41, 149, 169–70

Armories, 72, 74

Arrests: of strikebreakers, 43, 45, 70–71, 89, 103; of strikers and strike sympathizers, 102, 138–39, 144–45, 150, 156–57, 160, 166, 216, 222, 225, 244; of Mother Jones, 119, 139, 144; of Mrs. George Morton, 126; of coal and iron policemen, 127; of outlaws, 131; of Reuther brothers, 219; of Walter Reuther's assailants, 286 (n. 77)

Ascher Detective Agency, 120, 149–50, 152

Auto parts suppliers, 172, 188, 209–11, 215–23

Balch, Emily, 28

Baldwin, William G., 130, 169, 275 (n. 52)

Baldwin-Felts Detective Agency, 4, 119, 134, 143, 203; in West Virginia and Virginia, 128–41, 163–69; in Colorado, 140–43, 146

Battle of the Overpass, 184–88

Bennett, Harry, 6, 14, 170–72, 174, 176, 179, 181–82, 188, 193, 202, 231, 241, 288 (n. 107); relationship with Henry Ford, 173, 175–78; childhood of, 173–74; on Edsel Ford, 174, 190; and athletes, 175, 182–83; and boxing, 175; and navy, 175–76; and organized crime, 178, 192; and Ford Hunger March, 180–81; and Dearborn government, 183, 185–86; and Battle of the Overpass, 184–85; and attempted kidnapping of Walter Reuther, 187, 286 (n. 77); and 1941 Ford strike, 189–90; firing of, 191–92

Bergoff, Pearl, 6, 51, 65–69, 228, 230–31

Bergoff Brothers and Waddell, 4, 65–66, 68–69

Biracial unionism: in Deep South, 106–8

Black Legion, 14, 196–200

Blair Mountain, Battle of, 167–68

Bluestone, Irving, 225–26, 246

Bodybuilders, 46
Boer War, 44, 50, 146
Bogalusa, La., 107–8
Bogart, Humphrey, 200
Boston policemen's strike of 1919, 19, 27, 31
Bourne, Randolph, 21
Boy Scouts of America, 11
Brass knuckles, 67, 172, 184, 192, 212
Bride's Dances, 91–92, 267 (n. 52)
British general strike of 1926, 20
Brooklyn Rapid Transit strike of 1920, 65, 67–68
Brotherhood of Sleeping Car Porters, 112, 270 (n. 123)
Brotherhood of Timber Workers, 107
Brownsville Affair, 84–85, 265 (nn. 26, 27)
Bugas, John, 192
Bundy, Al, 233
Bunker, Archie, 233
Burns Detective Agency, 107, 154–56
Burroughs, Edgar Rice, 51
Butler, Nicholas Murray, 19–20
Byrnes Act, 230

Calumet copper strike, 13, 66, 114–15, 120, 149–54
Cane rush, 23–24
Carey, James, 241
Caterpillar Tractor strike, 243, 245–46
Chafin, Don, 133, 167, 276 (n. 63)
Chicago teamsters' strike of 1905, 13, 78, 81, 94–106
Children, 266 (n. 51); image of innocence, 91, 115, 117; in strike processions, 91, 116, 135–36; abuse of, 115, 122, 127, 136, 150–51, 156, 170, 222–23; and Mother Jones, 120, 135–36; killed in Ludlow massacre, 147, 149, 165; killed in Italian Hall tragedy, 149, 152–53, 169
Chrysler strike of 1937, 195, 206–9, 214–15, 225–26
Chrysler strike of 1950, 225–27

Cicotte, Eddie, 182
Citizens' Alliance, 152–53
Citizens League for Industrial Security, 215–16
Clinton, Bill, 246
Coal and iron police, 4, 120–23, 125–27
College athletes, 23; as strikebreakers, 15–16, 25, 27, 32, 254 (nn. 49, 53); in Ford Service Department, 32, 182
Colorado state militia, 143–48
Columbia University, 19; student strikebreakers, 15–16, 30–31, 255 (n. 72); cane rush, 24
Committee for Industrial Organization (Congress of Industrial Organizations; CIO), 154, 170, 194, 214–15, 224–26, 233; and African Americans, 112–13; and auto workers, 171–72; in South, 232
Commons, John, 87, 93
Company towns: in Louisiana, 108; in West Virginia, 129, 132, 135; in Colorado, 141–42
Corporations Auxiliary Service, 173, 203–5, 291 (n. 31)
Cossacks (Russia), 125; Pennsylvania State Constabulary compared to, 115, 125; Baldwin-Felts guards compared to, 128; state militiamen compared to, 144–45
Coughlin, Charles, 201
Coxey's Army, 120, 134
Crane, Stephen, 23, 44
Curry, Frank, 50, 62, 97–100
Czar Nicholas II, 11, 95

D'Anna, Anthony, 178
Davis, Richard Harding, 44, 46, 50, 76
Debs, Eugene V., 156, 159
Dewar, Rose, 97–98
Dewar, Thomas, 97
Dollinger, Genora Johnson, 203, 213
Donnelly, Michael, 87, 92–93
Du Bois, W. E. B., 79, 110–11
Dynamite, 35, 39, 44, 62, 159, 168

Effigies, 41–43, 55, 73, 92
Eisenhower, Dwight, 231, 235
Eliot, Charles W., 19
Emancipation Day, 91
Epidemic disease, 59–60
Ettor, Joe, 26
Eviction, 131–32, 136–37, 141–42, 150, 164

Farley, James, 4, 22–23, 50–62, 65, 68, 72, 98, 131, 259 (n. 70), 291 (n. 31); and masculinity, 6, 47, 54–56; background, 53; in 1906 New York gubernatorial campaign, 60–61; retirement of, 62–63; in *The Iron Heel*, 63; depicted as coward, 64; employs University of California students, 255 (n. 69)
Fascism, 230; and Ford Motor Company, 4, 14, 181, 187, 286 (n. 80); and Black Legion, 196; and Police Commissioner Pickert, 201; UAW-CIO opposition to, 208, 227
Federal Screw strike, 188, 220–24
Felts, Albert, 130, 141–42, 163–65
Felts, Lee, 130, 163–66
Felts, Thomas, 130–31, 133, 141, 163–64, 166, 168–69
Fitzpatrick, John, 92, 94, 295 (n. 99)
Flint Alliance, 212–13
Flint General Motors strike of 1936–37, 188, 194–95, 200, 209, 211–14, 218–19, 225, 227
Flophouses, 9, 12
Flying Squadrons: of coal and iron police, 122; of UAW-CIO, 188, 195, 211–15, 218–19, 221–22, 224–26
Football, 15, 23–25, 27, 32, 251 (n. 13), 254 (nn. 48, 49)
Ford, Edsel, 174–75, 183, 190–91
Ford, Henry, 182, 185, 192; relationship with Harry Bennett, 173, 176–78, 180, 193; relationship with Edsel Ford, 174–75; and Five Dollar Day, 176; approach to management, 177,
183; and America First Committee, 187; and 1941 Ford strike, 190
Ford, Henry, II, 191–92, 236, 288 (nn. 100, 102)
Ford Hunger March, 180–81
Ford Service Department, 171–72, 192–93, 241; compared to European fascists, 4, 14, 181, 187; in Dearborn, 170, 176–87; in Dallas, 171–72, 186; in Highland Park, 182; in Memphis, 186; in 1941 Ford strike, 189–90
Ford strike of 1941, 189–91
Foster, William Z., 110
Frankensteen, Richard, 179; at Battle of the Overpass, 184–85; and Johnny Andrews, 204–5; and Flying Squadrons, 211
Fraser, Doug, 179, 188, 205, 208, 246
Frazier, E. Franklin, 80
French Revolution, 39, 147

Gambling, 66–67, 92–93, 104
General Motors strike of 1945–46, 225–27
Goldman, Emma, 21
Gompers, Samuel, 19; on St. Louis streetcar strike, 38; and African Americans, 109; on 1919 steel strike, 111; on West Virginia, 128, 140
Great Migration, 78, 108–9
Grey, Zane, 46, 261 (n. 121)
Greyhound Bus strike, 243–45

Hadley, Arthur Twining, 20, 26
Hapgood, Powers, 122
Harding, Warren G., 163, 167
Harper, William Rainey, 19, 25
Hartford Valley, Ark., mine conflict, 13, 114, 154–63, 170
Harvard University, 18–19; student strikebreakers, 26–28, 32
Hatfield, Sid, 164, 166–68
Hearst, William Randolph, 60–61
Hibben, John Grier, 31

Hoffa, Jimmy, 188–89, 212
Holt, Fred, 158–59, 161–62
Homeless men, 9–10
Homestead strike of 1892, 4–6
Hughes, Charles Evans, 60–61

Immigrants, southern and eastern European, 82, 114–15, 170; compared to African Americans, 87; in packinghouse industry and strike, 87, 91–92, 267 (nn. 52, 56); in 1919 steel strike, 109; compared to American Indians, 118, 170; in Pennsylvania coal strikes, 118–19; in Colorado coal strike, 119, 145, 147–48, 278 (n. 101); in West Virginia mines and coal strikes, 129–30, 136; in Calumet copper strike, 149, 151–53
Indian wars, 34, 48, 83–84, 118–19, 146
Interborough Rapid Transit (IRT) strike of 1905, 15–17, 30, 43, 47, 58–60, 64
Intercollegiate Socialist Society, 21, 252 (n. 27)

James, Frank, 47
Jeffries, Jim, 64, 99
Johns Hopkins University: student strikebreakers, 32, 255 (n. 74)
Johnson, Genora. See Dollinger, Genora Johnson
Jones, Mother, 119–20; in West Virginia, 135, 139–40; in Colorado, 144–45
Jordan, David Starr, 30

Kelsey-Hayes Wheel sit-down strike, 208–11, 214
Keyes, Percy, 223
Ku Klux Klan, 196, 215

La Follette Committee, 3, 200, 203–5, 209
La Mare, Chet, 178, 183

Laski, Harold, 19–20
Lawrence textile strike of 1912, 26
Lewis, John L., 228
Linderfeldt, Karl, 119, 146–48
Lively, Charlie, 165–66
London, Jack, 9–10, 21, 63
Low, Seth, 30
Lowell, A. Lawrence, 19, 27
Ludlow massacre, 114, 119, 146–48, 157, 159
Lynching: threatened against strikebreakers, 43, 90, 101; and effigies, 43, 92; in South, 81, 108; in Springfield, Ill., race riot, 83; threatened against unionists, 108, 216, 218

Machine gun use in strikes, 189; by state militia, 73–74, 147; by Pennsylvania State Constabulary, 128; by Baldwin-Felts Detective Agency, 137–39, 142–43; by U.S. army, 160; in Battle of Blair Mountain, 167; by Detroit police, 202; by Pearl Bergoff, 228
Machinists' strike of 1901, 6, 30
Mahon, Archie, 51, 65–66
Martial law, 72; in West Virginia, 137–40; in Anderson, Ind., 218–19
Masculinity, 166; strikebreakers and, 6–7, 12–13, 22–23, 25, 45–48, 50–51, 54–56, 66, 76, 99–100; African Americans and, 13, 77, 80, 83–86, 90, 94, 97–100, 103, 105–7, 112; post-1945 redefining of, 14, 228–30, 233–34; crisis of, 21–23, 34, 45–46; college students and, 21–27, 29; impugning of strikebreakers', 26, 49, 63–64, 143; unionists and, 64, 89, 106–7, 112, 115–16, 136, 143; and Harry Bennett, 173, 175–76, 181, 183
Massachusetts Institute of Technology: student strikebreakers, 26, 31–32; and corporate research, 30
Matewan shoot-out, 163–66
Mazey, Emil, 193, 211

McCoy, Kid, 175, 182
McDowell, Mary, 92, 266 (n. 51), 267 (n. 56)
McParlan, James, 5, 163
Midland Steel sit-down strike, 205
Militia, state, use in strikes, 70, 72; in Virginia, 45, 71, 73; in Rhode Island, 70, 73–74; in Ohio, 72; in Connecticut, 74; in Pennsylvania, 75, 122–23; in Colorado, 120, 141, 143–48; in West Virginia, 137–40; in Michigan, 149–51, 153
Minneapolis millers' strike of 1903, 25
Motor Products strike of 1935, 199, 201–2
Mounted police: in Omaha, 90; in Detroit, 188, 201, 221–22, 224
Moyer, Charles, 153–54
Murphy, Frank, 200, 207, 210, 215, 219
Muscular Christianity, 22, 25

National Labor Relations Act (Wagner Act), 3, 187–88, 195, 207–8, 225, 232, 247
National Labor Relations Board, 3, 189, 226, 235; condemns Ford Motor Company, 188; representation elections, 190, 219, 230–31, 237, 239, 241, 246–47; back pay awards, 247
Nearing, Scott, 19
New England Telephone strike: of 1913 (near-strike), 12; of 1919, 26; of 1923, 26, 28
Nissan organizing campaign (Smyrna, Tenn.), 234, 236
Northrup, Cyrus, 25
Northwestern University, 82, 254 (n. 48)

O'Connor, Julia, 26
O'Hare, Kate Richards, 149–51
Operation Dixie, 232
Organized crime, 14, 66, 119, 177–78, 183–84, 192, 210, 212
Owen, Chandler, 110

Pacific Gas and Electric strike of 1913, 30
Packinghouse strike of 1904, 13, 78, 86–94
Paint Creek/Cabin Creek strike of 1912–13, 13, 114, 128–29, 133–40
Paris Commune, 39
Pennsylvania anthracite strike of 1902, 121–23
Pennsylvania State Constabulary, 127; formation and purpose, 74–75, 123; compared to Cossacks, 75, 125–26; in 1910 Philadelphia streetcar strike, 75–76; training of, 123–24; accused of sexual debauchery, 126
Pennypacker, Samuel, 123, 125
Perlman, Selig, 45
Permanent replacement of strikers legislation, 246–47
Philippines campaign, 9; compared to streetcar strike, 35; war correspondence and, 44; veterans as strikebreakers, 61, 122; African American troops in, 84; Karl Linderfeldt in, 146
Pickert, Heinrich, 197, 200–201, 210, 219, 225
Pinchot, Gifford, 127
Pinkerton, Allan, 4–5
Pinkerton Detective Agency, 4–5, 107; in streetcar strikes, 56; espionage in auto industry, 173, 203, 206, 217
Pittston, W.Va., mine strike, 243–44, 247
Police, 44, 49, 57, 73, 90, 105; injured in strikes, 39, 188, 222, 225; patrol wagons, 43, 56, 101; sympathy for strikers, 43, 70–72; and gambling, 67; and race riots, 82; African American, 91, 102, 104; collusion with auto companies, 193, 195, 201, 214–26; and Black Legion, 197, 199; denounced as anti-labor in Detroit, 200–202, 220, 225; censorship, 201, 290 (n. 23); in South, 241–42

Princeton University, 31

Prizefighting, 45–46, 64, 99–100; and Harry Bennett, 14, 173, 175; African American strikebreakers' participation in, 93, 104; Waddell-Mahon gunmen and, 150; and Ford Servicemen, 177, 179, 182, 184; decline of boxing club, 229

Professional Air Traffic Controllers Organization (PATCO) strike, 243, 245–46

Prostitutes, 120, 127, 185; in packinghouses, 92; and strikebreakers, militiamen, and mine guards, 115, 144, 149, 151, 170; and Pennsylvania State Constabulary, 126; accusations of white slavery, 126–27, 135; in mining camps, 132, 142

Pullman railroad strike, 19, 85

Pupils' strikes of 1905 in Chicago, 102

Race riots, 81–83, 94

Racism, 105; of unions, 78–79, 106, 109, 112–13; in South, 80–82, 106–8, 110, 241; in early twentieth-century North, 82–83; toward African American soldiers, 83–85; of packinghouse employers, 86–87, 92, 106; of white strikers and strike sympathizers, 91–94, 101–2; of police, 95, 105, 223; perceptions of African American boxers, 100; of ministers and priests, 102–3; of Chicago department stores, 104; of white strikebreakers, 104; of Ford Motor Company, 190

Railroad brotherhoods, 32, 79, 112

Railroad strikes of 1920 and 1921, 31–32

Randolph, A. Philip, 110, 112

Ravenswood Aluminum lockout, 234–35, 245

Reagan, Ronald, 231, 243, 245

Reed, John, 21

Reuther, Roy, 195, 206, 214

Reuther, Sophie, 187, 216–17

Reuther, Victor, 187, 193, 195, 286 (n. 77); and Boy Scouts, 11; compares Ford to General Motors and Chrysler, 172–73; on Harry Bennett, 175, 191; on Kelsey-Hayes Wheel sit-down strike, 211; in Battle of Bulls' Run, 214, 216–17; in Anderson, Ind., General Motors strike, 214, 216–18; in Yale & Towne strike, 219; on Federal Screw strike, 221; on contemporary labor movement, 233

Reuther, Walter, 195, 225; at Battle of the Overpass, 184, 188; on Harry Bennett, 187, 192; attempted kidnapping of, 187, 286 (n. 77); in Federal Screw strike, 188–89, 220, 222–23; in Yale & Towne strike, 219

"Right to work" legislation, 231

River Rouge plant, 172–73, 176, 178–81, 185–86, 188–91, 286 (n. 80)

Robeson, Paul, 190

Roosevelt, Franklin D., 8, 169, 210

Roosevelt, Theodore, 4, 22, 52, 84, 86

Russia (czarist): Nihilists of, 1; police system compared to American labor espionage, 3, 5, 128; Boy Scouts in, 11; students in, 20–21; revolution of 1905, 95, 125; compared to Pennsylvania and West Virginia coal districts, 115, 121, 125, 128

Sacco-Vanzetti case, 21

Salvemini, Gaetano, 286 (n. 80)

Schuettler, Herman F., 56, 95

Scudder, Vida, 26

Searchlights: use by Pinkertons, 56; use by mine guards, 134, 142

Sexual harassment: African American strikebreakers accused of, 93; of miners' wives and daughters, 115, 121–22, 127, 136, 142, 144, 149, 151, 156–57, 170; of hotel maid, 126; rape of miner's wife, 126–27

Shefferman, Nathan, 237–38

Sheridan, Ann, 200

Ships: housing of strikebreakers on, 12, 35–36, 43, 58–59

Slankard, Jim, 155, 157, 161–62

Smith, Gerald L. K., 187

Socialist Party, 18, 154, 159, 161

Sorensen, Charles, 177, 183

Sound trucks and cars, 201, 214, 217, 224

Southern organizing: early twentieth-century, 106–8; post-1945, 231–32, 234, 241–44

Spanish-American War, 34, 45, 49, 82, 86; compared to mine conflicts, 13, 114; compared to streetcar strikes, 35; militia veterans of, 72; African American troops in, 84–85, 99

Spanish Civil War, 201, 208

Stagg, Amos Alonzo, 25

Stanford University, 251 (n. 14); student strikebreakers, 30

State Fencibles, 49, 75

Steel strike of 1919, 108–12

Stevens Institute of Technology: student strikebreakers, 31, 255 (n. 72)

Stewart, Pete, 157, 161

Streetcar strikes, 34, 36–38, 51–52, 67; San Francisco (1902), 1–2, 64; Boston Elevated (1912), 28; convoy system in, 35; violence compared to war, 35, 72; impact on public, 36–37; San Francisco (1907), 36–37, 39–40, 43, 47–48, 61–62, 69, 71, 261 (n. 126); New Orleans (1929), 36–39, 49, 69–70; Richmond (1903), 38, 40, 44–45, 54, 57, 70–73, 259 (n. 76); New Orleans (1902), 38, 43–44, 60, 64, 70, 74, 258 (n. 54); Philadelphia (1910), 38, 47–49, 65, 75–76; Cleveland (1899), 38–39, 43–44, 49, 53, 62, 72; St. Louis (1900), 38–41, 45–46, 49, 60, 64, 99; Philadelphia (1909), 39, 65; Chicago (1903), 40, 43, 46, 48, 50, 54–57, 99; obstructing tracks and wires, 40–44, 48–49, 55, 257 (n. 23); Waterbury, Conn. (1903), 43, 54, 74, 259 (n. 76); Bay City, Mich. (1905), 45, 48; Indianapolis (1913), 45, 71; Brooklyn (1895), 51, 53; Providence (1902), 54, 70, 73–74, 259 (n. 76); Chicago (1915), 65, 69; Havana (1916), 66; Kansas City (1918), 69; impact of auto on, 69–70; Scranton, Penn. (1901), 259 (n. 76)

Sullivan, John L., 46, 99

Taft-Hartley Act, 231, 235, 239

Taylor, Frederick Winslow, 29

Tear gas use in strikes, 128, 190, 208–9, 219–21, 224–25

Tent colonies: in West Virginia, 132, 138; in Colorado, 142–43, 146–48

Tenure (academic), 19, 32

Tikas, Louis, 147

Turner, John Kenneth, 134–35, 138, 203

Unemployment, 7–10, 16, 53, 104–6, 238, 246; in auto industry, 179–80, 196–97; and Caterpillar strike, 245

United Automobile Workers (UAW), 181, 191–93, 199, 242; and Ford campaign, 4, 14, 172, 181, 183–90; and Flint strike, 14, 194–95, 200, 203, 206, 209, 211, 213–14; and Anderson, Ind., strike, 14, 211, 215–19; and Federal Screw strike, 188–89, 220–24; and African Americans, 189–90, 223; and 1937 Chrysler strike, 195, 200, 206–7, 209, 214; and Detroit police, 200–201; penetrated by spies, 204–7; elaboration of sit-down strike, 207–8; and Spanish Civil War, 208; and Kelsey-Hayes Wheel sit-down strike, 208–11; Flying Squadrons, 211–14, 218–19, 225; and Yale & Towne strike, 219–20; and American Brass strike,

224–25; and 1950 Chrysler strike, 225–26; and 1945–46 General Motors strike, 225–27; and Nissan campaign, 234; and Caterpillar strike, 245–46

United Mine Workers of America (UMW), 10, 115; and espionage, 5–6, 128, 163, 165; in Colorado, 116, 120, 141–46, 148; in Pennsylvania, 121–22, 124–26; in West Virginia, 128–29, 131–33, 135, 141–46, 148, 163–66, 168–69, 243–44, 247; in Arkansas, 154, 157–58, 160–63

University of California: student strikebreakers, 24, 30, 255 (n. 69)

University of Chicago, 251 (n. 14); firing of Edward Bemis, 19; student strikebreakers, 25

University of Michigan: student strikebreakers, 30; and Harry Bennett, 32, 175, 182–83

University of Minnesota, 19; student strikebreakers, 25

University of Pennsylvania, 19; student strikebreakers, 16, 255 (n. 72)

Urban League, 109, 111, 113

U.S. Army, 229; African American soldiers, 81, 83–86, 105; and 1919 steel strike, 111; in mine strikes, 148, 160, 163, 168

Vance International, 243–45

Veterans: as strikebreakers, 61, 146, 295 (n. 99); in Pennsylvania State Constabulary, 75; as union miners, 114, 145, 167; of World War II, 227

Vorse, Mary Heaton, 225–26

Waddell, James, 51, 65, 68, 150

Waddell-Mahon Detective Agency, 65–66, 149–51, 153, 203

Washington, Booker T., 79–80, 94, 111

Wellesley College, 26–28

Wells-Barnett, Ida, 103

Western Federation of Miners, 11, 115, 149–54

Western novel, 46–47, 229

Wheeler, Benjamin, 24–25, 30, 255 (n. 69)

White, Walter, 190

Whitehead, Jack, 6–7

Williams College, 32

Winchester rifles: use by strikebreakers on streetcars, 45; African Americans and, 81, 95, 100; coal and iron policemen and, 121; Baldwin-Felts guards and, 133; Arkansas mine guards and, 155, 158

Wister, Owen, 46

Women, 20, 35, 44, 50, 87, 106, 118, 132, 161–62, 205–6, 238; violence against, 11, 115, 125–27, 135–36, 144–45, 147–48, 151, 158–59, 165, 222; as strikebreakers, 11–12, 28, 97–98; college students, 27–29; as strike sympathizers, 28–29, 48–49, 116, 194–95, 200, 213, 218, 244; Boer, 44; in Western novels, 47; moral influence of, 91–92; in Battle of the Overpass, 184–85; in Yale & Towne strike, 219–20

Women's Emergency Brigade, 194–95, 213, 218

Women's Trade Union League, 28–29

Woodcock, Leonard, 202, 212, 227, 242

Yale & Towne strike, 219–21

Yale University, 20, 24; student strikebreakers, 25–26, 28

Youth culture, 116; collegiate, 16–18, 20, 23–24, 32–33